PENGUIN HANDBOOKS

CAKES

Barbara Maher was born in Berlin but grew up and was educated in Manchester. She studied textile design at the Manchester College of Art and Design, and later moved to London with her husband and three sons. Her interest in cooking and baking, which developed with her continuing role as hostess, reflects her continental background. She was joint winner of the André Simon Memorial Fund Book Award for 1982 with this book.

BARBARA MAHER
CAKES

Illustrated by
Thao Soun

Penguin Books

Penguin Books Ltd, Harmondsworth, Middlesex, England
Penguin Books, 625 Madison Avenue, New York, New York 10022, U.S.A.
Penguin Books Australia Ltd, Ringwood, Victoria, Australia
Penguin Books Canada Ltd, 2801 John Street, Markham, Ontario, Canada L3R 1B4
Penguin Books (N.Z.) Ltd, 182–190 Wairau Road, Auckland 10, New Zealand

First published by Jill Norman & Hobhouse 1982
Published in Penguin Books 1984

Copyright © Barbara Maher, 1982
Illustrations copyright © Thao Soun, 1982
All rights reserved

Made and printed in Great Britain by
Richard Clay (The Chaucer Press) Ltd,
Bungay, Suffolk

Except in the United States of America,
this book is sold subject to the condition
that it shall not, by way of trade or otherwise,
be lent, re-sold, hired out, or otherwise circulated
without the publisher's prior consent in any form of
binding or cover other than that in which it is
published and without a similar condition
including this condition being imposed
on the subsequent purchaser

Contents

INTRODUCTION	7
ACKNOWLEDGEMENTS	11
PLANNING THE BAKING AREA	13
BASIC INGREDIENTS	23
USING THE OVEN	37
BASIC PASTRIES	41
FRESH CREAMS, COOKED CREAMS AND FILLINGS	57
BOILING SUGAR	69
ICINGS AND DECORATIONS	71
PERFUMES, AROMATICS AND CANDIED FRUITS	82
SPONGES AND BISCUITS	87
CHOUX PASTRY	99
MERINGUES	108
YEAST BAKING	117
CHOCOLATE	143
GATEAUX AND TORTEN	158
POUND CAKES	181
TEA BREADS AND COFFEE CAKES	187
POTATO AND CARROT CAKES	193
TARTS AND PIES	203
TARTS AND PIES WITH FRESH FRUIT	220
FRESH FRUIT CAKES	240
DRIED FRUIT CAKES	268
WEDDING CAKES	286
CHEESE CAKES	298
NUTS	308
THE SPICE BOX	342
FRIANDISES AND BISCUITS	373
BIBLIOGRAPHY	387
INDEX	389

FOR TERRY

Introduction

> It was delightful – this business of having tea – and she always had delicious things to eat – little sharp sandwiches, short sweet almond fingers, and a dark, rich cake tasting of rum – . . . Carefully she cut the cake into thick little wads and he reached across for a piece. 'Do you realise how good it is,' she implored, 'Eat it imaginatively. Roll your eyes if you can and taste it on the breath. It's not a sandwich from the hatter's bag – it's the kind of cake that might have been mentioned in the Book of Genesis . . . And God said: "Let there be cake. And there was cake. And God saw that it was good." . . .'
>
> (Katherine Mansfield *Psychology*)

There is something irresistible about a home-made cake, which the pristine uniformity of the shop variety lacks. Home-made suggests excellence and perfect ingredients. The layers of a puff pastry case may puff and dip a little unevenly, the surface of a cheese cake may be cracked, or meringue peaks may have a soft honey tinge – it is not important. Who can resist the glistening brown triangles of caramel on a Dobos Torte or bright red strawberries, proudly lined by a careful hand, in a crusty flan? Even a casual dusting of icing-sugar is more inviting than the most complicated decoration. And what can tempt more than the yeasty aroma of a brown and sugary doughnut still warm from the oven?

Baking was my mother's forte and I was brought up in the teutonic tradition to enjoy cakes. Rationing of dried eggs and margarine made cakes a rarity in war-time England, and my birthday was usually celebrated with a flower cake – a bowl filled with soil, studded with candles and large blooms picked from the garden. When rationing was at an end and produce was again readily available, Rokitansky, my mother's Austrian 'bible', and her hand-written exercise books of handed-down recipes, appeared. We were treated to one new cake after another and each was greeted with my mother's cry, "This is the best I have ever made!". Zuckerkuchen, Gugelhopf, Streusselkuchen and Bienenstich, plain or cream-filled almond and hazelnut cakes were usual tea-time treats — Baumkuchen and Pfannkuchen were for special celebrations.

My own interest in baking started later when I began leafing through modern cookery books in search of recipes, but cakes made with margarine and coconut, or peanuts or vanilla essence had little appeal for me. I found what I was looking for in eighteenth, nineteenth and early twentieth century cookery books from Austria, Germany, Switzerland, France and Italy as well as England. Here were the light cakes of my childhood, made with ingredients of the best flavour and finest quality — butter and newly ground nuts, fresh eggs, fresh and dried fruits, chocolate, potato flour, curd cheese and cream, lightly flavoured with perfumes, liqueurs and spices.

I also became aware of the marked difference in styles and techniques. German and Austrian recipes frequently used nuts, often instead of flour; sugar quantities were usually quite small and were sometimes replaced by honey; separated eggs were used or yolks or whites on their own. I rediscovered forgotten cakes made with mashed potato and carrot, chestnut and quince pastes, and learned of the origins of more familiar pastries such as Strudel with its early Arab connections. The earlier German and Austrian cookery books contain numerous illustrations, but those of the nineteenth century have very few, for the interest in decoration had obviously waned in favour of greater simplicity and concentrated more on the quality of the cake itself.

Whilst the ingredients and flavourings of the French cakes were just as good, they were based mainly on sponge-type mixtures, and acted principally as frame-works for elaborate and complicated structures and decoration. Anatole France is reputed to have called pâtisserie a branch of architecture — itself one of the five beaux arts. The French confectionery books, lavish in their pictorial detail (they remained so), reflected this obsession with the grand visual element that was appropriate to the flamboyant life-style. Talleyrand the celebrated statesman and gastronome likened these confections to bouquets of beautiful fireworks, served at the end of a good meal. Of course there were smaller, simpler versions of the grand cakes too, which were known as petits fours.

Apart from the occasional sponge, English cakes tended to be of a richer and denser character; cake mixtures loaded generously with dried fruits (nuts were rarely used), sweet yeast bread doughs, plain and fruited, and non-yeasted mixtures such as pound cake were more typical, as well as the familiar fruit tarts and pies. The plainer confectionery was traditionally served at tea-time and apart from the heavy

INTRODUCTION

fruit cakes elaborately iced in the French style for festivities, decoration was minimal. Early in the twentieth century many more French recipes and techniques were adopted. Petits fours made with choux paste, meringue, puff pastries and sponges offered new opportunities to professional confectioners. Katherine Mansfield's description in a short story, *The Young Girl*, written in the 1920s shows the impact of these confections on the English tea-table.

> A tiny boy with a head like a raisin and a chocolate body came round with a tray of pastries – row upon row of little freaks, little inspirations, little melting dreams. He offered them to her, "Oh, I'm not at all hungry. Take them away".
> He offered them to Hennie. Hennie gave me a swift look – it must have been satisfactory – for he took a chocolate cream, a coffee éclair, a meringue stuffed with chestnut and a tiny horn filled with fresh strawberries. She could hardly bear to watch him. But just as the boy swerved away she held up her plate.
> "Oh well, give me *one*", said she.
> The silver tongs dropped one, two, three – and a cherry tartlet. "I don't know why you're giving me all these," she said, and nearly smiled. "I shan't eat them; I couldn't!" . . .

It was not until the 1950s that immigrant influences from Austria and Germany became evident in England. Delicatessen shops opened their doors to sell unfamiliar produce. Almonds, hazelnuts, walnuts, vanilla pods, poppy-seed and potato flour were sold along with *Aufschnitt* – cold cut meats, hams and sausages, pickled gherkins and matjes herrings. Continental cake shops also appeared and in Austro-Hungarian style served coffee along with a selection of their traditional pastries. *Mohrenkopf* – chocolate coated-sponge Othellos filled with freshly whipped cream; nut stuffed crescents; large Torten layered and piped with nut creams and chocolate cakes filled with cherries; Sachertorte, and yeast pastries rolled with poppyseed and cinnamon enticingly tempted the customers.

More recently both gâteaux and Torten have begun to appear on the dessert trolleys in restaurants, alongside the ubiquitous crème caramel and fruit salad; these sweet confections have added a new elegance to the dinner table, although many of the factory-made versions are of poor quality.

I derive as much satisfaction from baking, as I do from eating a home-made cake. It is a precise discipline whose chemical magic and visual appeal is most gratifying. Baking needs time, patience, practice and accuracy, but once the basic techniques have been understood and mastered, any cake is easy to make. Of course we all make mistakes, but with good ingredients also these can sometimes be turned to advantage. I have even seen a professional confectioner slice off and level the top of a sunken cake, which once filled and covered with cream, looked quite perfect.

* * *

This is not a book about fancy cakes or elaborate decorations, but about simplicity and good flavour. It offers a temptation for tea-time or with a cup of coffee, a morsel with a glass of wine, a satisfying snack for a hungry hiker or a dessert at an elegant dinner table.

It is planned as a working manual with recipes and detailed instructions of the basic techniques at the beginning for easy reference. Here you can learn how to make the different pastries or a sponge mixture, how to whip up an egg white correctly or how to glacé ice a cake. There are recipes for cake fillings and suggestions for simple cake decorations and flavourings. It is important to study these first sections carefully so that they can be used in conjunction with recipes elsewhere in the book. I have tested all the recipes in the book, and also baked the cakes in the photographs.

Weights and Measures

Measurements throughout this book are given in both imperial and metric units. It is important to use either all imperial or all metric measurements in a recipe, never a mixture of the two.

Conventional, fan-assisted and fan ovens

The baking temperatures and times given at the end of each recipe in the book are intended for conventional ovens.

Many new electric ovens are now fitted with a fan to assist the circulation of heat more efficiently. Because of this constant and even temperature, cakes are inclined to bake much too quickly and have a tendency to dry out. Usually it is necessary to reduce the temperature by between 20° and 25°C in every 100°C; but please consult the accompanying literature of your particular oven for precise information.

Acknowledgements

I have acknowledged various people throughout the text, but would also like to express particular appreciation to Mr. J. Brown of British Fermentation Products and Petty Wood and Co Ltd for professional information on yeast and dried fruits and nuts. Also Barker Ellis and Co Ltd for the loan of silverware. I thank Uta Schumacher-Voelker for allowing me to delve into her personal library and for her generous and enthusiastic advice. I thank Michael Raeburn for his early help and loan of many European cookery books. I thank my uncle, Harry Smith, who gave me inspired assistance in literary matters and also Sandra Lummis. I am delighted with Thao Soun's sensitive drawings – it was a pleasure to work with him. I also thank Christine Hanscomb for her fine and artistic still-life photographs.

I wish to thank all my friends who have tasted so willingly, but most particularly Claudia Roden, who persuaded me to write this book in the first instance. She has lent a willing ear to my ideas, made welcome suggestions and valuable criticisms, read and sampled enthusiastically over the years. I cannot express my gratitude enough to my publisher, Jill Norman, for having confidence in me and for nursing and encouraging my faltering footsteps along the way; I have appreciated her kindness and friendship. It has been an inspiring experience. I wish to thank my mother, who managed without Rokitansky for so long, for her helpful comments and critical tasting. Finally I thank my family, Terry, Nicholas, Anthony and Jeremy for acting as tasters in chief and for their patience and understanding whilst sharing me with the book which has been as much a part of their lives as it has of mine.

Planning the Baking Area

Basic Essentials, Equipment and Utensils

Work is made easier if all the machines, utensils, tins and ingredients are close at hand.

You need an open work space where you can roll out and knead, and if you have room to lay a marble slab it is ideal for handling goods which should be kept cool, such as puff pastries. Always buy the best quality equipment. Although the initial outlay is considerable, you will be repaid by many years of good service and there is no doubt that using the right equipment saves time and produces the best results. Look for a kitchen shop or a catering equipment specialist – they generally carry a more comprehensive range of utensils than most department stores and hardware shops, and also stock many of the better quality products.

ELECTRICAL EQUIPMENT

The invention of the electric mixer has revolutionized the modern kitchen. Most cake recipes may be prepared with a machine, and far less time is needed than when using traditional hand-mixing techniques. Although not essential, an electric mixer is a worth-while investment for the serious baker. As a mixer is heavy and awkward to lift, find a permanent position where it is convenient to use.

Large Electric Mixer. Heavy table model with stand and bowl. I find it useful to have a second mixing bowl, as many cake recipes call for part of the mixture to be prepared separately.

Small Electric Mixer. Portable, hand-held. This smaller, less powerful machine is suitable only for lighter mixtures and smaller quantities. The hand-held version is a useful supplement to the heavy table model, although not an alternative. Whisking custards and creams in a double boiler over the fire is far less arduous, and egg whites whip up in seconds as air is swiftly incorporated.

CAKES

Electric Blender or Liquidizer and Coffee Grinder. Free standing, or an attachment to a table mixer. These can ease many time-consuming tasks such as chopping and grinding nuts, breadcrumbs, herbs, spices and coffee beans. The length of time the motor runs determines the texture.

Food Processors. A food processor has the advantages of being compact, simple to operate and relatively inexpensive.

The basic concept of this machine is quite different from that of conventional mixers. It may be chosen as an alternative, although it is not as suitable for large families, since most can only cope with quite small quantities. However, larger 'family-sized' versions are beginning to be available. Small cakes, pastries, biscuits and even bread may be prepared with this machine, but no whisked aerated mixtures.

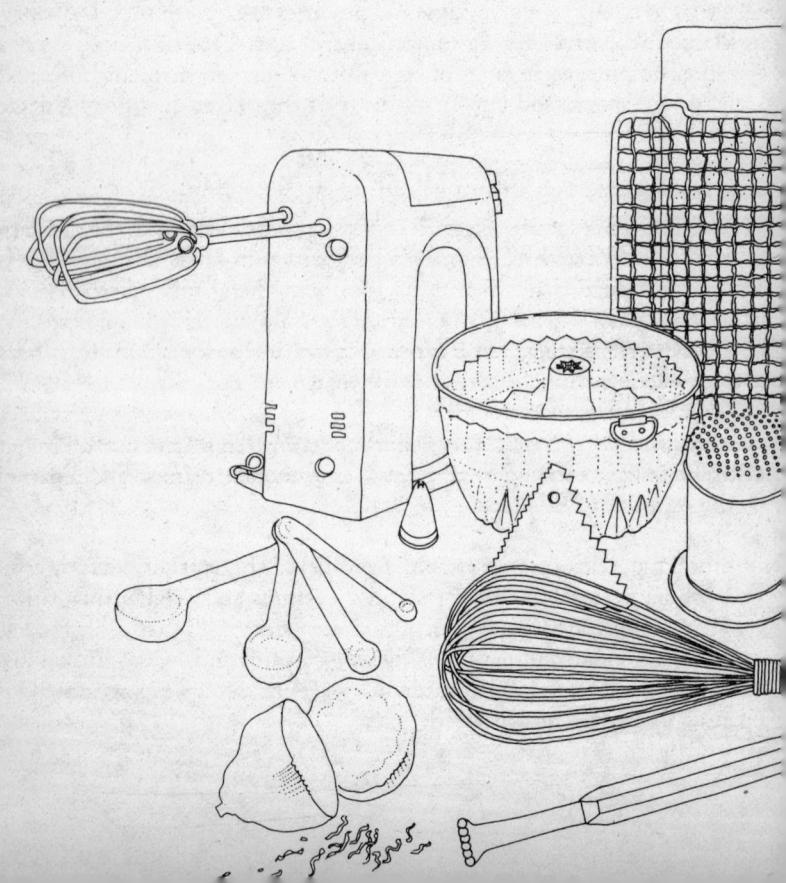

WEIGHING AND MEASURING EQUIPMENT

Marcel Boulestin said:

> The dangerous person in the kitchen is the one who goes rigidly by weights, measurements, thermometers and scales . . .

In baking, however, complete accuracy is essential and will determine success or failure.

There are three principal types of scales available in imperial and metric weights.

Spring Balance Scale. Simple to use and probably the most popular today, although the least reliable. Many versions are available, wall-mounted with a fold-away cover, and table models with a pan for the ingredients which sits on the top of the base.

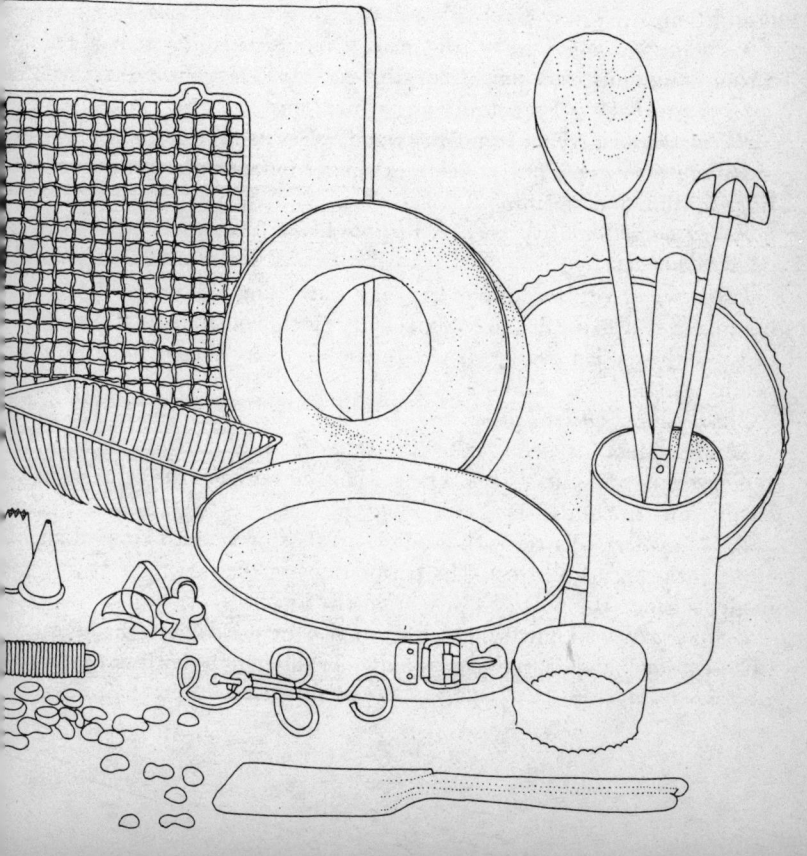

Sliding Weight Beam Scale. These table models have a large pan to hold the ingredients. A counterweighted lever balances the load being weighed. The weight slides along a notched scale.

Precision Scale with Separate Weights. These accurate scales are provided with individual metal weights.

A *set of measuring spoons* in plastic or metal is ideal for measuring small quantities. Draw a knife blade across the top of the heaped spoon to level off the surface: this gives a correct measurement.

A *measuring jug* in glass, clear polypropylene, or stainless steel, is essential.

BAKING TOOLS

Wooden or plastic spoons: Slotted and round, of various lengths and thicknesses. Wooden spoons should be fine-grained, hard and smooth.

Quirl: Large wooden swizzle stick for whipping small amounts of liquid/flour mixtures, etc.

Perforated draining spoon or wire spider: Stainless steel or tinned. For lifting doughnuts, etc. out of hot oil.

Large metal spoon: For folding egg whites into mixtures, etc.

Rolling pin: Heavy and smooth, wood, glass or pottery.

Spatula or scraper: Plastic, nylon or rubber for scraping bowls, stirring, folding and creaming.

Palette knife: Stainless steel. A flexible blade is essential for lifting cakes, icing, etc.

Pastry brush: For brushing pastry, egg wash, sugar glazes and greasing cake tins. Choose 2.5 to 3.5 cm (1 to 1½ inch) width; natural bristle brush with wooden handle. If you buy an ordinary brush, sterilize it before using.

Multi-purpose kitchen scissors.

Skewers: Metal or wood for testing cakes for readiness.

Citrus zester: Stainless steel. The six-hole cutter curls the zests from citrus fruits in thin slivers.

Lemon squeezer: Plastic with a bowl, or glass or wooden copy of an eighteenth-century version. The perforations in the lid of the plastic model separate the pips and pith from the juice.

Balloon whisks: Light wire with wooden or coiled wire handles. Choose a small and a large size, suitable for different quantities of egg whites, creams, etc.

PLANNING THE BAKING AREA

Cherry stoner: A spring-action steel stoning prong forces the stone out of the fruit.

Rotary hand beater: An alternative to a balloon whisk, though not as satisfactory.

Wooden chopping or pastry board: Choose a large, thick, hard wood board with clamp ends to prevent warping.

Marble slab: Polished. Keeps pastries or chocolate cool while working.

Mixing bowls: 25 to 30 cm (10 to 12 inch). See pages 34–35 (egg white volumes). Deep with rounded sides, made in glass, plastic or ceramic.

Copper egg-white mixing bowl: Used by the professionals, round-bottomed and unlined, a copper bowl gives the best results.

A selection of smaller bowls.

Strainer or sieve: Large and small sizes. Fine mesh in stainless steel or nylon with hooks to fit over the side of a bowl. For sifting and straining. (Nylon mesh should be used with soft and acidy fruits, as metal causes discoloration.) A conical strainer is useful for liquids.

Metal grater: Stainless steel. Box-shaped, conical or flat, with varied cutting edges, for grating citrus fruits, nutmeg, chocolate, etc.

Nut grinder: Hard nylon and die-cast base or heavy iron. Ground steel cutters of different sizes. Freshly ground nuts have the best flavour; may also be used for chocolate. Or use a food processor.

Pestle and mortar: For grinding spices and pounding nuts. Made in wood or stone.

Flour brush: Nylon bristles. To brush flour off the pastry table while working.

Flour/sugar dredger: Wood or metal.

Biscuit cutters: A selection of various sizes and shapes. Plain or crinkled, in steel, tin or plastic.

Pastry wheel: Wood or stainless steel, for crimping pies.

Decorating comb: Aluminium or plastic. To make patterns in icing, meringue, etc.

Apple corer.

Savoy piping bag: Nylon or cotton. A triangular bag into which a pipe is inserted for icing cakes, preparing éclairs, meringues, etc.

Icing tubes or pipes: Available in stainless steel, nylon and tin plate. Star, rope and plain patterns in various sizes. Choose smaller ones for icing and decorating, and up to 2 cm or $5/8$ inch for choux pastes, biscuits, etc.

Icing turntable: Tin or wood. To facilitate cake icing.

Cheese cloth or butter muslin bag: For straining cheeses, fruits, etc.

Oven cloths: For lifting hot tins and trays out of the oven.

Baking parchment: Non-stick siliconed baking parchment. Needs no greasing. Cakes lift off easily without sticking: sheets can be used several times. Ideal for lining tins, meringues, biscuits, etc.

Double boiler: Invaluable equipment for sauces and creams which need gentle heat over simmering water. Stainless steel, enamelled steel or aluminium. Stainless steel is most suitable. Enamelled steel is easy to clean, but must be handled with care as it chips easily. Aluminium is least suitable; when using a metal whisk or beaters it imparts a harmless though unpleasant taste and slightly stains the mixture.

Copper sugar boiler: With brass handle; tough and durable, an excellent heat conductor. Unlike other copper pans, must be unlined, as the boiling and melting points of sugar and tin are very close. Sugar and copper do not inter-react harmfully; the pan may only be used for boiling sugar in caramels, icings and sweet-making.

All the utensils suggested are useful, but not all are essential. With a little common sense one can improvise with existing equipment. A glass bowl set over a pan of simmering water will substitute quite satisfactorily for a double boiler; a sharp vegetable peeler will curl chocolate most effectively, and the top of a glass tumbler will serve as an equally efficient biscuit cutter.

THERMOMETERS AND TIMERS

Oven thermometer: Steel and nickel-plated. A correct oven temperature is of crucial importance in baking. Oven thermostats are not always reliable, so, although a thermometer might seem to be a needless luxury, it is in fact quite essential.

Sugar thermometer: Brass, with coloured alcohol or mercury gauge. Essential for caramels, icings and sweet-making. Also indicates various stages of boiling temperatures.

General kitchen thermometer: Brass. Measures temperatures of deep-frying fats as well as of sugar.

Timer: 1 hour or 5 hours. Useful for timing baking. Many ovens now have a clock built in.

TIN WARE

Tin utensils are efficient conductors of heat and produce excellent results in baking, although it is important to observe some basic rules in their use.

Tin melts at 232°C, 450°F, so never leave an empty tinned pan on a hot-plate.

Avoid scratching the surfaces by hard scouring or polishing, as heat is deflected from polished surfaces and cakes take longer to brown.

Grease and flour tins carefully before baking, otherwise the mixture will stick.

Tin is also inclined to rust, so wash and dry utensils very thoroughly after baking. (You may dry them off in a warm oven.)

Tin ware eventually warps and the surface wears away. Do not be tempted to use it, as cakes will stick and burn. Although it is worthwhile re-coating the surfaces of copper pans, it is cheaper to replace tinned steel utensils.

ALUMINIUM WARE

Although the virtues of stainless steel and aluminium as practical alternatives to copper are at last being recognized by the catering trade, their devotion to tin baking-ware still seems deeply entrenched. The self-sufficient housewife, however, is only too pleased to experiment with new materials which minimize tedious sink chores.

Though slightly more expensive than tin, the advantages of using aluminium in baking are worth the additional outlay.

Choose good quality heavy-gauge equipment. Non-toxic and matt, the metal is uniform in thickness so there is no fear of a protective cover wearing off, or of buckling and distortion. Heat is conducted efficiently and evenly, and provided the utensil is washed, rinsed and dried well, it will give a life-time of trouble-free service.

Though completely rust-proof, aluminium is prone to pitting, so avoid leaving hard water or foods to stand in the pan for any length of time.

Never scrape sticky waste with a knife. Soak in hot soapy water, and only if necessary use scouring powder and a brush or steel wool; follow with a thorough rinse and dry.

Aluminium baking utensils should be carefully greased and floured before using.

CAKES
PTFE ALUMINIUM WARE

Aluminium equipment is also available with a non-stick finish of Polytetrafluoroethylene or PTFE.

The non-stick finish must be lightly greased for all types of bakery, as some cake mixtures are inclined to adhere despite the coating. Although unaffected by most chemicals, it scratches very easily and the use of sharp metal tools must be avoided.

Never assume that non-stick means non-wash. Always wash utensils in clean, hot soapy water, rinse well and dry; otherwise minute particles of waste foods cling to the surface and build up a layer which destroys efficiency. (Should this happen, mix together one cup of water, half a cup of domestic bleach and 2 tablespoons of bicarbonate of soda, boil this mixture in the container, then wash, rinse and dry thoroughly.) Protect tins from scratching in storage by laying a cloth or a piece of kitchen roll between them.

TINS AND TRAYS

General Hints on Choosing Tins and Trays

Most baking tins and trays are made of light-coloured metals; occasionally, however, dark metal is used. These surfaces catch and retain heat more readily than light ones, so pies and pastries will brown more successfully. Baked goods such as biscuits and cakes may brown too rapidly and burn, so a slight adjustment in baking time and temperature has to be made. Lower the oven temperature by at least 15°C (25°F), and test the cake carefully for readiness.

Baking tins and trays which are thin and flimsy are inclined to develop hot spots to which cake mixtures will stick. Remember to choose a heavy quality gauge so that the heat may spread evenly.

Start with a small basic selection of utensils and enlarge it as your repertoire becomes more adventurous.

When preparing tins for baking, it is essential that the stipulated size and shape be used, since the quantity of cake mixture and the capacity of the tin are in direct relation to each other, and the cake might otherwise be spoiled.

Wire grid or pastry rack: Tinned or stainless steel, rectangular or round. Essential for cooling bakery, as air must be allowed to circulate around warm goods.

Two baking sheets: May have a 1 or 2 cm ($\frac{3}{8}$ or $\frac{3}{4}$ inch) high lip or be completely flat. For biscuits, tarts, meringues, etc.

Cake tins: Various sizes, straight-sided and 9 cm ($3\frac{1}{2}$ inch) deep, with fixed or removable base. Aluminium or tinned most suitable for rich cakes.

Spring-form tin: Tinned steel, with removable base and expanding spring-clip rim. 22, 24, 26, 28 cm ($8\frac{1}{2}$, $9\frac{1}{2}$, $10\frac{1}{2}$, 11 inch) diameter, 5, 6 cm (2, $2\frac{1}{2}$ inch) deep. Most versatile of all cake tins. Buy two or three of similar size for layered cakes. May also be bought with two extra bases, one with a *savarin funnel*, one with a *border pattern*.

Two sandwich tins: Fixed or loose bottom. 20, 23, 24 cm (8, 9, $9\frac{1}{2}$ inch) diameter, 2.5 cm (1 inch) deep for sponges, etc.

Loaf tins: 500 g, 1 kg weight.

Balmoral guttered cake tin: Half round and ribbed, long traditional shape for gingerbread, decorative for simpler cakes. 25, 30 cm (10, 12 inch) long, 12 cm (5 inch) wide.

Flan tins: Fluted or crinkled with loose or fixed base, raised or flat. Aluminium and tinned. Many sizes. For classic fruit flans and tarts.

Square shallow baking tins: Various sizes, 4 cm ($1\frac{1}{2}$ inch) deep. Square tins tend to darken bakery more heavily at the corners, unlike round tins which colour more evenly.

CAKE MOULDS

Patterned and funnelled cake moulds must be greased and floured even more thoroughly to prevent sticking. Use a pastry brush so as not to miss any indentations. PTFE aluminium is particularly suitable for these moulds.

Gugelhupf: Unusual, sculptured traditional shape with funnelled centre, for yeast and other bakery. Aluminium or tinned steel.

Savarin or ring: Plain-sided. An alternative to the spring-form base.

Plain or fancy bun or tartlet tins: Tinned steel, aluminium or PTFE aluminium (which is most practical). Twelve holes, 6 cm ($2\frac{1}{2}$ inch) wide.

Éclair sheet: Mostly tinned. Twelve holes, each 10 cm (4 inch) long.

General Care of Baking Equipment

Always keep baking equipment scrupulously clean. Dirty cake tins not only spoil bakery but are inefficient and wear out more quickly. Caked and dried on mixtures are very difficult to remove, so fill the kitchen sink with hot soapy water as you prepare to bake, then soiled utensils may be dropped in to soak as they are no longer required. To prevent hot water setting egg, flour and milk mixtures, rinse first with cold water. Make sure that kitchen tools and bowls are spotless before you start to bake. (Grease in a mixing bowl prevents egg whites foaming, as will a dirty spoon or spatula.)

Treat tins and trays with care: soak first in hot soapy water; only if really necessary give a light scouring with a powder and pad, bristle or nylon brush, and refrain from using heavy or sharp abrasives. (Remember that cakes take longer to brown in shiny tins.) Washing soda and strong alkalis should never be used on aluminium ware, as they cause pitting and corrosion.

A soiled pastry brush should be washed out and dried immediately; prevent bending or flattening by standing it in a container with the bristles uppermost.

Scrub and rinse wooden boards, spoons and rolling pins thoroughly.

Dry all utensils carefully and set in a warm place, such as a cooling oven, before storing away.

Line the oven floor with aluminium foil to protect it from burning and staining from fruit spillages, but take care that the foil does not come into contact with an exposed electrical element which, when heated, will fuse and burn out; also avoid covering gas jets and pilot lights.

Oven rack runners should be quite clean and lightly coated with pure petroleum jelly to ensure smooth easy movement, otherwise a delicate cake might be spoiled. Clean the oven very regularly for it will function more efficiently.

Basic Ingredients

Sugar and Syrups

Sugar is one of nature's most abundant gifts. Ripe fruits such as strawberries and pineapple contain sugar, as do maple sap, palm, malt, and the young germinating grains of barley, wheat and oats. The giant bamboo-like grasses of ripe sugar cane, grown in tropical climates, and the rather ordinary root vegetable, sugar beet, grown in more temperate zones, store the greatest quantities of starch and sugar, and they supply the major part of world demand today. Sugar is refined from the juices which are extracted from these plants.

Nowadays sugar, especially refined white sugar, has fallen into disrepute. Penalized for its carbohydrate 'fattening' properties and lack of mineral salts, slimming and health food pundits try to discourage the public from using it. However, it does play a valuable role in maintaining a balanced diet, by providing some of the energy which is necessary for the human body to remain healthy; but, as with any other foods, it can be harmful if eaten in excess.

Sugar refining consists of a series of separation processes which remove insects, bacteria, waxes and other non-sweetening properties; most of the valuable minerals and vitamins are also extracted, but as long as refined sugars are used principally as a condiment or balancing food and eaten in moderation, the loss of the extra properties is not particularly significant.

Sugar

> A sugar cane was found growing in the bedroom of King Subandu, and from this grew Ilshvaku, a prince who was the direct ancestor of the Buddha.

Few plants have been so honoured in folklore as sugar in this Indian fable. Although the Polynesians might possibly lay claim to the discovery

CAKES

Sugar Cane

of sugar, followed closely by the Chinese and the Indians, the Sanskrit name 'sarkara' originated in India.

'The reed which gave honey without the help of the bees' continued its westward journey as a result of the Persian invasion of the Indus in 510 B.C., and, in the fourth century B.C., having conquered Asia, Alexander the Great carried the sugar cane to Greece. Ancient Greece and Rome both imported sugar, as a medicine and a luxury product, and 'saccharum' is mentioned by Pliny the Elder in the first century A.D. The Persians remained for many centuries the great sugar experts, and by the fifth century A.D. they already had the expertise to extract solid sugar in loaf form. Two centuries later they in turn were invaded by the Arabs who, discovering the 'sacred reed', planted it abundantly in the countries they had conquered along the Mediterranean – in Egypt, Rhodes, North Africa, Cyprus, Syria and Southern Spain.

Having perfected the process of syrup extraction, the Arabs managed to produce a dark brown, sticky substance: a 'ball of sweet salt' or 'Kurat al Milh', the 'caramel' we know today. In 1099 the Crusaders brought the new 'spice' to their homeland, where it was sold at extortionate prices by the apothecaries, who had the sole right to sell and considered it to be the first and most indispensable medicine. By the fourteenth century, sugar was being imported from the Levant via the great trading port of Venice.

The subsequent conquest of the Arabs by the Portuguese a century later enabled Christopher Columbus to plant some trial sugar cane seedlings in the Canary Islands. The ideal combination of sun, rain and fertile soil produced an unprecedented crop which grew more rapidly than anywhere else, and caused an economic revolution throughout the world. Until now sugar had been a most expensive luxury, used as a spice but valued principally for its medicinal properties. As its production grew more common, it became an essential ingredient in the manufacture of a wide range of sweet-meats, particularly in the grand kitchens of Europe. A record of the time lists: 'tarts . . . conserves of old fruits . . . marchepan, sugar-bread, gingerbread, florentines . . . and sundry outlandish confections, altogether seasoned with sugar'. Travellers returning home from their grand tours of the continent asked for many of the sweet dishes which they had enjoyed abroad, thus stimulating even greater interest in the sweet spice.

With its increasing popularity among the wealthy, such items as lockable sugar boxes, spoons, tongs and sugar sieves, all cast in silver, became fashionable collectors' pieces. A more practical tool was the special iron sugar-cutter which was needed to break pieces off the sugar loaf. Large households bought their sugar in this way; the tall, conical loaf could weigh anything from 5–35 lb and stand as much as 3 feet high. Later, 'lump' sugar was bought from the grocer who chipped it off on demand.

VARIETIES OF SUGAR

There are several different types of sugar, and it is important for the baker to understand the differences between these varieties and avoid substituting them, as they may prevent success in baking.

Granulated Sugar. The medium-sized white crystal flows freely and is almost 100 per cent pure sucrose. Suitable for most sweetening purposes, rubbed-in mixtures, and preserving, it may also be used for baking where the liquid content and the cooking times allow the crystals to dissolve completely.

The principal product of the refining process, granulated sugar is the most popular and widely used, as well as the least expensive, of all the sugars.

Caster Sugar. This has the smallest crystal of the refined sugars; white and free-flowing, it dissolves more quickly than granulated sugar.

Ideal for meringue making, caster sugar is most suitable for creaming with fats for light cake mixtures. The small crystals introduce air in tiny

CAKES

bubbles and, by the friction of their many sharp corners, soften the fat so that an air-in-fat foam is formed.

It is possible to grind granulated sugar in a liquidizer to the finer texture of caster sugar, though the slight graining is more difficult to achieve and care should be taken when using it in recipes.

Icing Sugar. This is made by grinding refined sugar crystals to a fine powder. Smooth and powdery, it dissolves rapidly and is most suitable for making pastes, icings and butter creams used for decorating cakes.

Icing sugar must be sieved before use, as it very easily forms lumps which, when combined with other ingredients, are very difficult to disperse. Avoid substituting it for granulated sugar in baking, as its dense texture will alter the crumb in cakes.

If no icing sugar is available, granulated sugar may be pulverized in a liquidizer or coffee mill.

Preserving Sugar. This is specially prepared for use in jam and jelly making as well as for preserving fruit and pickles. The crystals are large, so that they dissolve more slowly than other sugars and do not form a heavy layer which is inclined to burn on the bottom of the pan. Since very little froth is produced, less stirring and skimming is necessary and this makes the final preserve clearer and brighter.

Cube Sugar. This is made from granular sugar, moistened, compressed, moulded into cubes and then dried.

Brown and Barbados Sugars. Made from the refining syrup left after refining white sugar, the degree of colour depends on the amount of refining that has been carried out.

Moist brown sugars known as 'pieces' and 'foot' sugars are particularly useful in baking, as they are so soft and easy to combine with other ingredients. Their distinctive flavour imparts richness to cakes, and the soft, moist quality helps to keep them in good condition for a longer time.

Muscovado Sugar. A raw cane sugar rich in natural molasses.

Avoid baking with brown sugars when weather conditions are hot and humid, as the result will be adversely affected.

BASIC INGREDIENTS
Syrups and Treacle

Syrups. Syrups give a close, moist texture to cakes. They are milder in flavour than treacle. The popularity of golden syrup is due to the fact that crystallization does not take place.

Molasses or Treacle. This is the syrup or mother liquor run out from muscovado sugar.

Both treacle and golden syrup are used in making gingerbread, because the syrup does not easily crystallize when the cake is baked, thus giving it a soft texture. A little syrup or treacle helps to keep a cake moist for the same reason.

Measuring Hints for Syrups and Treacles

If the syrup has been stored in a cool place, warm it slightly by standing the tin in hot water and it will run more freely.

Spoons and measures should be rinsed in boiling water before use so that the syrup may be cleaned off without wastage.

When weighing syrup or honey in the conventional manner, sprinkle the pan with flour first. However, since it is such a sticky substance to handle, I find the most practical method of weighing is to use the tin or jar in which it is packed.

Using Spring Balance Scales: Weigh the container without the lid. From this weight, deduct the amount of syrup needed, and check the resulting weight. Spoon out the amount of syrup required, and stop when the scales reach the latter weight.

Using Slide Weight Beam Scales: Weigh the container without the lid. From this weight deduct the amount of syrup needed. Make up weights to the resulting weight, and remove syrup from the container until the scales balance.

Melting Methods: When a recipe calls for syrup to be melted – weigh the saucepan first. Add the weight of the syrup needed, and then spoon the syrup into the saucepan until the desired weight has been reached.

Storing Sugar, Syrups and Treacles

Although sugar cane will deteriorate quickly once it has been cut, refined sugars will keep for an indefinite length of time. Store bags of sugar in a cool dry place. If the sugar should become damp, dry out in a cool oven and pour the sugar into an air-tight container. The texture and quality will not spoil even if it should become moist.

Particular care should be taken when storing demerara and brown sugars, as they are very susceptible to moisture. Store in tightly covered containers. If the sugar becomes lumpy, sprinkle lightly with a few drops of water and heat gently in a low oven for a few moments (take care not to overheat, or the sugar will melt). Alternatively, empty the sugar into a bowl, cover with a damp cloth, and leave to stand overnight.

Syrups and treacles will keep from 6 to 12 months. Some evaporation and crystallization may take place.

Sugar in Baking

Sugar with fat gives both sweetness and tenderness to doughs in baking; in small amounts it speeds the rising powers of yeast but inhibits them if used too liberally. When sugar is creamed with fat, air is trapped in the mixture by the fat-covered sugar crystals, thus imparting a light texture to the cake.

When both sugar and flour are present in the mixture, the sugar forms a syrup as it dissolves, and disperses the protein molecules of the gluten in the flour. The sugar enables the gluten to expand, by keeping it soft. This gives volume and lightness to the mixture. Too much sugar in the mixture will soften the gluten so much that it is unable to hold the risen shape of the cake, which will sink in the middle.

When eggs are also present in the mixture, sugar helps to delay the coagulation of the protein in the egg, again providing a finer, smoother texture. It is the sugar content in meringues which enables the mixture to achieve and retain a very high proportion of air.

Selecting Sugar

Always use the sugar which has been recommended in the recipe. The cake and the method by which it is made dictates the correct one to be used. There are some recipes which can be made with many types of sugar: each will produce a perfect, yet different, result.

Beware of substituting liquid sugars such as honey for solid sweeteners. There is a great difference in their sweetening powers, and the greater moisture content has to be taken into account.

BASIC INGREDIENTS
Flour

Selecting Flour for Baking

No one brand of flour is better than another, but the type of flour used in baking is important. Flour forms the main bulk or structure of many cakes – a light cake with a tender crumb needs weak flour; a vigorous and robust framework is better made with strong flour. Self-raising flour is suitable for plainer recipes, and plain flour with baking powder added suits richer cakes.

Always use the flour which has been recommended in the recipe.

TYPES OF FLOUR

Strong and Weak Flours. Grown in many parts of the world, wheat will flourish in different climates and soil conditions. It is these variables which determine the quality and quantity of protein in the flour. The long moist growing season in Britain and Europe lasts from the late autumn until the following summer. During this time the endosperm keeps swelling and produces a large amount of starch and only about 9 per cent protein; it is from this that weak flour is milled.

The growing season in the dry climates of North America, Canada and other parts of the world is considerably shorter, as the seed is sown in the spring. Less starch is able to develop though it has a similar amount of protein to that of 'weak' flour and thus produces proportionately more, 12 per cent of protein. This is 'strong' flour. When water is added to this protein, gluten is formed.

During baking the gluten, a sticky, elastic substance, is stretched into balloon-like bubbles by steam and expanding gases; these then set lightly and crisply to hold the cake in its risen shape. Since gluten absorbs water, the more protein there is in a flour the greater the yield of dough. Strong flour thus gives light, open-textured cakes with considerable rise.

Choose strong plain flour for making yeast cakes, puff pastries, éclairs, breads and batters. Choose weak plain flour for cakes with a finer, shorter texture and a smaller rise, such as light cakes, sponges, short pastries and biscuits.

Plain and Self-raising Flours. Apart from the gluten content, it is generally necessary to incorporate other raising agents with the flour.

Self-raising flour already includes this, but baking powder (a mixture of bicarbonate of soda and cream of tartar) has usually to be added to plain flour. In both instances a mixture of acid and alkaline chemicals react to form carbon dioxide gas when heated. As the gas is formed it expands and makes bubbles in the mixture. It is essential that the raising agent is distributed evenly and thoroughly when using plain flour. Sift the flour very carefully with the raising agent three or four times – this also ensures that the flour is well aerated. The raising agent in self-raising flour does not act quite as quickly as ordinary baking powder; when a cake mixture has been prepared with self-raising flour it may rest in a cool place without detriment for up to half an hour.

Superfine or Air-classified Flours. A new grade of flour is now available, known generally as superfine or supergraded. Slightly granular in texture, this flour has undergone a treatment known as air-classification. After the final sieving during the milling process, the remaining grains of flour are passed through a stream of air, and the finest particles of flour are removed so that those remaining are of a more uniform size. The flour feels much lighter and softer to the touch, is easier to sieve, and slightly easier to fold into a cake mixture. Since the gluten in dough is toughened by too much mixing, light and speedy handling when incorporating flour into a cake mixture is important; superfine flour gives an advantage in mixing, but there is little difference in the final result.

Wholemeal Flour. This contains all the rich and nutritive parts of the wheat grain, including the bran and the germ. It is free of chemicals; the only addition is caramel, which may be added to improve the colour. It contains more B vitamins and other minerals and has a much higher roughage content than white flour.

Avoid substituting wholemeal for white flour; use the recommended flour for the recipe, or choose a recipe which uses nuts and no flour at all.

Potato Flour (Non-wheat). As its name implies, this derives from potatoes, which are boiled and sieved before being dried. Potato flour is often used with other flours, and sometimes alone in sponges. (A section of this book is devoted to cakes made with this flour – see page 193f.) It has a quite distinctive light and creamy taste which particularly enhances the cake flavour.

BASIC INGREDIENTS

Cornflour. Cornflour derives from the endosperm of the maize grain and is almost pure starch. It is low in protein, but invaluable as a thickener for sauces. It is sometimes used with plain flours for making cakes (American 'cake flour' includes cornflour), and tends to produce a cake which is rather short, crumbles easily and melts in the mouth.

Arrowroot. This is a starch derived from the underground stems of plants growing in the Indies, tropical Africa and America. It dissolves slightly in water, quickly swells up in warm water or milk and is consequently easily digested. Arrowroot is very useful as a thickening base for creams and fine glazes for fruit flans and tartlets. It gives a clearer result than cornflour.

Storing Flour

Store flour in a cool dry place, on an airy shelf in the kitchen cupboard. It will keep better in its paper bag, which does not retain moisture. If the kitchen is inclined to be damp or the atmosphere rather steamy, empty the flour into an air-tight tin or a stoppered jar – but never add new flour to old, as faulty hygiene during storage can cause maggots and later tiny beetles or moths to appear (hatched from eggs in the cereal). Wash the container and dry very carefully first.

Plain flour will keep well for up to 6 months.

Self-raising flour may lose its raising potency if it is not used within 3 months.

Butter

BUTTER IN BAKING

Pastry made with butter has good flavour, is crisp and fairly short. Rubbed in with flour, butter coats small groups of flour particles with a waterproof layer but leaves a small amount of flour uncoated and able to absorb water. This in its turn makes an elastic mixture which gives crispness to the pastry.

For whisked cakes, butter is creamed with sugar to make a foam of air in fat. The butter must be quite soft for a speedy and good result, so that when the egg is beaten into the flour it smooths and stiffens the mixture and forms an emulsion with fat, otherwise it curdles and some aeration is lost. (This can be rectified by beating in a spoonful of flour.)

Choosing Butter for Baking

There are two types of butter most suitable for baking.

Sweet cream butter comes mainly from New Zealand, Australia, Ireland and the United Kingdom; it is smooth textured, mildly flavoured and strongly coloured. It is generally lightly salted, which has no adverse effect in baking and is most suitable for pastries and biscuits.

The paler coloured butter comes from Europe and Scandinavia; it has a rich creamy flavour, and a softer quality which makes it ideal for creaming in cake mixtures. It may be salted or unsalted, the latter being very suitable for cake fillings.

Cheaper creamery butter should be avoided; it is usually a blend of sweet cream butters of inferior texture and flavour, and is often heavily salted.

Storing Butter

Most salted butters keep for up to 6 weeks; unsalted up to 3 weeks. Keep in a cold place, closely wrapped. Stored in a freezer their life is longer; unsalted up to 6 months, salted up to 3 months. Thaw in the refrigerator and use within a week. Never store butter in warm conditions, for it quickly turns rancid and develops an unpleasant odour. It will ruin the flavour of any bakery.

Margarine

In the past, margarine has been substituted for butter as an economic measure. In my opinion this is a false economy, for margarine has almost no flavour and is of no benefit to baking, other than to fulfil the chemical functions. It is of course necessary for anyone whose diet or religious beliefs forbid animal fats.

Eggs, Egg Whites

> The excellence of the whole depends on the manner in which the eggs are whisked; this should be done as lightly as possible, but it is a mistake to suppose that they cannot be too long beaten, as after they are brought to a state of perfect firmness they are injured by a continuation of the whisking and will at times curdle, and render a cake heavy from this cause . . .
>
> (Eliza Acton, 1845)

Eggs

Egg is of crucial importance in a cake mixture. It gives good flavour and rich colour, and adds lightness by holding enough air not to need a raising agent. The yolk and white separately have useful properties: the yolk can hold fat in emulsion – helpful in richer cakes – and the white, when whisked, holds a considerable amount of air. Egg whites serve many other purposes in the baking kitchen; they act as a base for macaroons, as a bond for marzipan, in royal icing, fillings, and various glazes. Whipped separately, they are folded into cake mixtures and help to give an aerated rise; but certainly their simplest and most popular use is when they are whipped with sugar to make meringue.

Meringues taste magical and look magical, and even their preparation is considered by some to smack of magic; but their composition could not be simpler. The secret lies in the correct beating of the whites, and once this and the technique of folding in has been mastered the mystique will vanish. Chemistry is the only magic.

A Fresh Egg

When a fresh egg is cracked open it should have a thick and transparent white which hugs the yolk evenly all round. The white of a stale egg will be thin and watery and will not contain the yolk firmly, letting it spread and break up easily; the flavour too is stale and unpleasant, and the white will beat up only moderately well.

Eggs must be as fresh as possible for their flavour to be at its best. Shop-bought eggs, which are mostly battery-produced, are dated with the week in the year; the flavour is less good than that of free range eggs. These may or may not be dated – only buy undated ones where you are sure of freshness.

If you are doubtful about freshness, put the unbroken egg in a bowl of tepid water. An egg which lies on its side at the bottom is fresh, one that floats or rises with the rounded end up is probably stale.

Storing Eggs

In warm conditions eggs quickly lose freshness and become contaminated. Store whole eggs, in their boxes, in a cool pantry or low down in the refrigerator, and keep them away from strong-smelling foods, for the shells are porous and easily absorb odours.

Left-over egg whites will remain fresh for 4–5 days in the refrigerator; store in an airtight container with as little air as possible trapped inside (which speeds ageing) or they become stale, watery and thin textured. They can be frozen in individual ice-cube trays, one white to a cube – when frozen pack in freezer bags and store for up to 6 months.

Egg yolks keep less well than whites for only a day or two, and should not be frozen. Pour them into a small container and cover with a little milk or water; drain the liquid before using.

Egg Sizes

Egg sizes range from 1–7: size 3–4, standard size, are usually used for baking; sizes 5, 6 and 7 are smaller. A size 3 egg weighs about 60 g (just over 2 oz); a size 4 egg about 55 g (just under 2 oz).

The shell weighs approximately 6 g ($^3/_{16}$ oz)
The white weighs approximately 32 g ($1^1/_8$ oz)
The yolk weighs approximately 16 g ($^9/_{16}$ oz)

If you use larger eggs than standard, adjust the recipe accordingly.

How to Separate an Egg

Crack the egg sharply, on the side of a small bowl (not the main mixing bowl in case the egg is bad), and gently prise the two shells apart just enough to let the egg white slide out; tip one shell to hold the yolk, then slide the yolk into the other half, leaving the rest of the white to fall into the bowl underneath. Transfer the yolk to another small bowl and put the white into the mixing bowl.

Not a trace of yolk must be present in the whites, as this prevents them frothing when beaten. Use a half egg shell to scoop out any yolk if necessary.

BASIC INGREDIENTS
HANDLING EGG WHITES

When an egg white is over-beaten the snowy mass looks granular, starts to separate, and becomes lumpy and watery. Unfortunately it is completely spoiled at this point and it is impossible to retrieve the air. How do you avoid this?

Once you start beating, continue until the egg white has fully expanded – a stop midway will cause a collapse.

The stiff beaten white must be used straight away, as the aerated mixture disintegrates almost immediately. When sugar is beaten in, it holds the air much longer.

Egg white must only be beaten when it is needed – prepare the host mixture (with which it is to be combined) first.

Never stir or beat egg snow into a mixture (apart from lightening the main mixture with a spoonful at first) – only *fold* it in (see notes below).

The Bowl and Whisking Tool

The whipping bowl must be spotlessly clean and completely dry, as grease inhibits the rise of the egg white. A round-bottomed copper bowl is the most efficient type; enamel or glass is acceptable; plastic is least desirable. As egg whites expand in volume to more than three times their original size, quite a large bowl is needed. A pinch of salt or cream of tartar added to the egg whites helps them stabilize.

A 20 cm (8 inch) bowl will take 3 egg whites
A 25 cm (10 inch) bowl will take 5 egg whites
A 30 cm (12 inch) bowl will take 8 egg whites

The tool best designed for whisking is a large balloon-shaped wire whisk; a good alternative, needing less energy, is the hand-held electric mixer, which can be lifted up and round the mixture, so as to incorporate a maximum of air. Least satisfactory is the electric table-mixer, which cannot beat in enough air and makes a denser and compacter mass. An electric food processor is not at all suitable.

Whisking Egg Whites for Meringue or Whisked Cakes

Egg whites consist of albumen in water, and when warmed to room temperature and beaten, large air bubbles form in the albumen. With continued whisking they break down into smaller air bubbles. The mixture changes colour and texture, becomes opaque, increases considerably in volume, and stiffens eventually to stand in firm, snowy peaks. It will at least triple in volume. This aerated state gives lightness to a cake mixture and is the major ingredient of meringue.

How to beat the egg white: Start beating slowly at first until the whites begin to froth, then more vigorously; as you beat lift the beater up out of the bowl and back down through the mixture in a figure of eight movement, making sure that all comes across its path. The mass will then start to thicken, become dense and form into soft but firm snowy peaks. When the whisk is held up the snow will stand firm and upright on the tip. You should be able to turn the bowl upside down and the snow should remain intact. *Stop now*. If you beat more, the mixture will start to separate, become coarse, grainy, and slightly watery, and eventually collapse. There is no way of retrieving the air.

Folding in the Beaten Egg White

This is as important as whisking an egg white correctly, for the beaten-in air must be retained in both the main cake mixture and the snow. Use a large metal spoon, which cuts through the mixture better than a blunter tool. First stir 1 or 2 tablespoons of whisked white into the host mixture to lighten it; then tip in half the egg whites.

Lightness of hand and care are essential now. Slowly rotate the bowl as you work and cut down into the mixture, *never stir*; tilt the spoon and fold the mixture over very lightly, in a figure of eight movement, then lift it up and out high into the air. Continue until all the egg white has been used, making sure that each part of the mixture is incorporated. It will look spongy and well aerated but firm.

Pour the cake mixture straight into the prepared baking tin, rap the tin once, smartly, on the work top to dispel any air pockets, and bake in the preheated oven immediately.

Using the Oven

Failure in baking is often caused by an inaccurate oven temperature. An oven thermometer is invaluable. Adjust the heat control accordingly or move the shelves, but make sure that none is too close to the source of heat or the baking will burn.

When baking more than one cake at a time, make sure that no shelf is too close to the burners. Trays and tins should stand flat on the shelves, and be staggered so that one is not directly above the other. They must not touch each other, or the door, sides or back of the oven, as the air needs to circulate around them.

Prepare the oven before baking preparations are made. Switch on and set the thermostat to the required temperature 15 minutes before it is needed. A finished cake batter must be baked immediately in a preheated oven. Raising agents in a cake mixture, whether artificial or aerated, need heat instantly, in order to release the carbon dioxide and burst the starch grains. If the oven is not hot enough this action is unable to take place, the cake cannot rise, and it will turn out heavy and damp.

Avoid the temptation of opening the oven door before the cake has begun to set. Wait until at least three-quarters of the baking time has passed, and then be very gentle, for a sudden draught of cold air will cause the cake to collapse dramatically – particularly sponges and other cakes raised with air and containing little flour.

Test the cake for readiness. It should be well risen and evenly browned. Insert a warmed skewer into the centre: if it comes out dry the cake is ready, but if a little of the cake mixture still clings to it then the cake needs further cooking. Another method of testing the cake is to touch the surface gently – it should feel firm and springy; if the finger indentation remains it is not ready. Watch these final stages of baking, for when the cake starts to shrink away from the sides of the tin it is certainly ready. Lift the cake out of the oven very carefully; treat it with respect, for it is still sensitive and a sudden jerk or draught will cause a collapse. Never stand it near an open window or door.

Never stand a hot cake tin on a solid surface as the underside of the cake will become sodden and stodgy; always stand it on a wire cooling rack. This allows the air to circulate around the tin. Usually a cake has to stay in the tin for a few minutes while it settles down, then the tin sides and base can be removed and the cake left to cool on the rack. Some pastries are left to cool in the tin – see the individual recipes for details.

Remove the cake from the tin after about 5 to 10 minutes; gently run a knife blade down the side of the tin and carefully release the cake. Take care not to cut into the mixture. If it is of a fairly firm consistency and richness, the bottom tray should also be removed; very fine light-textured cakes are best cooled with the base in place. After removing the sides of the tins, lay the wire rack on top of the cake and lift them both up together and turn the cake over on to the rack. Remove the base. If the cake is to be iced use the base, which is smoother. Otherwise you need a second rack to turn it back over again with the top of the cake uppermost.

What Happens to the Cake in the Oven?

However careful one is while preparing a cake, for no apparent reason the final result is sometimes unsatisfactory. Even the most experienced baker can have a disaster. It is useful to understand a little of what happens to the cake in the oven, so that it is easier to decide what has gone wrong.

The heat of the oven and the moisture in the cake mixture cause the grains of starch in the flour to soften and burst so that they can absorb the melting fat. The moisture and flour (and fat when used) form a glutinous mixture which will stretch. Air which has been incorporated during the mixing, or the carbon dioxide which has been formed by the action of the moisture on the raising agent, will become heated and start to expand, forcing its way through the cake. This stretches the flour mixture, and the cake rises. If the heat in the oven is correct and the right ingredients have been used, the process is so regulated that, as the cake reaches its highest rising point, the heat is sufficient to set the mixture and a light well-risen cake will result.

A CHECKLIST OF THE BASIC ESSENTIALS

1. Read the recipe carefully and assemble all the ingredients in the kitchen at least half an hour before starting.

2. Set the oven thermostat to the correct temperature and switch on the oven at least 15 minutes before preparation begins.

3. Prepare the correctly sized baking tin — line or grease as instructed.

4. Make the cake mixture following the instructions precisely; pour into the cake tin straight away and bake immediately in the preheated oven.

5. Do not open the oven door too soon.

What Went Wrong?

Here are some suggestions which might account for failure.

The cake has not risen: Insufficient raising agent: if air is the raising agent then the basic mixture has been beaten too little, or the separated egg whites over-beaten and/or stirred not folded into the mixture; the oven temperature was set too high, so that the cake mixture was not fully stretched before it started to set.

Texture too coarse and grainy: Too much raising agent; wrong sugar; eggs and sugar whisked insufficiently in basic mixture; oven too cool.

A sunken middle: Oven temperature not hot enough to set the cake when it reached its peak; too much raising agent used, and the gluten in the mixture was overstretched and collapsed before it could set. Too much moisture can cause the cake not to set. This may be through using too many or too large eggs, too much liquid, too much fruit which has not been dried properly. A sudden draught of cold air, caused by opening the oven door too soon, creates a fall in temperature so that it is insufficiently hot to set the cake mixture.

The fruit has sunk to the bottom: Incorrect proportions of ingredients so that the mixture is too soft to support the fruit; the fruit was too heavy and large; oven temperature too cool to set the mixture quickly enough; the fruit was wet when used — a simple precaution is to dust the fruit with a little flour before incorporating it in the mixture.

The cake has a thick crust: Too high an oven temperature; cake cooked too long; inadequately lined tin for a large cake.

A damp and heavy cake: Incorrect proportions of ingredients: too much moisture or sugar, too much orange or lemon juice; oven not hot enough; mixture over-worked after flour addition; cake cooled too rapidly; not cooled on a rack where the air can circulate; the fresh baked, still warm cake was cooled in the refrigerator or sealed in a tin before it cooled completely.

Over-browning of the cake: Cooking too near to the top of the oven; the oven was overloaded; a large rich fruit cake was not covered with brown paper for part of the baking time.

CAKES

The cake top is peaked or cracked: A depression was not made in the centre of the cake before baking; too hot an oven; the cake was baked too near the top of the oven; too small a tin.

Basic Pastries

Dear Nelly! learn with care the pastry art,
And mind the easy precepts I impart:
Draw out your dough elaborately thin,
And cease not to fatigue your rolling pin:
Of eggs and butter see you mix enough,
For then the paste will swell into a puff,
Which will in crumpling sounds your praise report,
And eat, as housewives speak, exceeding short.

(King, quoted from *Food in England*,
Dorothy Hartley)

Shortcrust, Sweet Shortcrust and Sweet Shortcrust with Almond

Shortcrust is simple to prepare and the most versatile of pastries. I prefer the French versions (*pâte brisée* and *pâte sucrée*), which use more butter and egg yolks, and may be rolled quite thin. They have a light and crisp, though robust structure, which can contain and enhance any filling. English shortcrust, which may also use lard and water, has a more crumbly texture, and is inclined to be stodgy and less resistant to moisture.

Shortcrust is used for open and double-crust pies and tarts, or as a base for elaborate structures such as *Croquembouche* or *St Honoré* (pages 105, 103), for tartlets and barquettes (page 111). Sweet shortcrust is richer and has to be rolled thicker than the plain version. It is particularly good filled with fresh soft fruits and more elaborate creams.

General Hints for Making Basic Pastry Doughs

Lightness of hand and speed are the two most important factors necessary for successful pastry-making. It should take no more than 3 or 4 minutes to prepare, for if the pastry is worked too long the gluten in the flour will develop and the dough become too elastic, which causes difficulties in rolling, shrinkage in baking and makes the texture tough.

Cool conditions: Prepare pastry in a cool kitchen, preferably before you start cooking. Work on a marble surface if possible, though any surface will do provided it is kept really cool. Chill with a bag of ice-cubes in the summer if necessary. The fat should be slightly chilled, firm but not hard or it will not blend properly. Cool warm hands by holding wrists under running water for a few seconds.

Fingertip touch: Work with the fingertips, never the palms, and lightly toss the flour mixture as you rub, to retain air and keep it cool.

Avoid overworking: Ignore the occasional bigger piece in the crumb mixture, it will be blended more thoroughly later. If many large ones start to form when the crumb stage is passed, the paste has been over-worked and will never have quite the right texture (although chilling will help a little).

Adding water: Take care when adding water to the crumb mixture as the quality and moisture content of flour varies. Use two-thirds of the stated quantity to start with. This avoids over-working the pastry, and protects it from being too dry, and softening too much so that it toughens and hardens during baking. Add more water if necessary.

Excess flour: Will spoil the texture and flavour of the cake. Brush and scrape it away along with any excess dough whilst you work.

Greasing tins: Very lightly grease the baking utensil with butter or oil.

Baking temperatures: These basic pastries are usually baked in a fairly high oven to start, then the temperature is reduced to complete the cooking. The sharp heat sets the pastry into shape. Once *pâte sucrée* starts to brown, keep a watchful eye because the high sugar content causes it to scorch rather easily.

Preheat the oven to gas 6, 200°C, 400°F: bake the goods for 10 minutes to set, then turn down the heat to gas 4, 180°C, 350°F for about 20 minutes more. See the individual recipes for particular instructions.

Storing and Freezing Basic Pastries

Raw pastry will keep at least 3 to 4 days in the refrigerator if wrapped closely in greaseproof paper, aluminium foil or plastic film; no air must come in contact to spoil or dry it out. Take out about an hour before it is needed.

Wrapped similarly, it may also be stored in a freezer for up to 2 months; it dries out if kept any longer. Thaw out slowly.

Rolling the pastry

Raw pastry shaped into flan cases, tart tins or shells and then frozen is an even better alternative. Freeze separately on trays, then remove the tins and wrap the unbaked shells tightly.

Raw pies and tarts filled with fresh fruits such as apple (sprinkle with lemon juice to prevent discoloration), rhubarb and blackberry may be frozen successfully. Freeze unwrapped, then remove the container and pack as before. Transfer direct from the freezer to the preheated oven without thawing. (Be sure to cut a vent in a pie lid for the steam to escape before you put it in the oven.) The oven temperature should be gas 4, 180°C, 350°F. Cook for about $\frac{3}{4}$ to 1 hour.

Empty baked shells can also be frozen; re-heat from the frozen state at gas 3, 170°C, 325°F until crisp.

Avoid freezing baked and filled pastries; the pastry invariably becomes soggy when thawed and the filling may separate.

Shortcrust Pastry — Pâte Brisée

(1) Ingredients for a 20–22 cm (8–8½ inch) tin or 10 tartlet cases

130 g soft, plain flour	4½ oz soft, plain flour
pinch salt	pinch salt
80 g butter	3 oz butter
15 g caster sugar	½ oz caster sugar
1 egg yolk	1 egg yolk
1½ tablespoons iced water	1½ tablespoons iced water

(2) Ingredients for a 24–26 cm (9½–10½ inch) tin or 14 tartlet cases

175 g soft, plain flour	6½ oz soft, plain flour
large pinch salt	large pinch salt
110 g butter	4 oz butter
25 g caster sugar	1 oz caster sugar
1 egg	1 egg
2–3 tablespoons iced water	2–3 tablespoons iced water

(3) Ingredients for a 28–30 cm (11–12 inch) tin or 16 tartlet cases

260 g soft, plain flour	9 oz soft, plain flour
½ teaspoon salt	½ teaspoon salt
165 g butter	6 oz butter
35 g caster sugar	1 oz caster sugar
2 eggs	2 eggs

BASIC PASTRIES

3½–4 tablespoons iced water   3½–4 tablespoons iced water

Bake at gas 6, 200°C, 400°F for 10 minutes, then reduce temperature to gas 4, 180°C, 350°F for about 20 minutes unless otherwise shown.

Method of preparation: Sift the flour with the salt on to a cold surface and make a well in the centre. Cut the slightly chilled butter into small pieces and drop into the well, together with the sugar and egg yolk. Add a small quantity of water, then using the fingertips and thumbs lightly combine the ingredients. Work the flour in gradually, using a scraper as an aid, to make a breadcrumb texture, and moistening the paste more if necessary – it should be soft but not sticky. Roll into a ball. Blend thoroughly by pushing the dough away from you on the work surface, a small piece at a time, using the heel of the hand. It should be smooth and pliable. Press the dough pieces into a ball and lightly dust with flour. Wrap in aluminium foil or plastic film and chill for at least 30 minutes. The pastry is very elastic and easy to roll out; let it rest for a few minutes before lining the tin, so that the stretched pastry can spring back.

Sweet Shortcrust Pastry – Pâte Sucrée

(1) Ingredients for a 20–22 cm (8–8½ inch) tin or 10 tartlet cases

130 g soft, plain flour	4½ oz soft, plain flour
small pinch salt	small pinch salt
45 g caster sugar	1½ oz caster sugar
½ teaspoon lemon zest	½ teaspoon lemon zest
1 egg yolk	1 egg yolk
90 g butter	3 oz butter

(2) Ingredients for a 24–26 cm (9½–10½ inch) tin or 14 tartlet cases

165 g soft, plain flour	6 oz soft, plain flour
½ teaspoon salt	½ teaspoon salt
50 g caster sugar	2 oz caster sugar
1 teaspoon lemon zest	1 teaspoon lemon zest
1 small egg *or* 2 small egg yolks	1 small egg *or* 2 small egg yolks
110 g butter	4 oz butter

(3) Ingredients for a 30 cm (12 inch) tin or 16 tartlet cases

210 g soft plain flour	7½ oz soft, plain flour
½ teaspoon salt	½ teaspoon salt
70 g caster sugar	2½ oz caster sugar
1 teaspoon lemon zest	1 teaspoon lemon zest
2 eggs	2 eggs
150 g butter	5½ oz butter

Bake at gas 6, 200°C, 400°F for 10 minutes, then reduce temperature to gas 4, 180°C, 350°F for about 20 minutes unless otherwise stated.

Method of preparation: Sweet shortcrust pastry is prepared in the same manner as short pastry.

Sift the flour and salt together in a mound. Make a well in the middle and place in it the sugar, lemon zest and egg yolk. Lightly blend the ingredients until the sugar is absorbed, then work in the softened butter pieces and combine finally with the rest of the flour. Blend thoroughly by pushing the dough, a small piece at a time, away from you on the work surface using the heel of the hand, until the dough becomes smooth and pliable. Gather the pieces into a ball and dust with a little flour. Wrap in aluminium foil or plastic film and chill for at least 30 minutes before using.

Pâte sucrée has a more crumbly texture than short pastry, because of the greater sugar content. It must be well chilled before being used, and it is often easier to press it into the flan mould than to roll it out. Cracks and holes can be patched with small pieces of pastry.

Sweet Shortcrust Pastry with Almonds – Pâte Sucrée aux Amandes

(1) Ingredients for a 20–22 cm (8–8½ inch) tin or 10 tartlet cases

80 g butter	3 oz butter
40 g icing sugar	1½ oz icing sugar
1 egg	1 egg
40 g ground almonds	1½ oz ground almonds
1 teaspoon lemon zest	1 teaspoon lemon zest
120 g soft, plain flour	4 oz soft, plain flour
1 teaspoon lemon juice	1 teaspoon lemon juice

BASIC PASTRIES

(2) Ingredients for a 24–26 cm (9½–10½ inch) tin or 14 tartlet cases

100 g butter	3½ oz butter
50 g icing sugar	2 oz icing sugar
1½ eggs	1½ eggs
50 g ground almonds	2 oz ground almonds
1 teaspoon lemon zest	1 teaspoon lemon zest
150 g soft, plain flour	5½ oz soft, plain flour
1 teaspoon lemon juice	1 teaspoon lemon juice

(3) Ingredients for a 28–30 cm (11–12 inch) tin or 16 tartlet cases

140 g butter	5 oz butter
70 g icing sugar	2½ oz icing sugar
2 eggs	2 eggs
70 g ground almonds	2½ oz ground almonds
1½ teaspoons lemon zest	1½ teaspoons lemon zest
210 g soft, plain flour	7½ oz soft, plain flour
1½ teaspoons lemon juice	1½ teaspoons lemon juice

Bake at gas 6, 200°C, 400°F for 10 minutes, then reduce temperature to gas 4, 180°C, 350°F for about 20 minutes unless otherwise stated.

Method of preparation: Here the basic method differs from the previous two. Cream the butter and sugar until light and fluffy, then beat in the egg. Mix in the almonds, the lemon zest and then the sifted flour. Moisten with sufficient lemon juice to make a firm dough. Wrap in foil or plastic film and chill in the refrigerator.

A Note on Electric Food Processors

Although a food processor is not particularly suitable for cake preparation, it is ideal for making basic pastries. The process is in two stages:

(1) Blend the sifted dry goods (salt, sugar, flavour and almonds if used) with the cut up butter for 15 seconds – if it starts to go lumpy it has been over-mixed.

(2) Add the egg yolks and two-thirds of the water; blend for a further 10 seconds, check if the mixture is moist enough and add more water if necessary. (Usually less water is needed with this method.) Blend for a further 5 seconds to finish. The pastry will have blended into a well-combined, compact ball. It must rest overnight in the refrigerator,

CAKES

wrapped in foil or plastic film, to reduce elasticity. Take out an hour before it is needed.

It is easy to over-blend once the binding materials have been added, and you may prefer to finish off by hand as follows:

Make the crumb mixture as in (1), then tip the mixture into a bowl and stir in the yolks and water lightly with a blunt knife, judging the amount carefully. Combine into a ball, then knead by hand as for the hand method. Chill in the refrigerator for about 30 minutes.

German Pastry

(1) Ingredients for a 20–22cm (8–8½ inch) tin

120 g soft, plain flour	4 oz soft, plain flour
120 g butter	4 oz butter
60 g caster sugar	2 oz caster sugar
1 teaspoon lemon zest	1 teaspoon lemon zest
½ egg	½ egg

(2) Ingredients for a 24–26 cm (9½–10½ inch) tin

150 g soft, plain flour	5½ oz soft, plain flour
150 g butter	5½ oz butter
75 g caster sugar	3 oz caster sugar
1½ teaspoons lemon zest	1½ teaspoons lemon zest
1 small egg	1 small egg

(3) Ingredients for a 28–30 cm (11–12 inch) tin

220 g soft, plain flour	8 oz soft, plain flour
220 g butter	8 oz butter
110 g caster sugar	4 oz caster sugar
2 teaspoons lemon zest	2 teaspoons lemon zest
1 large egg	1 large egg

gas 5, 190°C, 375°F / 40 minutes

Sift the flour into a pastry bowl. Cut the cold butter into it and lightly crumb the mixture with the tips of the fingers. When all the coarse lumps have been broken, mix in the sugar and lemon zest. Using a knife or a spatula and part of the beaten egg, bind the pastry together; it

BASIC PASTRIES

should not be too moist. It may be used immediately, but will be easier to handle if it has been chilled for a little while in the refrigerator. Grease a baking tin or a round tin. Press the pastry lightly into it, covering the base and the sides evenly. Cover with prepared fruits (see pages 220–1).

Puff Pastry – Pâte Feuilletée

For many decades Claude Lorraine (1600–1682), the French landscape painter, was reputed to be the creator of puff pastry, but it was already known in Ancient Greece, and in 1311 Robert Bishop of Amiens mentioned *gâteaux feuilleteés* in a charter. Bartolomeo Scappi, the Italian chef, published in his book *Opera* a primitive paste, based on an Arab recipe, which was rolled and folded and layered with melted lard. Another dough known as *crostate*, not unlike Câreme's *vol au vent*, was basted during cooking with a feather dipped in butter.

In 1653, La Varenne introduced puff pastry to the French cookery book market, just eighteen years after Lorraine perfected it. Today the recipe is no different, and while many recipes have travelled across the channel from France to England, it would seem that puff pastry in fact originated in the East and was brought to the West by the Crusaders.

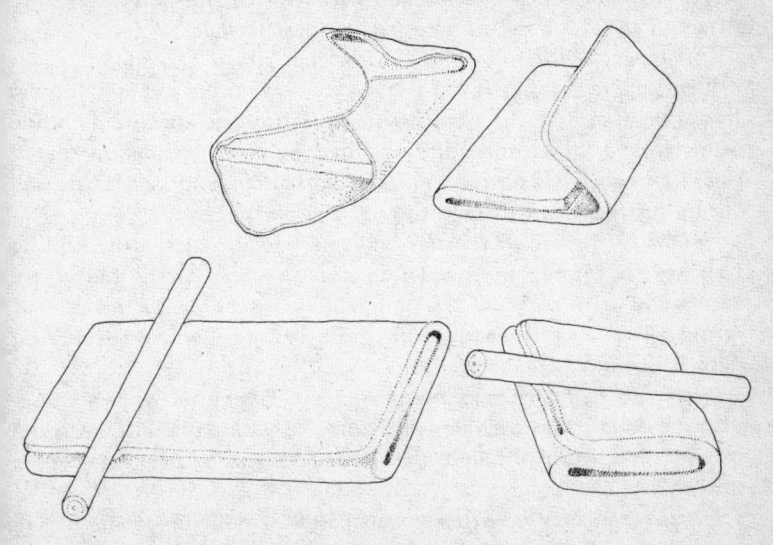

CAKES

Puff pastry needs a great deal of time and patience for its preparation, and I feel that for the special occasion it is worth the effort. It also demands absolute concentration or it can easily go wrong. Choose a peaceful period – in the evening when the children have gone to bed or while the house is empty. Most important of all is the need to work in a cool airy kitchen, for warmth causes many problems. A freezer is particularly useful for storing the prepared paste, which will keep fresh for up to 6 months.

I must also mention the ready-made fresh and frozen puff pastries which are available in the shops. Usually made with special margarines and shortenings, their flavour is not particularly good, but they are quite adequate on occasion, and the taste can be improved by rolling and folding in an extra layer of butter before using.

Notes about Making Puff Pastry

Use butter: I always bake with butter, though some prefer margarine; it is of course at the baker's discretion. However, for puff pastry you must use *unsalted* butter, *never* margarine, as the mixture is so simple (flour and fat in equal quantities, salt and water) that the flavour of the pastry depends entirely on the butter. Unsalted butter has a firm and stable texture which will layer successfully during the folding and rolling process without being squeezed out; salted butter chills less evenly, and although as easy to use as unsalted, has less flavour.

Use strong plain flour to give greater elasticity to the dough.

Work on a cold surface in cool surroundings, as butter and dough must always be of exactly the same low temperature and consistency while being worked. In warm conditions a marble slab is ideal; failing that, a bag of ice cubes laid on the work area for half an hour beforehand and during rest periods will help to keep the pastry cool.

Chilled rest periods are essential and must not be shortened. Rolling activates the gluten in the dough and also softens the butter; an over-active state prevents the dough from extending so that it may spring back when rolled and shrink during baking. Resting and chilling calm it down.

Never chill the pastry in the freezer or on ice. The butter will set harder than the dough, and with pressure from the rolling pin will break and splinter and push through the dough layers, rather than blend smoothly.

Geometric precision is necessary: puff pastry is built up of alternating layers of butter and dough, and to prevent uneven layering, which leads

BASIC PASTRIES

to imperfect pastries, it is important that rolling is precise. The sides must be straight, the corners square, and the thickness uniform.

Keep an accurate tally of the folds. Six folds have produced 729 layers — any more and the structure may fail to rise properly, and even disintegrate.

I have given the recipe instructions using large quantities (500 g (1 lb 1½ oz) flour, 450 g (1 lb) butter), so that half may be frozen if wished.

Pâte Feuilletée — French Puff Pastry

(1) 125 g flour makes 325 g dough

4½ oz flour makes 11 oz dough

125 g strong, plain flour
½ teaspoon salt
10 g unsalted, softened butter
50–100 ml iced water
3 drops lemon juice
115 g chilled butter

4½ oz strong, plain flour
½ teaspoon salt
scant ½ oz unsalted, softened butter
1½–3½ fl oz iced water
3 drops lemon juice
4 oz chilled butter

(2) 190 g flour makes 500 g dough

7 oz flour makes 1 lb dough

190 g strong, plain flour
½ teaspoon salt
20 g unsalted, softened butter
75–125 ml iced water
½ teaspoon lemon juice
170 g chilled butter

7 oz strong, plain flour
½ teaspoon salt
scant ¾ oz unsalted, softened butter
2½–4½ fl oz iced water
½ teaspoon lemon juice
6 oz chilled butter

(3) 250 g flour makes 650 g dough

9 oz flour makes 1 lb 7 oz dough

250 g strong, plain flour
1 teaspoon salt
25 g unsalted, softened butter
100–150 ml iced water
2/3 teaspoon lemon juice
225 g chilled butter

9 oz strong, plain flour
1 teaspoon salt
scant 1 oz unsalted, softened butter
3½–5½ fl oz iced water
2/3 teaspoon lemon juice
8 oz chilled butter

CAKES

(4) 500 g flour makes 1.25 kg dough

1 lb flour makes 2 lb 8 oz dough

500 g strong, plain flour	1 lb strong, plain flour
2 teaspoons salt	2 teaspoons salt
50 g unsalted, softened butter	1½ oz unsalted, softened butter
250–300 ml iced water	9–10½ fl oz iced water
1 teaspoon lemon juice	1 teaspoon lemon juice
450 g chilled butter	1 lb chilled butter

gas 7, 220°C, 425°F / Baking times vary, see the individual recipes

Basic pastry using the amounts in (4) above: Sift the flour and salt together into a bowl and rub in the 50 g (1½ oz) softened butter to make fine crumbs. Make a well in the centre, and add most of the water and lemon juice if used. Lightly combine all the ingredients to form a fairly stiff, smooth dough, adding more water if necessary, but avoid kneading too much. Roll into a ball, flatten slightly, and score the surface with a sharp knife to reduce elasticity. Place in the refrigerator to rest and chill for 2 hours, wrapped in foil or plastic film.

An electric food processor makes light work of this basic pastry. Sift the dry ingredients and blend with butter pieces and liquids until a ball is formed, but do not blend for more than 25 seconds. Flatten, score, wrap and chill as above.

Kneading the chilled butter: Lay the 450 g (1 lb) of chilled butter between two larger sheets of plastic film and beat with a rolling pin to flatten and soften it, into a 15 cm (6 inch) square.

Enveloping the butter: Roll the chilled pastry on a floured surface into approximately a 30 cm (1 ft) square. Lay the flattened butter in the centre, and fold in the sides of the pastry, taking care that the seams overlap and are secure. Press them gently with the rolling pin to ensure that the butter is sealed in well.

Lightly flour the work surface and the rolling pin while folding and rolling, but take care to brush away any excess from the outside and between the layers of pastry.

Rolling and folding: If at any time the dough should become too soft and difficult to work, wrap it up immediately and return it to the refrigerator to rest for a further 15–20 minutes.

If possible try always to roll in the same direction. Set the rolling pin 2.5 cm (1 inch) in from the edge of the pastry and roll, exerting gentle even pressure, to within 2.5 cm (1 inch) of the end – never beyond, as the trapped air may be pushed out. Too much pressure on the rolling pin will force the butter through the paste structure. Form a regular oblong strip 15 cm (6 inch) wide and 30 cm (1 ft) long. The butter should shine through the pastry, but not break it. Fold one narrow end into the middle and the other back over the top of it, to make a square of the three overlapping layers. This is the first fold.

Turn the paste through a right angle (and always in the same direction), so that the open ends are parallel to the rolling pin, and again roll the paste away from you into three layers as before. This is the second fold.

Make two slight indentations with your fingers (not the nails) in the paste on the side that is to be rolled next, to indicate the number of folds.

Resting and chilling: Wrap the paste in plastic film or moist greaseproof paper to prevent it forming a skin or drying out, and chill for 15–20 minutes.

Lightly beat the paste with the rolling pin, crosswise and lengthwise to start it moving before giving it two further folds. Wrap and chill for 15–20 minutes.

Make fifth and sixth folds. Chill for a further 30 minutes. The paste is now ready for use.

Roll the paste to the required size. Dip a sharp knife in boiling water and trim the edges cleanly and carefully without dragging the pastry. (Folded or crushed sides prevent the layers from separating and rising properly.) Cut to shape. Run cold water over the baking sheet, shake off the excess and lay the prepared cut pieces on to it with the underside uppermost. Cover, and rest the pastry for a further 30 minutes in the refrigerator to prevent it contracting and distorting in the oven.

Baking the pastry: The prepared pastry pieces should be well pricked with a fork before they are baked; this prevents them from rising excessively. Sometimes they do rise unevenly and start to topple over; in which case, 10 minutes before the baking time is complete, open the oven door gently and lightly push them down to level them. Lay a sheet of greaseproof paper over the top to keep them flat, and finish baking.

Blitz Puff Pastry – The Quick Method

The paste should be slightly softer than usual. Use the same ingredients as in the previous recipe.

Method: Cut all the butter into hazelnut-sized pieces, or grate if frozen (wrapping the end in foil) on a coarse gauge, into the sifted flour and salt. Using a fork, toss the butter pieces through the flour – they must stay whole. Make a well in the centre, pour in the water and lemon juice if used. Using a palette knife, lightly and briskly blend (but avoid rubbing) the butter into the flour, then shape into a ball. The texture will be rather coarse. Wrap the dough in plastic film and chill in the refrigerator for about 30 minutes. Roll, turn and fold in the conventional way; chill for 20 minutes after every two folds.

Puff Paste Trimmings

Naturally puff pastry loses some of its original lightness when it has to be rolled again; so waste as little as possible when cutting the first pieces. Use the trimmings for less important items such as tartlets, tart cases, barquettes, small biscuits and fleurons, etc. (These may also be kept for 2 or 3 days in the refrigerator.)

Assemble the off-cuts, overlapping them slightly, into a neat, rectangular shape and lightly brush every other edge. Dust with flour and gently roll to seal them together. Spread a small amount of softened butter over two-thirds of the paste and fold into three. Chill for 30 minutes and give it two more folds. Chill for a further 2 hours before using.

Freezing

Immediately after the sixth fold cut pieces to size and layer them between sheets of plastic film. They will keep very well in the freezer for up to 6 months. They may be baked from the frozen state without defrosting, in a preheated oven. Although baked pastry may be frozen, I find that with thawing and re-heating it loses flavour and lightness.

Strudel and Fila Doughs

Strudel and fila pastries remain today as probably the closest kin to the ancient pastries of the Greeks and Byzantines. Very fine paper-like doughs, prepared in quite a different way, had been known earlier, but it was probably the Turks who carried fila to the Arab world and Middle Europe on their conquering journeys.

Both are flour and water doughs, sometimes made with oil; while strudel, in typical Austrian fashion, is often enriched with butter and egg (even though greater fat content reduces elasticity). The simple basic pastes are both kneaded until very elastic and then stretched by hand until they are paper thin – in fact so thin, an Austrian saying suggests, that one should be able to read a love letter through them.

The fila of the Middle East is mostly wrapped around savouries – meats, vegetables, and cheeses – or filled with nuts flavoured with rose and orange flower waters. The most familiar strudel usually encloses fresh fruits – apples, cherries or plums – or curd cheese and nuts. The many savoury versions popular in the nineteenth century are now less common.

Apart from very moist fillings, particularly typical of Greece, fila pastries are mostly crisp and dry. Some large trays of sweet pastries, such as Baklava (page 337) are made, but it is the small, individual portions that are most authentic. 'Small is beautiful' is the motto, and each wrapped and rolled item shows the skill and patience of the host, which is much appreciated by the guest. The single sheet of pastry is first brushed over with melted butter, and then filled with a small amount of filling, before it is parcelled up. Baklava is built up of many layers of pastry also brushed with butter. In both instances the character is much like a puff pastry with its separate layers of fat and paste.

A successful strudel should have a crisp outside and be juicy inside, for although it is brushed with butter in the same way, the filling is generally spread over three-quarters of the single sheet before it is rolled; this soaks into the pastry, keeps it moist and prevents it rising in the way fila does. Strudels are occasionally layered, but invariably rolled; they are mostly large and are cut into individual portions only after baking.

The hospitable rituals of the Middle East are not a consideration to the Austrians, who prefer to concentrate on the contents and quality of the filling rather than on the appearance.

Strudel Dough

250 g strong, plain flour	9 oz strong, plain flour
a pinch of salt	a pinch of salt
1 egg	1 egg
100 ml water (approx.)	3½ fl oz water (approx.)
3 tablespoons oil or 20 g butter	3 tablespoons oil or 1 oz butter

Sift the flour and salt two or three times and lastly on to the pastry board. Make a well in the centre, drop in the egg, and add most of the warm water, in which the oil or butter has been dissolved. Mix to a dough. The texture should be fairly soft; add a little more water if necessary. At first the dough is inclined to stick both to your fingers and to the board, but when it starts to roll off more easily, lay it on a freshly floured area and wash and dry your hands. Flour them well, and knead the dough by punching and pressing with the flat of your hand until air bubbles start to develop and it becomes very smooth. Pat into a ball and let it rest on another floured corner, covered with a warm bowl, for 30 minutes.

Lay a small tablecloth or a piece of cotton material on the work top or table and dredge it heavily with flour. Place the dough in the centre and pat it lightly into a square shape. Dust it with flour and roll it out as thin as possible, first lengthwise until it is about 6 mm ($1/4$ inch) thick, then crosswise until it is about 3 mm ($1/8$ inch) thick. Brush lightly with melted butter if it starts to dry out.

From now on the dough is pulled and stretched by hand. Dust the hands with flour and hold them, thumbs inwards, so that the pastry lies over the backs of the hands. If only one person is working, then lay the rolling pin on the other end to hold the pastry down.

Working from the centre outwards, gently coax and stretch the pastry evenly until it is paper thin and almost transparent. Drop it back on to the floured cloth, then lift the side and start working round with the fingers until it is as thin as the rest. The thicker edges are cut away with a sharp knife or scissors.

Filling and Baking Strudel: Brush the strudel generously with melted butter. Cover two-thirds of the paste with filling. Fruit fillings need ground nuts or breadcrumbs as a base to absorb moisture (page 208), but with others this is unnecessary. Lift the cloth at either edge of the roll, if needed. Brush the surface well with a mixture of lukewarm melted butter and beaten egg; any leaking juices should be basted over a few minutes before it is ready. The crust when baked has a better taste and looks more attractive. Bake in a preheated oven, gas 6, 200°C, 400°F for about 40 minutes. Take out of the oven and while still hot dredge generously with icing sugar.

Fila Dough is discussed in greater detail on page 336.

Fresh Creams, Cooked Creams and Fillings

Fresh Creams

There are three different types of sweet cream in England.

Single cream for baking purposes is only useful to lighten double cream, as it will not whip on its own because it has been heated and cooled so as to keep the butterfat evenly distributed.

Whipping cream has a lower butter fat content, 35–42 per cent, than double cream, and whips very readily, but the flavour is not as rich.

Double cream contains at least 48 per cent butter fat. The thickness often varies, depending on the method of heat treatment used by the manufacturer. In addition, cream thickens as it ages, so when it is very fresh it often looks thin, and is difficult to whip (although it will eventually). It will not produce the same volume and thickness as cream that is two or three days old.

Whipping or double cream are both suitable for using as cake fillings. Keep cream in the refrigerator, as it is easier to whip when it is well chilled.

The rich flavour of double cream can be lightened by adding single cream or whipped up egg whites. Use one part single cream to two parts double cream. Use 4 stiffly beaten egg whites for 500 ml (17½ fl oz) double cream.

Crème Chantilly

To whip cream: Pour double or whipping cream into a bowl (stand over ice-cubes and water if it is a very warm day). Whip with either a balloon whisk or an electric mixer, gently at first until it becomes frothy, then faster. When the cream starts to thicken and the beater leaves thin traces on the surface, add the sugar and flavouring (see below) and continue

CAKES

whisking until the cream stands in soft peaks. (Any added ingredients must be cold, otherwise the cream will lose its fluffiness and turn thin.)

If it is to be used with a piping bag, stop now, as the pressure of pushing it through the nozzle has the effect of an extra beat. If it is to be spread with a spatula, give two more turns, but take care, for it very quickly becomes grainy, starts to separate and turns to butter.

Sweeten 500 ml (17½ fl oz) double cream with 60 g (2 oz) caster sugar.

Flavourings

* Replace 15 g (½ oz) sugar with the same quantity of vanilla sugar.
* Use 100 g (3½ oz) grated dark chocolate and 60 g (2 oz) caster sugar.
* Use 2 teaspoons instant coffee powder or moka syrup (page 85) and 60 g (2 oz) caster sugar.
* 2–3 tablespoons liqueur or spirit, such as Kirsch, Curaçao, Grand Marnier, Cointreau, and 60 g (2 oz) caster sugar.
* Purée 100 g (3½ oz) soft fruit such as strawberries, raspberries, well-ripened apricots, etc. and 60 g (2 oz) caster sugar; then fold into the beaten cream very carefully.
* Use 100 g (3½ oz) toasted nuts and 60 g (2 oz) sugar, or almond praline (pages 312–13) and 30 g (1 oz) sugar.

Using Gelatine to Stiffen Cream

Sometimes it is desirable to keep a cream layered torte for more than a day; it then becomes necessary to stiffen the cream with gelatine. The gelatine must be added to the liquid – never the other way round.

10 g (a sparing ½ oz) gelatine will set 500 ml (17½ fl oz) cream.

Sheet or leaf gelatine: Soak sheets in a bowl of cold water for five minutes to soften; lift out and squeeze away the excess water. Heat very gently in a pan until the leaves have dissolved. Cool completely at room temperature and fold thoroughly into the ready beaten cream.

Powdered gelatine: 10 g (a sparing ½ oz or 3 rounded teaspoons) will set 500 ml (17½ fl oz) whipped cream. Sprinkle the powder into a cup containing 75 ml (a generous 3 fl oz) of very hot, not boiling, water, and stir to dissolve. If it has not dissolved completely when the water has cooled, stand it in a pan of warm water over a low heat. It must all be dissolved. Cool down at room temperature and fold immediately into the beaten cream.

Storing Whipped Cream

Whipped cream will keep for several hours in the refrigerator. As it is inclined to exude a little liquid (owing perhaps to too much sugar) after 2 or 3 hours, pour it into a sieve, stand over a bowl and cover closely with plastic film so that the cream cannot absorb any food odours.

Cooked Custard Creams

Crème pâtissière is a cooked, custard-type filling now used generally as a lining for fruit tarts. In the eighteenth century Carême was especially fond of it and flavoured it with a variety of perfumes. Apart from the traditional vanilla, he used liqueurs and spirits, lemon zest or cedrat, orange and Seville orange, chocolate, café moka, hazelnut and almond pralines; the creams were used to fill his newly invented *vol-au-vent* cases. Many of his recipes also contained crushed almonds and macaroons as thickening; this heavier version is known as *crème frangipane*. When *crème pâtissière* is lightened with beaten egg whites, it becomes *crème St Honoré*, and is the classic filling for Gâteau St Honoré (page 103) and for choux puffs (page 101).

Crème Pâtissière with Vanilla

(1) 500 ml milk
vanilla pod
100 g caster sugar
5 egg yolks
50 g plain flour
pinch salt
50 g unsalted butter

17½ fl oz milk
vanilla pod
3½ oz caster sugar
5 egg yolks
2 oz plain flour
pinch salt
2 oz unsalted butter

(2) or to line a 24–26 cm (9½–10½ inch) flan case

250 ml milk
vanilla pod
50 g caster sugar
3 egg yolks
25 g plain flour
pinch salt
25 g unsalted butter

9 fl oz milk
vanilla pod
2 oz caster sugar
3 egg yolks
scant 1 oz plain flour
pinch salt
scant 1 oz unsalted butter

CAKES

Bring the milk to the boil and infuse with the split vanilla pod. Beat the sugar and egg yolks until the pale, creamy ribbon stage. Dredge in the well-sifted flour without beating too hard. Remove the vanilla pod from the milk and pour about a quarter on to the eggs and sugar while beating. Add this to the remaining milk and the salt, and return to the heat; continue beating vigorously on a brisk heat to avoid lumps forming, until the paste is thick and smooth and rolls off the pan sides. Pour into a bowl. Melt the butter in a small pan and let it brown, then stir it into the cream. Seal the surface with a little butter to prevent a skin forming while it cools. It will keep in the refrigerator, covered, for 2 or 3 days. Mix in 1 tablespoon Kirsch or rum to flavour if wished.

Alternative Flavourings

* *Lemon or Orange:* Omit the vanilla pod and prepare the basic cream as in the previous recipe. Finish by adding the grated zest of 1 lemon or 1 orange, and 100 g (3½ oz) crushed macaroons and 6 amaretti (page 376). Halve the amounts for quantity (2).
* *Chocolate:* Halve the sugar quantity and prepare the basic recipe. Finish by folding in 175 g (6 oz) finely grated, semi-sweetened dark chocolate and 100 g (3½ oz) crushed macaroons. Flavour with a tablespoon of rum or Maraschino. Halve the amounts for quantity (2).
* *Moka:* Prepare the basic cream using 75 g (2½ oz) brown butter instead of 50 g (2 oz). Add 2 teaspoons of moka syrup (page 85) and 100 g (3½ oz) crushed macaroons. Halve the amounts for quantity (2).
* *Hazelnut or almond praline:* Prepare the basic recipe using half the sugar quantity. Use 75 g (2½ oz) hazelnuts or 100 g (3½ oz) almonds with 100 g (3½ oz) sugar and make praline (see pages 312–13 for method). Crush well and fold into the cooked cream. Halve the amounts for quantity (2).

Crème Frangipane aux Amandes

(1) 600 ml milk
one vanilla pod
2 whole eggs
3 egg yolks
100 g caster sugar
100 g plain, soft flour
pinch salt
40 g softened, unsalted butter
20 g ground almonds

1 pt milk
one vanilla pod
2 whole eggs
3 egg yolks
3½ oz caster sugar
3½ oz plain, soft flour
pinch salt
1½ oz softened, unsalted butter
1 oz ground almonds

Optional flavourings: 1 tablespoon Kirsch, or 2 teaspoons orange zest or 1 teaspoon orange-flower water

(2) Or to line a 24–26 cm (9½–10½ inch) tin

300 ml milk
one vanilla pod
1 whole egg
2 small egg yolks
50 g caster sugar
50 g plain, soft flour
pinch salt
20 g softened, unsalted butter
10 g ground almonds

½ pt milk
one vanilla pod
1 whole egg
2 small egg yolks
2 oz caster sugar
2 oz plain, soft flour
pinch salt
scant ¾ oz softened, unsalted butter
scant ½ oz ground almonds

(Halve flavours as above.)

Bring the milk to the boil and infuse with the split vanilla pod. Using a wooden spoon, mix together in a pan the eggs, yolks, sugar, sifted flour and salt. Remove the vanilla pod, and pour the milk gradually over the mixture, beating all the time. Set the pan on the heat and while still stirring gently, cook for a further 2 minutes. Pour the cream into a bowl, and beat the melted and browned butter into it along with the ground almonds. Add flavouring if used. Moisten the surface with a little butter to seal it and prevent a skin from forming.

* *For a chocolate flavour:* Prepare the basic vanilla recipe and add 80 g (3 oz) melted and slightly cooled dark, plain chocolate.

CAKES

Crème St Honoré

6 egg yolks	6 egg yolks
30 g plain flour	1½ oz plain flour
30 g rice or potato flour	1½ oz rice or potato flour
pinch salt	pinch salt
1 teaspoon lemon zest or a vanilla pod	1 teaspoon lemon zest or a vanilla pod
250 g caster sugar	9 oz caster sugar
250 ml milk	9 fl oz milk
6 egg whites	6 egg whites

Beat the egg yolks in a bowl, and mix in the sifted flours, salt and lemon zest (if using), avoiding lumps as much as possible. Add 100 g (3½ oz) of sugar, then beat in the heated milk which has had the vanilla pod infused in it. Pour through a strainer into a double boiler and heat the mixture to below a simmer, stirring meanwhile. Draw off the heat and pour into a bowl. Whip the egg whites in a separate bowl to form stiff, creamy peaks, beat in half the remaining sugar, and then fold in the rest. Fold the meringue into the hot mixture with a metal spoon, retaining as much air as possible. Chill.

If the weather condition is hot, or the cream has to wait, it is advisable to stiffen it with gelatine. Use 2.5 ml (1/10 oz or 1 level teaspoon) gelatine for 250 ml (9 fl oz) milk (see page 58).

Mousseline Butter Cream using Egg Yolks (1)

This is a firm smooth cream that holds its shape even in the warmest weather conditions. It contains no egg whites, only yolks.

100 g granulated sugar	3½ oz granulated sugar
75 ml water	2½ fl oz water
4 egg yolks	4 egg yolks
1 drop pure vanilla essence	1 drop pure vanilla essence
225 g unsalted butter	½ lb unsalted butter

Dissolve the sugar and water in a sugar boiler and boil to the thread stage (110°C, 225°F). Lightly whisk the egg yolks and beat in the sugar syrup and the vanilla; carry on beating until it has cooled completely, by which time it should be light and foamy. In another bowl, beat the butter until soft and smooth, then gradually add the egg and sugar mixture. If the mixture starts to curdle (too much syrup) this can easily be rectified by adding a little more butter.

This cream will keep in the refrigerator for several days, sealed in an air-tight box or in a bowl covered with plastic film. It will also keep for several weeks in the freezer. Let it return to a working consistency at room temperature.

Optional liquid perfumes: 2 tablespoons fresh lemon or orange juice, spirit or liqueur, or 2 teaspoons moka syrup (page 85). Liquid perfumes should be beaten with the syrup into the butter.

Chocolate Mousseline Butter Cream

Melt 100g (3½oz) dark plain chocolate in 2 tablespoons of water and cool before adding to the cold egg cream.

Mousseline Butter Cream using Egg Whites (2)

This is a less rich, very light filling suitable for both filling and outside decoration. It is based on a cooked Italian meringue mixture, and will not melt in warm conditions.

2 egg whites	2 egg whites
100g icing sugar	3½oz icing sugar
175g unsalted butter	6oz unsalted butter
1 teaspoon vanilla sugar	1 teaspoon vanilla sugar

Assemble the egg whites and the sifted icing sugar in a bowl over gently simmering water. Whisk together until the meringue holds its shape; lift off the heat and continue beating for a few minutes, then allow to cool. In a separate bowl beat the butter until it is light and fluffy, then beat the meringue into it a spoonful at a time until all is well combined. As in the previous recipe, flavours should be added to the finished cream. Add liquid flavouring only a little at a time, for too much may cause the mixture to separate.

CAKES

Lemon or Orange Butter Cream

Prepare mousseline butter cream (2) but leave out the vanilla flavouring. Add to the finished cream the grated zest of 1½ lemons or 1 orange, and a few drops of juice.

Simple and Quick Butter Cream

Sometimes it is necessary to make a filling in a hurry. The flavour of this uncooked version is good, but it has a slightly grainy texture as the sugar has not been completely dissolved. Rinse the bowl in hot water before you start working so that the ingredients will combine more readily. Flavour as in mousseline butter cream (1).

2 egg yolks	2 egg yolks
50 g icing sugar	2 oz icing sugar
150 g unsalted butter	5 oz unsalted butter

Assemble all the ingredients in a bowl, including the flavour of your choice, and beat until the mixture is smooth. Chill the cream but keep it soft enough to work.

Chestnut Butter Cream

Prepare the recipe as above with vanilla flavouring, and add 120 g (4 oz) chestnut purée (page 332) to the finished cream.

Some More Elaborate Cake Fillings

Chocolate Ganache (1)

This is a simple but delicious filling made with double cream and chocolate. It is suitable for both spreading and piping.

375 g plain chocolate	13 oz plain chocolate
split vanilla pod	split vanilla pod
250 ml double cream	9 fl oz double cream

Break the chocolate into pieces and set on a plate in a warm oven to melt. Infuse the vanilla pod in the cream and bring to the boil. Withdraw from the heat, remove the pod, and gradually beat in the melted slightly cooled chocolate. Leave to cool, then beat again very thoroughly to lighten – the colour will become paler and it will double in volume. Ganache hardens as it cools, so use immediately.

If the weather is very warm, increase the quantity of chocolate – it will set harder.

Chocolate Filling (2)

150 g plain chocolate	5 oz plain chocolate
50 g unsalted butter	2 oz unsalted butter
2 egg yolks	2 egg yolks
3 egg whites	3 egg whites
20 g caster sugar	1 oz caster sugar
150 ml whipped cream	5 fl oz whipped cream

Melt and cool the chocolate. Whip it up with the butter and the egg yolks in a bowl set over simmering water until it is very thick. Draw away from the heat to cool. Whip the egg whites in a separate bowl until they stand in firm snowy peaks, then lightly beat in the sugar. Whip the cream stiffly, then fold it and the meringue into the chocolate mixture. Leave in the refrigerator, where it will thicken as it chills.

Chocolate Filling – Cocoa (3)

4 teaspoons cocoa	4 teaspoons cocoa
1 egg yolk	1 egg yolk
15 g caster sugar	½ oz caster sugar
200 ml single cream	7 fl oz single cream
250 ml double cream	9 fl oz double cream
1 tablespoon vanilla sugar	1 tablespoon vanilla sugar

Assemble the cocoa, egg yolk, sugar and single cream in a double boiler, and stir over heat until it has thickened; leave to cool. Beat the double cream to soft firm peaks, then combine with the chocolate mixture and the vanilla sugar.

Double cream may be omitted, but in that case a double quantity of chocolate cream should be prepared.

CAKES

Moka Coffee Crème

- 2 tablespoons moka syrup (page 85)
- 3 egg yolks
- 75 g caster sugar
- 2 teaspoons potato or cornflour
- 100 g unsalted butter
- 1 tablespoon powdered medium roast coffee beans

- 2 tablespoons moka syrup (page 85)
- 3 egg yolks
- 2½ oz caster sugar
- 2 teaspoons potato or cornflour
- 3½ oz unsalted butter
- 1 tablespoon powdered medium roast coffee beans

To lighten, optional: 100 ml (3½ fl oz) whipped double cream.

Spoon the coffee syrup into a double boiler, and add the egg yolks, the sugar and flour. Stir over simmering water until the mixture has thickened to ribbon stage, then allow to cool. Beat the butter until light and fluffy, mix in the coffee powder, then add the coffee cream spoon by spoon until all is well combined.

Finish by folding in the whipped cream, if using.

Walnut Filling (1)

- 120 g granulated sugar and 100 ml water *or* 200 ml honey
- 1 teaspoon cinnamon
- 1 teaspoon lemon or orange zest
- 175 g coarse ground or chopped walnuts
- 1 tablespoon rum

- 4 oz granulated sugar and 3½ fl oz water *or* 7 fl oz honey
- 1 teaspoon cinnamon
- 1 teaspoon lemon or orange zest
- 6 oz coarse ground or chopped walnuts
- 1 tablespoon rum

Boil the sugar and water to the thread stage (110°C, 225°F), or boil up the honey. Mix in the spice and zest, draw away from the heat and stir in the nuts. Moisten with sufficient rum to achieve a spreading consistency.

Walnut Filling (2)

Beat up 2 egg yolks, 100 g (3½ oz) caster sugar and 1 tablespoon of vanilla sugar until pale and creamy. Add 200 g (7 oz) finely chopped walnuts and blend in 150 ml (5½ fl oz) double cream. Sweeten to taste if necessary.

FRESH CREAMS, COOKED CREAMS AND FILLINGS

Hazelnut Filling (1)

A very simple one: moisten 50 g (1³/₄ oz) ground hazelnuts with a little egg white then beat in 2 whole eggs and 120 g (4 oz) sifted icing sugar.

Hazelnut Filling (2)

Beat 100 g (3½ oz) butter with 2 egg yolks; mix in 100 g (3½ oz) sifted icing sugar and 1 tablespoon vanilla sugar. Add 20 g (1 oz) finely chopped or ground hazelnuts, 70 g (2½ oz) chopped pistachios and 2–3 tablespoons red wine.

Nut and Chocolate Filling

3 whole eggs	3 whole eggs
140 g caster sugar	5 oz caster sugar
1 tablespoon vanilla sugar	1 tablespoon vanilla sugar
1 teaspoon cornflour	1 teaspoon cornflour
1 teaspoon coffee syrup (page 85)	1 teaspoon coffee syrup (page 85)
150 g unsalted butter	5½ oz unsalted butter
50 g grated, dark plain chocolate	2 oz grated, dark plain chocolate
40 g coarse chopped walnuts	1½ oz coarse chopped walnuts
40 g roasted hazelnuts (ground)	1½ oz roasted hazelnuts (ground)

Beat the eggs, sugar, flour and coffee syrup in a double boiler over the fire until they form a thick cream; set aside to cool. Beat the butter until pale and frothy, then mix well with the grated chocolate. Combine with the cooled cream, and finally fold in the chopped and ground nuts.

Almond Filling (1)

Beat 2 whole eggs with 2 egg yolks, then mix in 70 g (2½ oz) caster sugar and beat until the mixture is light and fluffy. Add the zest of half a lemon, 20 g (³/₄ oz) chopped candied lemon peel, 20 g (³/₄ oz) chopped pistachios and 70 g (2½ oz) finely chopped almonds.

Almond Filling (2) with butter

Mix 70 g (2½ oz) ground almonds with 1 egg. Beat together 70 g (2½ oz) butter and 70 g (2½ oz) icing sugar till fluffy, then beat in 4 egg yolks. Mix into the ground almond mixture.

Crème Pralinée – with almonds (3)

50 g granulated sugar	2 oz granulated sugar
50 g whole or flaked blanched almonds	2 oz whole or flaked blanched almonds
70 g unsalted butter	2½ oz unsalted butter

Gently heat the sugar in a copper sugar pan until it starts to caramelize; drop in the almonds and stir thoroughly until the nuts are completely coated. Pour on to an oiled baking sheet, spread out as much as possible, and leave to cool. Break up the praline to make a coarse powder. Beat the butter until pale and fluffy, then beat in the praline powder.

Almond Orange Filling (4)

75 g unsalted butter	3 oz unsalted butter
125 g icing sugar	4½ oz icing sugar
3 hard-boiled egg yolks	3 hard-boiled egg yolks
100 g ground almonds	3½ oz ground almonds
zest of 2 small oranges	zest of 2 small oranges

Beat the butter until soft and fluffy and add the sifted icing sugar. Sieve the egg yolks into the mixture and blend. Mix in the almonds and orange zest, and moisten with a little orange juice to make a good spreading consistency.

Boiling Sugar

Sugar syrups are occasionally needed as a basis for icings and creams. The process can be tricky, but there should be no problem if the basic rules are followed meticulously. Use preserving, cube or granulated sugar.

Use an unlined copper sugar pan, or, if this is not available, a strong, fairly large, thick based (not enamel) pan will do.

Use a sugar thermometer; keep it warm in a jug of hot water or it will break when dipped in the boiling syrup.

Always put the liquid in the pan first.

A pinch of cream of tartar will help prevent crystallization.

Sugar, Water and Cream of Tartar Quantities

Use approximately 150 ml water to 500 g sugar (5 fl oz to 1 lb), and a good pinch of cream of tartar. See the individual recipes for quantities. Dissolve the cream of tartar in 2 teaspoons of water and add to the sugar and water syrup as soon as the sugar has dissolved. A little more water does no harm: it just takes longer for the syrup to reach the correct temperature.

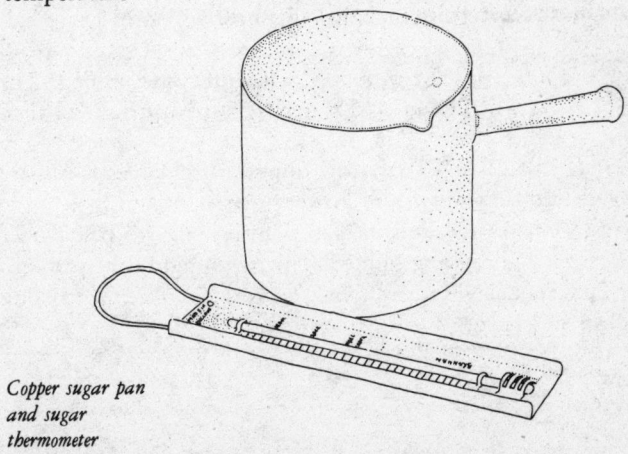

Copper sugar pan and sugar thermometer

Method

The sugar and cream of tartar must be dissolved completely in the water before it is brought to the boil. Set the sugar and water in a pan on a very low heat. Stir very gently with a wooden spoon, and take care not to splash the syrup against the sides of the pan, for if a sugar crystal drops back into the solution, the whole syrup may crystallize as it cools. Use a wet pastry brush dipped in cold water to keep the sides clean. When all the sugar has dissolved, add the cream of tartar, stop stirring, raise the heat and bring the syrup to the boil. Stand the sugar thermometer in the pan — read the measurements at eye level — and boil the sugar fairly vigorously until it reaches the correct temperature.

When the correct temperature is reached plunge the base of the pan in cold water for a moment to stop further cooking. Use immediately.

Sugar Temperatures

Thread (102°C, 215°F): About 20 seconds of boiling. Dribble a little syrup from the spoon, and when it falls in a fine thread it is ready.

Pearl (104°C, 221°F): About 25 seconds of boiling. The thread will be stronger and form a small pearl-like shape when it breaks.

Feather and Soft Ball (115°C, 240°F): About 2 to 3 minutes of boiling. Drop a little syrup into a cup of cold water and it will roll into a soft ball between the fingers.

Hard Ball (120°C, 250°F): Just over 3 minutes of boiling. A little syrup dropped into cold water will roll into a harder ball. A stick of wood dipped in cold water and then into the sugar will form a hard ball on the tip.

Small Crack (140°C, 280°F): About $3^1/_2$ minutes after boiling. The firm lump of sugar will flex in cold water, become brittle, and then snap.

Hard Crack (155°C, 310°F): About 4 minutes after boiling. A little syrup dropped into cold water will be very brittle.

Caramel (173°C, 345°F): Boil the syrup until it turns a pale amber colour, then arrest the cooking immediately by plunging the pan into cold water. The caramel will turn slightly darker. If cooked for too long it will blacken and burn.

Icings and Decorations

> Les gâteaux sont comme les chapeaux de dames, un rien les fait beaux et ce rien les fait vendre . . .
>
> (Pierre Lacam – *Le Memorial des Glaces*, 1902)

Carême's monumental extravaganzas were all very well in the eighteenth century, but a simpler approach is more appropriate today. A cake should be enhanced and complemented by its topping, not overwhelmed.

Icing sugar makes the simplest decoration: dredge icing sugar generously over the cake through a fine mesh sieve, or first lay a wire cake rack or a paper doily on top of the cake to make a more interesting pattern. Lightly place a saucer in the centre of a fresh fruit tart or gâteau, then dredge the cake with icing sugar, remove the saucer, and glaze the centre with strained apricot jam.

Whipped, sweetened and liqueur flavoured double cream is a sumptuous topping. Scatter chocolate flakes or curls on top, stud with toasted nuts, or top a few piped rosettes with fresh fruits.

A *plain icing or butter cream* can be studded with glacé fruits or nuts. More elaborate suggestions follow.

Apricot Glaze

A cake should always be insulated with an apricot glaze before it is covered with firm icing or chocolate, and the strained jam gives the strong bond needed to join the two different textures, otherwise the hard surface simply cracks away in large unsightly pieces.

Heat 100 g (4 oz) apricot jam with 2 tablespoons water in a pan over a gentle heat until slightly thickened. Strain through a wire sieve and brush over the cake whilst still hot.

2 tablespoons of dark rum or brandy can be added to 100 g or 4 oz of jam for extra flavour.

Prepare more than you require, for it will keep as long as any jam.

CAKES

Spun Sugar

This is a highly decorative voile of fine spun sugar threads which is very simple to make; however, it will not keep for long, especially in a humid or damp atmosphere. It can be used for croquembouche (page 105), barquettes (page 111), and any other festive cakes.

Method: Cook the sugar syrup to the hard crack stage (155°C, 310°F), plunge the pan in cold water for a moment, then leave the syrup to cool a little and thicken. Take a clean smooth wooden stick – a large wooden spoon or a new broom handle – and oil it well. Fix it to the work surface with the handle projecting out over the floor, and lay a clean oiled baking sheet beneath. You can use a very clean fork to spin the sugar threads, or a twig whisk, or cut off the ends of an inexpensive wire whisk. Dip the ends of the sugar thrower lightly into the syrup, let the excess drain off, then swing it continuously to and fro, with a flexed wrist, over the handle. As the strands fall they will form a series of fine hair-like threads. Repeat the process, but carefully slide the fragile veil off the stick at intervals and lay it on the oiled baking sheet. Spun sugar can be shaped by gently easing it into a mould or a bowl.

Glacé Icing

Glacé icing is suitable for most of the lighter cakes and biscuits, but not for piping as it is too soft (though it can be thickened). It will only keep for a few days, after which it starts to crack.

Ingredients for a 20–22 cm (8–8½ inch) cake

200 g icing sugar	7 oz icing sugar
2–3 tablespoons water	2–3 tablespoons water
4 drops pure vanilla essence	4 drops pure vanilla essence

Ingredients for a 24–26 cm (9½–10½ inch) cake

250 g icing sugar	9 oz icing sugar
4–5 tablespoons water	4–5 tablespoons water
6 drops pure vanilla essence	6 drops pure vanilla essence

Ingredients for a 28–30 cm (11–12 inch) cake

300 g icing sugar	11 oz icing sugar
5–6 tablespoons water	5–6 tablespoons water
7 drops pure vanilla essence	7 drops pure vanilla essence

ICINGS AND DECORATIONS

Sift the icing sugar into a small saucepan. Using a wooden spoon, stir in the almost boiling water until the texture is thick, smooth and creamy, and will coat the back of the spoon. Mix in the vanilla. Place the pan over simmering water and warm to lukewarm – no more or the aroma will be lost – so that it runs easily and dries. Use immediately, as it dries very quickly.

Be discreet with the water addition, for if the icing is too thin (add more sugar) it will soak into the cake; if too thick (add more water) it will not spread easily.

Avoid beating too vigorously, otherwise air-bubbles will form.

If coloured icing is required, dip a skewer into the bottle of edible colour – never drip it in directly as the colours are very intense.

Other Flavourings

Follow the method above.

* *Orange icing:* 200 g (7 oz) icing sugar
  1 tablespoon lemon juice
  2 tablespoons orange juice.
* *Lemon icing:* 200 g (7 oz) icing sugar
  2–3 tablespoons lemon juice.
* *Punch icing:* 200 g (7 oz) icing sugar; 2 tablespoons rum; 2 tablespoons orange juice; 1 teaspoon lemon juice.
* *Rum icing:* 200 g (7 oz) icing sugar; 3 tablespoons rum; 2 tablespoons water.
* *Coffee icing:* 200 g (7 oz) icing sugar; 2$^1/_2$ tablespoons water; 1 teaspoon coffee syrup *or* 2 teaspoons powder.
* *Liqueur icing (Kirsch – Cointreau – Maraschino):* 200 g (7 oz) icing sugar; 2–3 tablespoons liqueur; 2 tablespoons water.
* *Chocolate icing:* 200 g (7 oz) icing sugar; 2$^1/_2$ tablespoons water; 2 teaspoons cocoa powder *or* 20 g (1 oz) dark melted chocolate (cooled).

How to Ice a Cake with Glacé Icing

Make sure that the top of the cake is quite smooth and not risen in the centre – either turn it over and use the flat underside, or cut the uneven surface level.

Stand the cake on a wire rack so that excess icing can drip through.

Always decorate the cake top of a plain glacé iced cake first. Brush the top and sides with warm apricot glaze, and cool. Using a dry flexible spatula or metal knife (a wet one makes pools of water), coax the icing to the edge of the cake, turning it as you do to prevent the icing from spilling over the edge. Quickly smooth more icing round the sides and work as little as possible, so that the icing can spread out and level before it sets. Decorate the top immediately before it sets hard. A coating of toasted almonds, crushed, chopped or flaked, hazelnuts, walnuts or chocolate flakes give a professional finish to plain iced or apricot jam coated sides.

If the cake is to have decorated sides then they should be iced or glazed with apricot jam and decorated before the top is iced. Coat the sides of the cake with apricot jam, and cool. Coat with icing. Have the crushed nuts or chocolate ready in a large bowl; support the cake on the base of a cake tin (with the sides removed), and hold on the flat of the hand. Work low over the bowl and lift and press handfuls of nuts into the sides while rotating the cake on your hand. Alternatively, if you have an icing turntable, place it in the middle of a tray or large sheet of paper and swing it round slowly as you work. Ice the top as before and decorate.

Chocolate Icing

To ice a 22–24 cm (9 inch) cake

160 g plain chocolate	6 oz plain chocolate
250 ml water	9 fl oz water
1 tablespoon butter	1 tablespoon butter
140 g preserving or granulated sugar	5 oz preserving or granulated sugar

Melt the chocolate with 2 tablespoons water in a small fire-proof bowl in the oven or over a pan of simmering water. Stir in the butter until smooth. Boil the remaining water and sugar in a copper sugar boiler to the pearl stage (104°C, 221°F); draw away from the heat and plunge the pan into a bowl of cold water so that the sugar stops cooking. Pour immediately over the melted chocolate and stir with a wooden spoon until the right texture is achieved (a metal cooking spoon should stay lightly coated with icing). Not all the sugar syrup may be needed. When the icing starts to cool a little, pour it over the cake. Set in a hot oven for just a few moments for the icing to set and to take on a high glaze. Cool at room temperature – never in a cold place, as this causes a grey-white bloom to appear.

For a *moka flavour*, add 2 flat teaspoonfuls of instant powdered coffee to the chocolate mixture.

Soft Chocolate Icing

This soft shiny icing is suitable for large, light nut and sponge-type pastries and éclairs.

To ice a 24–26 cm (9½–10½ inch) cake

150 g plain chocolate	5 oz plain chocolate
60 g butter	2 oz butter
120 g icing sugar	4 oz icing sugar
50 ml cold water	1 fl oz cold water

Melt the chocolate in a double boiler, add the softened butter in small pieces, and sift in the sugar. Stir together until the butter has melted and the mixture is smooth. Draw off the heat and blend in the water a tablespoon at a time to cool. The icing should coat the back of the spoon. Pour over the cake while the icing is still lukewarm. Or dip the top of small cakes into the icing and cool on a rack.

For a *moka flavour*, add 2 flat teaspoonfuls of instant powdered coffee to the chocolate mixture.

Chocolate Fudge Frosting

50 g chocolate *or* cocoa	2 oz chocolate *or* cocoa
50 g butter	2 oz butter
350 g icing sugar	12 oz icing sugar
pinch salt	pinch salt
1 tablespoon instant coffee powder	1 tablespoon instant coffee powder
3 tablespoons single cream	3 tablespoons single cream

Gently heat together the chocolate and butter. When just melted, draw off the heat, add half the icing sugar, the salt and the coffee powder and beat until smooth. Whip in the remaining sugar and the cream.

CAKES
Boiled American Icing

This has an attractive rough finish.

220 g preserving or lump sugar
75 ml (5 tablespoons) water
pinch cream of tartar
1 egg white

8 oz preserving or lump sugar
2½ fl oz (5 tablespoons) water
pinch cream of tartar
1 egg white

Dissolve the sugar in the water, add the cream of tartar, and bring to the boil until the soft ball stage (115°C, 240°F). Plunge into a bowl of cold water for a moment. Whisk the egg white until snowy and stiff, then pour on the sugar syrup in a steady stream, whisking all the time. Continue beating until the mixture cools and starts to stand in peaks. Spread it immediately over the prepared cake surface, leaving a rough and peaked finish.

A Very Simple Egg Yolk Glaze

Beat 55 g (2 oz) icing sugar and 3 egg yolks until a smooth paste is formed. Leave to dry and harden for several hours.

How to Make and Use a Piping Cone

A small piping cone made from greaseproof paper and fitted with a plain metal nozzle makes delicate work easier.

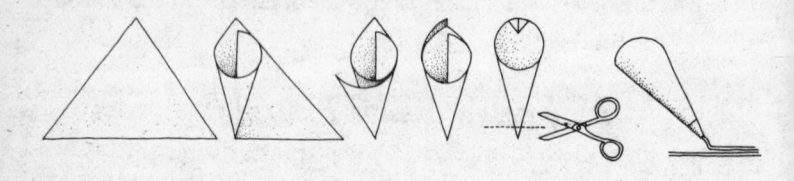

Fold a 25 cm (10 inch) square of greaseproof paper in half to form a triangle. Proceed as in the drawing. Fold over the top end then snip off the tip of the bag, enough to ease the nozzle in comfortably. Fill the cone, using a thin kitchen knife or small spatula, by drawing the icing up on to the knife and placing it point downwards into the bag. Press the knife against the side of the bag to ease off the icing. Take care not to overfill, otherwise the icing will spill out over the top. Fold the top of

ICINGS AND DECORATIONS

the bag over carefully and gently ease the icing down to the point; then fold in the sides at the top to give a flat cushion-type rest for the thumb.

Cover the bowl of icing with a damp cloth so that it remains moist, and beat again before refilling the bag.

How to Fill a Large Fabric Piping Bag

Never overfill the piping bag or the mixture will squeeze out over the top.

Hold the bag, fitted with the nozzle, about a third of the way down and fold the top edges back down over the hand. Fill the bag level with the top of the hand, then straighten up the folded down edges and gather them together with the other hand. Twist slightly to prevent the mixture from squeezing out. Always squeeze down from the top as you work. Turn the top edges back down over the hand again to refill the bag.

Decorative Ideas for Iced Cakes

Decoration and colour should always complement the flavour of the cake. Use nut decorations with nut and chocolate cakes or vice versa; punch, rum and fruit icings naturally blend with glacé fruits; crystallized flowers enhance plainer sponges and coffee, as do walnuts and chocolate.

Have the icing cone ready filled and the decorations prepared and laid out before the cake is iced; apply while the icing is still soft.

For Decoration Use:

* Half walnuts; whole or chopped hazelnuts; toasted flaked or halved or chopped almonds; pine-nuts; peeled chopped pistachios.
* Halved glacé cherries; angelica cut in strips or diamonds; candied lemon or orange peel cut in diamonds or squares; crystallized or stem ginger cut in a similar fashion.
* Crystallized violets; rose petals; mimosa balls.
* Tinted fruits and flowers made of almond paste.
* Chocolate curls and chocolate coffee beans.
* Silver and coloured dragees.

Glacé Icing with Crystallized Fruits

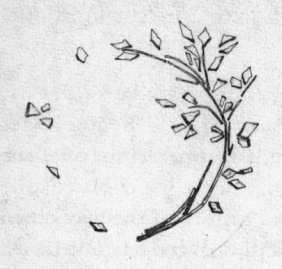

First prepare all the fruits: cut long thin pieces of angelica for the foliage, and citron, orange and lemon candied peels as flowers into diamonds, squares and triangles. Lay them out in the pattern formation on the work top beside you so that they can be transferred directly to the cake before the glaze has time to set.

Spread strained apricot jam all over the cake, then coat the sides and top with white or pale tinted glacé icing (see page 72 for amount). Lay the prepared fruits quickly in place and press them gently into the icing. (A small wooden cocktail stick is helpful.) Once a fruit has been laid down do not move it again, or the smooth glacé surface will be spoiled.

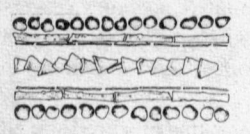

A Rectangular Loaf Glazed and Decorated with Glacé Fruits

Coat the cake with strained apricot jam first, then pour white glacé icing over the cake. Have ready prepared some long thin slices 0.5 cm ($^1/_4$ inch) thick of angelica, triangles of glacé pineapple, lemon or orange segments and glacé cherries. Lay an overlapping row of the triangular shapes down the centre and a row of the angelica slices either side. Lay two outside rows of glacé cherries.

The fruit can also be laid straight on to the cake without an icing. Coat the top of the cake well with strained apricot jam, lay the fruit in place, and brush a thin coating of the hot jam over all.

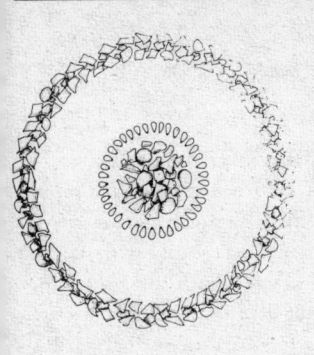

A Glacé Surface with a Border of Glacé Fruits and Pine Nuts

Any crystallized fruits are suitable, but use an occasional cherry to add brightness. Set the fruits (about 100 g (4 oz) altogether) in a border on the edge of the white glacéd cake and in about a 5 cm (2 inch) circle in the middle. Encircle this with pine nuts, points facing inwards.

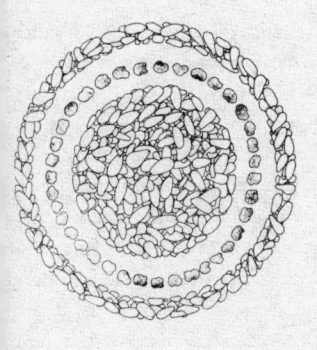

Chocolate Icing with Flaked, Toasted Almonds and Whole Hazelnuts

Lightly toast and cool 100 g (4 oz) of flaked almonds and 25 g (1 oz) of hazelnuts for the top of the cake and 100 g (4 oz) of chopped nuts for the sides.

Coat the cake with strained apricot jam, then mask only the sides with chocolate icing and press in the chopped nuts. (See page 74.) Coat the top of the cake with the icing, and press the toasted nuts in place as shown in the diagram.

A White Glaze with Chopped Hazelnuts or Walnuts and Chocolate Piping

Make a little more glacé icing than the amount stipulated for the cake. Reserve 4 or 5 tablespoons and thicken these to a piping consistency with icing sugar and 1 teaspoonful cocoa powder. Coat the cake with strained apricot jam and cover with the glacé icing. You need about 50 g (or 2 oz) chopped walnuts and 50 g (or 2 oz) walnut halves. Pipe the chocolate icing as shown on the drawing.

A Glazed Surface Decorated with Glacé Cherries or Hazelnuts, Toasted Almond Halves and Piped Icing

Coat the cake with strained apricot jam. Make white or pale tinted icing; thicken 6 tablespoons with a little more icing sugar and tint chocolate-coloured with 1 teaspoon of cocoa powder. Mask the top and sides of the cake with the pale icing. Place halved glacé cherries, or whole hazelnuts, around the cake, setting each 3 cm (1¼ inch) from the edge and placing one in the centre. Arrange the almond halves flat sides uppermost in fan shape as shown, with points inwards; press into the icing at the pointed end. Pipe first a plain scalloped line of chocolate-coloured icing round each cluster of almonds, then a smaller scalloped loop with a tiny bulb in each to finish. Pipe two plain lines and scallop with a bulb in the centre. Pipe all around the edge of the cake.

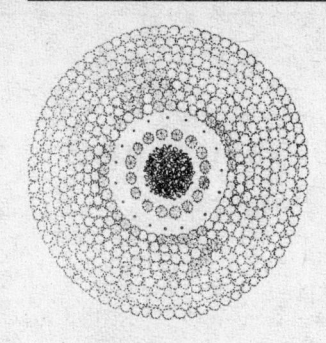

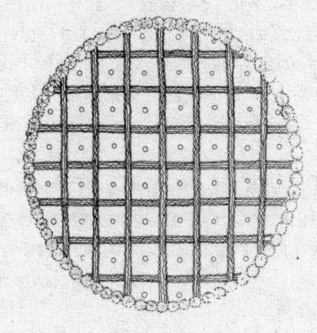

Piping Butter Creams

This technique is easier for the less experienced hand. Use a fabric or plastic coated piping bag fitted with any one of many piping nozzles of a coarser or larger size. Butter cream may be piped on to an iced cake but can also be used on a smooth covering of the same cream. The finished effect is bold and dramatic. Use either of the mousseline butter creams (pages 62, 63) or a double portion of the simple butter cream (page 64) to decorate a 24–26 cm ($9^1/_2$–$10^1/_2$ inch) cake. Fill the piping bag, fitted with a medium-sized star-shaped nozzle, and pipe as shown in the two illustrations. Decorate with silver cake balls or whole nuts.

Perfumes, Aromatics and Candied Fruits

The perfumed essences of orange flowers and roses were introduced by the Crusaders to the countries of the western world. Distilled flower waters had been used in the Middle East for centuries. The annual household shopping list of the Caliph Fatimide Aziz (976–96 A.D.) lists rose-water as an important commodity (oranges were apparently also mentioned around that time, but since the flowering period of the orange is relatively brief the water distilled from its flowers was probably not as common).

Flower waters gained in popularity throughout the world. In Shakespeare's time, they were infused at home; elder-flower, rosemary, damask-rose, violets, orange-blossom of the bigarade or bitter orange tree, and lavender were the great favourites. They were used for flavouring all foods, and custards in particular.

As with spices, the essences were used to excess at first, in both savoury and sweet dishes, but later were appreciated most by the pastry-chefs for flavouring their confectionery. By the eighteenth century Carême began to cast doubts on the value of perfumed essences, suggesting in preference the 'pleasant natural taste of orange, of citron, of seville orange, or lemon, of orange flowers or coffee, of vanilla, or green anise and saffron . . . it would be useful to have these various odours prepared previously, and kept close in glass bottles . . .'

Perfumed sugars were not unusual; since medieval times many sugars had been scented, sometimes as a result of their local growing conditions. Musscarat sugar (derived from the musk pouch of a type of mountain deer) was perfumed with musk, barbary sugar came from the kingdom of Barbary in North Africa, and caffetin or palm sugar came from the Genoese colony of Caffa, where the sugar was wrapped in mats of plaited palm leaves ('caffa' in Arabic). The large crystals of candi sugar were extracted from syrups of flowers and fruits such as rose and violet, lemon and red gooseberry, and Madeira sugar came from Portugal.

Of course, Carême's flavours were much stronger. He mentioned vanilla as a perfume only in passing, for it was very new then, but a century later Pierre Lacam was strongly recommending it in preference to the more dominating essences.

> Orange flower water is the perfume of the small pâtissier. He only uses vanilla for his creams and his éclairs. One pod must last eight days; if a little is used each day then it will be finished before eight. I say: do not economize with perfumes; it is the same principle as with butter. The large houses use less than six litres of orange flower water a year, as they use vanilla everywhere, and is not as expensive, and the cakes have more flavour. When I was young, I worked in a house where vanilla was unheard of, everything was prepared with orange flower water, *saint-honoré* and the rest. I wanted to mention it once, but was frightened of being dismissed. Today those patrons no longer sell those *saint-honoré* twice to the same person.

Vanilla Pod. The vanilla pod is probably the most important aromatic in the pâtissier's store cupboard today; its delicate sweet odour has none of the overbearing characteristics of the perfumed essences. It is the fruit of an unusual, rather capricious perennial climbing orchid (*Vanilla planifolia*), native to Mexico. Its golden flowers are insignificant, since all the plant's energy goes into producing dark green seed pods, up to 20 cm (8 inches) in length, which have a strong sweet permeating fragrance. These are picked before maturity and cured for some months until fermentation starts and the perfume develops even more. The outer casing is soft, shiny, black and liquorice-like, while inside are hundreds of tiny seeds stuck together.

The island of Réunion, a French colony, owes its fame to the vanilla pod. Cuttings of the root were brought in 1822 from the Jardin des Plantes in Paris to the island, where the climatic conditions were ideal. Whereas in Mexico a certain type of bee pollinated the flowers, producing fruits of fine quality, in Réunion the insects were missing and the culture was quite poor. It was only when a young native botanist attempted a method of cross-fertilization that the plants flourished. Within a short while a territory of some 4,000 hectares (10,000 acres) was covered, and in time the colony became the largest producer of vanilla in the world. Now it is cultivated in the Congo, Madagascar, Tahiti, the Seychelles, Martinique, and many other places.

Vanilla Sugar. Vanilla pod will keep for several months, for its aroma is very powerful.

It can be used time and time again, even after it has been steeped in a liquid. Wash it in cold water after use, and dry carefully.

Keep an airtight jar filled with caster sugar and plunge the pods into it. Two or three 4 cm (1½ inch) pieces will keep a kilo of sugar well perfumed – simply top up with more sugar as you use it. The pods should be replaced when they are dry and brittle and have no more perfume (usually after about nine months).

Vanilla Essence. Use only pure essences and extracts – these are made by macerating beans in a 35 per cent alcohol solution, but are difficult to find. Beware of substitutes, which are overpowering and have a synthetic and cloying sweetness.

Cinnamon. Cinnamon is the tender bark of a tree which curls into long quills or sticks. The best now grown commercially comes from Indonesia and Malaysia. The bark is peeled from the long green slender shoots and is dried in the sun. It is yellowish-brown in colour, very fragile, and when broken releases a spicy perfume, the essential oil, and has a hot, sweet taste.

Whole cinnamon sticks, like vanilla pods, may be washed and dried and used again.

Cinnamon Sugar. Gently crush 50 g (2 oz) cinnamon stick in a mortar with a tablespoon of caster sugar. Add another tablespoon of sugar and pound well. Sieve, and repeat the process with the leftover pieces of cinnamon. Sift once more and combine with 500 g (1 lb) caster sugar. Store in a tightly stoppered container.

Powdered cinnamon may also be used.

Orange and Lemon Peel Sugars. Take care to avoid touching the white pith under the skin of the fruit – this has a sharp bitter taste.

Grate the zest from 2 or 3 oranges or lemons. Mix 50 g (2 oz) zest thoroughly with 500 g (1 lb) caster sugar and spread it over a flat baking sheet. Dry out in a low oven heat. Store in a tightly sealed jar or tin.

Orange-flower Water and Rose-water. Today these are used with much more discretion and subtlety. They can be bought from pharmacists, drug-stores, delicatessen shops and ethnic stores.

Syrups

Moka Syrup. Grind 60 g (2 oz) dark, high roast, moka coffee beans to a fairly fine texture. Place in a jug, and pour over 225 ml (8 fl oz) boiling water. Cover with a lid and leave to infuse for 10 minutes. Heat together 250 g (9 oz) granulated sugar and 75 ml (3 fl oz) water in a copper sugar boiler to the hard ball stage (120°C, 250°F) then pour the solution over the coffee infusion. Pour the infusion back into the pan and bring to the boil gently (110°C, 230°F). Remove from the heat cover, and leave to cool. Strain through a fine muslin or filter paper, pour into a clean glass bottle and seal. It will keep for several months.

Instant Coffee Powder Syrup. Dissolve 6 heaped teaspoons of coffee and 2 tablespoons of cocoa powder in 250 ml (9 fl oz) boiling water. There is no need to let it infuse; simply proceed as above.

Candied and Crystallized Fruits

Shop-bought crystallized baking fruits are often of inferior quality; rather tough and chewy with very little taste, their greatest virtue is that they are ready chopped. Orange and lemon slices often have nothing to do with real fruit and are simply a sweet jelly flavoured with citrus, but crystallized half rinds, available in delicatessen and whole-food stores, obviously are real fruit. Pour boiling water over the rinds and scrape away the excess sugar. Dry carefully, then shred on a coarse grater before chopping small with a knife.

Candied Orange and Lemon Peel. If you take the trouble to prepare your own candied peels, the flavour and appearance are much better. Peel the skins very finely from 1½ or 2 fruits – avoid cutting any of the white pith, which is very bitter. Boil the skins in an unlined copper pan with 200 ml (7 fl oz) water and 25 g (¾ oz) granulated sugar for about 10 minutes until they have softened. By this time the syrup will have almost completely been absorbed by the skins. Remove them from the syrup and lay them on a board dusted with caster sugar. Roll them in the sugar, and then slice into narrow slivers; dredge with a little more sugar and dry out in the oven set on gas ½, 120°C, 250°F for about 20 minutes; they should not be too crisp. Store in an airtight jar, adding the excess sugar and a little more besides. The sugar can also be used for flavouring.

Candied Angelica. Should you be lucky enough to have an angelica plant in your garden, it is worth-while crystallizing some of the young spring stems yourself.

Slice about 500 g (1 lb) freshly cut leaf stems into 10 cm (4 inch) lengths. Drop them into a large heat-proof bowl, and pour over 500 ml (1 pint) of boiling water in which 100 g (4 oz) of salt has been dissolved. Cover, and leave to stand for 24 hours. Drain the pieces, peel off the skin, and wash them in cold water.

Dissolve 500 g (1 lb) of granulated sugar in 500 ml (1 pint) of fresh water, over a low heat, bring to the boil and simmer gently to reach 115°C, 240°F. Steep the angelica stems in the syrup and continue boiling for a further 20 minutes. Lift them out with a slotted spoon and drain on a wire rack in a cool place. Reserve the syrup. After 4 days re-boil the stems in the same syrup to 115°C, 240°F and keep boiling for a further 20 minutes. Leave to cool down in the syrup then drain again until quite dry. Toss in sugar and store in an airtight jar.

Sponges and 'Biscuits'

The word 'biscuit' in English applies to a thin, dry and brittle cake, but centuries ago a *piscot* was usually a slice of baked and dried unleavened bread, made of wheat flour and water, which was sometimes so hard it could barely be broken in the hand, and could even be kept for as long as fifty years. *Besquite, byscute, biscocten, zwybacken-brot* were variations, but by the early eighteenth century *biscotin* and *biscuit* in France referred to sponge cake as did *Biskuit* in Austria and Germany.

There are two methods of preparing a sponge batter, one where the egg whites are whipped up separately from the other ingredients, and the warmed method where whole eggs and sugar are beaten over heat until they expand. Possibly the earliest mention in Germany of the beaten white technique came in Marx Rumpolt's *Ein new Kochbuch* (1581). His 'Piscoten von lauter Eyerweiss' (biscuits made only with egg whites) gives a very clear description:

> Take whites of egg, and take a nice new pot, and good white flour: make a mixture in the pot and beat it well with a wooden spoon. Add aniseed and coriander and sweeten it well with white sugar. Pour in a little rose-water and a little salt. You can also add one or two egg yolks, which are fresh. Take an Oblat (wafer) which is wide and long, put the mixture from the bowl to it with a wooden spoon, push it quickly in the oven so that the mixture does not flow away; so will it rise high . . .

The method of beating whole eggs and sugar over heat was illustrated even earlier by Bartolomeo Scappi in his *Opera* (1572); the method was for a *zambaglione*, but whether he made a sponge cake in this manner is not certain. In 1699 a scholarly German writer, Mistress Schellhammer, wrote in *Occasional Confectionery* of a *new* method of beating a mixture of egg and sugar over heat – a sponge she called French sweet bread. There are illustrations of a round bottomed egg white bowl and tripod. Probably the first named sponge cake in France was *Biscuit de Savoie*, which must have also originated about the same time. It was made with the same biscuit ingredients but the egg yolks and whites were beaten up separately, to be combined finally with the flours; it also had a different texture because of a variation in the proportion of the ingredients. The technique was introduced to England when Hannah Glasse gave two recipes for Savoy biscuits in the *Compleat Confectioner* (1760), the first of which used the whisked egg white method.

A little later back in France, in 1778, the Marquis de Sade, imprisoned in the Bastille, wrote a complaining letter to the Marquise about the disappointing *Biscuit de Savoie* he had been sent, for by this time it was considered in France to be the most popular festive cake.

> The biscuit de Savoie is not at all what I asked for: In the first place, I wanted them candied all over, both on top and underneath in the same way as the little biscuits; in the second place, I wanted them with chocolate inside, and there's not the slightest trace of chocolate; they've browned them with the juice of herbs, but there's nothing that can be called the slightest trace of chocolate. The next time you're having things sent, please have them make some of these for me, and try to have someone you have confidence in see to it that there's chocolate in them. The biscuits ought to have the same taste as when you bite into a bar of chocolate. The next time you're sending, then: some biscuits of the kind I say: six ordinary ones, six candied, and two little pots of Breton butter, but good and well selected.

The text is translated by Edmund Wilson in 'The Documents on the Marquis de Sade' in 'The Bit between my Teeth' — but it would appear that Mr Wilson might not have realized that 'biscuit' in this instance was a cake.

Within a century, numerous recipes using both biscuit ingredients and the sponge technique featured in the basic repertoire of the pâtissiers' kitchens. Urbain Dubois, in *La Pâtisserie d'aujourd'hui* (1894), names many variations of 'appareils biscuits' with additions of fruits, spices and flavourings: 'biscuits glacés' mentioned later in the book are made with Italian boiled meringue and whipped cream for ice-cream desserts using the whipped egg white method.

Sponge Cakes

Notes on Preparing Sponge Cakes

All the ingredients for a sponge cake must be warmed to room temperature before you start baking.

A sponge is an airy mixture of whisked eggs, sugar, flour, sometimes butter and nuts. The open texture depends, as with whipped egg whites, on the amount of air beaten into it. There are two basic methods for making a sponge; the first heats and beats whole eggs and sugar in a bowl over hot water, before flour and butter are added; the second, which uses separated eggs, beats yolks and sugar in the cold state, before adding whipped whites and flour. The cake's texture in the first method is soft and springy, while that of the second is firmer and more suitable for layered cakes. The addition of butter makes for a richer cake which will keep for 5 or 6 days before it drys out.

Electric table mixer: Beating the sponge in a bowl over hot water can be avoided by using an electric mixer. While the hand method takes about 20 minutes, 10 minutes with the machine set at a medium to high speed will aerate the mixture almost as successfully.

Greasing and lining the tin: Use unsalted butter with a good flavour. Line the base of the tin with greaseproof or silicone paper and grease and dust a mixture of equal parts of caster sugar and plain flour over all; this keeps the crust soft. Shake off any excess. Pour the batter into the tin and spread it very lightly, using a spatula, taking care not to lose any air. The tin should be about two-thirds full.

Bake immediately for cakes raised with air collapse very quickly. The oven heat encourages the further expansion of the air-pockets in the mixture by steam, before the protein in the eggs coagulates with the flour to set the cake.

When the cake is ready it will have risen well and slightly domed; it will have browned and feel springy to the touch. It may also have shrunk away a little from the sides of the tin. If there is still some doubt, test with a warmed metal skewer or wooden cocktail stick – push it into the middle of the cake and if it comes out with cake mixture adhering it should be left in the oven for a few minutes longer.

CAKES

Plain Fatless Sponge

In this basic recipe the flour and sugar each weigh half the amount of the eggs.

100 g plain, soft flour	3½ oz plain, soft flour
4 (200 g) whole eggs	4 (7 oz) whole eggs
100 g caster sugar	3½ oz caster sugar
1 teaspoon lemon zest	1 teaspoon lemon zest

gas 4, 180°C, 350°F/30 minutes

(1) *The warmed method:* Sift the flour three or four times to aerate thoroughly. Choose a bowl that will fit snugly into the top of a pan and will give you plenty of room to work. Break the whole eggs into it and whisk in the sugar lightly; rest the bowl over the pan a quarter full of barely simmering water. Under no circumstances allow the bowl to touch the water, for the eggs will cook and the mixture overheat. Warming eggs and sugar speeds up the coagulation process of the eggs, which in turn helps build the volume of the mixture. Continued whisking causes a change to a pale cream colour and an increase in bulk of two or three times. You may prefer to use an electric table mixer, in which case make sure that the bowl is warmed before you start.

Whisk the mixture until it is thick and creamy. At this point, when a little of the mixture is allowed to fall from the whisk on to the surface it will leave a *ribbon trail* for two or three seconds. Lift the bowl away from the heat and continue whisking while it cools and thickens. Mix in the lemon zest. Dredge 2 spoonfuls of sifted flour across the surface, and with a large metal spoon fold it into the mixture (see page 36 for technique); as soon as it has dispersed repeat the process until all the flour has gone. Turn the mixture into a lined and greased 22–24 cm (8½–9½ inch) baking tin, or divide it between two shallow sandwich tins; lightly smooth the surface and bake in the preheated oven. The deeper cake takes about 30 minutes, the shallow about 20 minutes.

(2) *The separated egg method:* Reserve 2 tablespoons of sugar from the main quantity. Carefully separate the eggs. Whisk the egg yolks and the remaining sugar in a bowl by hand, or in the bowl of an electric mixer, until the mixture thickens and turns a pale creamy colour. Mix in the lemon zest. In another bowl beat the egg whites (page 36) with a pinch of salt until they stand in firm, snowy peaks. Beat in the reserved sugar. Lighten the egg and sugar mixture by mixing in 2 tablespoons of

egg snow; then, alternating with spoonfuls of sifted flour, fold in the rest as lightly and carefully as possible, taking care not to lose any air. Pour the batter into a prepared 22–24 cm (8$^{1}/_{2}$–9$^{1}/_{2}$ inch) deep cake tin or two shallow sandwich tins. Lightly smooth the surface, rap the tin once smartly on the work top to disperse any air bubbles, and bake immediately in the preheated oven.

Genoese Sponge

A plain sponge cake becomes Genoese when butter is added to it. Professional pâtissiers use it extensively in their bakeries; with the added butter and consequent longer keeping qualities it is popular as a base for petits fours and for layered cakes. An interesting book published for the trade in the early part of this century, *All about Gâteaux and Dessert Cakes* by H.G. Harris and S.P. Borella, gives nineteen Genoese recipe variations and 411 different named cakes using them; the cakes range from gâteaux selling at 1 shilling, 1s 6d, 2s and 2s 6d to a selection of 110 ornate fancy dessert cakes. The detail is fascinating, concentrating on precise measurements, on nozzle sizings and decorations rather than ingredients and flavours, but some of the patterns are attractive.

Genoese sponge has the advantage of keeping fresh for up to a week when wrapped and stored in a cool place; like fatless sponges it will also freeze very successfully. The best Genoese sponge is made with equal parts of flour, sugar and butter. For a less rich cake use half the amount of butter. You may follow either method to make the sponge.

Fine Genoese Sponge

120 g plain, soft flour
4 (200 g) whole eggs
120 g caster sugar
1 teaspoon lemon zest *or* 1 tablespoon vanilla sugar *or* liqueur
120 g unsalted butter (melted and cooled)

4 oz plain, soft flour
4 (7 oz) whole eggs
4 oz caster sugar
1 teaspoon lemon zest *or* 1 tablespoon vanilla sugar *or* liqueur
4 oz unsalted butter (melted and cooled)

gas 4, 180°C, 350°F/45 minutes

CAKES

Sift the flour well to aerate. Beat the eggs and sugars in a bowl, then stand over a pan a quarter filled with simmering water. (Or use an electric mixer if you prefer.) Whisk until the mixture becomes pale and creamy and increases in volume. When it leaves a trail, lift away from the heat and carry on beating until it has cooled and thickened. Add the flavouring of your choice. Sift some of the flour across the surface of the mixture, and, using a metal spoon, fold it along with about a third of the melted butter lightly and carefully into the mixture. Continue with the remainder until all is used. Pour quickly into a buttered, lined and floured 22–24 cm (8$^{1}/_{2}$–9$^{1}/_{2}$ inch) spring-form tin and bake in the preheated oven.

The butter may be melted and browned which adds a fine nutty taste.

Dressing up a simple sponge

What can you do with a simple sponge cake? It has great versatility.

* Fill with jam or lemon curd (page 237) and dust with icing sugar – an extra layer of whipped cream adds a little luxury.
* Try fresh soft fruits such as strawberries, raspberries and redcurrants. Slice or bake the cake in three layers. Sprinkle the base with a little kirsch or sherry; cover the base with a layer of sliced fruits and one of whipped cream, cover with the second cake layer, sprinkle and fill as before, and cover with the top cake layer. Dredge with icing sugar and arrange a few fruits on top.
* Try any of the butter cream or nut fillings given earlier; layer between, and spread over the outside; a simple decoration will add a touch of elegance.
* For a *coffee flavour*: flavour the basic sponge mixture with 2 tablespoons of coffee syrup (page 85) or 2 teaspoons of instant coffee powder dissolved in a little boiling water. Slice and fill with whipped, coffee-flavoured chantilly cream.

Simple Dark Chocolate Sponge

Use either the fatless sponge or the Genoese sponge recipe, but replace the lemon zest with 1 tablespoon of vanilla sugar. Sift 1 teaspoon of instant coffee powder and 1 tablespoon of cocoa powder with the flour. Add 1 teaspoon of lemon juice to the egg and sugar mixture, and then beat in 50 g (2 oz) of grated, dark, plain chocolate. Dissolve 1$^{1}/_{2}$ teaspoons of bicarbonate of soda in 1 tablespoon milk, and stir this into

SPONGES AND BISCUITS

the sponge mixture at the end. When the cake has cooled, split and fill with chocolate- or coffee-flavoured chantilly cream and glaze with coffee or chocolate icing (page 73).

For a *cocoa* alternative: replace the lemon zest with 1 tablespoon of vanilla sugar and replace between a quarter and a half of the flour in the recipe with unsweetened cocoa powder. Sift the cocoa and flour together before folding in.

Peach or Apricot Upside-down Sponge

An unusual fresh fruit suggestion. Tinned fruit can be used, but drain well of juices.

50 g moist brown sugar	2 oz moist brown sugar
25 g butter	scant 1 oz butter
5 large fresh peaches, halved and skinned *or* 750 g stoned and halved apricots	5 large fresh peaches, halved and skinned *or* 1 lb 10 oz stoned and halved apricots
basic sponge mixture, page 90	basic sponge mixture, page 90

gas 6, 200°C, 400°F/30 minutes

Grease and base-line a 22 cm (8½ inch) loose-bottomed cake tin, grease again. Melt the sugar and butter together, cool slightly and pour into the tin. Lay the halved peaches or apricots neatly into the base, stone side down. Prepare the sponge mixture and pour it over the peaches. Bake in the hot oven. When nicely browned and shrinking from the sides, lift out of the oven, leave to cool for 5 minutes, then turn the cake out on to a rack to cool, with the fruit uppermost. Serve as a dessert, with whipped cream.

Sponge Buns

All the basic sponge recipes can be baked in small bun moulds and have great appeal to children. Lightly grease the moulds and dust with a flour and sugar mixture; shake off the excess. Fill each up to three-quarters full of sponge mixture, dredge with granulated sugar, and bake in the preheated oven, gas 6, 200°C, 400°F, for 15–20 minutes. Glaze with a flavoured icing or melted chocolate, and decorate with hundreds and thousands, sugar coated chocolate dragees, chocolate vermicelli, glazed fruits, etc.

CAKES

Biscuit

'Biscuit' is the term often used for sponge goods in Europe, and in Germany and Austria in particular. They incline to be sweeter and very light, and are usually used for layered assemblies.

Plain Biscuit

140 g caster sugar	5 oz caster sugar
5 egg yolks	5 egg yolks
1 teaspoon orange or lemon zest	1 teaspoon orange or lemon zest
50 g plain flour	2 oz plain flour
50 g potato flour	2 oz potato flour
5 egg whites.	5 egg whites

gas 4, 180°C, 350°F/30 minutes

Beat the sugar and egg yolks (see separated egg method, page 89) until pale and creamy. Add the zest. Sift the flours thoroughly, then whip up the egg whites to form stiff snowy peaks and fold them, alternating with the flour, into the yolk mixture (page 36 for detail). Turn into a 22–24 cm (8½–9½ inch) greased, base-lined and dusted baking tin, or divide between two shallow tins and bake as above.

Almond or Hazelnut Biscuit

100 g caster sugar	3½ oz caster sugar
3 egg yolks	3 egg yolks
1 teaspoon orange zest	1 teaspoon orange zest
80 g blanched almonds or hazelnuts, ground	3 oz blanched almonds or hazelnuts, ground
3 egg whites	3 egg whites
50 g potato flour	2 oz potato flour

gas 4, 180°C, 350°F/30 minutes

Beat the sugar and egg yolks in a bowl by hand, or in an electric mixing bowl to the ribbon stage (see page 90). Add the zest, and mix in the finely ground nuts. Whip the egg whites in a separate bowl until they stand in peaks, then lighten the main mixture with a couple of spoonfuls of egg white and fold in the rest using a large metal spoon, alternating with portions of sifted potato flour. Pour into two greased, base-lined and flour and sugar dusted 22 cm (8½ inch) baking tins, and bake in the preheated oven.

Fillings for Biscuit

Walnut filling (2), page 66, gives a subtle taste to the biscuit: split the cake in three, fill, and cover with a vanilla or rum flavoured icing. *Dobostorte* on page 169 immediately springs to mind, with its thin layers of biscuit and chocolate mousseline butter cream; look also at the chapter on Gâteaux and Torten (page 158), which gives several cakes made with biscuit layers.

Biscuit de Savoie

> The dessert was now put on the table. In the middle there was a Savoy cake, in the shape of a temple with a melon-sectioned dome; and on the dome there was an artificial rose with a silver paper butterfly on a wire beside it. Two drops of gum in the heart of the flower imitated two drops of dew. Then on the left a cream cheese swam in a shallow bowl, and in another bowl on the right a pile of huge strawberries lightly crushed were running with juice . . .
>
> (Emile Zola, *Gervaise*)

The combination of separately beaten whites with potato flour and icing sugar gives a particularly delicate and light, close-textured cake.

200 g icing sugar	7 oz icing sugar
1 tablespoon vanilla sugar	1 tablespoon vanilla sugar
6 egg yolks	6 egg yolks
70 g plain flour	2½ oz plain flour
70 g potato flour	2½ oz potato flour
½ teaspoon orange-flower water *or* 1 tablespoon Grand Marnier	½ teaspoon orange-flower water *or* 1 tablespoon Grand Marnier
5 egg whites	5 egg whites
pinch salt	pinch salt
3 teaspoons lemon juice	3 teaspoons lemon juice

gas 4, 180°C, 350°F/30 minutes

Reserve 2 tablespoons of sugar, and beat the remaining sugars and the egg yolks to the thick ribbon stage. Sift the flours together three or four times, and fold them into the egg and sugar mixture a spoonful at a time with the flower water or liqueur, taking care not to lose the air. Whip up the egg whites with a pinch of salt, until they stand in firm snowy peaks, beat in the reserved 2 spoonfuls of sugar until the mixture is smooth, and then fold in the lemon juice. Fold the meringue into the first mixture, taking care as before. Grease a 24–26 cm (9½–10½ inch) spring-form tin with unsalted butter, line the bottom with greaseproof paper and grease again. Dust the base and sides with a flour and sugar mixture and turn the batter into the tin; fill two-thirds full and bake in the preheated oven. When it is golden brown and shrinking from the sides remove from the oven and stand on a rack for 5 minutes. Slide a knife round the sides of the cake to release, then turn out on to the cake rack to cool. Peel off the paper when cold.

Split the cooled cake into three layers and fill as wished. It will keep fresh for up to a week if kept in the refrigerator.

* *With Chocolate:* Sift 1 tablespoon of cocoa powder with the flours then prepare the first stage of the recipe above; beat 70 g (2½ oz) grated plain, dark chocolate into the aerated egg and sugar mixture before folding in the flours.

Biscuit de Savoie with Gooseberries

Prepare the basic sponge as above; bake and cool. Make a gooseberry filling as follows:

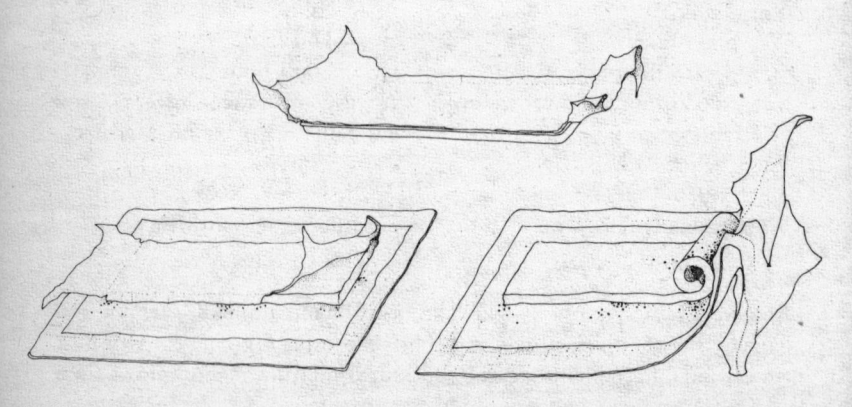

Top and tail 500 g (1 lb) green gooseberries and cook them with 150 g (5 oz) granulated sugar and 500 ml (1 pint) water until they have softened but still remain whole. Cool and drain the fruits, reserving the juice. Dissolve a 10 g (³/₈ oz) gelatine sheet or powder as instructed (page 58) and add it to 500 ml (1 pint) of the cold liquid.

Split the cake in two, reserve a few fruits as decoration, and lay the remainder over the bottom cake layer. Sprinkle a little Kirsch over the cake then, as the liquid starts to set, spoon it all over the fruit. Cover with the top cake layer and press well together. Whip 250 ml (9 fl oz) double cream, and spread it over the top and sides of the cake. Press toasted, flaked almonds all round the sides and decorate the top with gooseberries.

Roulades

Roulades and Swiss rolls are very popular. They can be made with jam, whipped cream, fresh fruit, or butter cream filling, and sprinkled with sugar. Use the plain, fatless sponge recipe for simple cakes — the Genoese or biscuit de Savoie with more elaborate fillings. The oven temperature has to be hot. Use a Swiss roll baking sheet 25 × 36 cms (10 × 14 inches) with 1 cm (¹/₂ inch) high sides. Butter and line with greaseproof paper, silicone or aluminium foil (I find this most efficient), leaving a few centimetres to hang over the sides and either end. Butter the paper; pour the cake mixture into the tin and smooth out. Set in the oven preheated to gas 8, 230°C, 450°F for about 10 minutes until it is well risen, feels slightly springy to the touch, and is golden brown. Lay a clean kitchen towel on the work top and lay on it a large sheet of greaseproof or silicone paper, dredged liberally with caster sugar. Take the cake out of the oven, turn it straight over on to the paper and peel off the baking paper (moisten the edges very slightly with water if it sticks). Trim away the crisp uneven edges of cake with a sharp knife.

For a jam roll: spread generously with 5 or 6 tablespoons of warmed jam to within 1 cm (¹/₂ inch) of the edge. Roll from the short side, using the towel and sugared paper as guide; tuck the first turn in neatly and firmly, then roll more lightly as you continue. Make sure that the join of the cake is underneath and leave to cool on a wire rack. Dredge with icing sugar before serving.

The cake must be cold before it can be used with other fillings; but since it crisps and hardens when cold it has to be rolled, unfilled, while still warm. Peel off the baking paper as before and trim away the edges. Lay a second clean sheet of greaseproof paper on the surface and roll the sponge from the short side, around the paper, using the towel to ease it along into a loose roll. Lay on a rack to cool, with the join underneath, and cover with a slightly damp cloth.

Raspberry, Kiwi Fruit and Pineapple Roulade

The most spectacular roulade I have seen was at the brothers Troisgros' restaurant in Roanne, France. It seemed impossible for us to eat anything more, but when the dessert trolley was wheeled in I could not resist trying a slice.

Prepare either a basic sponge mixture (page 90); or a biscuit de Savoie (page 95) made with all potato flour (it rolls like a dream!). Bake, roll up and leave to cool as instructed above.

Take 500 g (1 lb) of fresh, frozen or tinned raspberries. Reserve 150 g (5 oz) whole fruits and crush or purée the remainder; drain the excess juice. Spread the purée over the unrolled, cold sponge, scatter the whole fruits over and cover with 100 g (4 oz) toasted nibbed or flaked almonds. Roll it up carefully. Lay the roulade on a platter and dredge lightly with caster sugar. Peel and slice two kiwi fruit and lay the slices along the top, alternating with slices of fresh or tinned pineapple; set one whole raspberry in the centre. Serve with fresh whipped cream.

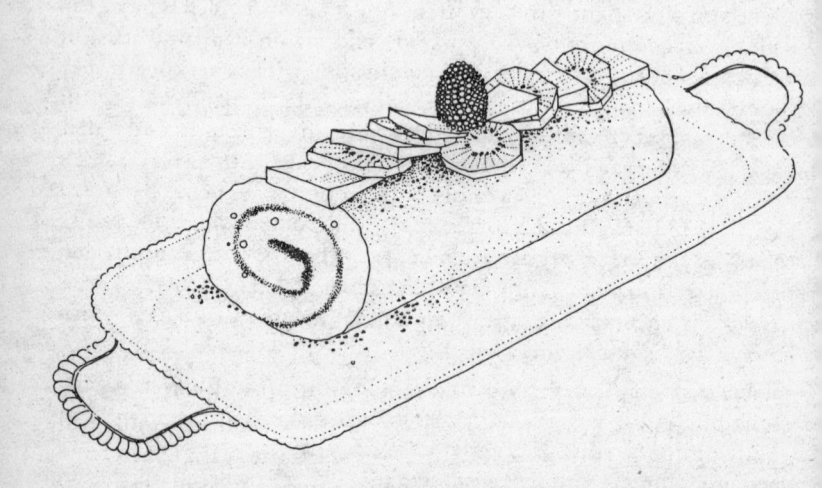

Choux Pastry

'Godber's has come,' announced Sadie, issuing out of the pantry. She had seen the man pass the window.

That meant the cream puffs had come. Godber's were famous for their cream puffs. Nobody ever thought of making them at home.

'Bring them in and put them on the table my girl,' ordered cook. Sadie brought them in and went back to the door. Of course Laura and Jose were far too grown-up to really care about such things. All the same, they couldn't help agreeing that the puffs looked very attractive. Cook began arranging them, shaking off the extra icing sugar. 'Don't they carry one back to all one's parties?' said Laura. 'I suppose they do,' said practical Jose, who never liked to be carried back. 'They look beautifully light and feathery, I must say.' 'Have one each, my dears,' said cook in her comfortable voice. 'Yer ma won't know.'

'Oh impossible. Fancy cream puffs so soon after breakfast.' The very idea made one shudder. All the same, two minutes later Jose and Laura were licking their fingers with that absorbed inward look that only comes from whipped cream . . .

(Katherine Mansfield, 'The Garden Party')

Cream puffs after breakfast might make 'one shudder', though I might even be tempted *for* breakfast! They are one of my favourites.

Cream puffs, Herzogbrot (Bread of the Duke), Paris Brest, Carolines, Salammbos, Mecca rolls, St Honoré, Lucca eyes and Religieuses – who would guess that these grand titles disguise one and the same pastry? They differ only in shape, decoration and flavour of filling. Few recipes in the pastry-cook's repertoire are as quick and easy to make, or visually as spectacular as these. No doubt Godbers were well pleased to have cornered the market in cream puff sales.

The delicate choux pastry shells are composed of a white roux made of flour, butter and water (milk or cream in Austria), and enriched with a high proportion of eggs: they are a miracle of kitchen chemistry. Eggs beaten into the white sauce trap air, and both the water in the whites and other liquids turn into steam while cooking in a high temperature, to expand and cause the paste to billow and puff to two or three times its size. As well as glazing the outside crust, the egg proteins coagulate in baking to help form part of the structure along with the flour, whose gluten has been softened and stretched by being beaten into the boiling liquid. Butter gives flavour and crispness to the crust.

Because of this delicate structure, choux pastry is vulnerable and liable to collapse if the rules are not observed. These particular points are the key to success:

1. Measure ingredients accurately.

2. Use strong flour — the gluten stretches more, giving a larger volume, and improves the crispness.

3. Do not overbeat the egg and flour mixture as this stops the pastry rising.

4. The mixture must not be too moist (do not use too many eggs).

5. Do not open the oven door too soon.

6. Do not remove from the oven until they are baked brown, feel light, hollow and very crisp.

Pâte à Choux

Basic Recipe (1)

130 g strong, plain flour	4½ oz strong, plain flour
pinch salt	pinch salt
2 teaspoons caster sugar	2 teaspoons caster sugar
100 g salted butter	3½ oz salted butter
250 ml water	8 fl oz water
4 whole eggs	4 whole eggs
1 teaspoon brandy, rum or orange-flower water (optional)	1 teaspoon brandy, rum or orange-flower water (optional)

Makes 22 small buns

Basic Recipe (2)

Use the same ingredients as above but replace half the water with an equal quantity of milk.

Method: Sift the flour with the salt and sugar two or three times and finally on to a sheet of greaseproof paper. Drop the butter, cut in pieces,

CHOUX PASTRY

into a large pan with the water or milk and water. Heat gently until the butter has melted, then raise the heat to bring the liquid to a rolling boil. Draw the pan aside, shoot in the flour all at once, and beat the paste vigorously over a low heat until it is smooth and the flour has cooked. It must not look grainy. It should roll cleanly off the bottom and sides of the pan into a ball (a floury film is left over the base). The whole operation takes only a few seconds.

Leave the mixture — the *panade* — to cool for 5 minutes, then beat in the lightly forked eggs very thoroughly, one at a time (you may prefer to use an electric mixer at this stage as it can be heavy work). Take particular care adding the last egg, as not all may be needed (though it can happen that in very dry conditions more egg will be needed). The mixture should be quite firm but elastic (it will drop from a spoon reluctantly when jerked slightly), or it will spread and fail to rise. Beat well until it has a glossy sheen. Add the brandy or rum — it helps crisp pastry as less fat is drawn into the mixture. At this stage the paste can be wrapped in a warm damp cloth to be used later.

If your oven is inclined to over-heat, use a layer of foil or a second baking sheet as added protection, to prevent the bottoms of the pastries from burning. Chill the tray under cold running water for a few moments; leave damp. Lay spoonfuls of the mixture (2.5 cm, 1 inch size for profiteroles; 5 cm, 2 inch for cream puffs) at well spaced intervals, or use a piping bag. Remember they expand to about three times their size. Lightly brush the surface with beaten egg to give a glaze. Bake in the middle of the preheated oven.

Small puffs, Éclairs, etc. are baked at gas 6, 200°C, 400°F for about 20 minutes.

Large Puffs, Rings, Paris Brest, etc. are baked on a longer and reducing temperature — gas 8, 230°C, 450°F for 15 minutes then gas 6, 200°C, 400°F for about 15 minutes more. This helps solidify the paste before it dries out and browns.

Choux pastry should be well browned all over (including the characteristic cracks). Professional pastrycooks invert a deep, metal tin over the pastries while baking; though not essential, this encourages them to swell even more, but take care when inspecting for readiness not to burn yourself.

Transfer to a wire rack to cool; pierce each pastry with a knife or skewer to release steam and retain crispness. Use within 2 or 3 hours, or store when cold in an airtight tin to eat the following day. They will crisp again, if heated for about 10 minutes at gas 2, 150°C, 300°F and taste almost as good as when completely fresh.

Choux pastry also freezes well. Pipe or spoon unbaked paste on to silicone paper, and freeze uncovered before packing. Add 5 minutes to the normal cooking time for frozen choux. Freeze baked unfilled pastries in airtight containers. Thaw in a cool oven, gas 2, 150°C, 300°F for 15 minutes.

Choux Grillés aux Amandes Pralinées

Gouffé tops unbaked choux with an almond layer as follows: Chop 100 g (4 oz) almonds finely and combine with 20 g (1 oz) granulated sugar – moisten lightly with water if necessary to prevent lumps from forming. Add one coffeespoon of rum and a little beaten egg. Mix well, and sprinkle this mixture over the choux buns. Bake as usual; cool.

Cream filling for Choux

Choux puffs can be filled with sweetened crème chantilly (page 57) which has been flavoured with a liqueur, almond praline (page 312), chocolate, coffee or a citrus zest. Éclairs are a more elaborate version.

Éclairs

Arthur Marshall, in the *Sunday Telegraph*, remembered:

> Tea was invariably elaborate and slap-up, with mother trying to outdo mother. In those days, trifles and jelly predominated and whipped cream was everywhere. Hostesses, wildly circulating among the guests, seemed to find it almost impossible to ask anybody a straight question. 'Would you like another éclair?' It took longer, was faintly irritating, and delayed the éclair.

Prepare *basic recipe (2)*. Fill a pastry bag fitted with a 1 cm (½ inch) piping nozzle and pipe twelve 4 cm (1¾ inch) lengths of paste on to a moistened baking sheet at 5 cm (2 inch) intervals. Bake as usual, prick to release the steam, and leave to cool on a wire rack. When cold split in half down the long side.

Crème pâtissière, flavoured with coffee or chocolate, or crème frangipane (pages 59, 61) make good fillings for éclairs. Lightly brush the pastry surface with strained apricot jam and coat with the appropriate icing (page 75). Lemon curd (page 237) is an unusual filling – ice with lemon glacé icing.

All éclairs should be kept refrigerated until needed and served the same day.

Profiteroles au Chocolat

An attractive after-dinner dessert.

Prepare a batch of choux buns, bake, cool, and fill with sweetened whipped cream. Make a small amount of caramel with 100 g (4 oz) of granulated sugar and 1 tablespoon of water, then dab each bun with a little and stick them all together into a pyramid shape. Just before serving drip spoonfuls of soft chocolate icing (page 75) over the profiteroles, covering some almost entirely.

Gâteau St Honoré Parisien

This cake is named after the patron saint of pastrycooks and bakers; but why the Bishop of Amiens in 660 A.D. should have been so honoured is not recorded. In 1894 Urbain Dubois remarked that this cake was almost an exclusive of the Parisian pastrycooks. Here is a version of his recipe. A ring of choux pastry is baked on to a shortcrust pastry base and the centre filled with a special cream; on top of the crown is set a ring of small caramelized puffs. The gâteau must be eaten the same day it is filled.

Roll out a 20 cm (8 inch) circle, 5 mm ($^1/_4$ inch) thick, of shortcrust pastry (page 44). Place on a lightly greased baking sheet. Moisten the rim with lightly beaten egg the same width as the choux pastry circle to be piped on. Prick the pastry all over the middle.

Prepare the choux pastry basic recipe (2). Pipe or spoon sixteen 2.5 cm (1 inch) puffs on to a separate baking sheet; then use the remainder of the paste to pipe or spoon a single circle on to the egg-washed edge of the shortcrust pastry. Place both trays in a preheated oven, set at gas 6, 200°C, 400°F. Bake for 10 minutes, then lower the temperature to gas 5, 190°C, 375°F and bake for a further 10 minutes with the door of the oven propped slightly ajar. Check the smaller puffs now, for they should be about ready. Take them out of the oven carefully and leave the larger cake to finish cooking for about 10 minutes more. Transfer the cooked puffs to a wire rack to cool, and prick each one to release the steam. When cold, fill each puff with a teaspoon of crème chantilly (page 57) — you will need about 80 ml (3 fl oz).

Make a caramel with 200 g (7 oz) of granulated sugar and 3 tablespoons of water (page 70). As soon as the caramel stage is reached, plunge the sugar boiler in cold water for a second to arrest the cooking; then stand the bottom in a bowl of hot water to keep the caramel liquid while you dip the tops of the small puffs into it. Scatter 50 g (2 oz) chopped pistachios over the surface. Then stick each puff on to the choux pastry crown with a little more caramel.

Crème St Honoré is used to garnish the centre hollow. See page 62 for quantities and methods.

Beat the egg yolks in a bowl. Mix in the sifted flours and salt and flavouring, avoiding lumps as far as possible. Add 100 g (3^1/$_2$ oz) of the sugar, then beat in the milk. Strain through a sieve into a double boiler, and heat the mixture to below a simmer, stirring meanwhile. Remove from the heat and pour into a bowl. In another bowl whip the egg whites to stand in peaks, beat in half the remaining sugar until glossy, then fold in the rest using a large metal spoon. Fold this meringue mixture into the warm mixture, using the same metal spoon and taking care to retain as much of the beaten-in air as possible. Set aside to cool.

If weather conditions are hot, or the cream has to be kept before being used, it is advisable to stiffen it with gelatine. Use 2.5 g (^{1}/$_{10}$ oz, ^{1}/$_2$ teaspoon) gelatine for 250 ml (8 fl oz) milk (see page 58 for method).

Pour the finished cream into the hollow crown of pastry and sprinkle a few chopped pistachios over the top for decoration. Leave the cake in the refrigerator until you are ready to serve it.

Gouffé has a few alternative suggestions: 'In many houses one replaces this cream with well flavoured chantilly, mixed with vanilla sugar. Failing good cream, one garnishes the hollow of the crown with crème italienne (meringue with whipped cream flavoured with Maraschino) or strawberry or raspberry bavarois or with chestnut cream. In this case the small puffs may be alternated with candied strawberries, or with green almond marzipan, even with small glacé fruits.'

CHOUX PASTRY

Paris Brest

This is a glorified puff, piped in a circle with a hole in the centre. It can be made either as one large circle, or twelve smaller circles, and filled with whipped cream or crème pâtissière. Use basic recipe (2) and 50 g (2 oz) flaked almonds for decoration: and crème pâtissière (1) (page 59), flavoured with almond praline.

gas 8, 230°C, 450°F for 15 minutes, then
gas 6, 200°C, 400°F for 15 minutes

Line a baking sheet with silicone-coated paper, and draw a 20 cm (8 inch) circle (or twelve 6 cm (2^1/$_2$ inch) circles). Either fill a piping bag fitted with a 1 cm (^{1}/$_2$ inch) nozzle, or for a more rustic look use a dessertspoon. Pipe a circle using the pencil line as guide, then pipe a second one inside this, touching the first; pipe a third circle on top of the two. If using a spoon, lay the mixture out in a similar way, and spoon another circle on top. (When cooked this is sliced off and acts as a lid.) Scatter the flaked almonds over the top and press in lightly. Bake in the preheated oven and reduce the temperature after 15 minutes. Remove from the oven when well risen and brown, and lay on a wire rack to cool. Pierce in several places to release the steam. When cold, slice off the top and fill the cavity with the prepared cream. Dredge with icing sugar to serve.

Croquembouche (A celebration cake)

This pyramid of choux pastry balls is popular today in France as a wedding cake, but a hundred or so years ago *Croque-em-bouches* were something quite different and choux pastry had little or nothing to do with them. They were, in fact, elaborate artifacts built up of almost any cake, fruit or sugar work over a mould. Carême's early moulds in *Le Pâtissier Royal* (1815) were plain, round and straight or tapered, not unlike a plain charlotte mould, and almost as high as they were wide. The cake constituents were stuck together inside the mould with sugar syrup, and when set the container was briefly heated and the moulded *croque-em-bouche* would drop out. The development of the technique over the next decades, particularly by Carême's disciples, Gouffé and Dubois, reached almost outrageous limits, with whimsical and extravagant compositions designed merely for looking at, and often proving structurally impossible; plaster of paris would have made more appropriate manufacturing material. By the end of the nineteenth century, this grandiose splendour in the kitchen started to give way to greater simplicity, with more emphasis on taste and flavour; and the 1920s saw Croquembouche as a pyramid made of choux balls held together with sugar syrup just as it is today. The pyramid often rests on an elaborate stand made of edible nougatine (nut brittle) or croquante (moulded caramel).

First make a mould: Use a large piece of brown wrapping paper about 67 × 58 cm (26^1/$_2$ × 23 inches) to make a conical mould 46 cm high × 20 cm diameter (18 × 8 inches). Fold and roll in much the same way as for the paper piping cone on page 76. Cut or fold in the bottom to make it level and leave the point intact. Pad the cone inside with newspaper for additional strength. Brush the outside of the cone with cooking oil.

Bake a flat shortcrust pastry base 28–30 cm (11–12 inches) in diameter (page 44) with: 260 g (9 oz) plain flour; 165 g (6 oz) butter; 35 g (1^1/$_2$ oz) caster sugar; 2 eggs; 3–4 tablespoons iced water; ^{1}/$_2$ teaspoon salt.

For the choux pyramid you need about 50 choux buns (make 3 or 4 smaller ones to place at the top of the cake). Prepare a double amount of basic recipe (1) or (2), and bake. Pierce each one to release the steam, and leave to cool on a wire rack.

Whip up 500 ml (1 pint) of double cream. Sweeten with 3 tablespoons of vanilla-flavoured caster sugar, and beat until it stands in firm peaks.

Split each choux bun and fill with a teaspoon of cream.

Make a sugar syrup with 700 g (1^1/$_2$ lb) granulated sugar, a pinch of cream of tartar and 250 ml (^{1}/$_2$ pt) water. Cook to the hard-crack stage (page 70) 155°C, 310°F. Cool the pan to arrest the cooking by plunging it in cold water for a second, then stand it in a bowl of hot water while you build up the pyramid of choux buns.

Assemble the pyramid: Dip the top of each cream-filled choux bun lightly into the caramel syrup. Starting at the base of the cone, work round making sure that each bun sticks to the next. Dust some of them with chopped pistachios or almonds. Build the buns up, reserving the small ones for the peak. As soon as the caramel has set, which takes only a few minutes, slide the cone from the inside and place the croquembouche on the pastry base. Pipe a few rosettes of whipped cream on the

CHOUX PASTRY

outside for decoration, and stud with a few crystallized fruits. Finish with a plume of spun sugar (page 72) and serve immediately. Guests will break off pieces of the caramelized and spun-sugar-coated puffs and 'crack it in the mouth' — croquembouche!

Meringues – 'Les Bijoux des Dames'

Comme ces sortes de gâteaux sont les bijoux des dames, les gourmands leur en font l'agréable hommage; les dames mangent d'autant mieux deux et trois de ces friands gâteaux, que leur composition est légère et aussi fondante que la crème fouettée qui les garnit et que, par cette raison, elles n'incommodent jamais l'estomac le plus délicat.

(Antonin Carême)

. . . being extremely light and delicate, and made of white of egg and sugar only, are really not unwholesome . . .

(Eliza Acton)

The basic mixture is 50 g (2 oz) caster sugar for 1 egg white (30 g or a generous 1 oz, size 3).

(1) Ingredients for a 20–22 cm (8–8½ inch) pavlova, circle or 14 meringues

100 g caster sugar	4 oz caster sugar
2 egg whites	2 egg whites

(2) Ingredients for a 24–26 cm (9½–10½ inch) pavlova, circle or 20 meringues

150 g caster sugar	6 oz caster sugar
3 egg whites	3 egg whites

(3) Ingredients for a 28–30 cm (11–12 inch) pavlova, circle or 28 meringues

200 g caster sugar	8 oz caster sugar
4 egg whites	4 egg whites

Notes on Preparing Meringues

All ingredients should be left in the kitchen for at least an hour before baking begins.

Measure out accurately. Sift sugars to disperse lumps. Prepare the baking sheet. Meringue is best baked on silicone-coated paper which

MERINGUES

needs no greasing; greaseproof paper and aluminium foil should be brushed with a light coating of oil. Draw a circle on the paper as a guide and leave space for expansion, as meringue is inclined to swell.

Method (for greater detail see notes, pages 35–6): whisk the egg whites until they stand in firm creamy peaks; sift half the caster sugar across the surface and lightly beat it in, retaining as much air as possible, until the mixture looks glossy, satiny and smooth. Sift part of the remaining sugar over, and fold in gently by hand using a large metal spoon; repeat until all the sugar is used up.

If the mixture is to be piped then all the sugar quantity may be beaten in, as it gives a firmer texture.

Spreading the meringue on the paper: I prefer a slightly rustic home-made look to the bland precision of the piped variety, which I use only for trellising and baskets.

As much as possible of the beaten-in air must be retained, so it is essential to work with a light and delicate touch.

Using a metal spatula as aid, pour or spread the mixture on to the prepared baking sheet to about 2 cm ($^3/_4$ inch) in depth. Very, very lightly push into shape and barely smooth the surface, it usually does so itself as it bakes. Alternatively, fill a large piping bag fitted with a large round nozzle and gently squeeze out a circle starting from the centre.

For small meringues use two spoons, the size depending on your requirements, and lay spoonfuls of meringue, well spaced, on the baking sheet.

Dredge the surface with sugar before placing in the oven.

Baking meringue: Meringues are dried out in the oven rather than baked. Preheat the oven to gas 1, 140°C, 275°F. They take anything from 1$^1/_2$ to 3 hours to dry, depending on their size, and the oven may be switched off and the meringue left in still longer. They will turn a pale golden coffee colour. Small meringues may be left all night in an oven switched on to the lowest heat with the oven door ajar.

Before lifting baked meringue out of the oven, check that the underside has also dried out. A gentle tap with a finger will tell you. It should sound hollow. If it is still soft, leave it in the oven for a little longer.

If syrup oozes from the baked meringue (too high a temperature) making it difficult to remove the paper, turn the meringue over and lightly moisten the paper with water. It will peel off with almost no difficulty.

Storing Meringue

All unfilled plain meringues can be kept for several weeks packed in a tin, wrapped up in plastic film or aluminium foil. They must be airtight and stored in a dry place, but take care, for they are very fragile and brittle.

Meringue Pavlova

Meringue Pavlova is charmingly named in honour of the Russian ballerina and her most famous role, the dying swan. What could be more appropriate for this light and crisp, airy froth of meringue? A pavlova is a large flat circular meringue which is filled or layered in different ways. I always have two or three in reserve, for they make an instant spectacular dessert using whipped cream and an available filling. Fill the cake about an hour before you need it so that the flavours can blend.

Suggestions for a pavlova using meringue mixture (2) on page 108

* Spread 250 ml (9 fl oz) crème chantilly flavoured with vanilla over the meringue surface, and sprinkle generously with 100 g (3½ oz) grated or flaked dessert chocolate, or chocolate caraque curls (page 148) for a more dramatic alternative.
* Flavour 250 ml (9 fl oz) crème chantilly with 2 tablespoons Kirsch or Grand Marnier, and slice a punnet (125 g, 4½ oz) of strawberries on top with a scattering of zest of half an orange to liven them up.
* Try 250 g (9 oz) raspberries and 250 g (9 oz) redcurrants (I like their sharpness); or a 500 g (1 lb) tin of preserved sour or morello cherries; or 4 large white peaches sliced and laid on crème chantilly flavoured with 2 tablespoons of Maraschino.
* Chestnut vermicelles (page 332, half the portion) and 250 ml (9 fl oz) whipped cream are a great favourite.
* Try mixing 100 g (3½ oz) almond or hazelnut praline (pages 60, 312–13) with the whipped cream, and scatter 50 g (2 oz) toasted whole nuts over the surface.

For a dramatic ensemble, two or three layers of meringue can be used with any one of these fillings, but assemble them two or three hours ahead of time and leave in the refrigerator to blend.

Small Meringues

Chocolate or coffee: Beat 3 egg whites, add 150 g (5^1/$_2$ oz) caster sugar and 2 teaspoons vanilla sugar, fold in 50 g (2 oz) grated dark chocolate or 2 teaspoons powdered instant coffee. Lay spoonfuls of the mixture on the baking sheet and bake in the preheated oven gas 140°C 275°F. When cool fill with chocolate- or coffee-flavoured whipped cream or butter cream (pages 58, 62–4).

Pistachio: Fold 50 g (2 oz) chopped pistachio nuts into a meringue mixture made with 3 egg whites and 150 g (5^1/$_2$ oz) caster sugar. Bake and fill with plain whipped cream.

Meringues à la Reine

Most famous of the small meringues must be these, named after Queen Marie Antoinette, who, it is suggested, made them herself.

Use the same ingredients as in the recipe above – 3 egg whites and 150 g (5^1/$_2$ oz) caster sugar, but replace the pistachios with 50 g (2 oz) blanched almonds, toasted and chopped. Make a meringue mixture and fold in the brown nuts. Pipe 'barquettes' or boat-shaped cases 7 cm (3 inches) in length and bake. Cool. Fill with 250 ml (9 fl oz) crème chantilly flavoured with 2 tablespoons Grand Marnier and the fresh zest of an orange. Pile into the boats and decorate with small pieces of crystallized fruits, such as cherry, plum, orange and lemon peel and angelica.

Zampa Kipfel

These unusual and elegant little morsels are a good accompaniment for fresh, soft fruits; the recipe comes from Mrs Joris's manuscript cookery book of 1886. Makes 25 pieces.

CAKES

100 g blanched, flaked or chopped almonds	3½ oz blanched, flaked or chopped almonds
2 egg whites	2 egg whites
100 g caster sugar	3½ oz caster sugar
2 teaspoons vanilla sugar	2 teaspoons vanilla sugar

Lightly toast the almonds in a warm oven and allow to cool. Scatter them over a sheet of greaseproof paper. Prepare the meringue: beat the egg whites to form stiff snowy peaks, beat in half the sugar and fold in the rest. Take a teaspoonful of meringue mixture and gently roll it in the roasted almonds until it is well coated. If you find the soft mixture too difficult to handle, continue beating over a pan of simmering water; after about 10 minutes it will have thickened to a firmer texture. This makes a more robust meringue. Lay the kipfel on a greased and floured baking sheet, and bake at gas 1, 140°C, 275°F for an hour.

Layered Nut Meringues

While layered cakes often incline to be on the rich and heavy side, these nutty meringue layers are very light, and their combination with butter cream fillings unusual. They make an excellent dessert. The cakes will keep for several days and improve as their flavours infuse. The meringue is crisp on the outside but softer inside.

Berliner Crème Torte

200 g raw almonds or walnuts	7 oz raw almonds or walnuts
50 g plain flour	2 oz plain flour
8 egg whites	8 egg whites
280 g caster sugar	10 oz caster sugar
filling (see below)	filling (see below)
20 g toasted nuts as decoration	1 oz toasted nuts as decoration

gas 3, 170°C, 325°F / 1 hour

Grease and flour three 24 cm (9½ inch) spring-form tins. Grind the nuts but leave rather coarse, and mix them with the sifted flour. Beat the egg whites to firm peaks and beat in half the sugar until the mixture appears smooth and satiny. Fold in the rest of the sugar, and finally the nuts and flour. Divide the mixture equally between the three baking tins and set in the preheated oven. When the cakes start to shrink away from the sides and feel slightly crisp, remove them from the oven and cool on baking racks. (The mixture can also be baked on greaseproof paper – draw circles and spread it over, then trim to size while still hot.)

Prepare vanilla butter cream filling or chocolate mousseline butter cream (pages 62, 63) or the following *coffee-flavoured filling with walnuts:*

200 g unsalted butter	7 oz unsalted butter
200 g icing sugar	7 oz icing sugar
150 g ground walnuts	5 oz ground walnuts
20 g powdered coffee	1 oz powdered coffee

Mix the butter and icing sugar until light and fluffy and blend in the nuts and coffee.

Sandwich the three cake layers with a similar thickness of cream to the cake; cover the top and the sides also. Decorate with toasted chopped or flaked nuts as appropriate.

Japonais

This is basically the same as the previous recipe, although hazelnuts are used. You can either make two 24 cm (9½ inch) circles, or pipe small ones allowing two for each cake. The layers should be no more than 0.5 cm (¼ inch) thick. Sandwich together when baked, with the smooth undersides facing upwards so as to achieve the traditional flat shape.

4 egg whites	4 egg whites
180 g caster sugar	6½ oz caster sugar
20 g vanilla sugar	1 oz vanilla sugar
150 g lightly grilled hazelnuts	5 oz lightly grilled hazelnuts
1 tablespoon plain flour	1 tablespoon plain flour
filling (see below)	filling (see below)

gas 2, 150°C, 300°F / 1 hour

Prepare the meringue, then fold in 100 g (3½ oz) of the nuts which have been ground and the flour. Spread on buttered and floured baking sheets and bake in the preheated oven. Cut the cakes to an even size while the cakes are still warm, using a cake tin as guide. Leave to cool. Prepare chocolate butter filling (2) (page 65).

Sandwich the large bases together or the small bases in pairs. Spread the cream round the sides and on the top. Finish the sides with the remaining hazelnuts, chopped, and place a whole nut in the centre.

Katalani Torte

Spices give an unusual tang to this meringue cake.

6 egg whites	6 egg whites
140 g caster sugar	5 oz caster sugar
140 g chopped or ground unpeeled almonds or hazelnuts	5 oz chopped or ground unpeeled almonds or hazelnuts
50 g grated dark chocolate	2 oz grated dark chocolate
1 ground peppercorn	1 ground peppercorn
1 ground allspice berry	1 ground allspice berry
1 ground clove	1 ground clove
½ teaspoon cinnamon	½ teaspoon cinnamon
1 tablespoon vanilla sugar	1 tablespoon vanilla sugar
whipped cream and grated chocolate to decorate	whipped cream and grated chocolate to decorate

gas 2, 150°C, 300°F/1 hour approx

Beat the whites of egg to form a stiff snow. Whisk in half the sugar. Chop or grind the unpeeled almonds and gently fold them into the egg-white mixture a spoon at a time, together with the rest of the ingredients. Grease and line three 21 cm (8½ inch) cake tins or make pencil circles on paper, divide the mixture between them and bake in the cool oven; cool on racks. When they are cold, layer and fill with 500 g (1 lb) bottled or tinned fruits such as white peaches or cherries, according to your choice, and set them one on top of the other. The flavour is improved if you fill the cakes some hours before you need them, as the fruits can soak into the layers which are rather crisp at first. Cover with whipped cream and sprinkle with coarse grated chocolate.

Snow Cake

(a whisked egg white cake)

In England whipped egg whites in baking are generally associated with meringues, but in Europe they have always played a much wider role.

MERINGUES

Many cakes, and nut cakes in particular, include separately beaten whites (a practice which started around the seventeenth century), and the air in them often substitutes in part for the lack of raising agent usually supplied by flour. This inexpensive nineteenth-century Austrian recipe exploits the aerated nature of whipped whites in a similar way, and its good flavour comes from the blend of butter, sugar and potato flour. The light and fluffy texture makes this plain cake an ideal tea-time treat; or, covered with chocolate or vanilla icing, a child's simple birthday cake. Mrs Beeton included a recipe for a Scottish snow cake in her book of 1866. Hers was made with arrowroot; I prefer potato flour.

120 g melted butter	4¼ oz melted butter
7 egg whites	7 egg whites
240 g caster sugar	8½ oz caster sugar
1 tablespoon vanilla sugar *or* grated zest ½ lemon	1 tablespoon vanilla sugar *or* grated zest ½ lemon
70 g potato flour	2½ oz potato flour
70 g plain flour	2½ oz plain flour
1 teaspoon baking powder	1 teaspoon baking powder

gas 3, 170°C, 325°F/40 minutes

Melt the butter and leave to cool. Beat the egg whites to form stiff, snowy peaks. Beat in half the sugars until the mixture is shiny and smooth. Using a large metal spoon, fold in the rest of the sugar. Sift the two flours together two or three times with the baking powder, and then fold into the mixture a little at a time, taking care not to lose any air in the mixture. Add lemon zest if used. Last of all fold in the melted, cooled butter. Pour into a greased and floured 24 cm (9½ inch) baking tin; bake in the preheated oven till the cake is pale and golden and starts to shrink away from the sides. Invert the cake on a cake rack to cool and leave the tin in place; after about 20 minutes turn the cake back over and leave it to cool completely. Serve sprinkled with icing sugar or ice with a lemon glaze (page 73).

Chocolate Egg White Cake

This is one of those useful cakes that needs only egg whites. The texture is somewhat akin to a soufflé and is inclined to drop, but the taste is pure and rich; it keeps very well for 5 or 6 days. It can be sliced into three layers and filled with strained apricot jam or, more festively, with chocolate ganache (page 64). Cover apricot cake with a chocolate glacé icing and the other with more of the cream. Avoid being over generous with the portions, as it is very rich.

180 g plain melted chocolate	6½ oz plain melted chocolate
100 g unsalted butter	3½ oz unsalted butter
8 egg whites	8 egg whites
170 g caster sugar	6 oz caster sugar
50 g plain, soft flour	2 oz plain, soft flour
50 g potato flour	2 oz potato flour

gas 4, 180°C, 350°F/30 minutes

Beat together the cooled chocolate and the butter. In another bowl whip up the egg whites to snowy peaks, beat in half the sugar, then fold in the remainder using a large metal spoon. Gently fold into the chocolate mixture and finally add the well sifted flours. Turn into a greased and floured 26 cm (10½ inch) cake tin and bake. Invert on a wire rack to cool but leave the tin in place. Brush over the cold cake with warm strained apricot jam, then cover with a chocolate glacé icing.

Yeast Baking

The Tackler's Story*

A tackler criticized his wife's bread making to such an extent that, in exasperation, she told him he had better make the bread himself.

'Reet', said he. 'Tha stay i'bed o Sunday morning an ah'll mek thee some proper bread'.

Sunday came. The wife stayed in bed, the tackler got up and went into the kitchen to make his bread. After a few minutes, he shouted up: ' 'ow much Yeast dost tha put in, lass?' 'Nay, lad,' returned the wife, 'tha' smekking t'bread, put in what tha thinks.'

For a long time, all was quiet in the kitchen; suddenly there was a great clatter. 'Hast gotten you bread in t'oven yet?' shouted the wife, wondering what was happening. 'Gotten t'bread in t'oven,' came back an anguished voice. 'It's tekking me all me time to keep it in t'kitchen.'

I can well sympathize with the tackler in his predicament. Overawed by the seemingly uncontrollable activity of yeast, I had always avoided yeast baking in much the same way as some people shun ordinary baking. But yeast, when one starts to explore its potential, is not difficult to work with; it is simply a matter of obeying the simple rules, of providing adequate nutrition for the yeast and offering the right conditions for growth.

The Effect of Yeast on Additional Ingredients

Bread obviously uses the leavening potential of yeast to the greatest advantage, with flour providing the main source of sugar and nitrogen; but yeast has the added qualities of good and distinctive flavour as well as giving a fine porous structure. These are more apparent in cakes.

Cakes are much richer than bread, as they contain such ingredients as butter, sugar, eggs, and fruits, all of which have an effect on the action

---

* Tacklers set up the looms in the cotton mills of Lancashire. They are reputed to be thick in the head.

of yeast. Sugar in larger quantities retards the action, so does fat; and eggs, which hold air so effectively, help to lighten the yeast mixture.

For these reasons when making cakes a greater quantity of yeast is generally used, the preparation technique differs, and the rising time may be longer.

It is sometimes suggested that to hasten the rise of the cake a little more yeast can be added.

I would avoid this since it can give a bitter flavour, coarsen the texture and reduce the keeping life of the baked goods. Follow the quantities given in the recipes.

Fresh Yeast

I much prefer fresh yeast to dried; it has a finer flavour and is easier to handle. Fresh compressed or baker's yeast can usually be bought in vegetarian or health food shops, but failing that, a small bakery might oblige.

It is essential that the yeast is really fresh, otherwise the action will be sluggish and the baked goods unsuccessful. Yeast should have a beige-white colour and smell of good rum or fresh fruit. It should smell neither sour nor of cheese. It should be cut in a block and have a moist and creamy texture, and should not crumble unduly and certainly not powder.

Wrapped in a package that allows a little air for ventilation it will keep fresh for a couple of weeks stored in the refrigerator.

Although I prefer to buy yeast fresh when I need it, it will also keep in a domestic freezer for at least 3 months. Date mark the packages carefully and use them in strict rotation. Defrost in the refrigerator for 24 hours before you need it, and keep for no more than 3 days; then use all immediately.

Dried Yeast

If fresh yeast is unavailable one can use dried 'live' or 'baker's' yeast. This comes in granular form, packed in small envelopes or tins. In England these packages unfortunately come un-dated as yet, and one cannot assess how long they have been on the grocer's shelves, but their life is reasonable for at least a year.

The concentration of dried yeast is twice that of fresh yeast. For cake-baking, where the mixture is very rich, *half* the quantity stipulated for fresh yeast should be used.

How to Use Dried Yeast

The granules, which have been hot-air dried (the water has been driven off), must be returned to a moist state before being used. They must be dissolved completely. Drop the dried yeast into a small amount of warm water or milk (the recipe will stipulate which), add one small teaspoon of sugar, stir, and leave for at least 10 minutes or until the liquid is creamy and froths a little. Whip it lightly to ensure that all the granules have dissolved, then use as directed. If it fails to 'work' the yeast is stale and should be thrown away.

The Yeast Sponge Batter for Cakes

Because sugar, butter, eggs, dried fruits and nuts inhibit and retard the natural growth of yeast cells, it is essential to prepare a preliminary sponge batter before the main mixture.

Warm the water, milk or cream to almost blood heat – no more than 80°F 25°C – an easy way is to mix one-third boiling and two-thirds cold to get the right temperature.

Crumble the yeast into the liquid in a warm bowl and add a teaspoon of sugar, taken from the amount listed in the recipe. Stir until the yeast has dissolved. (For dried yeast mix and leave to stand for at least 10 minutes in the usual way.)

Mix this with a small amount of sifted flour, about a quarter of the whole recipe amount. Beat vigorously to remove any flour lumps, and to incorporate air which encourages fermentation.

Cover. Leave to rise for 10–15 minutes, by which time the mixture should be fermenting, that is foaming and expanding.

The Main Points for Handling Yeast in Cakes

(1) Use fresh yeast if possible – half the amount if using dried yeast.
(2) Use strong flour; the higher gluten content gives a better rise.
(3) As heat encourages the activity of yeast, all the ingredients should be warmed so that the action is not held back. The liquid used for dissolving the yeast must be no more than 80°F, 25°C; otherwise too much heat will destroy some of the yeast cells.

CAKES

(4) The mixtures are generally prepared in two stages: First a batter is made which is allowed to rise; then the enriching ingredients are added, and a further rising is necessary.

(5) The dough should rise to about twice its volume. If allowed to rise more or left too long, or in too warm conditions, it will develop a taste of over-fermented yeast.

(6) The container in which the dough is set to rise should be warmed and so should the cover, though the dough itself will feel cool and clammy to the touch. It can be left in the mixing bowl, covered with a sheet of polythene or a damp cloth wrung out in warm water, or with aluminium foil. An oiled polythene bag is also good, but make sure that it leaves plenty of room for expansion.

(7) The rising periods are essential to success, as are both the temperature and location. Yeast hates to be disturbed – one rough jerk and the dough will collapse but it will rise again. An airing cupboard with a steady temperature of no more than 25°C, 80°F is ideal. Other alternatives are the plate-warming cupboard of a cooker, a warm boiler-room, or simply a warm corner in the kitchen. I have two ovens; I heat the upper one to 25°C, 80°F, then switch it off. The lower oven is switched on to gas $^1/_4$, 90°C, 175°F, and the rising warmth maintains the temperature in the upper oven. (Remember to keep a check with an oven thermometer.) You can also set the bowl of dough to rise on top of your cooker with the oven switched on underneath.

(8) Use unsalted butter to grease warmed cake tins, then dust with flour, which helps the cake turn out more easily when baked. Should it stick, wrap the tin in a cloth or aluminium foil, and the steam which is trapped inside the warm tin will create enough moisture to help release the cake.

(9) Bake in the preheated oven, and never open the oven door for at least the first 20 minutes or the cake will collapse.

(10) A yeast mixture can be left to rise overnight if need be. Obviously this must be in a cold place. After kneading or beating, cover with a damp cloth or aluminium foil to prevent a skin forming, and leave in the refrigerator. It will rise more slowly; the richer the ingredients the longer the mixture can be retarded. Finish the process as instructed.

Working and Kneading the Dough

Make sure that the yeast is completely dissolved and active before it is added to the other cake ingredients. Kneading and beating air into the dough is essential, to encourage the yeast activity as well as enhance the final structure. Enriched doughs are usually beaten initially with a wooden spoon or a spatula; or with an electric mixer and then kneaded vigorously.

With the cupped fingers of one hand lift the paste high, and slap it and pull it against the sides of the bowl. If the quantity is too large you will need to work on a lightly floured table. At first the dough will stick to your fingers, but the more it is worked the less sticky it becomes until finally it will detach itself entirely, become very elastic and smooth and have large air bubbles. You can test this by pulling it out about 30 cm (1 ft) between your hands and twisting it. It should remain whole. An electric mixer fitted with a dough hook is particularly successful if you lack sufficient elbow grease.

There is a marked difference between English and European yeast bakery. English recipes are usually based on a simple bread dough, often enriched with dried fruits and spices, and even with eggs and butter, for festive cakes. Elizabeth David has studied them very thoroughly in her splendid book *English Bread and Yeast Cookery*. In the shops today, apart from the simple sweet breads and buns, spiced or plain, the few popular enriched doughs to be found are Danish pastries and doughnuts. The doughnuts are travesties of their former quality, heavy and stodgy with an injection of cheap jam – no longer the light and airy puffs with a strong fresh yeasty smell that sported a distinctive wide hoop of white around the middle. Danish pastries leapt into fashion along with the espresso coffee bars in the 1950s and have since graced every pastry trolley and luncheon counter, every station buffet and café.

The Hungarians, Austrians and Germans have always been more imaginative than the English at baking; they used an abundance of eggs, butter, nuts, chocolate, fresh fruits and spirits, as well as the usual spices and dried fruits. The French used sweet brioche dough as a basis for numerous enriched variations.

Yeast cakes should be eaten quickly as they only keep fresh for 2 to 3 days.

Hefeteig – Basic Yeast Dough for Layered Cakes

This simple sweet dough is a perfect base for numerous layered variations.

115 ml milk	4 fl oz milk
20 g yeast	3/4 oz yeast
60 g sugar	2 oz sugar
300 g strong, plain flour	11 oz strong, plain flour
70 g butter	2½ oz butter
2 whole eggs (size 2)	2 whole eggs (size 2)
zest ½ lemon	zest ½ lemon
pinch salt	pinch salt

gas 5, 190°C, 375°F/25–30 minutes

Prepare the yeast batter (page 119) with the warm milk, yeast, a teaspoon of sugar and 75 g (2½ oz) of flour taken from the bulk. Beat very thoroughly, and set aside for 10 minutes to ferment. Beat the butter and sugar until light and fluffy, mix the eggs in singly, then add the lemon zest. Sift the remaining flour with the salt two or three times and finally into another bowl. Make a well in the centre, put in the butter mixture, draw a little of the flour into it and add the yeast batter. Beat well, then knead hard until the dough rolls off the sides of the bowl, is very elastic, throws large air bubbles, and is very shiny. It will take 10–15 minutes in an electric mixer fitted with a dough hook and about 30 minutes by hand. With a larger quantity it is easier when hand kneading to work on a floured work top. Cover the bowl, and leave for 20–30 minutes to rise and double its bulk.

Grease two trays 21 × 30 × 3 cm (8 × 11½ × 1½ inches), and dust with flour. Dust the work surface liberally and turn half the dough on to it. It will seem rather sticky and cling to the fingers, but if you lightly dust it with flour it will roll out perfectly and be very springy. Roll out to 3–4 mm (1/8–3/16 inch) thickness and approximately to the size of the baking trays (there is no need to be exact). Lap it over the rolling pin and lift it into the greased tray. Ease it gently into place with the floured hand; it will level out and fill the tray as it rises. Roll and prepare the rest of the dough. Stand it uncovered, in a warm place, to rise and double in bulk (about 20 minutes). Brush the dough surface with melted butter and sprinkle with 25 g (1 oz) toasted breadcrumbs or ground nuts, on each tray, if the filling is moist. Cover with filling (see variations) and bake in the preheated oven. Cool in the tray on a wire rack. Cut into rectangles and sugar if necessary.

Two fruit alternatives

* Skin 6 large peaches and remove the stones. Cut into 3 mm (¹/₈ inch) slices and sprinkle with a little lemon juice to stop discoloration. Lay the slices in even rows over the dough and scatter 50 g (2 oz) toasted flaked almonds over each tray. Bake. Cool, and dredge heavily with sugar before serving.
* Soak 50 g (2 oz) sultanas for 30 minutes in 1 tablespoon rum or Kirsch. Peel, core and slice thickly 1 kg (2 lb) Bramley cooking apples or Cox's dessert apples; sprinkle with lemon juice. Lay the fruits on to the prepared yeast dough and scatter over the drained dried fruits, a handful of seedless grapes, and 50 g (2 oz) nibbed almonds. Cover the top of the fruit with a sheet of aluminium foil to make the fruits more juicy, but remove it 5 minutes before the cooking is completed to allow them to brown slightly. Bake, cool and dredge with caster sugar to serve.

Streussel Kuchen

(a crumb covering on a yeast dough base)

Make either of the following streussel mixtures:

Cinnamon Streussel

220 g chilled, unsalted butter	8 oz chilled, unsalted butter
300 g plain flour	11 oz plain flour
1 tablespoon cinnamon	1 tablespoon cinnamon
220 g granulated sugar	8 oz granulated sugar

Almond Streussel

240 g chilled, unsalted butter	8½ oz chilled, unsalted butter
300 g plain flour	11 oz plain flour
120 g ground almonds	4 oz ground almonds
2 teaspoons cinnamon	2 teaspoons cinnamon
zest ½ lemon	zest ½ lemon
160 g granulated sugar	6 oz granulated sugar

Streussel is made like pastry. Cut the butter small into the sifted flour and rub to form fine crumbs; blend in the ground almonds (if using), spices, zests and sugar using a knife, until larger rather coarse crumbs are formed. Roll the pastry into a ball, wrap in foil or plastic film, and leave to chill and harden in the refrigerator. When it is really firm press it through a coarse sieve, or grate coarsely and dust lightly with flour to prevent it from sticking together.

Prepare the basic yeast dough on page 122, and once it has risen in the trays, brush the surface lightly with melted butter and scatter the streussel mixture thickly over the top. Set in the preheated oven and bake until the dough is golden and a testing skewer comes out dry. Cool on a wire rack in the tin and cut into slices when cold. Dredge with icing sugar before serving.

Zwetschken or Cherry Kuchen with Streussel

Prepare half the basic yeast dough quantity but use 15 g (½ oz) fresh yeast. Leave to rise. Roll out, and line a greased and floured 26 cm (10½ inch) spring-form tin. Leave to rise. Brush with melted butter, sprinkle with 50 g (2 oz) ground nuts or breadcrumbs. Stone and halve 1 kg (2 lb) of cherries, or stone 1 kg (2 lb) of plums and cut into quarters; lay the fruit close together on the dough, and dust with cinnamon. Prepare half the amount of cinnamon streussel (page 123) and scatter this over the top of the plums. Bake in the preheated oven at gas 5, 190°C, 375°F for about 30 minutes. Dredge liberally with caster sugar and cinnamon before serving.

Mohnkuchen

(Poppy seed on yeast dough)

This is a classic pastry. Use one portion of basic Hefeteig (page 122) and make the filling with:

200 g poppy seed	7 oz poppy seed
300 ml boiling milk	11 fl oz boiling milk
100 g butter	3½ oz butter
100 g sugar	3½ oz sugar
3 egg yolks	3 egg yolks
250 ml double cream	9 fl oz double cream
1 teaspoon cinnamon	1 teaspoon cinnamon
40 g chopped almonds	1½ oz chopped almonds
100 g sultanas	3½ oz sultanas
100 g raisins	3½ oz raisins
3 egg whites	3 egg whites

Grind the poppy seed in an electric coffee mill or with a pestle and mortar, and pour over the boiling milk; leave to infuse and swell. Beat the butter with the sugar until fluffy, then add the egg yolks and double cream. Add the poppy seed mixture and blend well together. Next add the cinnamon, almonds, sultanas, and raisins. Beat the egg whites to peaks and fold into the mixture lightly. Spread the mixture over the unbuttered yeast dough and bake in the preheated oven, gas 5, 190°C, 375°F, for 35–40 minutes.

When cold dust with caster sugar to serve, or cover with a thin layer of white, slightly lemon-flavoured icing. The poppy seed layer may also be covered with the cinnamon streussel mixture (page 123).

The poppy seed filling can also be baked on the butter pastry base (page 317 Bienenstich) at gas 3, 170°C, 325°F for one hour.

NOTE: It is possible to buy poppy seed which has been ready ground with sugar. In this case, omit the sugar from the recipe and do not boil the seed with the milk.

Curd Cheese Yeast Cake

Use the same yeast base as for the fruited cakes (page 122).

Cheese filling:

30 g butter	1 oz butter
250 g curd cheese	9 oz curd cheese
50 g sugar	2 oz sugar
2 egg yolks	2 egg yolks
1 whole egg	1 whole egg
3 tablespoons sour cream	3 tablespoons sour cream
zest 1 lemon	zest 1 lemon
40 g raisins	1½ oz raisins

Beat the butter until light and creamy. Mix in the sieved cheese and the remaining ingredients. Line a 26 cm (10½ inch) spring-form cake tin with two-thirds of the paste, pressing it out gently with floured hands to come 2 cm (¾ inch) up the sides.* Spread the cheese filling across the surface and brush with a beaten egg and milk mixture. Roll the remainder of the paste into long narrow strips and lay as a trellis over the cheese. Leave to rise. Bake at gas 5, 190°C, 375°F for 35–40 minutes.

* You can also put a layer of grated apple under the cheese.

Apricot Yeast Cake

The texture and quality of this yeast pastry is quite different from the basic one because of the cream and the greater number of eggs; it also keeps fresh for a longer time (4 or 5 days in the refrigerator). Cherries may be used if you prefer.

30 g fresh yeast	1 oz fresh yeast
100 ml milk	3 fl oz milk
50 g caster sugar	2 oz caster sugar
280 g plain, strong flour	10 oz plain, strong flour
pinch salt	pinch salt
100 g butter	3½ oz butter
4 egg yolks	4 egg yolks
50 g nibbed or flaked almonds	2 oz nibbed or flaked almonds
100 ml double cream	3½ fl oz double cream
2 egg whites	2 egg whites
1 kg fresh apricots	generous 2 lb fresh apricots

gas 5, 190°C, 375°F/approx 1 hour

Make a sponge with the yeast, the heated milk, a teaspoon of sugar and 70 g (2½ oz) sifted flour. Beat very well to aerate, then cover and leave to stand in a warm place.

Sift the rest of the flour with the salt into a bowl, and set in the oven to warm for a few seconds. Beat the butter and sugar together until pale and creamy, then add the egg yolks and the almonds and a spoonful of flour between each addition to prevent the egg curdling the mixture. Next add most of the flour (leaving aside 2 or 3 tablespoons), and the cream, spoon by spoon. Pour in the yeast sponge and beat the dough very thoroughly; add the last of the flour and beat until it becomes very shiny. Whip up the egg whites to stiff, foamy peaks and fold them into the yeast dough. The dough will now amalgamate perfectly and become very elastic. Cover, and leave to rise for about 30 minutes in a warm place.

Layer half the mixture, 1 cm (½ inch) deep, into a greased 24 cm (9½ inch) spring-form tin. Pull and tease the dough roughly into shape, or roll lightly on a floured board. Pack in half the stoned and quartered fruits generously, and dust sparingly with sugar if necessary. Cover with the rest of the dough, and finish off again with the apricots. Leave to rise once more in a warm place, but this time uncovered. It will take about an hour to double its bulk, because the weight of the fruits slows down the action. Bake in the preheated oven for a little more than an hour. Dredge with caster sugar before serving.

Gugelhopf

A cake shape which has altered little since the sixteenth century is the gugelhopf, with its straight or slanting, furrowed and moulded sides, and a central funnel through which the oven heat is able to penetrate the cake centre; 'Gugel' in earlier times meant 'cowl' or 'hood', and the cake itself was named after the mould.

The shape was popular throughout Austria, Germany and Alsace, and each region had its own name for the cake. In North and West Germany, and Berlin in particular, 'Napfkuchen', in coastal areas 'Topfkuchen' and 'Formkuchen'; 'Gugelhopf' and '. . . hupf' is Austrian, and 'Kougelhopf' Alsatian; 'Kugelhopf', 'Gugelhopfen', 'Gouglof' were other colloquial variations. In East German provinces 'Babe' or 'Bäbekuchen' were familiar names, and also turban or 'Turkenmütze' – the French 'Bonnet du Turc' which was mentioned in Diderot – d'Alembert's encyclopaedia in the eighteenth century. In England a pyramid fruit cake was baked in the same mould, and in America angel food cake.

The moulds themselves were made of various materials; tin in simple shapes, more elaborate ones of fired clay, and especially fine ones of copper. The cake ingredients also varied from region to region: in Austria, southern Germany and Alsace a yeast mixture was usual; 'Napfkuchen' were made with a conventional beaten mixture. In Alsace and southern Germany the cake had very little sugar and was often served at breakfast, with meat or as accompaniment to wine.

But where and when today's traditional gugelhopf cake, made with yeast dough and filled with sultanas, originated, I am not certain. It seems that it was baked in Poland from 1609 onwards, and apparently King Stanislas had a special weakness for it; a century later in 1719 Konrad Hagger in his *Neues Salzburgisches Koch-Buch* gives a recipe. Today it is most often associated with Alsace.

CAKES

Gugelhopf

(*a rich mixture*)

There are many gugelhopf recipes which use fewer eggs, less butter and often less sugar; they are inclined to be rather tasteless and bland and, like a tea-bread, can do with butter and jam or honey in addition. I prefer this richer version, which needs no embellishment so that the yeast dough can be best appreciated. The almonds, which are typical of the Alsatian cake, in Curnonsky's words 'crunch deliciously under the teeth'.

100 ml warm milk	3½ fl oz warm milk
20 g yeast	¾ oz yeast
75 g sugar	2½ oz sugar
300 g strong, plain flour	11 oz strong, plain flour
70 g raisins	3 oz raisins
30 ml Kirsch (optional)	1 fl oz Kirsch (optional)
100 g butter	3½ oz butter
1 whole egg	1 whole egg
3 egg yolks	3 egg yolks
1 teaspoon salt	1 teaspoon salt
30 g almonds for mould	1 oz almonds for mould

gas 6, 200°C, 400°F/45 minutes

Prepare a sponge with the milk, yeast, a teaspoon of sugar and 60 g (2 oz) of the sifted flour. Set aside to rise. Soften the raisins in Kirsch, drain and dust with flour. Beat the butter with the sugar till fluffy and pale,

Gugelhopf moulds

add the whole egg and the yolks, and a spoonful of flour to prevent the mixture from curdling. Turn into the well sifted flour and salt, draw in the flour and add the yeast sponge. Beat very well until a fine, silky homogeneous mass rolls off the sides of the bowl and has large air bubbles. Mix in the raisins. Sprinkle with a little flour, cover, and set in a warm place to rise and double in volume. Grease a 23 cm (9 inch) gugelhopf mould with melted unsalted butter, and stud with whole or split blanched almonds.

Knock back the risen dough and knead for a few more moments, then fill into the prepared mould; it will level itself out while it rises. Set it to rise in a warm place as before for about 35 minutes, or until the mixture has risen to within 2 cm (1 inch) of the top of the tin. Bake in the preheated oven until it is golden and a knife inserted will come out clean. Turn out on to a wire rack to cool. Dredge with icing sugar to serve, or cover with a fine clear glacé icing (page 72).

Gugelhopf can be frozen successfully. Wrap when lukewarm in aluminium foil or heavy duty polythene, and store in the freezer for up to 6 weeks. Thaw at room temperature for 2 hours; dredge with icing sugar to serve.

A Candied Orange alternative

Fresh home-made candied orange peel is essential for this orange cake; it is simple to prepare and the clear sharp taste makes all the difference to the flavour of the cake. (See page 85 for the method.) The sugar left over from dusting the candy can be used in the cake – but weigh it and take away the equivalent amount in the recipe.

Use the same ingredients as for the Gugelhopf, plus the zest of an orange and 1 tablespoon of orange juice. Beat the juice and zest of the fruits and the candied rinds into the mixture before adding the yeast sponge. Continue as instructed.

> The Monday of the Feast (September harvest) – for it lasted two days – was kept by women and children only, the men being at work. It was a great day for tea-parties; mothers and sisters and aunts and cousins coming in droves from about the neighbourhood. The chief delicacy at these teas was 'baker's cake', a rich, fruity, spicy dough cake, obtained in the following manner. The house-wife provided all the ingredients excepting the dough, putting raisins and currants, lard, sugar, and spice in a basin which she gave to the baker, who added the dough, made and baked the cake, and returned it, beautifully browned in his big oven. The

CAKES

charge was the same as that for a loaf of bread the same size, and the result was delicious; 'There's only one fault wi' these 'ere baker's cakes,' the women used to say; 'they won't keep!'. And they would not; they were too good and there were too many children about . . .

(Flora Thompson, *Lark Rise to Candleford*)

Potize

A circle coiled in snake fashion is characteristic of the Potize, Kärntner Reinling or Wickelkuchen. Here the very soft yeast dough is rolled out on a floured cloth, layered with a filling, and then rolled up using the cloth as aid, and coiled round to fit inside a spring-form tin. Filled with cinnamon and sugar, this popular peasant cake has established itself as a firm favourite among my friends and their children. It is quick and simple to prepare and still tastes good after 3 or 4 days.

150 ml milk	5 fl oz milk
15 g yeast	½ oz yeast
25 g caster sugar	scant 1 oz sugar
250 g strong, plain flour	9 oz strong, plain flour
1 teaspoon salt	1 teaspoon salt
50 g butter	2 oz butter
1 egg	1 egg
1 egg yolk	1 egg yolk

gas 6, 200°C, 400°F/20 minutes

Prepare the sponge batter with the warm milk, the yeast and a teaspoon of sugar and mix to a paste with 50 g (2 oz) of the sifted flour. Set aside, covered, to rise in a warm place. Sift the remaining flour and salt together two or three times. Beat the butter and sugar until pale and fluffy, then mix in the whole egg and yolk, the flour, and the yeast sponge. Knead well until the dough is very elastic, throws large air bubbles and draws away from the sides of the bowl. It will be very soft. Set aside to double its volume for about 40 minutes.

Dust a tea-towel liberally with flour and roll out the risen dough on it very lightly. (It will seem at first that the paste is far too soft, but provided that you use enough flour you will find it to be no problem at all.) Always keep the towel well dusted so that it cannot stick.

Roll the dough into a long narrow rectangle measuring about 120 cm (3 ft 6 inches) in length and 10 cm (4 inches) in width and 0.5 cm (¼ inch) thick. Spread generously with the filling (see below), and using the cloth to help, roll it up starting on the longest edge. Grease and flour a 26 cm (10½ inch) cake-tin; lift up the snake using the towel, and ease it gently into the mould. Start in the middle and work outwards and avoid crushing the roll in any way as it needs room to rise. Leave to rise once more for about 20 minutes, then brush lightly with beaten egg and set in the preheated oven. When cold dust with icing sugar.

Fillings

Try any one of the following:

* *Coarse sugar:* 125 g granulated sugar; 50 g sultanas; 50 g pine nuts; 1 teaspoon cinnamon
  (4 oz granulated sugar; 2 oz sultanas; 2 oz pine nuts; 1 teaspoon cinnamon)

Mix all the ingredients together. Brush butter on the dough.

* *Walnuts:* 140 g sugar; 100 ml water; 210 g ground walnuts; 1 tablespoon cinnamon; zest 1 lemon or orange
  (5 oz sugar; 4 fl oz water; 8 oz ground walnuts; 1 tablespoon cinnamon; zest 1 lemon or orange)

Boil the sugar and water in a copper pan to the thread stage (page 70), then stir in the ground walnuts, the cinnamon and the zest.

* *Almonds:* 100 g almonds; 100 g caster sugar; 100 ml honey; zest 1 lemon
  (3½ oz almonds; 3½ oz caster sugar; 3½ fl oz honey; zest 1 lemon)

Prepare an almond praline (page 312). Heat the honey and mix in the praline with the zest.

* *Poppy seed:* 40 g fine ground poppy seed; 200 ml double cream; 200 ml honey; 1 tablespoon cinnamon; zest ½ lemon
  (2 oz fine ground poppy seed; 7 fl oz double cream; 7 fl oz honey; 1 tablespoon cinnamon; zest ½ lemon)

Mix together the ground seed with the cream to make a thick paste. Beat in the honey, the cinnamon and the zest.

* *Chocolate:* 140 g granulated sugar; 200 ml water; 140 g grated chocolate
  (5 oz granulated sugar; 7 fl oz water; 5 oz grated chocolate)

Boil the sugar and water with the chocolate until it has thickened. Allow it to cool down a little before using it.

Roll out the pastry as before, and spread the lukewarm chocolate filling all over. Sprinkle with pine-nuts and vanilla sugar, and roll up the dough as before. Line the baking tin as for potize.

CAKES

Savarin and Baba au Rhum

Savarin was named in honour of the philosopher and gastronome Brillat-Savarin in 1840 by one of the Julien brothers, an eminent Parisian pastry chef. He experimented with the basic baba paste and left out the dried fruits, and also changed the shape and the syrup.

There are two basic methods for preparing these; the first mixes all the ingredients together and then leaves them to rise; the second prepares an initial sponge batter with a rising before the butter and sugar are incorporated. Having used both techniques, I find the second more satisfactory as the texture and taste of the dough is finer.

This quantity is enough for about 12 individual babas about 5 cm (2 inches) in diameter, or 1 large savarin 26 cm ($9^{1}/_{2}$ inches) in diameter.

The central funnel of the savarin mould should be at least 1 cm ($^{1}/_{2}$ inch) higher than the outer rim of the tin so that the cake can rise without spilling over. (If it is not, then insert a tube of aluminium foil but remember to grease it along with the rest of the tin.)

50 ml warm milk or 2 teaspoons cream	2 fl oz warm milk or 2 teaspoons cream
10 g fresh yeast	$^{1}/_{3}$ oz fresh yeast
250 g strong, plain flour	9 oz strong, plain flour
1 teaspoon salt	1 teaspoon salt
4 eggs	4 eggs
190 g unsalted butter	7 oz unsalted butter
1 tablespoon sugar	1 tablespoon sugar

gas 6, 200°C, 400°F/18—20 minutes

Heat the milk or the cream to blood heat and sprinkle on the yeast. Leave for 10 minutes. Sift the warmed flour with the salt into a warmed bowl. Make a well in the centre, pour in the foaming yeast, draw a little flour into it, add the eggs and knead the dough for a few minutes to blend the mixture, using either a strong wooden spoon or the hand. Remove the scrapings of dough from the bowl sides.

Beat the butter well to soften it, then spread it over the surface of the dough. (It will melt as the dough rises.) Cover the bowl and stand in a warm place for the yeast to ferment and the dough to double its volume.

Knock the risen dough back, then knead it very vigorously so as to incorporate the butter. At first it will separate into lumps coated in fat, but then it will blend into a coherent mass which throws air bubbles and is very elastic. Once it can be lifted in one piece, add the sugar and work for a moment so as to mix it in.

Baking the Savarin and Babas: Brush the savarin mould or the baba tins with melted, unsalted butter and dust lightly with flour; shake off any surplus. Press the paste into the moulds – they should be about one-third or half full. Do not smooth the surface, for it levels out as it swells. Leave the dough uncovered, and let it rise to double its volume again.

Bake in the preheated oven. The top will be golden-brown and feel rather crisp – a knife inserted into the middle should come out quite dry. Remove from the oven; ease round the edges with a knife if necessary and turn the babas immediately on to a wire rack. Savarin should rest for 5 minutes first. (Remember: if it sticks, wrap it in a cloth or foil – the vapour will help it turn out more easily.)

Freezing or Chilling

At this point, goods that are not needed can be slipped, while still warm, into a plastic bag and sealed. This prevents them from drying out and going stale. (The syrup is added later, only when the cake is to be used.) They will keep up to 10 days in the refrigerator (although they are at their best eaten on the same day), or 8 weeks in the freezer. Defrost in the refrigerator overnight.

Soaking Babas and Savarins with Syrup

Babas are traditionally soaked with rum and savarins with Kirsch. The syrup should be warm and so should the bakery. (Warm in the oven at Gas 2 150°C, 300°F, briefly if necessary.)

Babas: Arrange in a deep, large dish with the brown crust uppermost. Prick the surfaces liberally with a skewer or sharp-pronged fork, and douse with the prepared warm syrup (see below). Baste frequently for the next 30 minutes, until the babas are very moist and spongy but still hold their shape. Invert them on to a wire rack to drain.

Savarin: Prick the crusty side liberally before turning it into a deep dish with the crust side down. Pour over the syrup and baste often as before. Drain on a wire rack.

Serve with the rounded pale side uppermost. Slide the impregnated goods carefully on to the serving platter. Sprinkle a little neat rum or Kirsch (about 4 tablespoons) over the surface, then coat with 150 ml (5 fl oz) strained apricot glaze (page 71) to give a colourful sheen, and stud with halved glacé cherries and crystallized angelica; or pipe fresh chantilly cream into the centre. Fresh strawberries or other soft fruits are also a good filling, and so is crème pâtissière.

Syrup for Savarins and Rum Babas

It is customary to drench these in a good rum- or Kirsch-flavoured, sugar and water syrup, but in the past, and particularly in France, savarin syrups were far more exciting. Pierre Lacam mentions two in *Le Memorial des Glaces* (1902) – 'composition noyateuse', made with ground walnuts and apricot kernels, and 'composition spiritueuse' which is a very potent brew, made with:

> '2 litres of good kirsch; 2 litres of rose-water; 2 litres of anisette; 2 litres maraschino; 2 litres of crème de menthe; 1 litre orange-flower water; 1^1/$_2$ litre absinthe Pernod; 80 drops bitter almond essence
>
> One starts by putting the bitter almond at the bottom of the jar, pour very slowly the kirsch over this, which dissolves the essence; then pour over the other spirits in order, with the absinthe finally. Pour the whole into a glass or barrel which is always used for this purpose and happy tasting!'

More realistically, though, the following syrup from Austria is an interesting change and certainly lighter on the pocket. The candied oranges give an unusual flavour.

Syrup of Orange for Savarin

Prepare the syrup while the pastries are baking.

Boil 250 g (9 oz) of sugar with 250 ml (9 fl oz) of water and the finely cut zest of one orange until a light syrup forms. Strain, and pour over the hot savarin. Make a second syrup by boiling 150 g (5 oz) of granulated sugar with 300 ml (11 fl oz) of water until the thread stage (page 70). Divide 3 small oranges into segments and dip them into the sugar syrup. Drain on a wire rack and then decorate the savarin with them.

Syrup of Rum for Babas

I prefer this less sweet syrup with a strong liqueur taste. The amount of rum can be increased. Rum should be added to the syrup after cooking, so that the aroma and taste are not dispelled.

YEAST BAKING

500 ml water	17 fl oz water
200 g granulated sugar	7 oz granulated sugar
150 ml strong, dark rum	5 fl oz strong, dark rum
zest ½ lemon and ½ orange	zest ½ lemon and ½ orange

Put the water and sugar into a copper sugar pan and heat slowly until all the sugar is dissolved. Bring to the boil and cook to the thread stage (page 70). Remove from the heat and stir in the rum and zests. Pour over the babas while still warm.

Doughnuts – Faschingskrapfen

(*Doughnuts for Shrovetide and New Year*)

'As pretty as a Krapfen' – this was a compliment enough to make any young girl blush; and when her sweetheart offered to share one it was considered almost as significant as a marriage proposal. Such was the zenith of popularity of the doughnut in eighteenth-century Vienna. During Kaiser Karl IV's reign at the beginning of the century they were regarded as very special, and manufactured solely by the court sugar bakers to be served at great feasts. Each year at Fasching (Shrovetide), a competition was held to choose the finest Krapfen of the year. The doughnut became a symbol of great happiness.

Naturally the ordinary folk also craved the sweetmeat, and soon a sort of Krapfen epidemic broke out. Simple cooks became specialists, and set up in competition by advertising their wares in the local newspaper. Most successful was a lady named Kunigunde Rheinhertin who sold various types of Krapfen with an assortment of fillings and even made them to order. Her business expanded from one street stall to a chain, and despite the competition and the hostility of the court bakers she remained supreme – Krapfen became the national Viennese dish.

Although doughnuts crept into the northern regions as well, Pfannkuchen in Berlin and krapfes in France, they seem not to have captured the imagination of the English; but the Americans have more than compensated for this lack of interest. Brought to the New World by the Pennsylvania Dutch (who were in fact German), doughnuts, along with Johnny cakes and maple syrup, and French toast and orange sauce, now feature even on the American breakfast table. The national enthusiasm for the doughnut – it has even been called 'Yankee cake' – is reflected in the proliferation of recipes.

CAKES

In Europe doughnuts were usually round, while in America different shapes were popular. Most notable is the circle with a hole in the middle. Legend suggests that some time in the seventeenth century a 'Nanset Indian playfully shot an arrow through a fried cake his squaw was making. The squaw, frightened, dropped the perforated patty in a kettle of boiling grease — and the result was a doughnut' (*The Gold Cookbook* — Louis P. DeGouy).

Since the introduction of baking powder in the early 1900s almost all American doughnut recipes use the artificial raising agent; but in Europe they are still made with yeast in the style of the eighteenth century.

Faschingskrapfen were traditionally fried in my home on New Year's Eve. Much earlier in the day the preparations would commence. All the doors and windows were closed in the kitchen, and the oven was switched on to raise the temperature so that the dough would rise successfully. The utensils were warmed and so was the flour.

Once prepared, half the dough was rolled out and the circles cut and filled with jam. Eventually tidy rows of white, doughy pastries lay on the floury wooden boards. A complicated arrangement of boards, trolley and tea towels was then set up in the proximity of the open oven door, so that the yeast could set to work. The doughnuts rose and puffed and swelled, not without many an anxious glance under the drapery. At last they were ready to be fried, and eagerly we awaited the first samples. Of course they were numerous, they had to be, since nothing tastes quite as delicious as Krapfen dredged in sugar and still warm from the oil.

Later in the evening the family friends and relations would join us to herald the New Year with wine and doughnuts. There was rarely a Krapfen left for the following day!

Deep Frying Doughnuts

These pastries have to be deep fried. Use either corn or sunflower oil. Avoid ground-nut oil, as it has a low burning temperature which will give an unpleasant flavour to the goods. The oil should be heated to a temperature of 170°–175°C (330°–350°F). Always allow the oil to return to this heat before frying a further batch.

Doughnuts – *Faschingskrapfen*

550 g plain, strong flour	1¼ lbs plain, strong flour
350 ml milk	12½ fl oz milk
35 g yeast	1¼ oz yeast
2 tablespoons sugar	2 tablespoons sugar
10 egg yolks	10 egg yolks
140 g butter	5 oz butter
¾ teaspoon salt	¾ teaspoon salt
1 tablespoon rum or brandy	1 tablespoon rum or brandy
1 tablespoon orange juice	1 tablespoon orange juice
jam for the filling	jam for the filling
caster sugar for dredging	caster sugar for dredging

Warm the flour and the utensils as usual. Divide the milk into three parts.

Heat one part of the milk to the correct temperature (page 119), sprinkle on the yeast and 1 teaspoon of sugar, and set aside to dissolve. Beat well the yolks of egg with the second part of milk. Melt the butter in the third part of milk. Cool to tepid.

Drop the warmed flour and salt into a deep bowl and make a well in the centre. Into this stir the yeast mixture, the beaten egg mixture, and the melted butter mixture. Beat the dough well till it becomes fluffy and dense in texture, then add the rum and the orange juice. The dough should now have a fine, smooth texture, glisten and fall from the spoon.

Now take half the mixture and drop on to a well-floured board. Dust it with very little flour and roll very lightly with a rolling pin until the dough is the thickness of a little finger. Using a glass or a biscuit cutter, make impressions of small circles of 5–6 cm (2–2½ inches) in diameter. Do not cut into the dough. Drop a teaspoonful of apricot, strawberry or rose conserve (page 305) into the centre of each circle. Then cut several more of these circles and lay the topmost side, the one which has not been floured, over the jam circles.

Gently pinch round the edge of each doughnut to stick them together, and with a slightly smaller cutter cut each one out. They should be well sealed. Lay them on a warmed, flour-dusted board, making sure to turn upwards the side which had been lying on the board. The prepared doughnuts should then be covered with a light tea towel and the left-over bits returned to the remainder of the dough. Beat again with 2–3 spoonfuls of slightly warm milk.

Set the doughnuts to rise in a warm place as suggested on page 120. When they have risen on one side, turn them over so that the underneath may also rise.

To deep-fry the doughnuts: Heat the oil to the correct temperature (see above). Take the first batch of prepared doughnuts and gently lower the side which has risen first into the oil. Allow 4–5 seconds between each immersion; the pan will probably hold about 4 or 5 doughnuts at the most.

They cook very quickly and need to be carefully watched. Cover the pan and shake it gently about. After 3–4 minutes and as soon as the underside of the doughnuts starts to brown, turn them over. This time leave the lid off, and cook until the second side has browned as well. Carefully lift the doughnuts out of the oil with a perforated spoon, and lay to drain on kitchen paper. Then sprinkle with vanilla-flavoured sugar.

Lay the doughnuts on a white napkin or a round flat dish, and serve whilst still warm.

This quantity will make 40 doughnuts. They should rise as much as their width. They should also be so light that not even half of each one is immersed in the oil. This is how the characteristic white rim is achieved. The greater the rim the lighter the doughnut.

A Small Portion of Doughnuts

140 g strong, plain flour	5 oz strong, plain flour
100 ml single cream	3½ fl oz single cream
10 g yeast	⅓ oz yeast
½ teaspoon sugar	½ teaspoon sugar
2 egg yolks	2 egg yolks
25 g butter	1 oz butter
sparing ½ teaspoon salt	sparing ½ teaspoon salt

This makes 12 doughnuts. Prepare in the same way as for the previous recipe.

Dresdener Christstollen

I much prefer this classic German Christmas bread to the traditional English cake. Although it is filled with a similar extravagance of dried fruits and nuts, and is lavishly covered with butter and icing sugar, the

YEAST BAKING

pleasant dryness of the yeasted dough complements the riches without making them either too sweet or too cloying. Unlike other yeasted goods it will keep fresh for several weeks, wrapped tightly in foil or greaseproof paper and stored in an airtight tin. Keep it for at least a day before cutting. The quantities given are enough for two large loaves.

1 kg plain, strong flour	2 lb 3 oz plain, strong flour
80 g fresh yeast	3 oz fresh yeast
200 ml milk	7 fl oz milk
250 g caster sugar	9 oz caster sugar
350 g butter	12 oz butter
juice 1 lemon	juice 1 lemon
2 egg yolks	2 egg yolks
grated zest 1 lemon	grated zest 1 lemon
1 teaspoon salt	1 teaspoon salt
150 g blanched, slivered almonds	5 oz blanched, slivered almonds
100 g mixed candied orange and lemon peel	4 oz mixed candied orange and lemon peel
500 g raisins	1 lb raisins
225 g sultanas	8 oz sultanas
120 g melted unsalted butter	4 oz melted unsalted butter
icing sugar	icing sugar

gas 5, 190°C, 375°F/approx. 45 minutes

Sift the flour carefully two or three times and set in a bowl in the oven to warm for a few minutes. Prepare the sponge with the yeast, warm milk, 1 teaspoon of sugar and 60 g (2 oz) of the flour taken from the rest. Set aside to rise. Meanwhile melt the 350 g (12 oz) butter and cool slightly. Blend into the flour with the lemon juice, then add the yeast sponge. Beat, and add the sugar, egg yolks, lemon zest and salt. Beat all well together, and then knead until the dough is very firm, elastic and starts to roll off the sides of the bowl. Cover with a damp cloth, or transfer to a large oiled polythene bag. Stand in a warm place as before, for the first rise and for it to double its bulk.

Blanch, peel and sliver the almonds; chop the candied peels very fine: wash and dry the raisins and sultanas if necessary and dust them with a little flour. Mix all these ingredients together. Warm the fruits for a few moments in the oven before kneading them into the dough. Cold fruit can arrest the leavening activity.

Punch back the risen dough again, knead for a few moments, then pull the sides to the centre, turn it over and cover once more. Set to rise for a further 30 minutes and for it to double its bulk again.

Now turn the risen dough out on to a floured work surface, scatter the prepared fruit mixture over, and knead it in carefully. Divide the dough into two equal pieces; return one to the bowl and cover it so that it does not dry while the other is being finished. Roll out the dough into a slightly flattened pointed oval shape, large enough to fit on to a baking sheet but taking care to leave enough room to allow it to grow. Lay the dough on the buttered baking sheet. Roll with a rolling pin, pressing lightly across the full width from the centre outwards, on one side only, then brush the thinner half with a little water and fold over the other half leaving a margin of about 5 cm (2 inches) as a border, which also allows the dough to rise. Press well together; the water will bind it. This rolling and folding technique is essential to this bread, and its traditional shape is said to represent the Infant Christ wrapped in swaddling clothes.

Cover the stollen and leave to prove in a warm place and to double its volume again. Carefully brush over the surface with 60 g (2 oz) melted butter before placing it in the preheated oven to bake. This will take about 45 to 60 minutes depending on the size. Take out of the oven when it has browned nicely, brush while still warm with the remaining 60 g (2 oz) butter, and sprinkle with sifted icing sugar until the butter cannot absorb any more and a sugary crust has formed. Allow to cool before wrapping and storing.

Stephen's Beigli – A traditional Hungarian Christmas Roll

500 g strong, plain flour	1 lb strong, plain flour
200 ml milk (approx.)	7 fl oz milk (approx.)
20 g fresh yeast	¾ oz fresh yeast
1 teaspoon sugar	1 teaspoon sugar
250 g butter	9 oz butter
50 g icing sugar	2 oz icing sugar
2 eggs	2 eggs
pinch salt	pinch salt

gas 6, 200°C, 400°F/25–30 minutes
Makes 2 rolls

Make a sponge batter with 100 g (3 oz) sifted flour and 150 ml (5 fl oz) milk warmed to blood heat. Crumble the yeast into the mixture and add 1 teaspoon of sugar, beat vigorously to get rid of the lumps, cover, and set aside to ferment. Beat the butter and icing sugar until light and fluffy, then whisk in the eggs one at a time. Sift the rest of the flour twice with the salt, and then into a mixing bowl; make a well in the centre, pour in the butter mixture, draw a little of the flour into it, then add the sponge batter. Beat well, then knead hard, adding more milk if it seems too stiff (but not too much, for if the dough is too soft it will crack when baked). Continue kneading until the dough becomes very elastic and throws large air bubbles. Cover the bowl, or place the dough in a large oiled polythene bag, and set in a warm place to rise (page 120) for about 2 hours or until it at least doubles in bulk. Knock the dough back and divide into two pieces. Roll each piece out on a floured board into a rectangle $1/2$ cm ($1/4$ inch) thick. Cover again with a slightly damp cloth, and leave to rise for another hour in a warm place. Meanwhile make either a walnut or poppy seed filling.

Walnut filling

200 g granulated sugar; 300 g ground walnuts; 100 g sultanas; zest 1 lemon
(7 oz granulated sugar; 10 oz ground walnuts; 3 oz sultanas; zest 1 lemon)

Dissolve the sugar in 2 tablespoons of water over a low heat, then add the ground walnuts and cook for 5 minutes. Remove from the heat and stir in the sultanas and lemon zest. Cool, then beat until creamy before using.

Poppy seed filling:

300 g poppy seed; 200 ml milk; 200 g granulated sugar; 100 g sultanas; 4 tablespoons strained apricot jam; 1 teaspoon lemon zest
(10 oz poppy seed; 7 fl oz milk; 7 oz granulated sugar; 3 oz sultanas; 4 tablespoons strained apricot jam; 1 teaspoon lemon zest)

Grind the poppy seed and pour over the boiling milk; leave to infuse and swell. Dissolve the sugar over low heat in 2 tablespoons of water, stir in the sieved poppy seed and draw off the heat. Stir in the sultanas, apricot jam and lemon zest. Leave to cool, then beat until creamy before using.

Spread the filling over the yeast pastry base to within 2 cm ($3/4$ inch) of the edge (taking care not to overfill, or the roll will crack as it bakes).

Roll the dough up carefully and set on a greased baking sheet with the open edge underneath. Brush all over the surface with lightly beaten egg, which will give a marbled effect to the baked cake. Set the roll to rise again but in a cool place this time, for 30 minutes more. Prick the sides of the roll with a fork in several places, to help stop the cake cracking, brush again with egg and set in the preheated oven. Do not open the oven door until at least three-quarters of the cooking time has passed.

Leave the cake to mature for at least a week before cutting. It gets softer as it ages, and stays fresh for at least a month.

Beigli yeast dough can be made into a horseshoe shape and served for afternoon tea.

Chocolate

'There!' cried Mr Wonka, dancing up and down and pointing his gold-topped cane at the great brown river. 'It's *all* chocolate! Every drop of the river is hot melted chocolate of the finest quality. The *very* finest quality. There's enough chocolate in there to fill *every* bathtub in the *entire* country! *And* all the swimming pools as well! Isn't it *terrific*? And just look at my pipes! They suck up the chocolate and carry it away to all the other rooms in the factory where it is needed! Thousands of gallons an hour, my dear children! Thousands and thousands of gallons!' The children and their parents were too flabbergasted to speak. They were staggered. They were dumbfounded. They were bewildered and dazzled. They were completely bowled over by the hugeness of the whole thing. They simply stood and stared. 'The waterfall is most important!' Mr Wonka went on. 'It mixes the chocolate! It churns it up! It pounds it and beats it! It makes it light and frothy! No other factory in the world mixes its chocolate by waterfall! But it's the *only* way to do it properly! The *only* way!' . . .

(Roald Dahl, *Charlie and the Chocolate Factory*)

While chocolate in its liquid form was known to the natives of the Caribbean and Latin America long before the New World was discovered, tablets of chocolate are a recent invention of the last hundred years. The first written mention of 'chocolatl' was from Bernal Diaz in the mid sixteenth century, in the *History of the Conquest of New Spain*, his account of the conquest of the Aztec empire. Montezuma II offered him a rather strange, but rich and stimulating, brown decoction, and the seeds from which it had been made came from the chocolatl tree. The seeds had been dried in the sun and roasted in pots, then crushed and kneaded into cakes and whipped with carved wooden beaters into 'a potation flavoured with vanilla and other spices and so prepared as to be reduced to a froth of the consistency of honey which gradually dissolved in the mouth and was taken cold'. 'Chocolatl' was considered by Montezuma to be as great a luxury as gold, and it was served with due

CAKES

ceremony in goblets of beaten gold. It is said that 50 pitchers were prepared for his daily consumption, while 2,000 jars were also made for the male members of his court. The female members were forbidden it, possibly because of its reputed strong aphrodisiac qualities. Chocolate beans were also used as valuable currency – a 'tolerably good slave' would fetch as many as 100 beans – and as late as 1850 they replaced bills of money.

The conquistadors brought the beans back to Spain with them, and the drink immediately gained favour among the privileged classes. They discovered that when taken hot and sweetened with sugar, the drink was even more appetizing. 'The Spanish ladies of the New World love chocolate to the point of madness; not content with drinking it several times in a day, they sometimes order it to be brought to them in church,' commented Brillat-Savarin much later. As a result of this practice a heated argument developed among the clergy as to whether drinking 'chocolatl' breached the laws of fasting. Having decided that it did not, anyone might fast with a clear conscience during Lent by drinking chocolate as if he had only partaken of a glass of cold water.

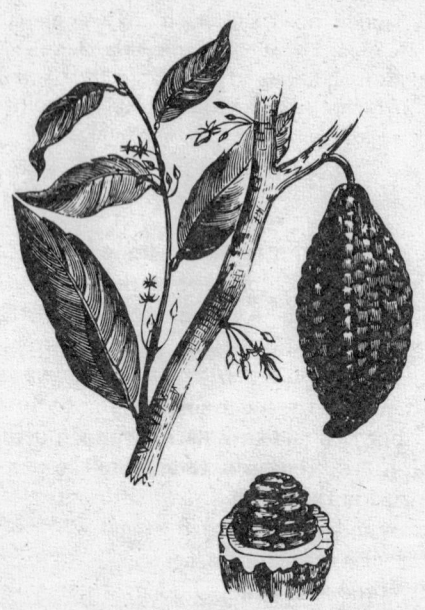

Chocolate plant
(Theobrama cacao)

CHOCOLATE

For over a century the recipe was kept a closely guarded secret, but eventually the Spanish monks introduced it into France, Germany, and Italy; and in 1660 when Maria Theresa, Infanta of Spain, married Louis XIV, chocolate became the fashionable drink in the Court of France. It was also recommended as an effective drug, and Cardinal Richelieu was the first person said to have used it to lessen the 'vapours' from his spleen.

Ten years later, however, chocolate was blamed as the cause of many unpleasant and strange ailments, none more bizarre than that of the Marquise de Coëtlogen who 'took so much chocolate being pregnant last year that she was brought to bed of a little boy who was black as the devil!' However, chocolate once more regained favour in 1693 at the Court of Louis XIV, who offered it to his guests on 'receiving' days, which time became known as the 'chocolat' – 'J'entrai alors au chocolat de son Altesse Royale'. The recipe was complicated, as this prescription of Philippe Sylvestre Dufour in his tract *Traitez nouveaux et ancieux du café, du thé, du chocolat* (1685) shows.

> Sept cens cacaos,
> Une livre et demy de Sucre.
> Deux onces de Canelle.
> Quatorze grains de Poivre de Mexique,
> apellé Chilé ou Pimiento.
> Demi once de Cloux de Girofle
> Trois gousses de Vanille,
> ou en sa place deux onces d'Anis
> Le gros d'une noissette d'Anchiote.
>
> Quelques uns ajoute-t'il y mettent un
> peu d'eau de fleurs d'oranges, un grain
> de Musc ou d'Ambre gris, ou de la
> Poudre de Scolo pendre. De ces choses
> Colmenero en bannit les cloux de Girofle,
> le Musc, l'Ambre et les eaux de senteur,
> et la poudre de roses d'Alexandria.
> Delact dit qu'en Amerique on y met encore
> le fleur d'un abre resineux, odorante
> comme celle de l'Orange, et une gousse
> appelée Tlixochitla. Il y en a qui y font
> entrer le Mays ou le Panis el l'Orejevala.

By this time, of course, chocolate was also well established in England, the first chocolate house having been opened in 1657 in Queens Head

Alley, Bishopsgate. The bitter chocolate was generally bought in cakes or rolls, which were sliced or scraped and then boiled in water with a little sugar. Away from the fire the brew was whirled vigorously with a hand-mill — a swizzle stick which produced a lively froth. (This little wooden stick or 'quirl' is the equivalent of the traditional Mexican 'molinillo', which has a roughly carved end that is twirled between the palms to beat the chocolate to a froth.) Samuel Pepys seven years later recorded a visit 'to a coffee house to drink jocolatte; very good'.

Chocolate houses such as the 'Cocoa Tree' became popular as rendezvous for the rich and famous, who also founded various political, gaming and literary clubs on the premises. The Exchequer, equally quick to realize the potentials of the new luxury, levied taxes on cocoa in its various stages — on the raw beans, ground-nibs and even chocolate in a liquid state. The taxes were so punitive that the beans were considered worth smuggling, along with 'brandy for the parson, baccy for the clerk!' At last, in 1853, Gladstone reduced the taxes considerably, and the industry expanded.

A little earlier, in 1828, the invention of the cocoa press by Van Houten in Holland had enabled cocoa butter to be extracted from the crushed beans. This made the rather greasy and gritty drink into a much more palatable one; at the same time it was found that the taste of eating chocolate which still contained cocoa butter was very much better. This new awareness paved the way for the invention of a more refined version. Although a rough form of a rather bitter chocolate had been made, attempts to blend it with milk had not proved successful; but in 1875 the two Swiss, Daniel Peter and Henri Nestlé, collaborated in an experiment using Nestlé's milk, and a new delicious eating chocolate in tablet form was invented, which gained immediate popularity. Five years later Rudolp Lindt discovered how to make chocolate that would melt in the mouth.

> At the beginning of the 'eighties the outside world remembered Fordlow Feast to the extent of sending one old woman with a gingerbread stall. On it were gingerbread babies with currants for eyes, brown-and-white striped peppermint humbugs, sticks of pink-and-white rock, and a few boxes and bottles of other sweets. Even there, on that little old stall with its canvas awning, the first sign of changing taste might have been seen, for one year, side by side with the gingerbread babies, stood a box filled with thin, dark brown slabs packed in pink paper. 'What is that brown sweet?' asked Laura, spelling out the word 'Chocolate'. A visiting cousin,

being fairly well educated and a great reader, already knew it by name. 'Oh, that's chocolate,' he said off-handedly. 'But don't buy any; it's for drinking. They have it for breakfast in France.' A year or two later, chocolate was a favourite sweet even in a place as remote as the hamlet; but it could no longer be bought from the gingerbread stall, for the old woman no longer brought it to the Feast.
(Flora Thompson, *Lark Rise to Candleford*)

Selection for Baking

I prefer plain or bitter chocolate; it has a strong, clean and distinctive flavour that blends well with all types of pastry.

Take care in your selection, as there are several inferior cooking chocolates on the market which taste bland and uninteresting. Price is a good indication of quality – the cheaper it is the less real cocoa fat it is likely to contain (vegetable fats, synthetic additives, preservatives and artificial colourings replace it). The pure flavour and true colour of real cocoa fats far outweigh the economic benefits of the cheaper varieties. Buy either imported cooking or baker's chocolate, or the best plain, bitter or unsweetened dessert chocolate.

Avoid replacing chocolate with cocoa powder or drinking chocolate, for cocoa, which is dry and powdery, may alter the balance of ingredients in a cake calling for chocolate and spoil the texture; melted chocolate might make the cocoa cake too wet. Do not use drinking chocolate, which is made with both milk powder and sugar as well as cocoa powder and is bland and oversweet.

Storage

Store chocolate and cocoa in a dark, dry cool place where the temperature is fairly constant; wrap in foil or greaseproof paper or in an airtight box. It will keep almost indefinitely in these conditions without becoming rancid, though frequent temperature changes will cause a harmless greyish-white bloom to appear on the surface. The flavour will not be spoiled. Cocoa powder does not keep quite as well, and after about 12 months is inclined to go mouldy and taste musty and sour.

Melting Chocolate

Chocolate should *never* be melted in a pan set directly over the fire, for it quickly loses its fine flavour and burns very easily.

Break the chocolate into small pieces and drop into a double boiler or a dry bowl set over hot water. The base of the bowl must not touch the water. Allow to dissolve without stirring (it takes about 10 minutes). Be careful not to let it reach a temperature any higher than blood heat (37°C, 98°F) or it will lose its gloss when it cools. Draw away from the heat and stir gently. Cool the chocolate to about 22°C, 80°F, before adding it to the other cake ingredients unless directed otherwise.

To melt chocolate in a warm oven, break it on to a flat plate and leave in the oven for about 5 minutes at gas ¼ 100°C, 225°F.

If the chocolate gets too hot and stiffens, stir in a little vegetable shortening — not butter.

Keep the warmed chocolate over a bowl of warm water until you are ready to use it for decorating purposes.

For a plain chocolate covering: melt 100 g (3½ oz) chocolate in 2 tablespoons of water and stir in a walnut-sized knob of butter. Pour straight over the cold cake and spread with a hot knife. (Cool at room temperature or it will lose the sheen.)

Chocolate Decorations

There are several types of chocolate decoration available in the shops, such as flaked rolls, shavings and vermicelli. Although they make quick and convenient substitutes, their flavour leaves much to be desired. I like to keep a stock of my own home-made decorations in the store cupboard. They should be kept cool or they lose their shape.

Grated chocolate. Chill the chocolate well before grating or it will stick to the utensil. Grate on the coarse side of a grater or with the grating blade in a rotary hand grinder. The grating blade (not the chopping blade which melts the chocolate) on a food processor is also successful. To catch the flying flakes use a large bowl (not plastic which charges with static electricity) lined with a sheet of greaseproof paper which makes it easy to transfer.

Caraque curls or flakes. Warm the chocolate very slightly, otherwise it splinters and will not curl. Either leave at room temperature for a while, or hold briefly, wrapped in foil, in the hand. Use a small sharp kitchen knife, vegetable peeler or metal cheese-slicer, and shave off slivers from the long thin side.

The traditional confectioner's method is more successful. Melt the chocolate in a bowl over hot water and leave to cool for a moment or two; pour it on to a lightly oiled marble slab or laminated surface and spread out thinly to 3 mm ($1/8$ inch) thickness with a spatula. Leave to cool and harden, then holding a knife blade at either end in an upright position use a gentle sawing action as you pull the knife towards you. The chocolate should curl; if not, it is too cold, so lay the palm of the hand momentarily on the chocolate surface and try again. (A wide-bladed metal decorator's scraping tool is also good for this job.) Lay the curls on a baking sheet and leave to cool and harden. Store in an airtight container between layers of greaseproof paper or foil, and keep in a cool place.

When using caraque as a decoration, a final dusting of icing sugar gives a pleasing effect.

Sachertorte

Apart from Black Forest kirschtorte this is probably the best-known chocolate cake in the world, and is instantly recognizable with its simple flat shape, and a plain undecorated chocolate covering with 'Sacher' piped across the centre; it seems incredible that it should have been coveted, to the point of legal action being taken to claim the rights to the original recipe.

The name is closely associated with the Sacher family of Vienna. Franz Sacher had relinquished his position as chef to the Austrian Chancellor Clemens Lothar Metternich in 1840, so that he could open a delicatessen shop and hotel in the Weihburggasse. His three sons took over the various responsibilities on his retirement, and the youngest, Edouard, established himself in the gastronomic history of Vienna as the founder of the hotel which was named after him, in the 1880s. As an exclusive speciality of this hotel, Franz Sacher's Torte helped establish its fame and reputation. The hotel became a rendezvous for the aristocracy, for the Hungarians and Bohemians and eventually even the Archduke and Duchess. And the Torte also ousted the Linzertorte from its hitherto premier position as favourite.

The closely guarded secret of the Sachertorte recipe meanwhile inspired an extraordinary variety of 'authentic' versions. The most popular were based on an equal weight mixture, and others included almonds. Maybe at last the truly authentic recipe has come to light.

CAKES

This recipe was given to a lady attending cookery classes conducted by Anna Sacher, Eduoard's wife in 1883. It used the old measures, which I have converted to grammes.

Anna Sacher's Sachertorte (1883)

140 g dark, plain chocolate	5 oz dark, plain chocolate
100 g butter	3½ oz butter
140 g caster sugar	5 oz caster sugar
4 egg yolks	4 egg yolks
4 egg whites	4 egg whites
70 g plain flour	2½ oz plain flour

gas 3, 170°C, 325°F/60 minutes

Set the chocolate in the oven on a plate to warm and melt gently. Cool slightly. Beat the butter and the sugar in a bowl until pale and fluffy, then beat in the chocolate. Beat in the egg yolks one at a time and combine well. Whip up the egg whites to a stiff snow and mix lightly into the chocolate mixture with a metal spoon. Fold in the sieved flour carefully, taking care not to lose any air. Have ready a 22 cm (8½ inch) spring-form tin, greased and floured; pour in the mixture, rap the tin on the work top to dispel any air pockets, and bake in the preheated oven. Cool on a wire rack and then cover with a plain chocolate icing (page 74); you may like to coat the cake first with apricot jam to insulate it against the chocolate.

Roulade au Chocolat

This is a particular favourite of my family — it is not too sweet, and the coarsely chopped almonds give a pleasant crunch to the pastry. The almonds may be omitted if wished. Sponge roulades are generally rolled while still warm, but this is unnecessary here, as butter, chocolate and nuts keep the cake moist as it cools.

50 g butter	2 oz butter
100 g plain chocolate	4 oz plain chocolate
50 g caster sugar	2 oz caster sugar
7 egg yolks	7 egg yolks
50 g raw almonds	2 oz raw almonds
7 egg whites	7 egg whites

CHOCOLATE

| 30 g icing sugar | 1 oz icing sugar |

gas 4, 180°C, 350°F/15 minutes

Melt the butter and cool to lukewarm. Melt the chocolate also and leave to cool. Then beat the cooled chocolate thoroughly with the caster sugar and the egg yolks; mix in the coarsely ground raw almonds. Beat the egg whites in a separate bowl until stiff peaks have formed and, using a metal spoon, gently and lightly fold in the sifted icing sugar and the melted butter. Combine this mixture with the chocolate mixture. Have two Swiss roll tins 25 × 36 cm (10 × 14 inch) ready lined with greaseproof paper and butter them lightly; spread the mixture over, 1 cm (3/8 inch) thick, and bake in the preheated oven. When lightly browned, take out of the oven and cool slightly before lifting on to a cake rack. Cover with a damp cloth, leave to cool, then trim the edges, fill with whipped cream, roll up and glaze with melted chocolate.

Mohr im Hemd – Moor in a Nightshirt

This is a Moorish delight, irresistible to most!

100 g butter	4 oz butter
100 g caster sugar	4 oz caster sugar
6 egg yolks	6 egg yolks
100 g raw almonds, coarsely chopped	4 oz raw almonds, coarsely chopped
1 teaspoon instant coffee powder or syrup	1 teaspoon instant coffee powder or syrup
100 g plain chocolate, grated	3½ oz plain chocolate, grated
6 egg whites	6 egg whites

Cream

250 ml double cream	9 fl oz double cream
50 ml single cream	2 fl oz single cream
2 tablespoons caster sugar	2 tablespoons caster sugar
rum or vanilla to flavour	rum or vanilla to flavour

gas 4, 180°C, 350°F/approx 1 hour

Cream the butter and sugar until light and fluffy; beat in the egg yolks one at a time and mix well between each addition. Next add the almonds, coffee and grated chocolate. Whip the egg whites to form stiff peaks, and fold them into the chocolate mixture. Grease and dust with caster sugar a 24 cm (9½ inch) cake tin or a savarin mould, pour in the mixture, and bake in the preheated oven. Leave to cool for a few minutes before inverting on to a cake rack to cool, but leave the tin in place. When it has chilled completely, cover with the prepared cream (see below).

Cream: Beat together the double and single cream until stiff, then fold in the sugar and flavour to taste.

Napoleon Torte with Spices

Wohlbewerth's mit Fleiss zusammengetragenes Kochbuch aus dem Jahr 1778 ('The well valued, assembled with much industry cookery book of 1778') is an old Viennese book in which this spiced 'Dorte von Schiocolati' is listed. 'Half a pound of almonds with six whole eggs and three yolks are stirred; add lemon peel, cinnamon, clove, ginger and stir for a whole hour. Then add grated chocolate and bake, sprinkle with sugar and decorate with a flower, then it is ready!'

Here is a modern interpretation which bakes into a rather flat shape with a dense though slightly crumbly texture. Be generous with the apricot jam, which soaks in and gives moisture, but cut sparingly as it is very rich.

140 g plain chocolate	5 oz plain chocolate
140 g butter	5 oz butter
3 egg yolks	3 egg yolks
140 g raw, coarse ground almonds	5 oz raw, coarse ground almonds
½ teaspoon ground cloves	½ teaspoon ground cloves
½ teaspoon cinnamon	½ teaspoon cinnamon
pinch ginger	pinch ginger
140 g caster sugar	5 oz caster sugar
zest ½ lemon	zest ½ lemon
40 g potato flour	2 oz potato flour
3 egg whites	3 egg whites

gas 3, 170°C, 325°F/50–60 minutes

Melt the chocolate in a double boiler and leave to cool. Beat together the butter and egg yolks until light and creamy. Coarsely grind the almonds, and combine with the spices, sugar, zest and sifted flour in another bowl. Mix with the melted chocolate until all the lumps have dispersed. Beat into the butter and yolk mixture one spoon at a time. It will have a very dark and shiny texture. Whip the egg whites separately; blend a spoonful of the stiff snow into the chocolate mixture to lighten it, then gently fold in the rest. Turn into a greased 24 cm (9½ inch) cake tin, and bake in a preheated oven. Cool on a cake rack, then split and fill with strained apricot jam. Spread jam on the top as well, glaze with chocolate or vanilla icing, and decorate with a few toasted almonds. Serve with stiffly whipped cream.

Chocolate Almond Slices

For a touch of the exotic, replace half the almonds with pistachios. Each tray makes about 25–30 slices.

65 g plain chocolate	2½ oz plain chocolate
100 g butter	4 oz butter
140 g caster sugar	5 oz caster sugar
4 egg yolks	4 egg yolks
1 teaspoon lemon zest	1 teaspoon lemon zest
½ teaspoon cinnamon	½ teaspoon cinnamon
1 crushed clove	1 crushed clove
4 egg whites	4 egg whites
140 g blanched, ground almonds	5 oz blanched, ground almonds
50 g flaked almonds for decoration (optional)	2 oz flaked almonds for decoration (optional)

gas 4, 180°C, 350°F/20 minutes

Melt the chocolate in a bowl over hot water and set aside to cool. Beat the butter until light and fluffy; blend in the chocolate, sugar, egg yolks, zest and spices. Whip up the egg whites into peaks, and gently fold them into the mixture with alternate portions of ground almonds. Pour into two greased and floured 31 × 21 × 2 cm (12 × 8 × ¾ inch) tins. The finish is optional:

(1) Brush the surface lightly with beaten egg and decorate with slivered almonds. Bake until the cake starts to shrink away from the sides of the tin; remove from the oven and cut into even slices while still warm. Leave in the tin to cool.

(2) Leave undecorated and bake, then cut into slices while still warm and leave in the tin to cool. Sandwich pairs with strained apricot jam and whipped cream. Then cover with glacé icing and decorate with red glacé cherries and angelica.

CAKES

Chocolate Ganache Torte

The crispy, chocolate biscuit texture of the pastry is a perfect foil for the cream filling.

210 g butter	7½ oz butter
280 g plain flour	10 oz plain flour
1 tablespoon cocoa	1 tablespoon cocoa
140 g caster sugar	5 oz caster sugar
140 g dark chocolate, grated	5 oz dark chocolate, grated
4 egg yolks	4 egg yolks

gas 4, 180°C, 350°F/15–20 minutes

Rub the butter, sifted flour and cocoa to make a fine crumbly texture. Blend in the sugar and the chocolate lightly, using a knife, combine and work in the egg yolks quickly and thoroughly. Divide the pastry into four parts and press each out on a silicone-coated sheet of paper pencilled with a 24 cm (9½ inch) circle. (The texture of the pastry is too light to roll.) Bake in the preheated oven, watching it carefully for chocolate pastry is inclined to burn. Cool on wire racks.

Prepare the chocolate ganache filling (page 64) with 170 ml (6 fl oz) double cream and 200 g (7 oz) plain chocolate.

When the layers are cold, sandwich them with the ganache filling and spread a layer on top. Decorate with chocolate curls. Leave overnight before cutting.

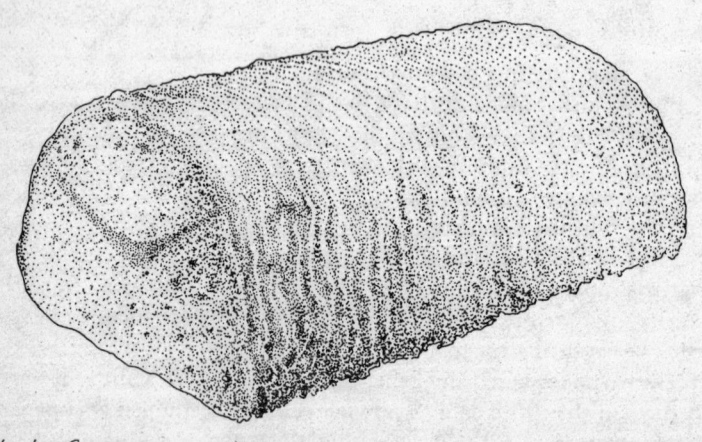

Chocolate Caracas

CHOCOLATE
Chocolate Caracas

Goethe had a special weakness for chocolate, and sent to the nineteen-year-old Ulrike von Levetzow a verse, wrapped with some small bars of 'Gesteinsproben' chocolate, with a reminder that these were the best in Vienna:

> Geniesse dies nach deiner eigenen Weise,
> wo nicht als Trank, doch als beliebte Speise!
>
> (Enjoy this in your own way, if not as a drink,
> then as a favourite dessert!)

I think he would have approved of this recipe.

60 g plain chocolate	2 oz plain chocolate
40 g butter	1½ oz butter
80 g ground almonds	3 oz ground almonds
40 g icing sugar	1½ oz icing sugar
5 egg whites	5 egg whites
6 egg yolks	6 egg yolks
30 g caster sugar	1 oz caster sugar
40 g plain flour	1½ oz plain flour

gas 4, 180°C, 350°F/60 minutes

One portion of chocolate ganache (page 64) made with 170 ml (6 oz) double cream and 200 g (7 oz) plain chocolate.

Melt the chocolate in two tablespoons of water and set aside to cool. Melt the butter and leave to cool. Blend together the ground almonds, sifted icing sugar and 1 egg white to make an almond paste. Beat in the egg yolks one at a time. Whip up the remaining 4 egg whites in another bowl to form stiff peaks, then beat in the caster sugar until the mixture turns glossy. Fold the two mixtures together, using a large metal spoon, and taking care not to lose any air from the beaten whites. Fold in the chocolate and the cooled melted butter, and finally the sifted flour. Pour into a greased 35 cm (14 inch) long, narrow, guttered cake mould, tap it lightly to disperse any air-pockets, and place in the preheated oven.

Turn out on to a wire rack to cool when baked. Cut a triangle out of the rounded top surface, along the length; fill the cavity with chocolate ganache and replace the triangle on top. Cover the triangle and the rest of the top with the remaining ganache. Drag a fork across the surface to make a pattern, and dredge with a little icing sugar. This cake keeps in a cold place for up to 2 weeks.

CAKES

Chocolate Truffle Cake

Biscuit

140 g caster sugar	5 oz caster sugar
5 egg yolks	5 egg yolks
1 teaspoon orange zest	1 teaspoon orange zest
50 g plain flour	2 oz plain flour
50 g potato flour	2 oz potato flour
5 egg whites	5 egg whites

Chocolate mousseline butter cream

75 g granulated sugar	2½ oz granulated sugar
50 ml water	2 fl oz water
1 drop pure vanilla essence	drop pure vanilla essence
3 egg yolks	3 egg yolks
170 g unsalted butter	6 oz unsalted butter
75 g plain chocolate	2½ oz plain chocolate
1 tablespoon water	1 tablespoon water

Truffles

100 g plain chocolate	3½ oz plain chocolate
60 g unsalted butter	2 oz unsalted butter
1 teaspoon instant coffee powder	1 teaspoon instant coffee powder
1 tablespoon double cream	1 tablespoon double cream
60 g dark chocolate, grated	2 oz dark chocolate, grated

gas 4, 180°C, 350°F/30 minutes

Prepare the biscuit as on page 94. Divide the mixture between two 24 cm (9½ inch) spring-form tins and bake until light and springy to the touch. Lift out of the oven on to wire racks, release the sides, and remove the bases after 10 minutes. Leave to cool. Make the butter cream (see pages 62–3 for method). Chill.

To make the truffles, warm the 100 g (3½ oz) plain chocolate in a bowl over hot water, lightly stirring until smooth. Beat the butter well in another bowl until creamy, then beat in the cooled chocolate and the coffee powder. As soon as the mixture starts to thicken, beat in the cream, then roll small balls of the mixture and coat them with the grated chocolate shavings. Set on a wire rack to harden.

Assemble the cake: Spread 2 tablespoons of butter cream over one cake layer, and sandwich with the other. Coat the top and sides of the cake

American Devil's Food Cake

This has a lovely rich moist texture, where cocoa is hard to discern from real chocolate. It is traditionally filled and covered with a chocolate fudge icing (page 75), but the seven-minute frosting (page 176) makes a pleasing contrast. You can bake it in two 22 cm (8½ inch) spring-form tins or a savarin mould, or two 500 g (1 lb) loaf pans.

Mixture (1)

100 g cocoa powder	3½ oz cocoa powder
150 g soft, brown sugar	5½ oz soft, brown sugar
1 large egg	1 large egg
125 ml milk	4½ fl oz milk

Mixture (2)

110 g butter	4 oz butter
150 g soft, brown sugar	5½ oz soft, brown sugar
1 tablespoon vanilla sugar	1 tablespoon vanilla sugar
2 eggs	2 eggs
225 g plain flour	8 oz plain flour
3 teaspoons baking powder	3 teaspoons baking powder
125 ml milk	4½ fl oz milk

gas 4, 180°C, 350°F/45 minutes

(1) Mix the cocoa and sugars in a small pan, then beat in the egg and add the milk. Cook gently, stirring all the time, until the mixture has thickened and starts to bubble. Set aside to cool.

(2) Cream the butter and sugar until fluffy, add the eggs and beat vigorously. Sift together the flour and the baking powder, and add it in stages alternating with the milk until all is well combined. Blend in Mixture (1). Pour into the ready greased mould and bake. Leave in the tin for 5 minutes before turning out on to a wire rack to cool. Split and fill with frosting, and coat the top and sides of the cake. Scatter chocolate flakes or curls over the top.

Gâteaux and Torten

The most desirable after-dinner dessert or special occasion cake is a gâteau or Torte, and the hostess who treats her guests to a home-made confection earns a warm accolade. The English, with their historic love of plain or fruited cakes and tarts, paid scant attention in the past to the ingredients of a celebration cake and concentrated exclusively on the most elaborate sugar icings and decorations. Now the customs of Europe have been adopted with great enthusiasm. There is an appreciation of fine flavours and complementary tastes, of layers of delicate creams, light sponges or meringues, of fresh fruits and nuts; and of the refined decoration which is an essential part of the whole.

Elaborate Confections

GATEAUX

In France *grands gâteaux* and *sujets d'ornaments* remind of grand occasions, of banquets and entertaining. In the nineteenth century, cakes were much influenced by the *pièces monteés* (assembled pieces) of Carême, and though they were made of fine ingredients, inordinate trouble was taken to achieve perfect replicas of quite extraordinary subjects.

Pâte d'Office or Confectionery Paste.

'Sift on a marble slab, a pound and a half of fine flour, with a pound of sugar, making a hollow in the middle, to contain the whites of eight eggs; mix it up into a stiff paste; but if too stiff, add some more whites of eggs; when of a proper consistence, knead it with your wrists till perfectly smooth. This paste is to form the carcass or frame-work of your Pièces Montées, which are to be cut out of it, of the size and shape of the dish you mean to use; it must be rolled a quarter of an inch thick: it will likewise be useful to roll it in bands or fillets, as supporters to the whole. You bake them on plates slightly buttered, in an oven of a moderate heat; when half done, draw them out, and cut them to your fancy; you are to construct with them castles, pavilions, Chinese temples, hermits' cells, pyramids, cottages, Turkish pavilions, monuments, and any other thing the fancy may suggest. When they are cut and exactly fitted together, put them back in the oven to finish baking.'

(G.A. Jarrin *The Italian Confectioner* 1829)

While Carême's preoccupation with sculpture and architecture was still evident in France, representations were generally shifting to more mundane arrangements: baskets of mushrooms, bunches of asparagus or grapes, tortoises, tin drums or a box of dominoes — even a ham bone baked in a special mould. Urbain Dubois dedicated 'gâteau ananas moderne' to Chiboust, a friend and colleague with whose diligence and single-minded artistic toil he was impressed. The sponge cake, baked in two conical moulds, was sandwiched, cut to shape and filled with a cream filling, then decorated with tinted creams, leaves, pistachios and icings, all laboriously worked over and over to achieve the desired effect of a large pineapple standing on a cake-base with simulated rings of fruits around the bottom. The almost obsessional attention to detail is shown best here:

Cristal-Palace

Bake a triple-layered sponge in a conventional round mould and fill with a candied orange and curaçao filling. Cover the gâteau with strained apricot jam, then mask it with a thin smooth layer of Italian meringue; decorate the upper and lower rims with small, flat and even circles of meringue; place the cake at the mouth of the oven for the meringue to set; then, decorate each circle with a piece of orange peel dipped in apricot. — Decorate the sides of the cake with a piped lattice pattern in chocolate meringue. Ornament the middle with a pretty bunch of frosted cherries set on a pastille made of pale-green iced marzipan; encircle it with a string of small, white marzipan balls covered with icing.

(Urbain Dubois, *La Pâtisserie d'aujourd'hui*, 1894)

TORTEN

'A *Torte*,' said a family friend, 'is a tart with the garnation upstairs!' In the confectionery trade it is 'a built up round structure decorated with soft eating materials; particular care is taken with flavouring, which should be a liqueur or a spirit. It can be said that a good torte is one with a pleasing decorative appearance inside and out.'

CAKES

The Austrian and German torten of the nineteenth century suffered less from the French decorative zeal; the concern was more for the flavour, and while the cake shapes basically remained traditional circles and squares, the decorations too had simplified to crystallized fruits and flowers, or marzipan fashioned into fruits, figures, leaves and petals. Interest in the cake flavour had begun in Germany over a century earlier, at the start of the 1700s, when the devastating effects of the Thirty Years War were being overcome, and a completely new approach to cuisine and confectionery was evolving. Until then cake had been quite simple, with little decoration, but in 1691 the *Vollständiges Nürnbergisches Koch Buch* of Wolfgang Moritz Endter gave the following recipe: '2 eggs, sugar, rose-water beat together and add flour to a kneading consistency; roll out a base and a long strip to make a border as high as you wish. Then press the long strip into a mould and dry well. Then stick the strip round the base with gum arabic and rose-water. Dry again. Fill with marzipan as above. Bake for an hour on low heat, when cold ice on cover with citronat and flowers and gilding if wished.' (The marzipan — almond 1 lb (450 g): sugar $^5/_8$ lb (285 g): 16 stiff whites: Stir into almonds and sugar 2 loth ($1^1/_4$ oz, 35 g) flour.)

The decorated *coffer* or mould into which the cake pastry was pressed was probably carved of wood. Sometimes, to reduce the cost of the marzipan, the hollow was filled with bottled fruits and only a thin layer of the almond paste laid on top to be indented with yet another mould.

An eighteenth century pastry design by Conrad Hagger

Thirty years later Conrad Hagger, the chef de cuisine to the Prince-Archbishop of Salzburg in 1719, had developed this idea extensively, as his book for the professionals *Neues Salzburgisches Koch Buch* illustrates. Like Endter, Hagger used carved mouldings, but these had become a decorative art in themselves and some cakes were even made in several parts, to be assembled later. A hollow framework of pastry was built up and the spaces filled with tinted juices and jellies, in others the pastes were coloured differently to create changing patterns. The carved and moulded marzipan surfaces were outstanding, and astonishingly modern in their symmetry.

While the decorative element remained strong, another aspect was developing. Hagger introduced layered cakes for the first time, and though he used the usual bottled fruits he also mentioned 'cremb' fillings. The basis of egg yolk and cream, with sugar, cinnamon, rose-water and fine ground almonds, was cooked and could be coloured in various ways – with chocolate and cinnamon, pistachio, spinach, red wine, redcurrants, sour cherries and saffron. By the early nineteenth century cream fillings were a commonplace, and often the cream was whipped and then beaten into the egg and sugar mixture. Crème pâtissière was being used, and so were jams. Garnishes too saw a change, icings being coloured and small spiced biscuits used as decoration.

Cornets and piping nozzles

Dripping cake batter through a type of funnel on to a baking sheet was a method known quite early on, but 1716 saw a further development of the technique. Marperger in his *Vollständiges Küch- und Keller- Dictionarium*, the first German culinary encyclopedia, mentioned, 'One can let this paste flow through a cone on to paper, in such shapes as one will, as a rose or a heart, oval, round, flat and also in other shapes.' Just over a century later another culinary expert, Anna Dorn, instructs that the icing made with 'a whipped egg white and enough sugar to make it thick' be squeezed through a *Spritze* on to the cake; probably these syringes were made of paper.

Undoubtedly the best description of a newer tool was in Charles Elmé Francatelli's *The Modern Cook: A practical guide to the culinary art 1860*. He mentioned a cornet or a biscuit forcer of paper, but adds a footnote: 'These biscuit forcers are also made of tin, resembling a funnel in shape; they have a bag of wash-leather, or canvas cloth, affixed round the upper part, with a string running through the top, which, when the bag is filled with batter, is drawn tight, this effectually preventing it from escaping at the upper end, while it is forced out at the point below. The use of this utensil, however, is objectionable, from the leather or canvas contracting a nauseous odour. In other respects it answers the purpose well enough.'

Until now cornets had been used only for piping icings and cake pastes, but within fifty years a very significant change in confectionery decoration was to take place.

Butter Cream

In 1895 Carl Krackhart in a confectionery book mentioned only one butter cream filling for the six-layered sponge Prinzregententorte, but seventeen years later he remarked on how popular the creams had become, and at the expense of whipped cream fillings. Possibly the new laws of pasteurization had changed the quality and texture of cream to such an extent as to make the chefs seek an alternative ingredient. Butter, which had been used in fillings to a very minor extent, now seemed more suitable. Whereas whipped cream tasted good, its potential as piping material was fairly limited. It lacked precision and definition and hardened very quickly; while butter on the other hand was totally malleable. The opportunities offered by both butter and the piping technique became obvious, and the further development of the metal nozzle was logical.

The fine tin nozzles were pressed into various shapes, which gave much greater scope and took far less time than the rather clumsy die-cast or engraved moulds of the past. The selection of pressings gave the pâtissier almost as much potential as an artist with a paint-brush. In *La Pâtisserie d'aujourd'hui* (1894) Dubois mentions the delicacy and accuracy that could be achieved by piping the leaves and petals of roses. Varying thicknesses of lines, dots, tassels, twisted rope effects and rosettes could be piped, and stars were a new form which achieved great popularity.

Until the twentieth century in England little interest had been shown in layered or filled cakes, though there was an exceptional interest in elaborate sugar decoration — pastillage.

Pastillage still exists today, principally in the trade for confectionery fairs and for festive and celebration cakes. Home bakers are now influenced by the simple methods and flavours of continental Europe.

GATEAUX AND TORTEN
Flockensahnetorte

This combination of pâte sucrée with choux pastry and rum-flavoured cream was given to me by the Swiss chef pâtissier Hans van den Klinkenberg. It is best eaten the day it is assembled, but the layers may be baked a day early.

Pâte sucrée (page 45)

For a 26 cm flat base with:

130 g plain flour
90 g butter
45 g caster sugar
1 egg yolk
pinch salt
1/2 teaspoon lemon zest

For a 10 1/2 inch flat base with:

4 1/2 oz plain flour
3 oz butter
2 oz caster sugar
1 egg yolk
pinch salt
1/2 teaspoon lemon zest

Streussel topping (page 123)

110 g caster sugar
pinch salt
110 g butter
150 g plain flour
1/2 teaspoon lemon zest

4 oz caster sugar
pinch salt
4 oz butter
5 oz plain flour
1/2 teaspoon lemon zest

Pâte à choux (page 100)

125 ml water
50 g butter
75 g strong, plain flour
pinch salt
2 eggs

4 1/2 fl oz water
2 oz butter
2 1/2 oz strong, plain flour
pinch salt
2 eggs

Sahne crème

3 egg yolks
50 g caster sugar
1 teaspoon lemon zest
pinch salt
1 tablespoon vanilla sugar
1 tablespoon rum
12 g gelatine sheet
500 ml double cream

3 egg yolks
2 oz caster sugar
1 teaspoon lemon zest
pinch salt
1 tablespoon vanilla sugar
1 tablespoon rum
3/8 oz gelatine sheet
17 fl oz double cream

You also need 2 tablespoons strained apricot jam; 3 tablespoons cranberry jam; 50g (2oz) toasted flaked almonds (optional).

Make the streussel topping see page 123 for method.

Bake the pâte sucrée base and cool on a wire rack. Grease and flour three flat baking sheets and spread three 22cm (8½ inch) circles of choux paste about 2mm (under ¹/₁₀ inch) in depth. Snip each choux layer with scissor points at 5cm (2 inch) intervals (this helps the choux rise), scatter one with streussel topping, and bake the layers in the hot oven set at gas 8, 230°C, 450°F for 10 minutes.

They will rise and puff rather unevenly but brown well. Leave to cool on a wire rack.

To make the Sahne crème, beat the egg yolks, caster sugar, lemon zest, salt and vanilla sugar until pale, mousse-like, and doubled in bulk. Whip in the rum. Soften the gelatine sheet in cold water, lift it out and melt over heat. Or dissolve powder — see page 58.

Whisk the double cream until stiff and fold in the cooled gelatine which should just be starting to set. Fold in egg mixture and combine lightly.

Assemble the cake as follows: Brush the sheet of pâte sucrée with strained apricot jam. Cover with a plain layer of choux pastry. Spread half the quantity of rum cream over the choux pastry and cover with the second choux circle. Dot a few small teaspoons of cranberry jam on to this, and cover with the rest of the rum cream. Lay the Streussel-covered choux circle on top. Press the layers gently together, then, using a spatula, ease the surplus cream up the sides of the cake. Dress the top of the Streussel mixture with toasted almonds, and dredge with icing sugar before serving.

Black Forest Kirschtorte

Chocolate, cherries, cream and Kirsch is the irresistible combination that has made this cake so popular today. The late nineteenth and early twentieth centuries saw a proliferation of black cherry and chocolate cakes from the cherry-growing regions. Some included nuts, fruit jam occasionally replaced fresh fruit, and cocoa chocolate — there was no specific recipe and none contained Kirsch. It is hard to establish when Kirsch crept in, and it was an inspired idea. This potent eau-de-vie, distilled from morello or wild cherries, with a delicate perfume, reminds one a little of the bitter almond.

GATEAUX AND TORTEN

Any basic sponge mixture is suitable as a framework for this cake. Flavour a double quantity of the basic fatless sponge (page 90) with 100 g (3½ oz) of grated, plain dark chocolate; or use chocolate Genoese (page 92), which keeps a little longer. My favourite is the recipe for Roulade au chocolat with almonds (page 150), which rises only a little but is very moist and has the additional pleasing crunchiness of the nuts.

Sponge layers (page 150)

100 g plain chocolate, melted and cooled	4 oz plain chocolate, melted and cooled
50 g caster sugar	2 oz caster sugar
7 egg yolks	7 egg yolks
50 g raw ground almonds	2 oz raw ground almonds
7 egg whites	7 egg whites
50 g melted and cooled butter	2 oz melted and cooled butter
30 g icing sugar	1 oz icing sugar
1 teaspoon instant coffee powder	1 teaspoon instant coffee powder
1 tablespoon cocoa powder.	1 tablespoon cocoa powder

Line the bases of two 22–24 cm (8½–9½ inch) spring-form cake tins with greaseproof paper, and grease and dust with equal parts of sugar and flour. Divide the mixture between them, and bake in the preheated oven at gas 4, 180°C, 350°F for 30 minutes. Leave to stand in the tin on a rack for a few minutes before turning out to cool. Strip off the papers.

Fruit, syrup and cream: Fresh or tinned, pitted morello or sour cherries can be used. Use 1 kg (2 lb) fresh fruit or an 850 g (1½ lb) tin or jar of cherries, and avoid the temptation of setting them in jelly – as James Beard says, 'to trap them in insipid rubbery gelatine is an abomination'. Wash fresh cherries carefully and remove the stones. Place in a pan and sprinkle over 100 g (3½ oz) of granulated sugar. Leave to draw for a short time, then simmer on a low heat until they soften. Strain and reserve the juices, and leave the fruits to cool completely before using. Drain preserved fruits and check for any stones. Reserve 4 or 6 good-looking fruits for decoration.

Never be mean with the Kirsch or the flavour will fail to penetrate. It must be diluted with the fruit juice before it is sprinkled on to the sponge cake. Mix 75 ml (2½ fl oz) of strained cherry juice with 120 ml (4 fl oz) of Kirsch, or more to taste.

Whisk 500 ml (17 fl oz) of double cream to make soft peaks, beat in 2 heaped tablespoons of caster sugar until the peaks are stiff, and fold in 3 tablespoons Kirsch.

Assembly: Split each sponge into two; sprinkle a third of the Kirsch syrup over one, and cover with a quarter of the whipped cream. Press half the fruit into the cream surface. Lay a second sponge on top, sprinkle with more syrup, spread another quarter of the whipped cream and top with the remaining cherries. Lay the third sponge on top, sprinkle with the rest of the syrup, and cover with the third quarter of whipped cream. Top with the last sponge layer and spread the surface and sides with the remaining whipped cream. Decorate with grated chocolate or chocolate curls, and pipe rosettes of cream around the edge. Stud a cherry into every other rosette.

Keep the cake in the refrigerator; but should you intend keeping it for more than 1 or 2 days, add a little gelatine to the whipped cream (page 58).

Kirschtorte

The texture and flavour of this cake makes a complete contrast to the previous one. It is a Swiss speciality. Covered, it will keep for up to a week. Be generous with the Kirsch or the taste will be undistinguished.

Biscuit layer

140 g caster sugar	5 oz caster sugar
5 egg yolks	5 egg yolks
5 egg whites	5 egg whites
30 g potato flour	1 oz potato flour
1 teaspoon lemon zest	1 teaspoon lemon zest
70 g plain flour	$2^1/_2$ oz plain flour

Macaroon layer

5 egg whites	5 egg whites
165 g caster sugar	6 oz caster sugar
180 g raw, ground almonds	$6^1/_2$ oz raw, ground almonds
2 tablespoons plain flour	2 tablespoons plain flour
2 tablespoons cornflour	2 tablespoons cornflour

Prepare the biscuit layer (see page 94). Pour the mixture into a 26 cm ($10^1/_2$ inch) spring-form tin, and bake in a preheated oven, gas 4, 180°C, 350°F, for about 30 minutes. Cool on a rack. Make a macaroon mixture (page 373), and fold in the almonds and well sifted flours. Bake two layers 26 cm ($10^1/_2$ inches) in diameter at the same temperature for about 15 minutes until they are pale gold in colour. Remove from the paper immediately and cool on a rack.

Meanwhile make either of the mousseline butter cream fillings on page 62, and finish by beating in 1 tablespoon of strained redcurrant or raspberry jam, to give colour, and 4 tablespoons of Kirsch (more if you prefer a stronger flavour).

Make a syrup by boiling 6 tablespoons of water and 3 tablespoons of granulated sugar to the thread stage (102°C, 215°F). Remove from the heat, and when cool stir in 6–8 tablespoons of Kirsch.

Assemble the layers: Spread the first macaroon base with butter cream. Cut the biscuit flat and even if necessary. Prick it with a fork, sprinkle with syrup, turn over and set on to the butter cream, spooning over a further 3 tablespoons of Kirsch. Spread a layer of butter cream on the biscuit and sandwich with the second macaroon. Spread the remaining butter cream over the top and sides of the whole cake, and press 2 tablespoons of toasted coarse ground or flaked almonds into the sides. Dredge the surface heavily with icing sugar, and draw a diamond design in the cream with a long knife blade. Allow the flavours to soak in for a day before cutting.

* The Kirschtorte becomes a Hungarian *Mikado Torte* when it is filled with a chocolate mousseline buttercream.

Le Bernois of Pierre Lacam

This was very much in vogue at the turn of the century at the Hotel Royal in Dieppe. Composed of four different pastes, the layers are actually baked together, customarily in a moule à manqué (a straight-sided round tin). I prefer a rectangular 1 kg (2 lb) loaf tin. The pistachio marzipan can be prepared the day before and chilled in the refrigerator overnight. Pistachios may be bought ready shelled. They should be plunged in boiling water and peeled like an ordinary almond. Gently dry the prepared nuts in a cool oven, gas ½, 120°C, 250°F, before grinding, and use as directed.

Prepare *shortcrust pastry (1)* (page 44). Roll out thinly and cut one piece to line the base of the loaf tin and a second to line the top.

Make *Pistachio marzipan*: Moisten 30 g (1 oz) of ground peeled pistachios and 20 g (1 oz) of ground blanched almonds with a little egg white; add 50 g (2 oz) of icing sugar or more until it has the texture of marzipan and can be rolled with a rolling pin. Roll out two sheets of paste to fit the tin; these act as insulation for the soft layers.

Paste 1: Mix together 50 g (2 oz) of slightly coarse ground blanched almonds and 2 egg whites; beat in 50 g (2 oz) of caster sugar and 2 teaspoons of vanilla sugar. Whip 2 small egg whites to form stiff snowy peaks, and fold the almond and sugar mixture into it with 1 tablespoon of flour.

Paste 2: Work 65 g (2½ oz) of butter until light and creamy, then beat in 4 eggs one at a time. Add 65 g (2½ oz) of caster sugar, 1 teaspoon of vanilla sugar, and finally 50 g (2 oz) of self-raising flour.

Assemble the cake: Line only the base of the greased tin with the first shortcrust pastry layer. Pour in half paste (2) and smooth out carefully; cover with a sheet of pistachio marzipan. Pour in all of paste (1); level out and cover with the second sheet of marzipan. Spread over the remainder of paste (2) and cover with the second shortcrust pastry sheet.

Bake in the preheated oven set at gas 4, 180°C, 350°F for about an hour. The pastry will have browned slightly and the sides will have shrunk away. Test with a skewer. Unmould after about 5 minutes and leave to cool on a rack. When cold, glaze the top and sides with a lemon-flavoured icing (pages 72–3), and stud with some whole and chopped pistachios.

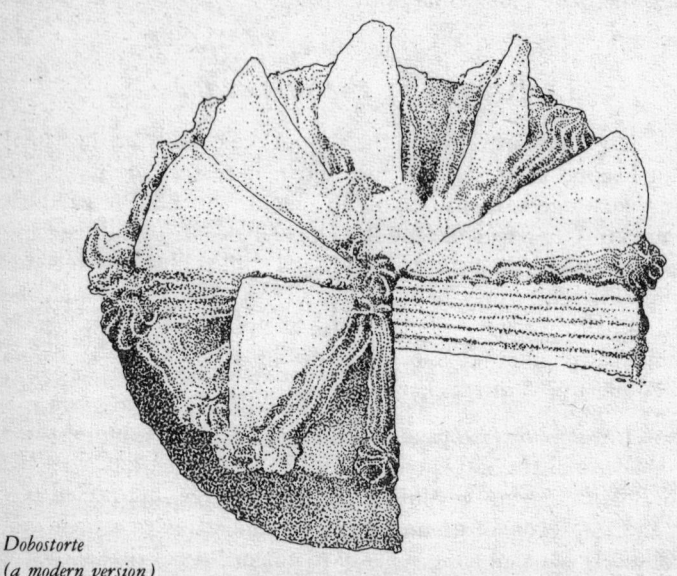

Dobostorte
(a modern version)

GATEAUX AND TORTEN

Dobostorte

Named after Dobos, the famous Hungarian pâtissier born in Budapest in 1924, this spectacular cake with the caramel sheet on top '. . . looks rich, is rich and enriches everyone who eats it'. Assemble the cake layers as soon as they have cooled, for they become crisp and harden after a short time.

Biscuit

140 g caster sugar	5 oz caster sugar
5 egg yolks	5 egg yolks
5 egg whites	5 egg whites
50 g plain flour	2 oz plain flour
50 g potato flour	2 oz potato flour
1 teaspoon lemon or orange zest	1 teaspoon lemon or orange zest

Chocolate Filling (2) page 65

150 g plain chocolate	5 oz plain chocolate
50 g unsalted butter	2 oz unsalted butter
2 egg yolks	2 egg yolks
3 egg whites	3 egg whites
20 g caster sugar	1 oz caster sugar
150 ml whipped cream	5 fl oz whipped cream

gas 7, 220°C, 425°F/5–6 minutes

Prepare the biscuit sponge (see method page 94). *Bake 6 layers:* Butter and flour one or two baking sheets and carefully spread a thin even circle of the mixture about 24 cm (9½ inches) in diameter. Use two trays on different shelves in the oven, and depending on the source of heat, one will be ready sooner. Bake for 5–6 minutes in the preheated oven until a pale golden colour. Remove from the oven, and using an inverted cake tin as a guide, quickly, while the cake is still hot, trim the edges of the circle even, and transfer immediately to a cooking rack. (This also prevents the sides from hardening.) Grease and flour the tray again and repeat the process. Meanwhile the other tray will be ready; remove it from the oven and follow the same procedure until all the mixture has been used. Prepare the chocolate filling.

A traditional Dobostorte has a flat, thin, almost transparent sheet of caramel on top. Sandwich five of the sponge layers with the chocolate cream and reserve some for the sides. Set the remaining sponge layer on top.

Make the caramel glaze: Heat 65 g (2½ oz) of granulated sugar in a copper sugar boiler until golden, then add a further 100 g (3½ oz) of sugar and cook until it has thickened. Pour immediately on to the cake top. Smooth it all over very quickly with a hot spatula (it hardens fast), then, using a sharp long-bladed oiled or buttered knife, cut through the caramel firmly and divide the cake into 14 equal sections. When the caramel has cooled the cake can be cut without difficulty. Smooth the rest of the chocolate cream on the cake sides. Serve with whipped cream on the side.

A Modern Variation

Lay one sponge layer on to a sheet of greaseproof paper on a wire rack. Make the caramel as above, pour over and cut as instructed, but through the sponge as well. Leave to cool. Sandwich the rest of the cake layers with 170 ml (6 oz) cream, reserving a little for piping decoration. Thinly coat the sides and top as well. Lightly mark out 14 sections as above, then fill a piping bag fitted with a star nozzle with the reserved cream and pipe a long whirl in the centre of each portion. Fill the piping bag afresh with whipped cream and pipe into the triangular spaces. Set a caramel coated triangle, fanwise and tilted slightly, on each piped chocolate whirl, and press 50 g (2 oz) flaked toasted almonds into the piped cream for decoration. Decorate with chocolate beans.

La Périgourdine

Bake a Genoese sponge (page 91) and cool. Cut out the centre in one piece to about 1.5 cm (⅝ inch) in depth, and to within 2 cm (¾ inch) of the edge. Hollow out the base a little more and discard the crumbs. Prepare mousseline butter cream (1) (page 62) and flavour with 100 g (3½ oz) of chopped walnuts and 2 tablespoons coffee liqueur (such as Tia Maria) or dark rum. Reserve a small amount of the butter cream for decoration, and fill the rest into the hollowed cake. Replace the sponge centre to cover the cream. Brush with strained apricot jam and mask the top with coffee icing (page 73). Press toasted flaked almonds into the moist icing around the sides if you wish, and space walnuts at 2 cm (¾ inch) intervals in a circle on top of the line of the original incision. Pipe stars of cream in the spaces between the walnuts.

An Alternative Version

Fresh soft fruit and liqueur-flavoured whipped cream are delicious. Use redcurrants, wild or cultivated strawberries, or raspberries. Whip 250 ml (½ pint) double cream to soft peaks, then whisk in 2 tablespoons of caster sugar and one of Kirsch. Crush 3 or 4 of the fruits to colour the cream and fold with the rest of the fruits into the cream. Fill the cake hollow, replace the centre, brush with strained apricot jam, and ice over the whole with a delicate lemon-flavoured white glacé icing (pages 72–3). Decorate with fresh fruits.

Marjolaine

Marjolaine is a delicious confection, a favourite among the well-known French chefs of today. Shaped in a long narrow rectangle, three light and fluffy creams are thickly sandwiched between thin layers of nut sponge, and the outside is coated in chocolate shavings or cocoa powder and dusted on top with icing sugar. Fernand Point took several years to perfect a version in the 1930s, and two of his protegées, François Bise and Louis Outhier, later developed others.

During the nineteenth century both Urbain Dubois and Pierre Lacam gave recipes, which must have inspired Point. In Dubois' recipe, four layers of a light hazelnut almond meringue are sandwiched and covered with moka butter cream and glazed with coffee icing; Lacam fills his with a pralined butter cream and inscribes the name on the surface. The modern interpretations are combinations of both recipes, using both creams and a chocolate one in addition; and Outhier's is also flavoured with orange.

Use two 34 × 23.5 cm (13½ × 9 inch) Swiss roll tins. Cut the cakes down the middle while they are still hot to make four 34 × 12 cm (13½ × 4½ inch) strips.

Cake layers

150 g blanched almonds	5 oz blanched almonds
120 g hazelnuts	4 oz hazelnuts
220 g caster sugar	7 oz caster sugar
20 g plain, soft flour	1 oz plain, soft flour
6 egg whites	6 egg whites

gas 6, 200°C, 400°F/6–7 minutes

Toast the almonds and hazelnuts on separate trays in a hot oven for 10 minutes. Rub the skins off the hazelnuts and grind them quite fine, together with the almonds, then add the sugar and sifted flour. Beat the egg whites in a separate bowl to form stiff, snowy peaks, sprinkle some of the nut mixture over the surface, and fold in very lightly, using a metal spoon and taking care not to lose any air. Sprinkle and fold in the rest of the nut mixture twice more. Pour into lightly greased and floured Swiss roll tins, spread carefully across the surface, and bake in the preheated oven for 6–7 minutes or until they have browned slightly. Cut in half immediately and trim the sides even, then cool on a wire rack.

The cream fillings:

(1) Prepare *chocolate ganache (1)* (page 64) with 250 ml (9 fl oz) of double cream and 375 g (13 oz) of plain, dark chocolate and a split vanilla pod.

(2) Prepare *Mousseline butter cream with egg whites (2)* (page 63) with 4 egg whites; 200 g (7 oz) icing sugar; 2 teaspoons vanilla sugar; 350 g (12 oz) unsalted butter. Divide the completed mixture into two equal parts.

(3) Flavour one part with 100 g (3½ oz) almond praline (page 312), using half the quantity).

Assembling the cake: Spread one cake layer with half the chocolate ganache (1); cover with the second cake. Spread all the mousseline butter cream (2) over this. Cover with the third cake and smooth almond praline cream (3) over. Top with the remaining cake layer. Spread the top and sides of the cake with the other half of the chocolate ganache, dust liberally with cocoa powder and sift icing sugar on top. Chill for a day to allow the flavours to blend.

Malakoff

In 1855 the French stormed and took the Malakoff tower of Sebastapol during the Crimean War; enough people, including nineteen generals, were killed, to make it a glorious triumph. One of the victors, Marshall Jean J. Pélissier, later adopted the title of Duke of Malakoff. It was customary in France to commemorate success, however gruesome, in food.

Today Malakoff is often made with sponge boudoir biscuits, layered with almond cream and served slightly chilled. I prefer the original version, with home-made biscuit layers.

GATEAUX AND TORTEN

Biscuit

180 g caster sugar	6 oz caster sugar
4 egg yolks	4 egg yolks
4 egg whites	4 egg whites
150 g plain flour	5 oz plain flour

Almond filling

110 g unsalted butter	4 oz unsalted butter
150 g caster sugar	5 oz caster sugar
3 egg yolks	3 egg yolks
150 g ground, blanched almonds	5 oz ground, blanched almonds
200 ml double cream	7 fl oz double cream
3–4 tablespoons Kirsch or rum	3–4 tablespoons Kirsch or rum

To finish you also need 250 ml (9 fl oz) whipped double cream, 75 g (3 oz) caster sugar, and a few toasted almonds.

Prepare the biscuit (page 94) and pour into a 22–24 cm (8^1/$_2$–9^1/$_2$ inch) spring-form tin that has been base-lined, greased, and dusted with a flour and sugar mixture. Bake at gas 4, 180°C, 350°F for 30 minutes. Cool on a wire rack. Leave to settle for several hours, covered, then split into three thin layers.

Make the almond filling by beating the butter and sugar until pale and creamy. Beat in the yolks one at a time then the ground almonds and double cream.

To assemble the cake: Sprinkle each sponge layer with a little Kirsch or rum, spread the filling over two layers, then sandwich the three together. The top is left plain. Leave to rest overnight, covered, so that the layers absorb all the flavours. Whip the cream with the sugar and spread over the top and sides lavishly. Scatter on a few flaked, toasted almonds for decoration.

Lacam make a chestnut cream (page 64) as an alternative, and of course chocolate, moka, praline or orange creams are also good.

CAKES

Hazelnut gâteau praline

300 g hazelnuts	11 oz hazelnuts
150 g granulated sugar	5 oz granulated sugar
150 g caster sugar	5 oz caster sugar
2 eggs	2 eggs
8 egg yolks	8 egg yolks
150 g melted butter	5 oz melted butter
zest ½ lemon	zest ½ lemon
6 egg whites	6 egg whites
60 g plain flour	2 oz plain flour
500 ml whipped cream	17 fl oz whipped cream
2 teaspoons coffee powder (optional)	2 teaspoons coffee powder (optional)

gas 4, 180°C, 350°F/30 minutes

Spread the nuts on a baking tray and set them in the hot oven to toast. When the skins start to flake, take the tray out and rub the nuts between coarse towels to remove the skins. Leave to cool, then grind half the quantity coarsely and the remainder finely.

Make a praline with the granulated sugar and the *coarse* nuts (pages 60, 312–3), and crush when cold. Set aside.

Cake mixture: Beat the caster sugar and the whole eggs until light and creamy, then add the egg yolks one at a time. Mix in 60 g (2 oz) of praline, the *ground* hazelnuts, and the cooled melted butter. Add the lemon zest. In a separate bowl beat the egg whites to stiff snowy peaks, and fold into the mixture with alternating spoonfuls of the sifted flour. Divide the mixture between three greased and flour-dusted 26 cm (10½ inch) spring-form tins, and bake in the preheated oven.

Meanwhile whip up the cream until stiff and fold in 60 g (2 oz) of praline and the coffee powder. Cool the cakes on wire racks, then spread the cream between the layers and smooth it on the top as well. Sprinkle the remaining praline as decoration.

Himmelstorte (Heavenly cake)

This comes from Frau Maurer in Bad Homburg, Germany. 'Es schmeckt himmlisch,' she comments – it does!

250 g plain flour
pinch baking powder
125 g butter
125 g caster sugar
4 egg yolks
zest 1 lemon
50 g chopped almonds (optional)
5 teaspoons cinnamon
150 g caster sugar
250 g cranberry or redcurrant jelly
450 ml double cream

9 oz plain flour
pinch baking powder
4 oz butter
4 oz caster sugar
4 egg yolks
zest 1 lemon
2 oz chopped almonds (optional)
5 teaspoons cinnamon
5 oz caster sugar
9 oz cranberry or redcurrant jelly
16 fl oz double cream

gas 4, 180°C, 350°F/15 minutes

Sift the flour and baking powder well. Beat the butter and sugar until pale and fluffy, and add the egg yolks one at a time. Sieve in the flour and add the lemon zest, blend together and then knead well. The mixture is rather stiff. Divide into four portions. Press one layer into a greased 24 cm (9½ inch) spring-form tin, scattering the almonds over the top. Bake. Remove from the oven and cool on a wire rack. Cool the tin, grease as before and press in a second portion of pastry. Scatter a mixture of cinnamon and sugar over; bake as for the first layer. Repeat with the two remaining batches of pastry.

When the cakes are cool, spread a thin layer of jam over three of them and sandwich together with lightly sweetened whipped cream. Set the almond-coated layer on top. Leave covered in the refrigerator for 2 days before serving dredged with icing sugar. The cake will keep for up to a week.

Lady Baltimore Cake

This original recipe was created by Mrs Alicia Rhett Mayberry, of Charleston, the central character in Owen Wister's early nineteenth-century novel, *Lady Baltimore*. Described in detail by Wister in the book, it became one of the most popular American cakes. Multi-layered, filled with a mixture of frosting, nuts, figs and raisins, it is finished with white mountain frosting.

The *egg white snow cake* on page 114 is the basis of this layered cake. Divide the mixture between three 24 cm (9½ inch) spring-form tins and bake at gas 3, 170°C, 325°F for 40 minutes.

7 egg whites	7 egg whites
240 g caster sugar	8½ oz caster sugar
zest ½ lemon	zest ½ lemon
70 g potato flour	2½ oz potato flour
70 g plain flour	2½ oz plain flour
120 g melted butter	4¼ oz melted butter
1 teaspoon baking powder	1 teaspoon baking powder

7 minute frosting and filling

175 g icing sugar	6 oz icing sugar
2 tablespoons water	2 tablespoons water
¼ teaspoon cream of tartar	¼ teaspoon cream of tartar
speck of salt	speck of salt
1 egg white	1 egg white
35 g chopped pecan nuts	1½ oz chopped pecan nuts
3 dried figs	3 dried figs
70 g raisins	2½ oz raisins
½ teaspoon pure almond essence	½ teaspoon pure almond essence

Make the icing by beating the icing sugar, water, cream of tartar, salt and egg white in a bowl; stand over a pan of simmering water and beat until stiff enough to stand in peaks — about 4 minutes with an electric hand beater. Remove from the heat, and beat until a spreading consistency is reached. Reserve a good third, and add the chopped nuts, thinly sliced figs, chopped raisins and almond essence to the remainder. Fill the bottom and second layers with this mixture, and cover the top and sides with the plain icing. Decorate with whole pecan nuts and a few toasted chopped almonds.

Bûche de Noël

In France the Bûche de Noël or Christmas log is traditional fare, and the most spectacular type of roulade. The following recipe is taken from H.G. Harris and S.P. Burella, *All about Gâteaux and Dessert Cakes*.

'Gâteau Bois'

The base for this gâteau is generally a piece of Genoese, sandwiched and built up to the necessary thickness, and sometimes coated with a sheet of almond paste. The easiest way, however, is to use something in Swiss roll form as a base. The following is submitted as best of all: Make a small Viennois roll (see Genoese), and in place

GATEAUX AND TORTEN

of jam spread it with crème au beurre well flavoured with almond or aveline praline and kirsch. When rolled, trim one end straight, and then cut a length diagonally across the roll so that one side is 7 inches [18 cm] long and the other not quite 6 inches [15 cm]. The ends should be dipped in hot highly-boiled apricot conserve, and when set, into cream-coloured fondant or water icing sufficiently thin for the concentric rings to show through.

The boles can be formed from almond paste, or better still, from a much smaller roll shaped straight at one end and diagonal at the other, the straight ends treated exactly as the larger roll, and adjusted in place as shown. They are generally held in position either with a little very highly boiled apricot, caramel sugar (boiled just beyond the crack), or pinned with a strip of firm angelica. A small pencil-shaped piece of barley sugar or even a length of thin macaroni gives even greater security, and can be used as desired. The final coating of the gâteau is variously effected. Chocolate is almost always the colour chosen, but coffee can be used. Butter cream is the richest, and on that account sometimes objected to. To sum up, all of the following forms of chocolate will give good results, in addition to coffee crème au beurre:

(1) Chocolate crème au beurre.

(2) Chocolate fondant, with one-third its weight of fresh butter well beaten into it whilst warm, and allowed to get cold and set.

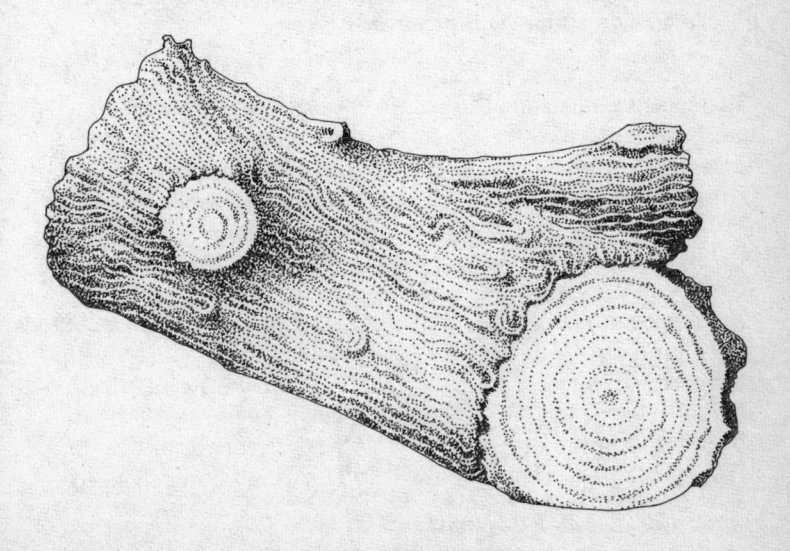

CAKES

(3) Chocolate coloured and flavoured fondant, with one-third its weight of butter, as above.

(4) Chocolate coloured and flavoured royal icing, well beaten and firm.

The covering must be done with a finely-cut star tube, and the lines, although running from end to end, must not be too straight, showing here and there small loop-like excoriations in the bark. A few pieces of finely-chopped pistachio and browned almonds or coconut may be used to give colour effect; coloured fine granulated sugar serves the same purpose, carefully used . . .

Spiced Coffee and Pecan Cake

He had opened a hanging-cabinet, and taken thence the requisites for his coffee-making: a cylindrical Turkish mill, a long-handled pot, a double receptacle for sugar and ground coffee, all in brass. 'Palmitin, stearin, olein,' he went on, shaking the coffee berries from a tin box into the mill, which he began to turn. 'You see I make it all myself, it tastes twice as good.' . . . They were seated . . . at a bamboo tabouret which held an oriental brass tray, upon which Behrens had set the coffee-machine, among the smoking utensils . . . The Hofrat ladled coffee and sugar into the long-handled pot, added water, and let the brew boil up over the flame of the lamp. It foamed brownly in the onion-pattern cups, and proved on tasting both strong and sweet . . .

(Thomas Mann, *The Magic Mountain*)

3 teaspoons cinnamon	3 teaspoons cinnamon
pinch ginger	pinch ginger
2 teaspoons nutmeg	2 teaspoons nutmeg
2 teaspoons allspice	2 teaspoons allspice
250 g plain flour	9 oz plain flour
1 teaspoon salt	1 teaspoon salt
1 teaspoon baking powder	1 teaspoon baking powder
2 tablespoons bicarbonate of soda	2 tablespoons bicarbonate of soda
100 g butter	3^1/$_2$ oz butter
185 g brown sugar	6^1/$_2$ oz brown sugar
2 whole eggs	2 whole eggs
180 ml sour cream	6^1/$_2$ fl oz sour cream
100 g pecan nuts, chopped	3^1/$_2$ oz pecan nuts, chopped

gas 3, 170°C, 325°F/35 minutes

Filling

One portion of moka coffee cream (page 66) with whipped cream.

Grind the spices in a mortar, then sift with all the dry ingredients, apart from the sugar. Set aside. Whisk together the butter and the sugar until light and fluffy, then add the eggs, and mix in the sour cream. Beat in the chopped nuts and the sifted flours, taking care not to overbeat. Divide the mixture between two greased 24 cm (9½ inch) spring-form tins, and bake in the preheated oven. When the cake starts to shrink away from the sides, remove from the oven and cool on a wire rack. Make the coffee cream and add some pecan nuts if you like, then fill the cake, cover the top and coat the sides. Decorate with a few pecan nuts.

Le Lacam

This cake was dedicated to Pierre Lacam, the nineteenth-century pastry chef, by one of his best friends, in recognition of his forty years devoted to pâtisserie.

250 g ground almonds	9 oz ground almonds
25 g hazelnuts	sparing 1 oz hazelnuts
3–4 walnuts	3–4 walnuts
250 g caster sugar	9 oz caster sugar
1 tablespoon vanilla sugar	1 tablespoon vanilla sugar
3 whole eggs	3 whole eggs
3 egg yolks	3 egg yolks
1 tablespoon rum	1 tablespoon rum
1 tablespoon Kirsch	1 tablespoon Kirsch
1 teaspoon aniseed	1 teaspoon aniseed
1 drop bitter almond essence	1 drop bitter almond essence
1 teaspoon lemon zest	1 teaspoon lemon zest
60 g potato flour	2 oz potato flour
60 g plain flour	2 oz plain flour
3 egg whites	3 egg whites

gas 4, 180°C, 350°F/50 minutes

Grind all the nuts together, then mix with the sugars. Beat in the eggs one at a time, then the egg yolks, and beat to a fine mousse. Next beat in the liqueurs, aniseed, essence and lemon zest. Sift the flours together well. Whip the egg whites in a separate bowl until they stand in firm snowy peaks, and gently fold them into the mixture along with alternating spoonfuls of flour. Turn the mixture into a buttered and floured 24 cm (9½ inch) spring-form tin, and bake in the preheated oven for about 50 minutes. In the words of Lacam, 'This cake is better made in the evening which encourages the finishing that consists of sprinkling, or rather imbibing, with a teaspoon of the following preparation composed especially by the author of the recipe. Once well sprinkled, ice the cake with vanilla icing with chopped pistachios. It will keep for some time, weeks, and be useful as a gâteau de voyage. So as not to lose its aroma it is good to wrap it in tinfoil which also keeps it fresh.'

This is the liqueur which as Lacam says, 'will make the liqueur Savarin pale and that of Cussy blanch!'

1 tablespoon of rum: very strong in flavour and aroma, 2 tablespoons Kirsch: 2 tablespoons aniseed: 1 teaspoon Maraschino: 1 teaspoon cognac: 1 tablespoon Curaçao: 1 teaspoon orange zest: 1 drop bitter almond essence: 1 drop walnut essence.

Pound Cakes

To make Pound Cakes. From the same.

Take a Pound of double refined Loaf-Sugar beaten and sifted; then beat eight Eggs and stir the Sugar in them; then melt a Pound of Butter, and stir that in with the rest, and then stir in a Pound of Flour, some Mace finely beat, with some Nutmeg grated, and some Sack, and Orange-Flower-Water; beat these all together for an hour and a half till all is well mix'd; then stir in some Currans plump'd a little. To make good the name of the Cake, there should be a Pound of a sort. Some put about a quarter of a Pound of Caraway Comfits; but every way is good. Bake these in little Pans, in a gentle Oven, and when they are quite cold, turn them out, and keep them in oaken Boxes, with Papers between them, in a dry Place.

(Richard Bradley, *The Country Housewife and Lady's Director*, 1736)

Pound cake or Victoria sandwich in England, *Sandtorte* in Germany, *quartre quarts* in France, is probably the easiest tea or coffee cake to prepare. It has a fine buttery texture which can be flavoured in many different ways, it keeps very well, and it is a good substitute for biscuits and cookies. Pound cakes are equal weight cakes – that is, each dry ingredient weighs the same as the eggs. 'A pound all round' was the popular description. James Beard has these affectionate words to say:

> I remember that when I was young, my mother always had a pound cake in the larder. One week it would be a caraway seed cake, with the little pungent flecks pushing through the smooth golden-yellow cake. Another week it might be a citron cake, with thin slivers of citron on the top (never mixed in, lest they sink to the bottom). Sometimes there were chopped walnuts in our cake, or ginger, which gave it an exotic, spicy flavour. Pound cake was our standby. We had it for tea, toasted for breakfast, and as a foundation for fruit desserts, with fresh or poached berries, poached plums or peaches, and slathers of heavy cream poured over everything . . .
>
> (*Beard on Food*, 1974).

CAKES

There are two basic methods of preparation. The simple and speedy one, using an electric mixer, beats the butter and sugar first, then the whole eggs are added and finally the flour. The result, although perfectly satisfactory, is a rather heavy pound cake. The second method, where the egg-whites are whipped up separately with part of the sugar, gives a much lighter and more aerated cake with a finer taste. I find the extra effort well worth while.

Use a long guttered cake mould, a gugelhopf tin, or, for the smaller quantity, a simple 1 kg or 2 lb rectangular loaf tin.

Self-raising flour may be used in preference to the plain and potato flour mixture, though the flavour is less good, but leave out the baking powder.

Pound Cake (Basic Mixture)

Ingredients for a 20–22 cm (8–8½ inch) mould

125 g plain flour	4½ oz plain flour
125 g potato flour	4½ oz potato flour
1 teaspoon baking powder	1 teaspoon baking powder
250 g butter	9 oz butter
240 g caster sugar	8½ oz caster sugar
2 tablespoons vanilla sugar	2 tablespoons vanilla sugar
4 large eggs (250 g)	4 large eggs (9 oz)
1 teaspoon lemon zest or 1 tablespoon rum	1 teaspoon lemon zest or 1 tablespoon rum

gas 4, 180°C, 350°F/1¼ hours

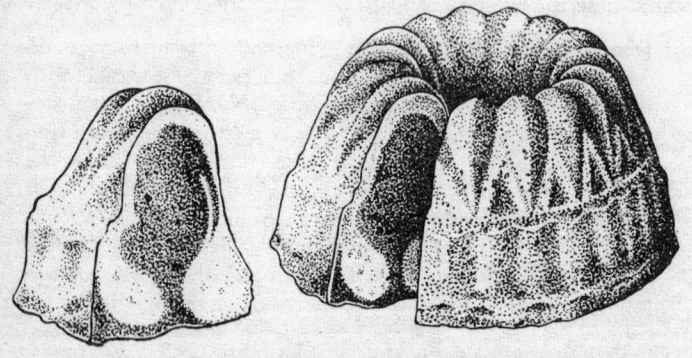

Pound Cake in a gugelhopf mould

Carefully sift the flours with the baking powder three or four times. Cream the butter and half the sugar until pale and fluffy, then beat in 3 egg yolks and 1 whole egg one at a time, beating the mixture thoroughly in between. (Should the mixture curdle, beat in a tablespoon of flour to stabilize it.) Add the lemon zest or rum. Sift and lightly beat in the flours a little at a time, taking care not to beat the mixture for too long or the cake will be heavy and stodgy. Beat the 3 egg whites in a separate bowl to hold firm peaks, sift in spoonfuls of the remaining sugar, and beat to give a shiny smooth texture. Beat a few spoonfuls of the egg white into the mixture to lighten it, then using a large metal spoon, gently but swiftly fold in the meringue. Have the cake mould ready greased and floured, pour in the cake mixture and bake in the preheated oven. Leave in the tin for 10 minutes to settle, before turning out on to a rack to cool. Dust with icing sugar to serve.

The variations on Pound cake are numerous. For simple embellishment, add to the basic mixture:

* For 'brawn brack' (a seed cake) 1 tablespoon of caraway seed.
* For a spicy cake, add 1 teaspoon of ginger powder and 50 g (2 oz) chopped, preserved ginger.
* For a spirited tang, add 2 tablespoons of rum or brandy.
* *Marbled with chocolate or spices:* Pour half the pound cake mixture into the cake-tin; blend into the rest either (a) 2 tablespoons of cocoa or 50 g (2 oz) plain grated chocolate; or (b) a mixture of ½ teaspoon each of cinnamon, allspice, mace, nutmeg and a pinch of cloves. Pour over the first mixture and gently drag a fork through the whole to create a marbled effect. For a striped alternative spoon thin alternate layers of the mixtures into the tin.

Austrian Coffee Cake

Bake the basic recipe and cool. Replace in the cake tin and prick all over with a skewer, then pour over 250 ml (9 fl oz) cold, strong black coffee mixed with sugar and brandy or rum to taste. Leave to soak. Mask the cake with whipped, vanilla flavoured crème chantilly, and sprinkle over toasted, flaked almonds.

* For an orange flavour you can substitute orange juice for the coffee in the previous version. Flavour the basic mixture with the zest of one orange, bake and cool. Return to the mould and pierce with a skewer.

Press out the juice of 3 oranges and 1 lemon and strain; pour over the cake and leave to soak before cutting.

Fresh Fruited Pound Cake

This uses apples, apricots, cherries, rhubarb or Zwetschken plums, prepared as below. The raw prepared fruits are laid on the surface of the cake mixture and sink down while it bakes.

750 g (1 lb 8 oz) apples: peel, core, quarter the fruits. Make small incisions in one side and sprinkle first with lemon juice, then with caster sugar. Lay on the cake cut side uppermost.

500 g (1 lb) apricots: wash, dry, halve and stone; pack in tightly together.

750 g (1 lb 8 oz) cherries: prepare as apricots, but leave the stones.

500 g (1 lb) rhubarb: string older fruit, and cut into 3 cm (1¼ inch) lengths of even thickness. Pack tightly.

750 g (1 lb 8 oz) Zwetschken: wash and dry carefully; halve and stone, pack close with the skin side down.

Dried Fruit Pound Cake

Use a mixture of raisins, sultanas and currants, weighing 250 g (9 oz) in all. Check that the fruits are clean and dry, then dredge with a further 50 g (2 oz) of flour to coat them and prevent the fruit sinking to the bottom of the baking cake. Shake off the excess flour into the basic flour quantity. Make the cake and fold in the prepared fruits. This quantity will fill two 1 kg (or 2 lb) loaf tins.

English Fruited Pound Cake

This is more elaborate, and is made with 6 eggs and 370 g (13 oz) each of butter, sugar and flour. Add 100 g (3½ oz) sultanas, 100 g (3½ oz) ground or nibbed almonds, 100 g (3½ oz) lemon and fine cut orange candied peel, and 2 tablespoons of rum. Clean the fruits and dredge with 50 g (2 oz) flour. Shake off the excess. Prepare the basic mixture and fold in the nuts and glacé fruits with the spirit. Pour into a 20 cm (8 inch) lined and greased deep loose-bottomed cake tin and bake. (This cake may take a little longer to cook.)

POUND CAKES

Vienna Nut Cake

Prepare the basic mixture. Fold 100 g (3½oz) grated bitter chocolate or 6 flat teaspoons of cocoa powder, and 150 g (5½oz) peeled and coarsely ground hazelnuts into the cake batter. Bake and cool. Brush the cold cake with strained apricot jam, and glaze with rum flavoured icing (page 73).

Sugar Cake

This family adaptation of pound cake is a children's favourite. The quantities are slightly adjusted to allow for the butter slivers and sugar on the surface. It is baked in two shallow 31 × 21 cm (12 × 8½ inch) rectangular cake tins with 2.5 cm (1 inch) high sides. The salt in the butter gives a pleasant flavour.

175 g salted butter, melted	6 oz salted butter, melted
4 large eggs	4 large eggs
225 g caster sugar	8 oz caster sugar
1 teaspoon lemon zest	1 teaspoon lemon zest
225 g self-raising flour	8 oz self-raising flour
50 g salted butter	2 oz salted butter

gas 5, 190°C, 375°F/20–30 minutes

Gently melt the butter and leave to cool. Beat the eggs and 110 g (4 oz) of the sugar together until very frothy, and mix in the lemon zest. Sift the flour two or three times, then fold into the mixture, alternating with the melted butter. Spread the mixture into the greased tins. Place thin slivers of the 50 g (2 oz) butter at regular intervals over the surface, and dredge generously with the remaining sugar. Bake in the preheated oven until the cake starts to shrink from the sides. Remove from the oven, and cut while still hot into rectangular fingers about 7 × 3 cm (3 × 1¼ inches). Leave to cool in the tins. Store in an airtight container. Each tray makes 30 slices.

Making Toast with Pound Cake

Pound cake is good eaten as it is, but after several days a few tired left-over pieces can be transformed into a mouth-watering treat.

Cinnamon toast: Cut a slice just over ½ cm (¼ inch) thick and toast one side only. Turn over and spread thickly with unsalted butter, then sprinkle with a generous mixture of demerara sugar and cinnamon. Replace under the grill, but watch carefully until the sugar starts to melt and bubble and blend with the butter and spice. Cut into thick strips and serve warm when the top has started to caramelize.

Orange toast: Mix cinnamon and a little orange zest with granulated sugar and moisten with orange juice. Proceed as for cinnamon toast.

Tea Breads and Coffee Cakes

Sweetened breads are particularly good served plain, lightly toasted, spread with unsalted butter and jam or a dollop of clotted cream; they make a traditional offering with a cup of tea or coffee, or even a chilled glass of white wine. Yeast cakes in the Viennese manner, such as doughnuts and Gugelhopf, and sour-cream coffee bread are still much loved by the coffee-drinking Americans, while in England the traditional tea accompaniment is yeasted and non-yeasted breads, spiced and fruited or with nuts. Elizabeth David has an excellent collection of English recipes in her *English Bread and Yeast Cookery*. The following are some non-yeasted suggestions. All these breads and cakes will keep for at least a week, if close-wrapped or stored in an airtight container.

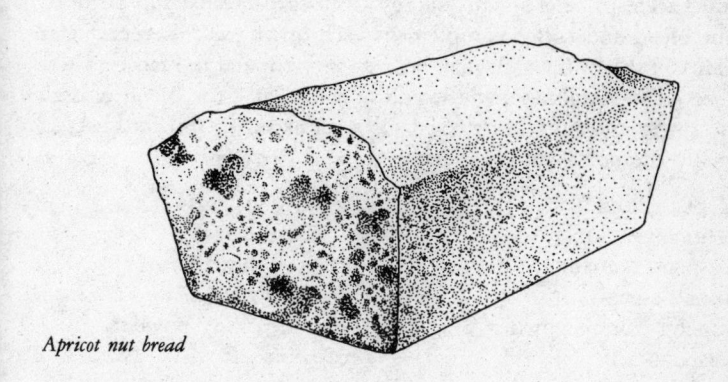

Apricot nut bread

Raisin Bread

This has a very light and fluffy texture. Because there is only one egg white and no raising agent, the flour has to be sifted very carefully indeed to aerate it well, and the egg yolks and sugar have to be beaten very thoroughly. It takes about 10 minutes with an electric mixer.

70 g raisins	3 oz raisins
1 tablespoon flour	1 tablespoon flour
140 g caster sugar	5 oz caster sugar
5 egg yolks	5 egg yolks
1 whole egg	1 whole egg
zest 1 lemon	zest 1 lemon
140 g plain flour	5 oz plain flour

gas 4, 180°C, 350°F/50 minutes

Dredge the dried fruit with the 1 tablespoon flour and shake off the excess. Beat together the sugar, egg yolks and whole egg until the mixture is very pale and fluffy and has at least doubled in bulk. Mix in the lemon zest. Sift the flour, then sift it into the cake mixture in stages. Fold in very lightly, and finally fold in the raisins. Butter and dust with flour a 1 kg (or 2 lb) loaf tin, pour in the mixture and bake. Turn out to cool on a rack, and serve cut in thin slices.

Walnut Bread

Walnuts seem to be especially successful in cake-breads; and buttered walnut bread and coffee complement each other well. Recently this speciality of the Rhine valley has become very popular in France, where it is served in restaurants at the end of the meal — the blend of dark sugar, spices and nuts has proved to be an excellent foil for cheeses, especially the goats' milk varieties.

500 g plain flour	1 lb plain flour
250 g molasses sugar	9 oz molasses sugar
1/2 teaspoon cinnamon	1/2 teaspoon cinnamon
2 crushed cloves	2 crushed cloves
1 teaspoon baking powder	1 teaspoon baking powder
1/2 teaspoon salt	1/2 teaspoon salt
150 g walnut halves or quarters	5 oz walnut halves or quarters
2 eggs	2 eggs
350–400 ml milk	12–14 fl oz milk
sultanas (optional)	sultanas (optional)

gas 4, 180°C, 350°F/1 hour

Sift together the flour, sugar, spices, baking powder and salt. Stir in the nuts. Lightly beat the eggs and blend them into the mixture, adding enough milk to form a strong elastic paste. Add a handful of sultanas if wished. Grease a 1 kg (2 lb) loaf tin, pour in the bread mixture and bake. Cool on a wire rack, and cut in slices to serve.

Prune and Walnut Loaf

This is useful for travellers because it is moist and keeps its shape well.

250 g dried prunes	9 oz dried prunes
250 ml red wine or water	9 fl oz red wine or water
2 teaspoons lemon zest	2 teaspoons lemon zest
120 g caster sugar	4 oz caster sugar
50 g coarsely ground walnuts	2 oz coarsely ground walnuts
250 g plain flour	9 oz plain flour
1 teaspoon baking powder	1 teaspoon baking powder
½ teaspoon cinnamon	½ teaspoon cinnamon
pinch cloves	pinch cloves

gas 4, 180°C, 350°F/1–1¼ hours

Soak the prunes in hot water for about an hour; drain. Heat the wine with 1 teaspoon of lemon zest and 1 tablespoon of sugar, and drop in the prunes. Cover the pan and simmer gently until the fruits have softened a little. Cool and drain, but reserve the liquid. Remove the stones and cut the fruit into thin slivers. Combine in a bowl with the nuts and the remaining sugar and lemon zest. Sift the remaining ingredients carefully and stir lightly into the fruit mixture, damping it with some of the prune liquid, until the texture is rather soft and moist. Pour into a greased and floured 1 kg (2 lb) loaf tin, and bake in the preheated oven.

CAKES

Butterbrot mit Schokolade

Butter bread without butter!

6 egg yolks	6 egg yolks
170 g caster sugar	6 oz caster sugar
100 g blanched, ground almonds	3½ oz blanched, ground almonds
2 teaspoons lemon zest	2 teaspoons lemon zest
120 g dark, grated chocolate	4 oz dark, grated chocolate
100 g plain flour	3½ oz plain flour
½ teaspoon cinnamon	½ teaspoon cinnamon
2 ground cloves	2 ground cloves
6 egg whites	6 egg whites

Egg yolk glaze

40 g icing sugar	1½ oz icing sugar
2 egg yolks	2 egg yolks

gas 4, 180°C, 350°F / 1 hour

Beat the egg yolks and sugar until very pale and creamy; beat in the almonds and lemon zest, then add the chocolate. Sift the flour thoroughly with the spices. Beat the egg whites to stiff snowy peaks, and whip 2 or 3 tablespoons into the mixture to lighten it. Gently fold in the remainder, using a large metal spoon, and alternating with siftings of flour. Turn into a well greased 1 kg (2 lb) loaf tin or a gugelhopf mould, and bake in the preheated oven. Leave to cool in the tin for 5 minutes before turning out on to a rack. When cold, coat with the egg yolk glaze (page 76). Leave to harden for several hours, then scatter sugar crystals over as decoration.

Apricot Nut Bread

180 g chopped dried apricots	6 oz chopped dried apricots
300 g plain flour	11 oz plain flour
1 teaspoon baking powder	1 teaspoon baking powder
1 teaspoon salt	1 teaspoon salt
225 g caster sugar	8 oz caster sugar
140 g flaked almonds	5 oz flaked almonds
zest and juice of 1 large orange	zest and juice of 1 large orange
2 eggs	2 eggs

50 g butter, melted
150 ml sour cream

2 oz butter, melted
5 fl oz sour cream

gas 4, 180°C, 350°F/1¼ hours

Soak the apricots in water for several hours to soften; then chop. Dry well and dredge with a small amount of flour. Sift together the flour, baking powder and salt. Stir in sugar, almonds and orange zest. In a separate bowl lightly combine the eggs with the cooled melted butter and the orange juice; mix in the sour cream. Blend the liquids with the dry mixture and combine well. Pour into a greased and floured 1 kg (2 lb) loaf tin and bake. Leave to cool in the tin on the rack for 10 minutes before turning out to finish cooling.

Brazil Nut Bread

Here is a recipe from Elisabeth Lambert Ortiz.

100 g self-raising flour
100 g sugar
pinch salt
275 g Brazil nuts, finely ground
275 g pitted dates, finely chopped
1 tablespoon finely chopped fresh ginger root
4 eggs

3½ oz self-raising flour
3½ oz sugar
pinch salt
10 oz Brazil nuts, finely ground
10 oz pitted dates, finely chopped
1 tablespoon finely chopped fresh ginger root
4 eggs

gas 4, 180°C, 350°F/45 minutes

Sift the flour, sugar and salt into a large bowl. Stir in the nuts. Toss the dates in a little extra flour, shake off the excess, and add to the other ingredients. Add the ginger and mix. Lightly beat the eggs and fold them into the rest, mixing thoroughly. Butter a 1 kg (or 2 lb) loaf tin; pour in the cake mixture and bake in the preheated oven until the top is lightly browned and a skewer comes out clean. Cool for a short while in the tin before turning out on to a cake rack. Serve cold sliced as a tea bread, or if liked, buttered or with cream cheese. It can be sliced in half lengthwise and filled with whipped cream, then masked with cream and fresh fruits such as pears, peaches or pineapple.

CAKES

Astrig's Sour Cream Coffee Bread

Sour cream gives this cake an almost yeasty texture. It is very light.

170 g butter	6½ oz butter
130 g caster sugar	4½ oz caster sugar
1 tablespoon vanilla sugar	1 tablespoon vanilla sugar
2 eggs	2 eggs
1 carton sour cream (150 ml)	1 carton sour cream (5 fl oz)
270 g plain flour	10 oz plain flour
pinch salt	pinch salt
2 teaspoons baking powder	2 teaspoons baking powder
½ teaspoon baking soda	½ teaspoon baking soda

Filling

100 g caster sugar	3½ oz caster sugar
1 teaspoon cinnamon	1 teaspoon cinnamon
50 g chopped, toasted hazelnuts, almonds or walnuts (optional)	2 oz chopped, toasted hazelnuts, almonds or walnuts (optional)

gas 4, 180°C, 350°F/1 hour

Cream the butter and sugars until light and fluffy. Add the eggs one at a time, then beat in the sour cream. Sift the flour, salt, baking powder and soda thoroughly, then beat them into the mixture. Mix the filling ingredients together. Have ready buttered a deep round gugelhopf or savarin mould. Spread a third of the cake mixture in the bottom and scatter part of the filling all over; spread over the cake remainder and sprinkle with the last of the filling. Bake in the preheated oven.

Potato and Carrot Cakes

Today it seems strange that carrot should be considered as a cake ingredient, but in past centuries root vegetables were almost as common as fruit in sweet dishes. Turnips, carrots, parsnips and later potatoes; marrow, spinach, sorrel and even lentils were used. Most were already familiar to the Greeks and Romans, to whom a sweet, sour spicy taste was not unusual. But by the fifteenth century root vegetables were generally considered as food of the poor, though Martino, the celebrated Italian cook, gave a recipe for what was obviously a dessert — a sweet turnip cake in Platina's *De honesta voluptate*. Here the thin slices of cooked vegetable were layered with a Bel Paese type cheese and flavoured with butter, sugar and sweet spices.

The introduction of the potato is much more recent, with its origin in South America. In Europe its first mention was in the *Cronica de Peru* of Pedro Creca (1553): Gerard refers to it in 1596 in his *Catalogus* and illustrates it a year later in his *Herball*. Austria, Germany, Switzerland and France apparently knew nothing of the potato until the early seventeenth century, although Rumpolt in *Ein new Kochbuch* (1581) gave a single recipe for *Erdepfel* (earth-apples) – 'Peel and cut fine/boil in water/and dry out well through a hair cloth/chop small/and roast in bacon/which is cut small/add a little milk/and let it simmer/so will it be good and taste well.' This seems very early for the potato in Germany, and may of course have been the sweet potato which Sir John Hawkins had introduced to Europe in 1565.

Root vegetables and potatoes in particular were quite common in England a century later. Richard Bradley in *The Country Housewife and Lady's Director* (1736) shows his enthusiasm: 'The potatoe . . . is a very useful root, being either boil'd or roasted in hot embers; and after it is boiled, to be broiled or after boiling it tender, and beaten in a Mortar, it is used to thicken Sauces and for making of rich Puddings, as I am inform'd by a skilful Person in this way . . .' Candied orange and lemon peels, orange and rose-flower waters, spices, sugar, herbs, eggs, hard-boiled egg yolks, and cream were ingredients common to potato pudding, red-beetroot cakes, sorrel tart, biscuits of potatoes and parsnip cakes, though here 'the sweetness of the Parsnip Powder answers the want of sugar'. Ousting the parsnip from popularity, the potato soon played a major role in the kitchen; and by the late 1800s other virtues were being appreciated, as the eminent American physician William Salmon pointed out: it stopped fluxes of the bowels, was full of nutrients and cured consumption; it also increased seed and provoked lust, causing fruitfulness in both sexes!

Potato was generally boiled and mashed when used in dessert dishes, but early in the nineteenth century a method for making potato flour was mentioned by Carême: 'Wash and scrub 15 pounds of floury potatoes [which gives 2 lb flour]. Grate them into a large bowl of water and then change the water. After about 3 hours in which time the earthy taste of the potato is removed, wash twice more: Spread out on a silk sieve and set in an oven to dry out. In time you will get a very white flour with a good flavour. Sift before use.' He also commented with some surprise that 'one day when I was in a hurry, I carried this out swiftly and dried the potato off and used it thus . . . This recipe may be of great use to voyagers and those who live in the country or are unable to obtain it.' Potato flour offered another benefit to the baker, for apart from the delicate and distinctive flavour of the root, its moisture-absorbing properties were valuable, and particularly in nut, fruit and carrot cakes. By the end of the nineteenth century potato flour was widely in use.

Carrots also, as dessert, were especially popular in the late nineteenth century. Mrs Beeton had two favourites: carrot jam, made with sugar,

Virginian Potatoes from Gerard's Herball

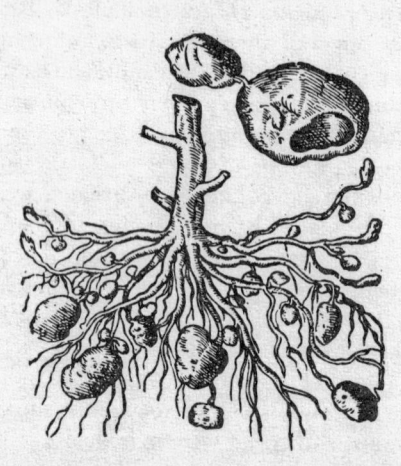

lemon, butter, beetroot and brandy; and carrot pudding with breadcrumbs, butter, cinnamon and glacé cherries. There was compôte; carrots crystallized whole for use as cake decoration, or grated raw in a crème pâtissière type of filling on a yeast pastry base. Most successful, though, was the combination with ground almonds and eggs which probably originated in Italy.

While potato flour cakes have stayed with us throughout this century, carrot cakes have only become popular again in England as a result of the recent interest in health foods; in America, however, they have been a national favourite for considerably longer.

Potato flour is used in many recipes throughout this book, but in the following the fine, mousse-like structure and delicate but distinctive flavour of the flour is particularly noticeable. Those cakes using cooked potato have a less pronounced taste, but an exceptionally moist, rather heavier texture; they are also quite economical. While floury potatoes naturally give the best results, I have found that even moist ones work well. But do avoid those which have a very gluey texture.

Boil potatoes in their skins, pour away the water when they are just cooked, and close cover with a clean folded tea-towel and the lid for a few minutes. Peel while still warm. Leave to cool. Grate when cold.

Potato and carrot cakes keep fresh for at least a week when wrapped in foil or stored in an airtight box.

Potato Cakes

Potato Flour Sponge

The Jewish Passover — *Pesach* — falls about the same time as Easter, and celebrates the Exodus of the Jews from Egypt in Pharoah's time. In their haste they were unable to let the bread rise. The Festival of Deliverance lasts for eight days, during which time it is customary to eat cakes made with nuts or potato flour, and any baking containing raising agents such as wheat flour breads, yeasts and baking sodas is forbidden. Matzoh, the traditional wafer of the festival, is the closest in character to the one that the fleeing Jews baked. It is made with wheat flour, but special care is taken not to let the freshly reaped grains come into contact with water until the very last moment, when the mixture of flour and water is immediately baked for at most 18 minutes before leavening activity begins. Potato flour cakes are a much tastier alternative.

CAKES

Unless you have unflagging energy, this really is a job for the electric mixer. This late nineteenth-century Austrian recipe calls for one hour's hand-mixing, while with the machine it takes only about 15 minutes. It also uses a gugelhopf mould, but I find the cake holds its shape and is less likely to collapse in a wide square tin. It is a very delicate, simple, inexpensive and delicious cake.

100 g potato flour	3½ oz potato flour
6 egg yolks	6 egg yolks
210 g caster sugar	7½ oz caster sugar
zest and juice of 1 lemon	zest and juice of 1 lemon
6 egg whites	6 egg whites

gas 2, 150°C, 300°F / 1 hour 10 minutes

Grease a 21 cm (8½ inch) square cake tin very carefully with melted butter and dust thoroughly with potato flour. Sift the flour three or four times to aerate really well. Whip up the egg yolks and caster sugar for about 5 minutes until the mixture is very pale, thick and creamy, and has trebled in bulk. Add the lemon zest and juice and continue beating for a further 10 minutes or so; at first the mixture will be thin but it then thickens again and expands still further. In a separate bowl, beat the egg whites until they stand in soft, firm peaks, and then, using a large metal spoon, fold them into the other main ingredients without losing any air. Sieve the sifted potato flour on to the mixture in three or four stages and gently fold it through. Pour into the tin, rap it sharply on the work-top to disperse any air pockets, and set it in the heated oven. Remove from the oven when it starts to shrink away from the sides of the tin and has coloured slightly. Place on a cooling rack but leave moulded for 5 minutes or so; then turn on to a sheet of greaseproof paper dusted with caster sugar, and back over again on to the rack with the sugared side up. The cake drops a little, but the texture remains very light and mousse-like though not moist.

* For a *chocolate version* beat 1 teaspoon cocoa powder and 60 g (2 oz) dark, grated chocolate into the egg and sugar mixture before folding in the whites and flour, but leave out the lemon and add the grains of half a vanilla pod.

POTATO AND CARROT CAKES

Zephyrs

These are very short and melt in the mouth.

80 g butter	3 oz butter
1 egg yolk	1 egg yolk
80 g caster sugar	3 oz caster sugar
125 g potato flour	4 oz potato flour
40 g plain flour	1½ oz plain flour
1 teaspoon baking powder	1 teaspoon baking powder
1 egg white	1 egg white
2 tablespoons rum	2 tablespoons rum

gas 4, 180°C, 350°F/20 minutes

Beat the butter until creamy, add the egg yolk and the sugar and whip together until fluffy. Sift the two flours and the baking powder together, then beat into the mixture carefully and not too vigorously. In a separate bowl, whip up the egg white to form snowy peaks, and fold into the mixture along with the rum. Leave in the refrigerator for an hour to chill; then using two teaspoons place walnut-sized mounds of the mixture well apart on a flat buttered baking sheet. You can also add a few broken nuts to the paste. Makes about 30 pieces.

'Ertoffeltorte'

Potatoes were used only on very special festive occasions in eighteenth-century Austria, for they were still an expensive delicacy. A lb of potatoes then cost 360 *Kreuzer*, which was 6 *Gulden*; a lb of shrivelled, dry potatoes 4½ *Gulden* — an exorbitant price when you consider that a highly skilled cabinet-maker earned only 24 *Kreuzer* a day. Even sugar, at 34 *Kreuzer* a lb, seemed relatively cheap. A cake of the time which used 3 lb of potatoes, 24 eggs and 2 lb of sugar must have been for a very special celebration.

CAKES

Here is a less extravagant modern interpretation, and if you can find floury potatoes for this, so much the better.

90 g butter	3 oz butter
90 g caster sugar	3 oz caster sugar
6 egg yolks	6 egg yolks
140 g cold, cooked potato, grated	5 oz cold, cooked potato, grated
1 tablespoon rum	1 tablespoon rum
zest 1 lemon	zest 1 lemon
1 teaspoon cinnamon	1 teaspoon cinnamon
6 egg whites	6 egg whites
2 tablespoons potato flour	2 tablespoons potato flour

gas 3, 170°C, 325°F/45 minutes

Beat the butter until creamy, then beat in the sugar until pale and fluffy. Add the yolks one at a time, and then the grated potato. Add the rum, lemon zest and cinnamon, and beat very well for at least 15 minutes with an electric mixer. Whip up the egg whites into stiff but snowy peaks, and fold them lightly into the mixture along with the sifted potato flour. Turn into a greased and breadcrumbed 24 cm (9½ inch) spring-form tin, and bake. Leave to cool in the tin on a cake rack for 15 minutes before turning out. Like all fresh potato cakes, this is inclined to drop. When cold, dredge with icing sugar to serve.

POTATO AND CARROT CAKES
Rosa's American Potato Cake

This recipe from Mrs S.R. Dull's *Southern Cooking* (1928 and 1941) uses mashed 'Irish' potatoes. Oddly enough, North America knew nothing of the potato until about 1700, almost a century later than Europe. It was grown first in Londonderry, New Hampshire, in 1719 from roots carried from Ireland. The name persisted, particularly in the south where it was used to distinguish it from the sweet variety.

80 g raisins	3 oz raisins
40 g chopped raw almonds	1 1/2 oz chopped raw almonds
130 g plain flour	4 1/2 oz plain flour
1/2 teaspoon cinnamon	1/2 teaspoon cinnamon
1/2 teaspoon nutmeg	1/2 teaspoon nutmeg
1/2 teaspoon cloves	1/2 teaspoon cloves
40 g cocoa powder	1 1/2 oz cocoa powder
1 teaspoon baking powder	1 teaspoon baking powder
170 g caster sugar	6 oz caster sugar
1 tablespoon vanilla sugar	1 tablespoon vanilla sugar
200 g butter	7 oz butter
90 g warm, mashed potato	3 oz warm, mashed potato
2 small eggs	2 small eggs
60 ml milk	2 fl oz milk
zest 1/2 lemon	zest 1/2 lemon

gas 4, 180°C, 350°F/approx. 1 hour

Dust the raisins and nuts with a tablespoon of flour. Divide the rest of the flour into two equal parts, and sift one together with the spices and cocoa, and the other with the baking powder. Set aside. Cream the sugars and the butter until light and fluffy, then beat in the mashed potato and the egg yolks. Mix in the spiced flour and blend well. Then stir in the milk and add the rest of the flour. Just mix to combine, no more. Stir in the nuts, raisins and lemon zest. Beat up the 2 egg whites to form stiff, snowy peaks, and then, using a large metal spoon, fold lightly into the mixture. Grease and flour a 1 kg (2 lb) square tin or a large gugelhopf mould, and pour in the cake batter. Bake in the preheated oven.

CAKES

Carrot Cakes

Austrian Carrot Cake

The taste and texture of this cake improves considerably if it is kept for 2 or 3 days before being cut.

5 egg yolks	5 egg yolks
250 g caster sugar	8 oz caster sugar
250 g raw, finely grated and strained carrots	8 oz raw, finely grated and strained carrots
250 g raw, coarse ground almonds	8 oz raw, coarse ground almonds
2 tablespoons rum	2 tablespoons rum
zest 1 lemon	zest 1 lemon
50 g potato flour	2 oz potato flour
1 teaspoon baking powder	1 teaspoon baking powder
1 teaspoon cinnamon	1 teaspoon cinnamon
pinch cloves	pinch cloves
5 egg whites	5 egg whites
pine kernels for decoration (optional)	pine kernels for decoration (optional)

gas 4, 180°C, 350°F/50 minutes

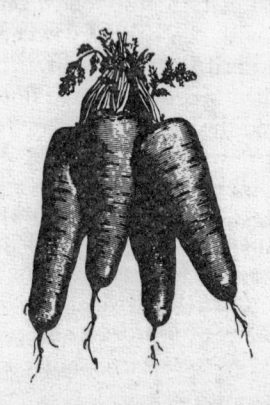

Beat the egg yolks and sugar until pale and creamy. Mix in the carrots, almonds, rum and lemon zest. Sift the flour well with the baking powder and spices, and combine lightly with the mixture. Whip up the egg whites to form stiff, snowy peaks, and fold into the carrot mixture taking care not to overbeat or lose any air. Pour into a 26 cm (10½ inch) spring-form mould which has been greased and dusted with a flour and sugar mixture, and sprinkle over the pine kernels, if using. Bake, then leave to cool in the tin for 10 minutes before turning out on to a rack. Dredge with icing sugar to serve; or cover with plain glacé icing (page 72) instead of using pine kernels.

Portuguese Carrot Roll

This cake has the moist texture of a carrot pudding. For a drier version the carrots can be grated raw.

2 egg yolks	2 egg yolks
250 g caster sugar	8 oz caster sugar
500 g raw carrots, cooked, mashed and drained, to make 250 g boiled carrots *or* 250 g raw, grated carrots	generous 1 lb raw carrots, cooked, mashed and drained, to make 8 oz boiled carrots *or* 8 oz raw, grated carrots
zest 1 orange	zest 1 orange
2 egg whites	2 egg whites
50 g plain flour	2 oz plain flour
1 teaspoon baking powder	1 teaspoon baking powder
1 teaspoon cinnamon	1 teaspoon cinnamon

gas 8, 230°C, 450°F/10 minutes

Mix the egg yolks with the sugar, carrot and orange zest. Beat the egg whites to make firm peaks. Sift the flour thoroughly with the baking powder and cinnamon. Carefully fold the egg white and flour into the mixture in alternate spoonfuls, until all is well blended. Have ready greased and dusted with a sugar/flour mixture a Swiss roll tin 34 × 23 cm (13½ × 9 inch); pour in the batter, spread lightly over the tin and bake in the preheated oven. When the cake starts to shrink very slightly from the edges of the tin and feels softly springy to the touch, remove from the oven and turn over immediately on to a cloth or a sheet of greaseproof paper strewn with caster sugar; ease a spatula round the edges if necessary. Roll up very carefully on to itself, as it needs no filling. It can be covered with a plain white glacé icing when cold, or served with Cointreau-flavoured whipped cream. If raw grated carrots have been used, strained apricot jam or a whipped cream filling add richness.

American Carrot Loaf

Some time ago I attended a children's birthday party held in a California park. The picnic was laid out on tables conveniently situated by the swings and roundabouts, with pride of place given to the birthday cake. The huge square cake was lavishly spread and piped with a thick covering of sweet, buttery cream cheese, and inside the delicious blend of walnuts, orange zest and brown sugar was coloured a rich brown, speckled with orange. This splendid carrot cake, despite its nutty sophistication, was enthusiastically devoured by the young guests.

250 g plain flour	9 oz plain flour
2 teaspoons baking powder	2 teaspoons baking powder
1 teaspoon bicarbonate of soda	1 teaspoon bicarbonate of soda
1/2 teaspoon salt	1/2 teaspoon salt
1 teaspoon cinnamon	1 teaspoon cinnamon
220 g raw carrots	8 oz raw carrots
100 g chopped walnuts	3 1/2 oz chopped walnuts
220 g soft, brown sugar	8 oz soft, brown sugar
3 whole eggs	3 whole eggs
zest 1 orange	zest 1 orange
100 g melted butter	3 1/2 oz melted butter
icing sugar	icing sugar

gas 4, 180°C, 350°F/1 hour

Sift together the flour, baking powder, bicarbonate of soda, salt and cinnamon two or three times; set aside. Grate the peeled carrots finely and drain away any excess liquid. Combine with the walnuts and sugar in a bowl, then beat in the eggs one at a time. Add the orange zest, and the cooled melted butter. The mixture will be very liquid at this stage. Gently add spoonfuls of the flour until all is well combined. Pour into a greased and floured guttered loaf tin or a 21 cm (8 1/2 inch) square tin, and bake in the preheated oven. Turn on to a rack to cool. Dredge with icing sugar to serve, or cover with a cream cheese and butter cream made as follows:

Beat 20 g (1 oz) of unsalted butter until pale and soft, then beat in 140 g (5 oz) of sieved cream cheese and 150 g (5 oz) of sifted icing sugar. Flavour with a scraping of vanilla pod.

Tarts and Pies

To make an Amblongus Pie

Take four pounds (say 4½ pounds) of fresh Amblongusses, and put them in a small pipkin.

Cover them with water and boil them for 8 hours incessantly, after which add 2 pints of new milk, and proceed to boil for 4 hours more.

When you have ascertained that the Amblongusses are quite soft, take them out and place them in a wide pan, taking care to shake them well previously.

Grate some nutmeg over the surface, and cover them carefully with powdered gingerbread, curry powder, and a sufficient quantity of cayenne pepper.

Remove the pan into the next room, and place it on the floor. Bring it back again and let it simmer for three-quarters of an hour. Shake the pan violently until all the Amblongusses have become a pale purple colour.

Then, having prepared the paste, insert the whole carefully, adding at the same time a small pigeon, 2 slices of beef, 4 cauliflowers, and any number of oysters.

Watch patiently till the crust begins to rise, and add a pinch of salt from time to time.

Serve up in a clean dish, and throw the whole out of the window as fast as possible.

(Edward Lear, 1812–88)

Tarts and Pies in History

There is probably no early cookery documentation as explicit of both cooking and culture as the writings of Muhammed al-Baghdadi, who died in 1239. His descriptions of dishes and their preparation are as comprehensive as any today, and the following sweetmeat – which must surely class as a tart – is typical of many others cited by him.

Judhab al-Rutab – Take a tinned copper dish, and spray with a little rose-water. Spread a thin cake therein, and cover with

CAKES

newly-gathered *khastaua* dates. Sprinkle with fine-ground pistachios and almonds, and toasted poppy, to form a layer. Add another layer of dates, and so continue until the dish is half-filled, making the top layer of almonds and pistachios. Pour on half a *ratl* of syrup and an *uqiya* of rose-water which has been coloured with half a *dirham* of saffron: cover with a thin cake. Hang over it a fat chicken stuffed with sugar, almonds and pistachios kneaded with scented rose-water, and smeared with saffron inside and out. When thoroughly cooked, remove.

The method of suspending the chicken over *judhab* is as follows. Hang it up in the oven, and watch: then, when the fat is about to run, place the *judhab* under it.

(1 ratl = 12 uqiya = 16 ounces = 1 pint. 1 uqiya = 10 dirham)

All the ingredients were quite common in Arab cuisine, but what the 'thin cake' consisted of is unclear; it was probably flour and water, which the fatty, dripping juices of the stuffed chicken moistened and flavoured during cooking, in much the same way as butter does fila. Whether the

Pastry Cooks at work — Bosse

roasted chicken was served together with the sweet tart is a matter for conjecture, though it was certainly an oriental custom to serve sweet and savoury dishes together.

The earliest form of pastry was made with flour, oil and honey, not unlike fila or strudel, and was invariably used as a foundation or wrapping for a savoury filling. Gradually, as it was influenced by the gastronomic Romans, improvements in the flavour were made with the use of eggs, butter and salt, and soon these dish pies enclosed cooked meat seasoned with bacon and spices and eventually cream and fruit.

In the Middle Ages tarts and pies were invariably served at festivities, on saints' days and birthdays, at weddings, christenings and funerals, as indeed were most cakes. And as Alexis Soyer pointed out: '. . . so early as the thirteenth century the flans of Chartres, the patties of Paris, and the tarts of Dourlans, were in great reknown . . .' The patties of Paris were hawked through the streets and were extremely popular, so much so that the Chancelier de L'Hôpital, whose duty it was to suppress luxuries, prohibited the crying of them (as a temptation to gluttony) but not their sale. In England also a street crier in 1393 peddled 'Kokes and here knaues crieden hote pyes hote.' In the Middle East, pastries were only ever served for festivals, never at meal times, though occasionally an exception was made for an honoured guest, and then a pastry was offered with a cup of coffee as a hospitality ritual.

Tart and Pie Fillings

Over the centuries some rather bizarre fillings have been used. A medieval 'fysshe tarte', mentioned by Dorothy Hartley in *Food in England*, very much resembles the thirteenth-century *Judhab*. Here the pork-pie type crust or coffer of paste was filled with layers, first a black mixture of figs, raisins, prunes and ginger, then a layer of white fish with currants in it, and another of the fig and prune mixture dotted with white, blanched almonds. The whole was gilded with gold leaf, and a fish-tail stuck out of the top.

Jerusalem artichokes were recommended in the seventeenth century by Charles Rose, a master cook to Charles II. He sieved the boiled vegetables and mixed them with butter, egg yolks, sugar, salt, cinnamon and green citron peel. There was mint with sugar, dried fruits, candied peels and spices. Borage flowers, marigolds and cowslips mixed with egg yolks and sweet curds were popular in the sixteenth century; and while Florence White in *Good Food in England* (1932) suggested that any other flowers might be cooked in a similar way, she admonished the reader 'before using any part of a plant for food to study Mrs Grieve's and Mrs Leyel's Modern Herbal'. In nineteenth-century France, Carême also followed the Oriental tradition of mixing savoury with sweet — a strange combination of spinach, crème pâtissière, amaretti, sugar, salt and hazelnuts.

> *Tourte de Crème aux Epinards et Pralinée* — Pick, wash, and blanch two large handsful of freshly gathered spinach, chop it very fine, put it in a stewpan with 75 g fresh butter over a moderate fire, stirring it continually until it dries, add 4 spoonfuls of crème pâtissière, 1^1/$_2$ dl double cream, 75 g pounded sugar, 50 g butter macaroons pounded, a pinch of orange flowers (candied) and a grain of salt; mix the whole and put it in a tourte (open flan), mask the top with 50 g of filbert kernels, chopped and mixed with 50 g sugar and a little white of egg. Bake in a hot oven.

It seems to be the Americans who, more than anyone else in recent times, have taken to tarts and pies in a big way. Evan Jones has called them 'pie fanatics', and has even suggested that 'a meal without pie may be no meal at all'. Apart from the vast range of familiar fruit pies, and the less familiar such as lime, huckleberry, green currant and pumpkin, there are some with unusual names. Shoofly or Gravel pie is made with molasses and topped with a Streussel mixture — a speciality of the Pennsylvania Dutch (who are reputed also to have invented the fruit pies of America). Jefferson Davis is a sponge-like mixture laden with dried fruits and nuts and topped with meringue; Funeral Pie is a lemon-flavoured raisin concoction which is baked when people die. In addition the best recipes of the various ethnic backgrounds have been assimilated; Linzertorte from Austria, Frangipane from France, Banbury from England and countless others.

> Katy produced the second basket, and there, oh, delightful surprise! were seven little pies — molasses pies, baked in saucers — each with a brown top and crisp candified edge, which tasted like toffee and lemon-peel, and all sorts of good things mixed up together.
>
> There was a general shout. Even demure Cecy was pleased, and Dony and John kicked their heels on the ground in a tumult of joy. Seven pairs of hands were held out at once to the basket; seven sets of teeth went to work without a moment's delay. In an incredibly short time every vestige of pie had disappeared, and a blissful stickiness pervaded the party.
>
> (Susan Coolidge, *What Katy Did*)

Some Hints on Preparing Double Crust Tarts and Pies

Use a flat oven-ware or enamel pie plate, or a fireproof dish. Metal containers conduct the heat better than glass or porcelain. Grease lightly with butter or oil. For a 20 cm (8 inch) pie-plate use the basic pastry quantity (3) (page 44) and about 750 g (1 lb 6 oz) fruit.

Divide the pastry into two pieces, one slightly smaller than the other. Knead the smaller into a round ball and roll out into a circle a little larger than the plate. Roll the second half into a circle for the cover; leave the pastry to rest for a few minutes and prepare the filling. (Meanwhile the pastry has time to relax and lose some of its elasticity.) Fold the pastry over the rolling pin and gently lift on to the greased plate, taking care not to stretch it. Smooth away any air bubbles from the centre to the edge. Cut off the surplus dough from around the edges with a sharp knife. There are several ways in which fruit juices can be prevented from soaking the pie-crust base (see pages 208, 221).

Prepare the fruits: peel, core and chop or slice hard fruit; pit stone fruits and dry thoroughly. Remember to slice apples and pears thickly so that the good flavour and texture is not lost in cooking. Heap the fruit into the pastry and dot with a few small pieces of butter. Sprinkle sugar and spices between the layers only – never underneath the fruit or on top, as the crusts will become soggy. Smooth the fruit into a flat dome. Dampen the pastry edges with cold water.

Lift on the pastry cover without stretching it, and firmly press together the two edges. Trim, crimp and flute them. Decorate the top with small cuttings of left-over paste, using cold water to stick them. Make a hole in the centre, or cut slits to allow the steam from the cooking fruit to escape. Brush the crust with beaten egg-white or a little milk, and dredge with caster sugar.

Place the plate on a tray which has been preheated along with the oven – the tray helps cook the bottom crust completely. Bake shortcrust and sweet shortcrust pastries for $^3/_4$–1 hour. After 15 minutes reduce the heat from gas 6, 200°C, 400°F to gas 4, 180°C, 350°F.

Fruit Flans

A flan is a free-standing open-faced tart made with pastry, not sponge as is often found today. A flan may be baked together with the raw fruits, so that their flavours and those of the paste blend, but sometimes flan cases are baked blind (empty), then either lined with cooked fruits and

CAKES

covered with a thickened syrup, or filled with fresh soft fruits, glazed and piped with cream.

Use either a flan ring laid on to a baking sheet or a flan tin with fluted sides and a loose base. You can also make the flan without sides, in which case roll the pastry 1 cm (³/₈ inch) thick and cut into a circle; this is only suitable baked blind.

Generally a short or sweet crust paste is used, but sweet almond is also good.

The base of the flan case, whether cooked or raw, *must always be protected from moist fillings*. The base may be brushed with lightly beaten egg white; or with strained apricot jam (page 71) or redcurrant jelly; or scattered with breadcrumbs, chopped nuts, or toasted flaked almonds. In addition a lining of crème pâtissière or crème frangipane (pages 59, 61) gives an elegant touch.

Lining a Flan Case with Pastry and Baking Blind

A fluted metal flan case with a removable base gives the best results, for metal conducts the heat well and the loose bottom facilitates unmoulding. A flan case with a fixed base must be greased very thoroughly, and while a china flan dish may look attractive, pastry does not cook particularly well in it and is very difficult to unmould successfully. *Baking blind* means baking a pastry shell without a filling.

Prepare the pastry in the usual way; wrap it up in foil or plastic film and leave in the refrigerator for at least an hour to rest and harden. Lightly grease the utensil with melted butter.

Roll out the pastry 0.5 cm (¹/₄ inch) thick and 2 cm (³/₄ inch) wider than the flan ring. Leave to rest for a few minutes for it to shrink back and lose some of the elasticity.

Roll the dough round the rolling pin to lift it over the prepared ring, and press it into the ring without stretching. Short pastry is inclined to break – this is not serious, for it can be patched. Smooth the pastry gently over the bottom and up the sides so that no air-bubbles are trapped underneath, and make sure that the inner bottom edges are only the same thickness as the sides and the bottom. Trim the edges neatly.

Prick the pastry lightly with a fork all over. This releases any air and prevents the pastry from rising – the holes seal up during baking. Cover the surface with a sheet of greaseproof paper and weigh it down with rice, dried haricot beans or clean pebbles.

Bake on a hot baking sheet to give a good crispy base to the flan.

TARTS AND PIES

When cooked, remove the paper and weights (they can be used time and time again). Brush the base lightly with beaten white of egg, which will prevent the fruit juices from saturating it, and return it to the oven for another 5 minutes to dry out the bottom.

A *fully baked flan case* is baked blind on a reducing temperature for about 30 minutes. Start at gas 6, 200°C, 400°F, and reduce this after 10 minutes or when the pastry starts to set to gas 4, 180°C, 350°F.

See *Vol au Vent* page 230 for details of handling *Puff Pastries*.

For filled flans follow the specific recipe instructions.

A *par-baked flan case:* Sometimes it is necessary to par-bake the pastry base before it is filled. Prepare with greaseproof paper and weights as above, then bake in a preheated oven gas 6, 200°C, 400°F, for 10–15 minutes until the pastry has set and has coloured very slightly.

How to Line a Deep Flan Case with Pastry

Sometimes a deep flan case is needed for cheesecakes or two layered fillings such as the Quince Torte (page 254). The deeper spring-form tin is the most suitable for these, as the side can be removed without disturbing the pastry. Usually the cake is left to cool in the tin. The process is in two stages: first only the pastry base is par-baked, then the deep tin sides are lined with raw dough, the filling is poured in and the flan is baked. Sweet shortcrust pastry, with or without almonds, is used – you need a larger amount of pastry than usual.

For a 22–24 cm (8$^1/_2$–9$^1/_2$ inch) cake tin use quantity (2), page 44.

Divide the pastry into two equal parts, and roll out one half on the greased base of the tin to about 3–6 mm ($^1/_8$–$^1/_4$ inch) thick. Prick with a fork at regular intervals; cover with a sheet of greaseproof paper or aluminium foil, and weigh down with beans or pebbles. The sprung side is left off.

Bake in the preheated oven, gas 6, 200°C, 400°F, for 10–15 minutes. The pastry should be set and very slightly coloured. Lift out of the oven and remove the lining paper and weights.

Roll the rest of the pastry to the same thickness as the base, and cut two equal strips – the same depth as the tin and half the circumference. Lightly brush the sides of the tin with melted butter, then clip it on to the pastry-covered base. Gently ease a pastry strip into place around half of the rim and press it carefully into the pastry base to seal it. Line the rest of the tin with the second strip. Trim the edges. It is now ready to receive the filling.

Tartlet Cases

A small tart is made in much the same way as a large one, but the baking time is shortened by about half – that is 20–25 minutes at the same temperature for a filled case and 7–10 minutes for an empty shell.

Tartlet tins can be bought individually or moulded in sheets of a dozen.

Blind tartlet cases: Prepare the basic pastry as usual. Roll it out to 3 mm (¼ inch) in thickness, and cut circles using a sharp metal cutter a size larger than the tartlet tins. Turn the tins over on to the reverse side, grease very lightly with butter, then press the paste firmly down on to the tops of the moulds. Prick them all over. Bake the pastries until they are golden. Remove from the oven, turn them over immediately while they are still hot, and drop them back into the tins ready to receive the filling. Leave to cool.

Filled tartlet cases: Prepare the basic pastry, roll and cut into circles as above. Press the pastry into the greased tin moulds and fill as for the larger cases. Bake as instructed.

Glazing Fruit Flans

Glazing tinned or preserved fruits for a 26 cm (10½ inch) flan.
250 ml (9 fl oz) strained fruit syrup (from the tin); 3 level teaspoons arrowroot; sugar and lemon juice to taste.

Blend 6 tablespoons of the cold fruit syrup with the arrowroot. Bring the remaining syrup to the boil and stir in the thickening. Taste, add lemon juice and sugar as needed, and stir until the glaze becomes very clear; it will have a thick consistency as it cools down. After about a minute of cooling, glaze the fruits, basting from the outside to the centre. Should the glaze start to thicken too much before it is all used, re-heat it. Prick air bubbles and leave to set and cool. This takes 10–15 minutes.

Glazing raw fruits for a 26 cm (10½ inch) flan. For strawberries, raspberries, loganberries, red-currants.

Take 6–8 small, damaged or misshapen fruits; cut them up and cook in 250 ml (9 fl oz) water with 100 g (3½ oz) sugar to the thread stage (page 70). Strain and use with 3 level teaspoons of arrowroot as above. Adjust the flavour with lemon juice.

Apricot glaze is also sometimes used (page 71).

TARTS AND PIES
Pecan Pie

Pecan nuts are less familiar in Europe but quite common in the United States — they apparently first grew wild in the South, and then were improved by a 'black gardener named Antoine who grafted 16 trees on a plantation in Louisiana sugar country to produce the best pecans the South had known'. To me the nut itself resembles most closely a neat and tidy walnut (though the shell is quite different and it is less oily and has quite a different flavour); mixed with molasses or corn syrup, eggs and butter for a filling, it makes a quite irresistible pie. Recipes vary, and I prefer this one from Evan Jones's *American Food: The Gastronomic Story* which both lays nuts on the surface and combines them chopped with the mixture. He suggests that the mystery flavour is a sip of Kentucky bourbon — failing that, rum can be substituted.

For a very moist, sweet and treacly pie, use molasses and dark muscovado sugar. Golden or corn syrup and light brown sugar will give a less rich taste and the pecan flavour will be more outstanding.

shortcrust pastry for 22 cm tin (page 44)	shortcrust pastry for 8½ inch tin (page 44)
150 g pecans, coarsely chopped	5 oz pecans, coarsely chopped
1 tablespoon flour	1 tablespoon flour
75 g butter	3 oz butter
110 g dark or light muscovado sugar	4 oz dark or light muscovado sugar
3 eggs	3 eggs
pinch salt	pinch salt
250 ml corn syrup, treacle or molasses	9 fl oz corn syrup, treacle or molasses
1 tablespoon Kentucky bourbon	1 tablespoon Kentucky bourbon
20 pecan halves	20 pecan halves

gas 6, 200°C, 400°F for 20 minutes then
gas 4, 180°C, 350°F for 40–45 minutes

Make the pastry with quantity (1) to line a 22 cm (8 inch) pie plate; roll out the dough and line the plate. Prick with a fork. Roll the remnants into a long strip 2 cm (¾ inch) wide; moisten the edge of the pastry on the plate sides and set the pastry strip on to it. Press firmly to make sure that it has sealed, and cut slightly with a knife to make a pattern all round. Weigh down the pastry with greaseproof paper and beans and bake blind. Leave to cool while you make the filling, for which you can use a food processor.

Dust the chopped nuts with the flour and set aside. Cream the butter and add the brown sugar slowly, beating constantly until all is absorbed and the mixture is fluffy. Add the eggs one at a time, beating continuously, then add the salt, syrup, and bourbon. Fold in the chopped pecans, and pour the filling into the pastry shell. Bake for 30 minutes, take it out of the oven and decorate the surface with the pecan halves. Replace in the oven and bake until the top is firm and risen. Serve lukewarm or cold, with flavoured whipped cream.

Yorkshire Treacle Tart

In England we usually associate treacle tart with the nursery and with school dinners. It can be rather too sweet, but this version has a little more character. Nuts may replace the crumbs.

125 g white breadcrumbs	4½ oz white breadcrumbs
125 g mixed cake-fruit (sultanas, raisins, currants)	4½ oz mixed cake-fruit (sultanas, raisins, currants)
1 teaspoon ground cinnamon	1 teaspoon ground cinnamon
pinch ground ginger	pinch ground ginger
1 medium cooking apple	1 medium cooking apple
zest and juice 1 lemon	zest and juice 1 lemon
2 tablespoons golden syrup	2 tablespoons golden syrup
sweet shortcrust pastry for 23 cm flan	sweet shortcrust pastry for 9 inch flan

gas 7, 220°C, 425°F/20–30 minutes

Mix the breadcrumbs, fruit and spices together. Peel and grate the apple, and pour the lemon juice over it to prevent it from discolouring. Mix with the dry ingredients; add the lemon zest and finally the syrup. Have the pie-plate ready lined with the pastry, and pour in the filling. Bake in the preheated oven and serve lukewarm or cold, with whipped cream.

TARTS AND PIES

Tartelettes Amandines

Battez pour qu'ils soient mousseux
   Quelques ouefs;
Incorporez à leur mousse
Un jus de cédrat choisi;
   Versez-y
Un bon lait d'amande douce;
Mettez de la pâte à flan
   dans le flanc
De moules à tartelette;
D'un doigt preste abricotez
   Les cotés.
Versez goutte à goutelette
Votre mousse en ces fruits, puis
Que ces fruits
Passent au four et, blondines,
Sortant en gais troupelets
   Ce sont les
Tartelettes amandines!

('Du bon pâtissier Ragueneau',
from Edmond Rostand, *Cyrano de Bergerac*)

In English cake recipes almonds are often eked out or replaced by breadcrumbs, flour or sometimes even essence; in France the tendency is to extravagance. Jane Grigson, in *Food with the Famous*, mentions the almond tart that Sydney Smith ate in Montreuil in France. The Reverend Sydney Smith born in 1771 was a popular preacher. He was especially fond of good food, for which he developed an even greater passion after his trips to France. As a dinner companion he was much sought after, being not only an appreciative guest but also, as the Honourable Mrs Norton said, 'wisest of witty men, and the wittiest of wise men'.

Sydney Smith actually preferred savoury dishes to sweet desserts, but he was rather fond of this tart, made with a large number of almonds and sweet and sour creams.

CAKES

Sydney Smith's Almond Tart

125 g butter	4½ oz butter
175 g caster sugar	6 oz caster sugar
2 whole eggs	2 whole eggs
2 egg yolks	2 egg yolks
75 ml double cream	2½ fl oz double cream
75 ml soured cream	2½ fl oz soured cream
125 g ground almonds	4½ oz ground almonds
125 g blanched almonds, coarsely ground	4½ oz blanched almonds, coarsely ground
1 tablespoon orange-flower water or brandy	1 tablespoon orange-flower water or brandy

gas 6, 200°C, 400°F for 20 minutes, then
gas 4, 180°C, 350°F for 15–20 minutes

Cream the butter and the sugar. Beat in the eggs and yolks, the creams and the almonds. Blend in the flavouring. Line a 24 cm (9½ inch) flan case with sweet shortcrust pastry (page 45). Spread the almond filling over the base. Set in the preheated oven and bake. Sprinkle the warm tart with icing sugar and melt it under the grill, taking care that it does not caramelize. Serve hot or warm with cream; or serve cold.

> Jam tarts, particularly raspberry tarts, are the food which children in Thackeray relish most. It is virtually impossible for him to imagine childhood without them. Tarts were prominent in his own schooldays, as he recalls in *Cruickshank's Gallery*, and the scene in a school playground where an adult visitor, probably military, hands out a sovereign tip which is converted into jam tarts, recurs frequently in his writing. Tarts meant, for him, innocence and vulnerability. Thus Fanny Bolton, out for a treat at Vauxhall with her adored Pen, owns to a 'partiality for raspberry tart', which Pen quickly gratifies, and Dobbin longs for Amelia 'as the poor boy at school who has no money may sigh after the contents of the tart-woman's tray'.
>
> (John Carey, *Thackeray – Prodigal Genius*, 1977)

Decoration of tarts was of great importance to the housewife, and quite early on, particularly in the north of England, a competitive element soon became apparent as each one strove to outdo the next in producing a more elaborate and more attractive design. Dorothy Hartley gives these illustrations (See page 215) in *Food in England*.

TARTS AND PIES

The 'Red Cross' was filled with redcurrant jelly and covered with curd cheese; the 'Star' was called 'Epiphany' when made for the Church social, and one could use as many as twelve different jams if one wanted to show off. The 'Well' was very effective with greengage round blackcurrant, and it was a 'good pattern' if you wanted to use up a small scrape of jam in the middle – it could be done in any colours. The 'Cross' used two or four jams; the 'Lattice' had only one jam, and if over apple, the lattice was wide and 'nailed down' with cloves where it crossed. 'Whorl' and 'Slits' depended on the amount of pastry available. They were rolled and folded in a particular manner.

Francatelli's instructions were more professional.

> Mosaic boards, for tartlets, may be had of all sizes and patterns at any turner's shop. To cut out impressions from these, it is necessary to use small circular flats of raised pie paste, which must be

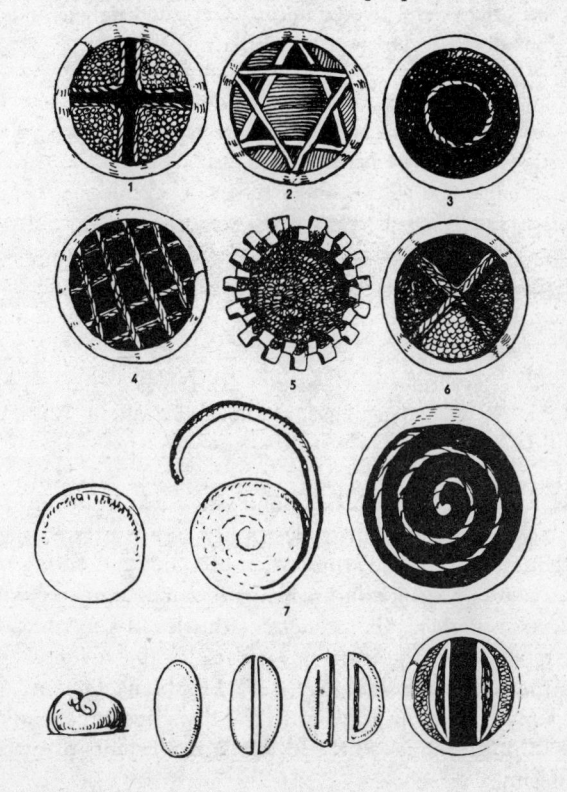

placed on the board, and pressed into the design, by rolling it with a paste-pin; the superfluous paste must then be cut or shaved away, and the mosaic of paste that remains in the design shaken out of the board.

Linzertorte

In Austria and Germany one particular jam tart, Linzertorte, became the most popular cake of all; it was served, and still is, for all festive occasions. Its success can be rated by the proliferation of recipes in old cookery books, and along with the multi-layered Prinzregententorte and Baumkuchen it remains a classic.

Linzertorte is made of almond pastry and has a distinctive latticed top. Almonds and spices were coveted in early German kitchens and almond cake was considered to be the finest offering.

> Wer ein gut muss wil haben
> das mach von sibennlei sachn
> du must haben, milch, salz,
> und schmalz, zugker, ayer,
> und mel saffran. Dar zue so
> wirt es gell. Ain mandel muss machn.

(From Allerley kochen von Maister Hannsen des von Würtenberg Koch, 1460).

> To make a good mousse, there are seven things you must have, milk, salt, and fat, sugar, eggs, and flour with saffron. With that it will be yellow. To make an almond mousse.

In 1581 Rumpolt mentioned almond cakes, but it was in 1719 that Hagger first named Linzertorte specifically and illustrated the lattice surface, though only a vague suggestion of a 'suitable' filling is made. The proportion of almonds in his recipe is small compared with later ones, reflecting perhaps the economic realities of the time. Earliest historical reference in the town of Linz itself came a century later in 1804, in the *Linzer Kochbuch* by Maria Elisabetha Meixner, and no mention is made of its origin; but in the many recipes she gives are a variety of fillings. She uses bottled fruits, redcurrants or grapes, and redcurrant jam.

Here is a modern interpretation.

200 g plain flour	7 oz plain flour
½ teaspoon cinnamon	½ teaspoon cinnamon
pinch cloves	pinch cloves
1 teaspoon cocoa	1 teaspoon cocoa
200 g butter	7 oz butter
200 g raw ground almonds, hazelnuts or walnuts	7 oz raw ground almonds, hazelnuts or walnuts
200 g caster sugar	7 oz caster sugar
1 egg	1 egg
1–2 tablespoons Kirsch	1–2 tablespoons Kirsch
250 g cranberry, raspberry or redcurrant jam	8 oz cranberry, raspberry or redcurrant jam
egg yolk for brushing the top.	egg yolk for brushing the top

gas 6, 200°C, 400°F/30–40 minutes

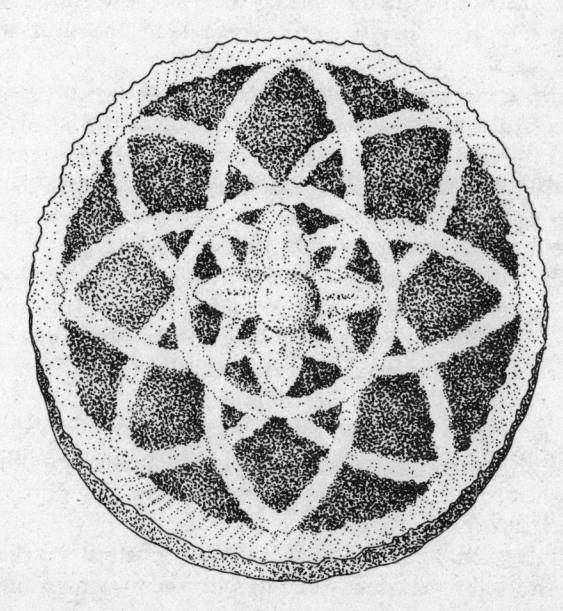

Linzertorte

Sift the flour, spices and cocoa into a large bowl. Add the butter, cut in small pieces, and rub to fine crumbs. Mix in the almonds and sugar and combine to a fine paste with the lightly beaten egg and Kirsch. Roll the pastry into a ball, wrap in foil or plastic film and leave to rest in the refrigerator for an hour.

Divide the pastry into two parts, of a third and two-thirds. Set aside the larger amount for the base of the cake and roll out the rest into a 24 cm (9½ inch) circle; use the cake tin as a template.

Use either a 22 cm (8½ inch) cake tin to cut the first line 2 cm (¾ inch) in from the edge, or judge by eye and cut with a sharp knife – there is no need for it to be too precise. This first band is reserved for finishing off the outside edge of the cake when the lattice pattern has been completed.

Cut each band to the same thickness; see diagram 1. Cut a solid 6 cm (2½ inch) diameter circle from the centre of the paste.

Assembling the cake: Roll out the larger amount of pastry on the base of a 24 cm (9½ inch) spring-form tin, clip the outside ring in place, and push the pastry a little way up the sides. Prick the paste all over with a fork then spread the fruit jam evenly across it. Cut 4 long narrow strips of paper – newsprint will do – and lay them on the work-top as shown in diagram 2. Set the pastry-lined tin in the middle; the papers will act as a guide to centre the flower points.

The lattice: Place the solid disc in the centre of the flan. Then starting with circles 2 and 3, lay the pastry strips on to the jam surface as in diagram 3 – the dotted line first then the solid line. Moisten the ends of the pastry with a little milk so that they bind well with the base. Lay circles 5 and 6 as in diagram 4 for the open daisy pattern, cutting the strips and easing the pastry into place as needed.

Brush all the lattice strips with lightly beaten egg; then set the outer circle 1 on top of all the lattice edges. Gently press into place and tidy up any loose ends if need be. Set circle 7 outside the solid centre circle. Roll out another piece of paste and cut another solid 4 cm (1½ inch) circle to cover the middle. Pinch up the edges to make it attractive and set it in place. Cut a small motif or leaf shapes for the centre as decoration.

Brush all the new lattice work with lightly beaten egg yolk to give a sheen when baked. Bake in the preheated oven. Dot a little more jam into each lattice hole.

The cake should be kept for at least a week before it is cut, and will stay fresh for several weeks. The flavour improves with time.

TARTS AND PIES

Fresh Cranberry Jam for the Filling

200 g fresh cranberries	7 oz fresh cranberries
2 twists of lemon zest	2 twists of lemon zest
125 ml water	4½ fl oz water
110 g granulated sugar	4 oz granulated sugar

Put the fruit, zest and water in a pan, bring slowly to the boil, cover and simmer for no more than 10 minutes. Stir it now and then, and watch that it does not burn. Draw off the heat and stir in the sugar. Leave to cool.

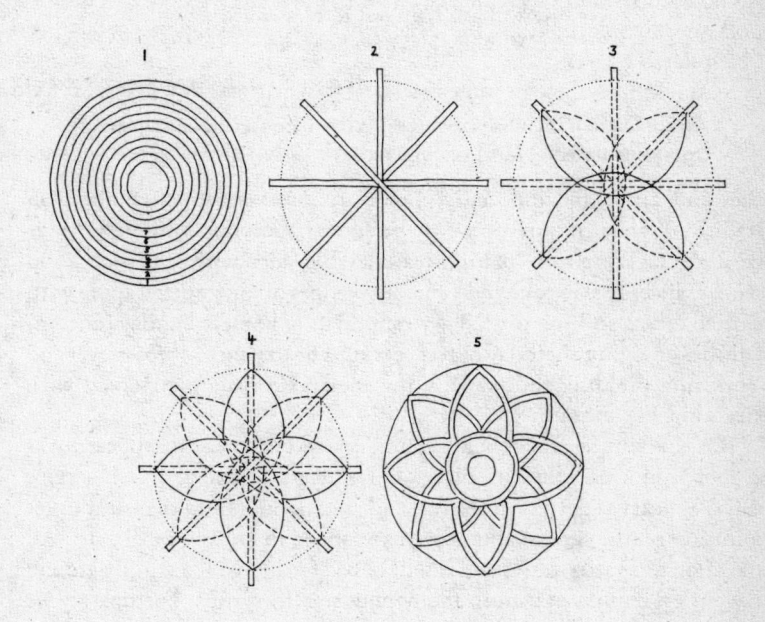

Tarts and Pies with Fresh Fruit

> '. . . when I undress me
> Each night, upon my knees
> Will ask the Lord to bless me
> With apple pie and cheese!
>
> (Eugene Field, *Apple pie and cheese*)

> An apple pie without some cheese, is like a kiss without a squeeze!
> (Saying from the North of England)

Pies and tarts, and especially apple tart, are very much an English tradition. They conjure up a cosy picture of Victorian winter evenings beside a crackling fire – of high-tea at a table laden with sandwiches and scones, slices of slab cake and generous wedges of juicy spiced apple with clotted cream spilling over. They remind us of homely Sunday lunches, families enjoying their day of rest, eating a hearty meal of roast beef and Yorkshire pudding followed by the inevitable fruit pie, served with steaming hot custard.

But this simple and delicious home-made tart is fast disappearing as a poor imitation takes its place. It frequents canteens or self-service cafés, appears as dessert in the fish and chip parlours and the hamburger joints, or on the supermarket shelves wrapped in foil and cardboard. All too often the pastry tastes and smells of bad fat and wraps soggily around flavourless chunks of fruit in anonymous starchy syrups. Fortunately we have no need to tolerate these imitations – a fruit tart is quite simple to make. Good quality fruits and a fine pastry are the basic essentials.

Most fruits are successful in a pie or a tart, but those still considered to be mainly seasonal are particularly welcome. The first arrival is early rhubarb; nothing grand is needed for those pink and red stalks – just a hint of cinnamon, sugar, orange zest and a wrapping of sweet crust. The gooseberry is another 'pie plant' – the small sour fruits appear around Whitsuntide and need a good amount of sugar. The large, sweet dessert varieties come a little later. From then on a parade of berried fruits swiftly follows; raspberries and strawberries (they are best eaten as they are on an open-faced pre-cooked tart); redcurrants and blackcurrants, succulent and juicy. Next come blackberries (and try bilberries or blueberries, those rich, dark purple fruits with a juicy bitter sweetness – spice them with pepper as James Beard does, or with cinnamon, and remember to polish your teeth afterwards!). Then there are peaches and apricots from abroad, plums, and of course apples and pears; they taste delicious with pistachios and almonds. Finally the edible quince, a large aromatic golden-yellow pear-shaped fruit.

For tarts and pies choose well-ripened, well-shaped and strong-coloured fruits – and taste them. The flavour is of the greatest importance; if they have no taste when raw it is unlikely to be better when cooked. Sugar and complementary flavours are also vital, but avoid colourings – one rhubarb recipe actually uses beetroot! Always be generous with fruit, there is nothing worse than a 'mean' pie.

Many recipes call for fruit to be stewed or stewed and pulped before it is used as a filling. For very hard fruits such as quince (page 251) this is essential, but I dislike the method in general, since sieving makes most fruits taste bland, they are inclined to lose colour, and are too reminiscent of the shop varieties.

Bottled and canned fruits may be used, but should be drained and dried very thoroughly or the juices will saturate the pastry.

Here are a few unusual recipes using fruits.

Rhubarb

Rhubarb is not really a fruit at all but a vegetable; and although it was in common use throughout the East (in China, Tibet, Turkey and India) from as far back as the fourteenth century B.C. it was not well known in the West until the eighteenth century. Hannah Glasse says of rhubarb tarts: 'These tarts may be thought very odd, but they are very fine ones and have a pretty flavour; the leaves of rhubarb are a fine thing to eat for a pain in the stomach, the roots for tincture, and the stalks for tarts.'

Gâteau à la Rhubarbe

Prepare almond pastry (1) (page 46) for a 20 cm (8 inch) tin; line a tart plate and prick all over with a fork. Cut 700 g (1½ lb) rhubarb into short lengths and pack tightly in the base. Sprinkle with 2–3 tablespoons of sugar, and bake in a pre-heated oven for about 30 minutes at gas 7, 220°C, 425°F. The pastry must not get too brown. Take out of the oven and sprinkle 2–3 tablespoons of white wine over the rhubarb, together with a further 2 tablespoons of sugar and a few butter flakes. Bake for a further 5–10 minutes.

You may prefer to soften the rhubarb beforehand. In this case soak the fruit in sugar overnight; then boil up the juice separately and drop in the fruit sticks and leave them to soften for a while. Drain them before laying them on to the pastry base.

Gooseberries

In 1822 John Loudon published a weighty *Encyclopaedia of Gardening*. It was full of worthy garden lore as relevant today as it was then. Among the various soft fruits he discussed was the gooseberry (the name a corruption, he suggested, of gorseberry since it resembled a prickly gorse bush), and of these there were more than 300 different varieties. Gooseberry prize meetings were a popular event of the time, and almost every cottage gardener in Lancashire and Cheshire had his gooseberry bushes and aspirations of winning a coveted prize.

Published annually, the *Manchester Gooseberry Book* listed those meetings, and in 1819 no fewer than 136 were recorded. The Top-Sawyer Seedling was the largest berry that year, weighing 26 penny weights (17 g, $^3/_5$ oz). Exhibits included 46 red, 33 yellow, 47 green and 41 white varieties; and 14 newly named seedlings, said to be 'going out' – that is about to be sold to growers.

Choice varieties of seeds were grown in pots of rich light soil for a year, then planted out to be cultivated for a year or two. The strongest young bushes were then given special attention – rich soil, careful watering, pruning and thinning to produce the largest specimen fruits. As well as normal watering, each of the 3 or 4 individual fruits remaining had a saucer of water placed beneath it to 'suckle' it.

Gooseberry and Almond Flan

> Two gooseberry pies being supposed, their paste made at the same time, and indeed of one mass, the gooseberries gathered from the same bushes and of equal age, the sugar in just proportion and clotted cream to eat with both, it follows that the largest is preferable. I love gooseberry pie . . . I think the case is plain.

TARTS AND PIES WITH FRESH FRUITS

So said Robert Southey, the early nineteenth-century poet and man of letters. As for Parson Woodforde, he complained of violent pain from eating gooseberry pie, though it was more likely to have been caused by his earlier excesses.

> I gave them for dinner a dish of Maccarel, 3 young Chicken boiled and some Bacon, a neck of Pork rosted and a Gooseberry Pye hot. We laughed immoderately after dinner . . . What with laughing and eating hot Gooseberry Pye brought on me the Hickupps with a violent pain in my stomach which lasted till I went to bed.

I think that both gentlemen might have found the following flan even more appetizing than the one with which they were familiar.

pâte sucrée (page 45) for a 26 cm tin	pâte sucrée (page 45) for a 10½ inch tin
150 g butter	5 oz butter
380 g caster sugar	13 oz caster sugar
4 egg yolks	4 egg yolks
200 g blanched almonds, ground	7 oz blanched almonds, ground
100 ml white wine	4 fl oz white wine
6 egg whites	6 egg whites
50 g plain flour	2 oz plain flour
500 g gooseberries	1 lb gooseberries

gas 4, 180°, 350°F/1½ hours

Prepare the pastry; roll out 3 mm (⅛ inch) thick and line only the base of the tin; prick all over and bake blind for 20 minutes. Roll the rest of the pastry into a long strip the depth of the tin, and line the sides of the cooled tin.

Beat the butter and half the sugar until pale and creamy. Add the egg yolks one at a time, next the almonds and the white wine. Whip up the egg whites in a separate bowl until they stand in peaks, beat in half the remaining sugar and fold in the rest. Fold in the well sifted flour. Blend this mixture with the first, losing as little air as possible, and fold in the washed and top and tailed gooseberries. Turn into the prepared flan case and bake. The mixture rises into a gentle dome and browns slightly. Leave to cool in the flan tin before unmoulding.

Dredge with icing sugar to serve or brush with apricot jam and glaze with white glacé icing (page 72).

CAKES

Apples

Tarte Tatin

The most familiar of all French apple tarts, Tarte Tatin, is unlike any other, for the filling is baked underneath and the whole tart turned over afterwards. In this way the apples retain their succulence, the sugar and fruit juices have caramelized to a shiny golden brown colour, and the pastry cannot overcook or burn.

The Demoiselles Tatin owned an hotel at the turn of the century, in Lamotte-Beuvron in the Sologne, in the Loire region of France. Jane Grigson, in *Food with the Famous*, gives a fine description of the Hotel Tatin, the sisters and the tart. She says:

> . . . it is difficult to understand how the tart became so famous; Lamotte-Beuvron is buried in the Sologne, a district of woods and meres. It had a canal and a fairly important main road, but I suspect the success of the tart was due to the arrival of the railway. This meant that wealthy Parisians could easily come down for a few days' shooting in the woods which are one of the richest areas of France for game . . . Restaurants of high quality flourish in the autumn, with sociable parties from the shooting boxes, and extra guests. And the game season is also the apple season, with the 'Reinette d'Orléans' as the major local variety.
>
> We went to eat at the Hotel Tatin, watched coldly by the stuffed deer and other trophies of the chase. I was surprised by the *Tarte Tatin*, by its darkly caramelized appearance, its air of rusticity; it was a completely different thing from the elegantly arranged, softly golden tarts of the smart French pâtissiers . . . In the end, there are no doubt as many versions as there are cooks, but I like to know how things are at the source . . . I make a tarte that is

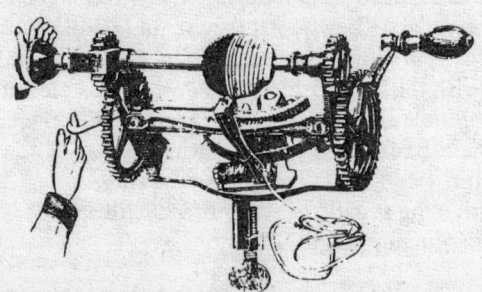

A Victorian mechanical apple peeler

TARTS AND PIES WITH FRESH FRUITS

somewhere between the two, reflecting presumably the moderated rurality in which most country-dwellers now live, whether in England or France.

Here is the recipe in her own words.

'The first thing to consider is the mould. It must be metal and a good 2–3 cm [¾–1¼ inches] deep. A straight-sided moule à manquer is ideal. I have even used a heavy sauté pan which has a handle tough enough to withstand high oven temperatures: but the handle makes the tart difficult to turn out. You could quite well use a cake tin, so long as it was not too deep. The ingredients for a 22–25 cm [8½–10 inch] tin are as follows:

60 g butter	2 oz butter
2 teaspoons vinegar (optional)	2 teaspoons vinegar (optional)
5 heaped tablespoons caster sugar	5 heaped tablespoons caster sugar
8 large Reinettes or Cox's Orange Pippins	8 large Reinettes or Cox's Orange Pippins
shortcrust made with 130 g plain flour (page 44)	shortcrust made with 4½ oz plain flour (page 44)

Spread the butter over the base of the tin, then add the vinegar if you like and the sugar, shaking it evenly. Set the tin over a moderate heat until the mixture begins to caramelize to a pale golden brown; keep stirring. You can let the caramel turn to a toffee hardness and colour, because the juices from the apple will liquefy it to the right consistency later.

Remove the tin from the stove, and allow it to cool while you peel, core and slice the apples. It is up to you whether you arrange an elegant bottom layer of concentric circles. I don't. I just put them in evenly in a rough kind of way. At La Varenne cookery school in Paris, they peel, core and halve the apples, and then arrange these halves on their sides, as it were, with the cored side of one half pressed against the rounded outer curve of the next half. The apples at Lamotte-Beuvron were higgledy-piggledy.

It is quite wise to attend carefully to the first layer, making it more or less even. Then put in the rest of the apple as you like, aiming for a depth of roughly 2 cm [¾ inch]. Firm eating apples will not greatly subside, neither will they turn to a snowy pulp, but you will achieve a better result if you aim at an even depth without too many gaps.

Roll out the pastry, and cut a circle to fit closely inside the tin. Prick it if you like, but it does not much matter. Fit it in place, pressing it down lightly on the apples. Put the tart in the oven at gas 8, 230°C, 450°F for upwards of half an hour, according to how brown you want the final result to be.

Remove it from the oven, run a knife round the edge of the tin, and invert the whole thing on to a heavy serving dish. A certain amount of juice may flow, so do this quickly. Serve with plenty of cream.

Note: When good eating apples run out, Golden Delicious may be substituted. They do not produce so rich and fragrant a result as Reinette or Cox's, but are quite satisfactory.'

Pumpkins

The pumpkin in England shows its hollow face for ghostly candlelit Hallowe'en festivities and little else. In Europe it ranks mainly as a vegetable and in America as a fruit. In warmer climates it grows abundantly – road-side stalls flanked by huge piles of ripened pumpkins are a familiar autumn sight in California.

As vegetables they cook like marrow; stuffed, or chopped and braised. They may be pickled, and also make a fine creamy soup. But the most popular role is as a fruit baked in a pie – the traditional Thanksgiving dessert of America. Like the marrow, it has a rather bland and boring taste which needs some delicate flavouring to bring it to its best.

An unusual Middle Eastern version of a tart sandwiches two layers of a creamy pumpkin mixture with one of minced meat well laced with brandy. In England apples blend well with pumpkin, currants, mixed peels and spices. The Germans inevitably combine them with ground almonds and lemon zest on a yeast or puff pastry base. Another version, using almonds again, includes sultanas with a conventional cake mixture made of butter, eggs and breadcrumbs. And a rather imprecise French recipe mixes the sieved fruit with a 'lump of butter', a 'glass of sugar', a 'packet of yeast', and 2 or 3 egg yolks, into which the stiffly beaten whites are folded.

James Beard's pumpkin pie, which follows, varies somewhat from the traditional American recipe by using almost double the number of eggs to give a much richer, more custard-like texture; he also substitutes candied for powdered ginger, and laces it with 'sherry, cognac or rum to make it more pungent; these touches', he suggests, give 'the taste of true greatness . . . a far cry from the usual mealy and sticky pumpkin pie'. (I find that it improves still further with the addition of a little sugar – 100 g, 3½ oz.) James Beard recommends serving the pie warm, never chilled – offer cream as well.

Pumpkin should be peeled, sliced and have the seeds removed before boiling in lightly salted water until it is soft. It can also be steamed. Push through a fine sieve to purée.

James Beard's Pumpkin Pie

Beat together 500 ml (1 pint) pumpkin purée and 100 g (3½ oz) caster sugar with 4 eggs, 175 ml (6 fl oz) double cream, ½ teaspoon cinnamon, a pinch of cloves and one of mace, 2 tablespoons sherry or liqueur, and 20 g (1 oz) fine cut candied or preserved ginger. Pour into a 22 cm (8½ inch) par-baked sweet shortcrust flan case (see page 45), and bake at gas 5, 190°C, 375°F for 25 minutes until it has just set. Serve warm, never chilled.

Fruit Flans

Simple Ideas for Cooking Fruits in Raw Pastry Cases

* Stone and halve fresh greengages and lay them stone side up on to a crème pâtissière base.
* Stuff the cavities of stoned and halved plums or apricots with split blanched almonds; embed them in crème frangipane. Seedless grapes or half muscat grapes are also good this way.
* Slice apples into thick pieces and toss with fresh blackberries, sugar, cinnamon or vanilla. Lay evenly on to the base.

Bake in the oven set at gas 4, 180°C, 350°F for about an hour, but check after 45 minutes to see that neither the fruit nor the pastry is burning. Cover with foil if necessary until the baking is completed.

Apricot Streussel

A classic Streussel Kuchen is traditionally made with yeast pastry (page 123), but the crumbly Streussel also makes a delicious coating over fruits and shortcrust pastry. Apples are the usual favourite, but try apricots for a change.

Line a 26 cm (10½ inch) cake tin with sweet shortcrust pastry (page 45). Brush with strained apricot jam. Halve and stone 500 g (1 lb) fresh apricots and lay them skin side down on to the jam surface. Prepare a butter Streussel (page 123) with:

220 g butter	8 oz butter
300 g plain flour	11 oz plain flour
220 g granulated sugar	8 oz granulated sugar
1 tablespoon cinnamon	1 tablespoon cinnamon

Sprinkle over the apricots, and bake in the oven set at gas 4, 180°C, 350°F for about 1 hour; the Streussel should remain pale in colour. Dredge with icing sugar before serving.

Flans with Berries

Late August, given heavy rain and sun
For a full week, the blackberries would ripen.
At first, just one, a glossy purple clot
Among others, red, green, hard as a knot.
You ate that first one and its flesh was sweet
Like thickened wine: summer's blood was in it
Leaving stains upon the tongue and lust for
Picking. Then red ones inked up and that hunger
Sent us out with milk-cans, pea-tins, jam-pots
Where briars scratched and wet grass bleached our boots.
Round hayfields, cornfields and potato-drills
We trekked and picked until the cans were full,
Until the thinkling bottom had been covered
With green ones, and on top big dark blobs burned
Like a plate of eyes. Our hands were peppered
With thorn pricks, our palms sticky as Bluebeard's . . .

(Seamus Heaney, *Blackberry-picking*)

All soft fruits, and particularly those growing wild, have a special charm. I remember the occasion when I wished to offer dinner guests a rare treat. A friend in the trade kindly arranged for a tray of wild strawberries to be flown over from Paris especially. My guests' response far surpassed expectations as they gasped with astonishment and pleasure, and within seconds the wild strawberry desserts had vanished. (I can only accept their word that they were delicious since not a morsel remained for me to sample.)

Wild blackberries and wild woodland strawberries apart, the larger more flamboyant cultivated cousins are every bit as good; and so are raspberries, whether early in the summer or late into autumn, or the purple-coloured bilberries, with their greyish bloom, and the sharp redcurrant clusters or the large and handsome deep purple loganberries. Glossily layered in an open flan, they all look as good as they taste. And they certainly taste better unbaked.

Use blind baked flan cases (page 208) and remember to insulate them (page 208). Heap the small clean fruits extravagantly into the insulated case, or pack in the bigger ones neatly, their points upwards. You can spoon over a light coating of fresh fruit glaze (page 210) if you like, leave to set, then pipe generously with sweetened whipped crème chantilly.

Vol au Vent

'Tarts, always tarts' — Carême often said; 'we seem unable to find anything to replace the beasts!' One day he had the idea while making some tarts at Allain, in the Rue Gaillon, to leave away the sides on one. He cut a circle out of the puff pastry, laid it on a baking sheet and notched it all round. He then cut a circle on the surface and brushed it with beaten egg. He pushed it in the oven and instructed the baker to keep an eye on it. Suddenly the man cried out, 'Antonin, elle vol au vent!' Carême dashed to the oven and saw with amazement the new creation. (He had forgotten to give the paste the 7th fold and the pastry was leaning to one side). 'Tut, tut,' he said, 'I know what I must do to straighten it.' He made another one, and named it 'Vol au Vent'.

(Pierre Lacam, *Le Memorial des Glaces*)

Today these pastries are mostly filled with savoury creams, although Carême obviously enjoyed the sweet varieties.

Strawberry Vol au Vent

Here is an unusual flan variation, based on Carême's Vol au Vent.

For a 20–22 cm (8–8¹/₂ inch) vol au vent use pâte feuilletée (4) (page 52), with 500 g (1 lb) strong flour. Make the pastry (see pages 52–3 for the method). Roll into a rectangle about 50 × 30 cm (20 × 12 inches) and 1 cm (³/₈ inch) thick.

Use a cake-ring as a template and cut two circles to size with a very sharp knife, dipped in boiling water. Turn one pastry circle over on to a flat dampened baking sheet. Brush cold water in a 4 cm (1¹/₂ inch) border around the edge. To cut the pastry lid from the second pastry circle, use a template about 4 cm (1¹/₂ inches) smaller (a cake-tin or bowl will do – or judge it by eye). Make a sharp cut as before.

Brush the outer ring from the second circle lightly with flour, fold it in half and then quarters and unfold it carefully on to the damp pastry rim. It is important not to stretch the outer ring when you lift it over onto the base. Ease it into place, taking care not to damage or crush the edges (which would prevent it from rising evenly). Prick the middle only with a fork. To seal the two layers of dough, hold the back of a knife upright at an angle and press indentations at 2 cm (³/₄ inch) intervals around the circumference. Brush with beaten egg.

Lay the remainder of the second pastry circle on another damp baking sheet: prick with a fork and brush with lightly beaten egg. Leave both to rest in the refrigerator for an hour.

Just before setting the pastries in the preheated oven, cut a line about 3 mm (¹/₄ inch) deep in the bottom pastry disc where the inner edge of the top disc joins it; this will make a lid when it has baked. (During baking it rises to the same level as the outer rim.) Prick the outer cake rim in 4 or 5 places with a fork or a skewer, to help the pastry rise evenly, and set in the preheated oven straight away.

Oven temperatures should be gas 7, 220°C, 425°F for 20 minutes then gas 4, 180°C, 350°F for 30–40 minutes until it is brown and crisp. If it starts to look too dark, cover with a loose sheet of aluminium foil.

Lift the pastries out of the oven. Cut the lid out along the cut line and lift out. It will probably break. Use a fork to scrape any uncooked pastry lightly from underneath; replace in the oven for 5 minutes to dry out. Leave to cool. The broken lid can either be used as an additional layer between the cream and fruits, or eaten by the cook!

The filling: Whip up 250 ml (9 fl oz) of double cream and 2 tablespoons of single cream into soft peaks. Sweeten with 3 tablespoons of caster sugar and flavour with 2 tablespoons of Grand Marnier. Whip further, until the cream holds stiff peaks. Carefully spoon the chantilly into the vol au vent case and press the second pastry lid into place, level with the top of the shell.

Rinse lightly, dry and hull 500 g (1 lb) or more of wild strawberries, raspberries or redcurrants, or a mixture, and heap them on to the surface of the pastry case. Scatter some fresh orange zest on top.

You may finish the fruit with a fresh glaze if you wish (page 210).

Millefeuille with Crème Chantilly

This is reputed to be another of Carême's creations.

gas 7, 220°C, 425°F/20 minutes

Roll 325 g (11 oz) of puff pastry (see page 51) into a large rectangle 2 mm ($^1/_{12}$ inch) and 40 × 30 cm (16 × 12 inches) across. Cut into 3 equal strips with a sharp, hot knife. Allow to rest overnight in the refrigerator. Next day lay on a moistened baking sheet, and prick all over to stop them puffing excessively. Bake in the preheated oven for about 20 minutes, until they are golden brown in colour.

Have prepared 250 g (9 fl oz) of crème chantilly or crème pâtissière (pages 57, 59). Spread half the cream over a layer of pastry, the rest over a second layer and lay it on top of the first. Cover this with the last sheet of millefeuille. Lightly press the pastry into the cream so that it will cut more easily.

Fresh strawberries and raspberries are good with this; either fold them into the pastry cream or embed them in the bottom layer of cream. Save a few to decorate the top, and dredge heavily with icing sugar. Cut with a serrated knife.

Flan de poires frangipane

Fruit flans can be most disappointing. Although the circles of bright fruits might look very appetizing, too often they are layered in tough and tasteless pastry and disguised by a thick and chewy coating of gelatine. Loss of flavour with raw fruits is less likely, but tinned and bottled varieties, which are a little bland and innocuous to start with, suffer badly.

Choose fruits with a strong taste, enhance them with other flavours, but avoid the temptation of mixing too many together. This recipe of Urbain Dubois is a fine example.

Prepare sweet shortcrust or sweet shortcrust pastry with almonds (pages 45, 46) and line a flan ring 26 cm (10$^1/_2$ inches) in diameter.

250 ml red wine	9 fl oz red wine
250 ml water	9 fl oz water
225 g granulated sugar	8 oz granulated sugar
zest ½ lemon and ½ orange	zest ½ lemon and ½ orange
2 cloves	2 cloves
split vanilla pod or cinnamon stick	split vanilla pod or cinnamon stick
5 ripe, firm pears	5 ripe, firm pears
1 tablespoon brandy (optional)	1 tablespoon brandy (optional)

Combine wine with water and sugar, and stir over heat until the sugar is dissolved. Add zests and spices, simmer together for 20 minutes, then remove from the heat. Drop the peeled, halved and cored pears into the syrup, which should just cover them. Bring back to a bare simmer, leave uncovered and stew for 10–15 minutes more until they are tender but still firm when tested with a knife. Do not boil, or the fruit will disintegrate.

Lift out the fruits with a draining spoon. Remove the spice stick or pod and then boil the liquid quite vigorously to reduce it by about two-thirds and thicken; this takes about 10 minutes. Lift the pan off the heat and add the brandy if used; a drop or two of cochineal colouring can also be added to the liquid at this point, which enhances the colour of the pears without affecting the flavour. Replace the pears and ladle the juice over them so that the flavours can be better absorbed; leave to cool for at least 20 minutes for the fruits to become firm.

Spread the prepared flan with a layer of frangipane cream (page 61), and par-bake in a preheated oven set at gas 4, 180°C, 350°F for 15 minutes. Remove from the oven, fill with more cream, and pack in the prepared pears closely together. Bake for a further 35–40 minutes. While still hot, cover the fruits with the chilled pear syrup; or alternatively caramelize them by sprinkling granulated sugar over the surface and grilling at a high temperature until it melts, browns and bubbles.

Apricots are also suitable for this tart.

A Fine Apple Tart from Basel

This flan of southern Germany and Austria is more sophisticated than Clafouti; here cream is substituted for milk, flour is excluded, and the fruits are embedded in a thick egg custard. As a result the flavour is greatly improved, the cake eats well cold, and it keeps fresh for 3 or 4 days.

This is a Swiss version using apples, grapes and an egg-custard batter.

sweet shortcrust pastry (2) (page 45)	sweet shortcrust pastry (2) (page 45)
50 g white breadcrumbs	2 oz white breadcrumbs
2 tablespoons grated hazelnuts	2 tablespoons grated hazelnuts
50 g butter	2 oz butter
750 g cooking apples	1¾ lb cooking apples
3 tablespoons sugar	3 tablespoons sugar
50 g seedless grapes	2 oz seedless grapes
1 tablespoon Kirsch	1 tablespoon Kirsch
2 egg yolks	2 egg yolks
2 tablespoons caster sugar	2 tablespoons caster sugar
1 teaspoon vanilla sugar	1 teaspoon vanilla sugar
200 ml double cream	7 fl oz double cream
cinnamon sugar, made with 2 tablespoons caster sugar and ½ teaspoon cinnamon	cinnamon sugar, made with 2 tablespoons caster sugar and ½ teaspoon cinnamon

gas 7, 220°C, 425°F/40 minutes

Roll the pastry 3 mm (⅛ inch) thick and line the base and sides of a 24 cm (9½ inch) buttered spring-form tin. Prick well with a fork. Mix the breadcrumbs and the nuts and sprinkle over the base. Melt the butter in a pan and drop in the peeled, cored and not too thinly sliced apples to stew gently with 3 tablespoons of sugar until they are half cooked. Macerate the washed grape halves in Kirsch. Drain and cool the apple slices and spread over the pastry. Sprinkle with the grapes. Make a batter by beating the egg yolks, 2 tablespoons caster sugar and the vanilla sugar to a thick cream; mix in the double cream, pour over the apple and grape mixture and bake. Serve lukewarm, or chilled and sprinkled with cinnamon sugar.

Apple Flan with a Rich Almond Paste

Peel, core and cut into thickish slices 750 g (1¾ lb) Bramley cooking apples, Cox's or Golden Delicious, and stew very gently in a pan with a knob of butter, 1 teaspoon of lemon zest, 1 teaspoon of cinnamon and 3 or 4 tablespoons of brown sugar. Add just a small amount of water to stop the apples catching and burning. Draw off the heat and leave to cool a little. Drain any excess juice, then sieve or process the apple. Leave to cool.

Prepare sweet shortcrust pastry (2) (page 45) and line only the base of a 22 cm (8½ inch) spring-form tin with two-thirds of the paste: prick; bake until just coloured at gas 5, 190°C, 375°F for about 15 minutes. Brush while still warm with beaten egg white. Roll out the remainder of the pastry and cut a strip the depth of the tin; line the sides of the cool tin. Pour the cooled apple purée into the shell, and set in the oven preheated to gas 4, 180°C, 350°F for about 20 minutes.

Meanwhile make the almond paste with:

100 g butter; 100 g caster sugar; 100 g ground almonds; 2 eggs; 1 teaspoon lemon zest; 50 g plain flour
(4 oz butter; 4 oz caster sugar; 4 oz ground almonds; 2 eggs; 1 teaspoon lemon zest; 2 oz plain flour)

Cream the butter and sugar together until pale and fluffy. Mix in the almonds. Beat in the eggs and the lemon zest and finally the flour. Spread this mixture over the part baked apple flan and bake for a further 40 minutes. When cold, cover with strained apricot jam and coat with vanilla glacé icing.

Fresh Peach or Greengage Flan

sweet shortcrust or almond pastry (see pages 45, 46)	sweet shortcrust or almond pastry (see pages 45, 46)
7 fresh peaches	7 fresh peaches
100 g caster sugar	3½ oz caster sugar
200 ml double cream	7 fl oz double cream
2 egg yolks	2 egg yolks

gas 5, 190°C, 375°F for about 20 minutes, then reducing to gas 4, 180°C, 350°F

Prepare the pastry for a 22 cm (8½ inch) flan tin and par-bake it blind (page 208) until it has set but not yet coloured – about 10–15 minutes. Take it out of the oven and brush lightly with white of egg so as to protect the pastry from the moist fruits; return to the oven for a further 5 minutes. Meanwhile prepare the fruits. Skin the peaches by dropping them into a bowl of boiling hot water for a few seconds to release the skins. Cut them into quarters and lay them tightly together in the case stone side up. Sprinkle half the caster sugar over the top and put the tin back into the oven to bake for a further 20 minutes.

Make a batter by beating together the double cream with the rest of the caster sugar and the egg yolks. Pour or spread the mixture over the fruits, making sure that all are covered. Return to the oven and bake until the cream has set – about 30 minutes. Serve either hot or cold. Pipe with whipped cream if serving cold.

A Flan with Glazed Orange Slices

This is a colourful and striking dessert. It keeps well for at least 10 days.

Prepare *pâte sucrée* to fit a 24 cm (9½ inch) flan case (page 45) with: 165 g (6 oz) plain flour; 110 g (4 oz) butter; 50 g (2 oz) caster sugar; 1 small egg; ½ teaspoon salt; 1 teaspoon lemon zest. Bake blind. Cool and brush with strained apricot jam.

Prepare *Orange Mousseline Butter Cream (1)* (page 62) with: 50 g (2 oz) granulated sugar; 50 ml (2 fl oz) water; 2 egg yolks; 110 g (4 oz) unsalted butter; 1 tablespoon fresh orange juice and zest of 1 orange. Pour into flan shell and smooth: leave to chill.

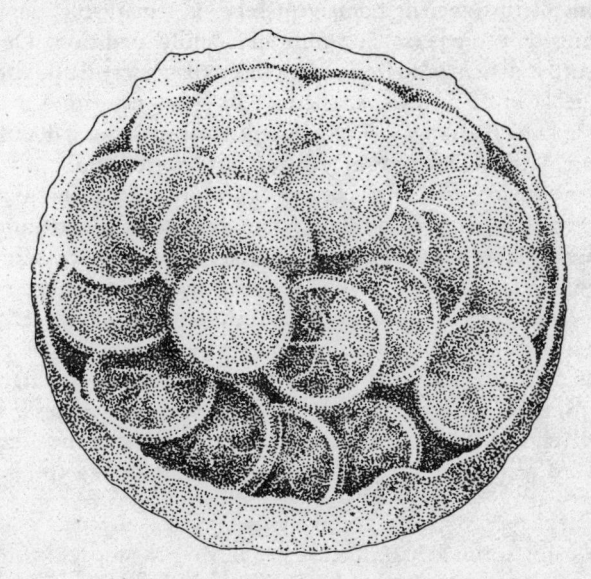

Prepare *Orange Syrup* with: 125 ml (4½ fl oz) orange juice; 125 ml (4½ fl oz) lemon juice; 330 g (12 oz) granulated sugar; 3 small, thin skinned oranges. Dissolve the sugar in the strained juices in an unlined copper pan on a low heat before bringing to the boil; then simmer gently for about 20 minutes. Meanwhile wash and dry the oranges carefully; using a sharp knife, cut out 1 mm (less than $^1/_{16}$ inch) channels through the skin and pith, at 1 cm ($^1/_2$ inch) intervals, working down from the point where the fruit joins the stem, to the base. This makes the glazed fruit less chewy. Cut the oranges into thin 3 mm ($^1/_8$ inch) slices. Drop them in the syrup and simmer for a further 15 minutes until they are well glazed. Reserve the syrup, and lay the fruits to drain and dry on a wire rack.

Arrange the dried and set orange pieces in overlapping circular rows on the mousseline butter cream in the flan case.

Boil the reserved syrup until it thickens, withdraw from the heat, and stir in 3 tablespoons of an orange liqueur, for example, Grand Marnier. Pour the syrup over the oranges in the flan case and chill before serving.

Lemon Meringue Flan

Lemon tarts, lemon pies, lemon pudding are essentially one and the same. An empty pastry shell is filled with a lemon (or orange) curd or cheese made with eggs, sugar, butter and lemons. But the number of variations of this ancient homely preserve is remarkable, sometimes depending only on personal whim and family tradition. Of course lemon curd is delicious on its own in a shortcrust pastry shell, but with a meringue layer it tastes even better. In Victorian times a type of meringue known as 'royal icing' was a popular glaze for a double-crust pie or tart. Urbain Dubois uses it on his 'tarte conversation'. A very stiff mixture was made with a little beaten egg white and a generous amount of sifted icing sugar. Ten minutes before the end of the cooking time, the icing was lavishly spread over the surface and the pie was returned to the oven. Today we prefer to lay the meringue over the open fruits.

Lemon meringue flan is a great English favourite. The slightly acid sharpness of the lemon filling contrasts pleasingly with the crunchy pastry and sweet, fluffy meringue. An additional layer of frangipane cream (page 61) between the lemon and the meringue makes it special. I have given two lemon fillings, one a type of custard, the other more like a curd or cheese. Prepare the lemon filling before you bake the pastry.

Traditional Lemon Curd or Cheese

220 g granulated sugar	8 oz granulated sugar
juice and zest of 4 lemons	juice and zest of 4 lemons
100 g unsalted butter	sparing 4 oz unsalted butter
3 large eggs.	3 large eggs

Makes about 750 g (1½ lb)

Put the sugar and lemon zest in a bowl set over simmering water or a double boiler. Crush the zest with the sugar so that the oils penetrate, then add the butter cut in small pieces and the strained lemon juice. Leave the mixture over the water until the butter has melted and the sugar dissolved. Whip up the eggs in another bowl, then strain them into the lemon mixture. Mix well with a wooden spoon, then cook gently, stirring often, until the curd thickens and becomes creamy. This will take about 10–15 minutes. Pour into warm sterilized jars and seal while hot, or, if using straight away, lightly brush a little butter over the surface to prevent a skin forming while it cools.

Lemon filling (2)

150 g caster sugar	5 oz caster sugar
3 egg yolks	3 egg yolks
zest and juice 3 lemons	zest and juice 3 lemons
65 g unsalted butter	2½ oz unsalted butter
3 tablespoons cornflour	3 tablespoons cornflour
250 ml milk	9 fl oz milk

Place the caster sugar, egg yolks, lemon zest and juice in a pan over hot water and heat gently, stirring all the time. When it has become transparent and the sugar has melted, beat in small lumps of the butter until all has combined. In another bowl mix the cornflour with a little of the milk and set the rest to boil in a pan. Pour on the cornflour mixture and stir over heat until it has thickened. Amalgamate the two mixtures until the consistency of a crème pâtissière (page 59) has been reached. Cool.

Shortcrust pastry: Prepare the pastry to line a 26 cm (10½ inch) flan case (see page 44). Bake blind until set and very lightly coloured, start at gas 6, 200°C, 400°F and reduce the oven heat to gas 4, 180°C, 350°F.

Pour the lemon mixture into the prepared flan case, and bake in the preheated oven to set it for 10 minutes. Lift out of the oven and reduce the heat still further to gas 2, 150°C, 300°F.

Make the meringue 5 minutes before the cooking is complete, using 3 large egg whites and 165 g (6 oz) caster sugar flavoured with vanilla (see page 83 for method). Spoon or pipe the meringue on to the set filling. Dredge with caster sugar and return it to the oven for about 45 minutes to dry out, brown slightly and become crisp.

Meringue flans can be made with other flavours as well. Apart from a coffee filling (page 60), substituting orange for lemon is an obvious choice. Fresh skinned and sieved peaches in a blind-baked case look attractive piped with a meringue trellis, and so does mango with its strong exotic taste and brilliant orange colour – chopped pistachio nuts sprinkled over the top blend well with both flavours. Finely chopped hazelnuts blend very well with rhubarb.

Rhubarb and Hazelnut Meringue

Sprinkle 100 g (4 oz) of toasted hazelnuts over a chilled, pre-baked flan made of shortcrust or sweet shortcrust pastry in a 23 cm (9 inch) base (pages 44–5). The fruit should be prepared a few hours before it is needed by cutting it small and drenching it with 100 g (4 oz) caster sugar and a dusting of cinnamon. Half a kilo (1 lb) of fruit is about the right amount. Drain the fruit juices and lay the fruit in the pastry case. Set in the oven and bake for about 30 minutes at gas 5, 190°C, 375°F. Reduce the temperature to gas 2, 150°C, 300°F. Make a meringue using 3 egg whites and 165 g (6 oz) caster sugar and spread this over the rhubarb. Bake in the cooler oven until it has browned slightly and crisped.

Fruited Meringue

Although the above meringue flans are very familiar, fruits cloaked in the meringue itself are quite unusual. They will keep for only a couple of days, but make a delicious, light dessert for a dinner party.

Small soft fruits such as blackberries, ripe gooseberries, raspberries, bilberries, redcurrants and strawberries are most suitable. The quantity of fruit can vary depending on the amount you have available, but there should be enough to cover the base of the flan. 500 g (1 lb) is a rough guide.

Wash and dry the fruit if necessary, making sure that no moisture remains. (Tart or sour fruit might need a small amount of sugar – dust lightly and shake off any surplus.)

Line a 26 cm (10½ inch) flan tin with pâte sucrée or shortcrust pastry (pages 44–5) and bake it blind. Chill.

Make a meringue mixture with 3 egg whites and 165 g (6 oz) caster sugar. Whip up the egg whites to stand in firm snowy peaks. Sift half the sugar over the surface and whip until the mixture has thickened. Fold in the rest of the sugar using a large metal spoon. Reserve a small amount of the meringue to pipe a simple trellis pattern if you wish. Fold the fruits into the remainder and spread over the prepared flan case. Smooth the reserved mixture across the top or pipe it as suggested. Lightly dust caster sugar all over, and bake in the preheated oven, gas 7, 220°C, 425°F, for about 15 minutes, checking after 10 minutes as the mixture must not cook too long or it will run. The meringue should be golden and have brown peaks. Serve cold, and use a wet knife to cut portions.

Grape Meringue Tart

The sweet tartness of the grapes blends particularly well with the meringue.

Prepare shortcrust or pâte sucrée (pages 44–5) and line a 26 cm (10½ inch) flan case. Bake it blind and chill.

Prepare a meringue in the usual way with 4 egg whites and 210 g (8 oz) caster sugar. Wash, dry and seed if necessary 500 g (1 lb) black, green, muscat or seedless grapes, and fold into the meringue alternately with the 100 g (3½ oz) raw, fine ground almonds. Spread the mixture on to the baked, chilled flan case and bake in a preheated oven at gas 4, 180°C, 350°F for 1 hour.

Fresh Fruit Cakes

'Air and fruit,' wrote the Marquis de Sade from his prison cell in the Bastille in September 1784,

> are the two things I live by and, especially in this season, I would as soon have my throat cut as forgo them. If you saw the abominable, debased, and stinking vittles that are served us here, you would understand that anyone who is used to a more delicate diet must needs supplement it with purchases of his own . . . so please take note of this list.
>
> A basket of fruit, made up of
> Peaches 12
> Nectarines 12
> Poires de beurre 12
> Bunches of grapes 12
> (half of all these to be ripe, and the rest ready to eat in 3 or 4 days)
> Two pots of jam
> A dozen cakes from the Palais Royal (six of them orange-flavoured) and two pounds of sugar.
> Three packets of candles for the night.

The irresistible temptation of fruit began in the Garden of Eden and still has the same appeal. Through the centuries it has inspired cooks, artists, writers and poets.

> The apple trees, with irregular green apples slightly flushed with brown where they faced the south, clustering in twos and threes along the branches in the orchard, like love-birds with their heads under their wings, filled the orchard, rustling their boughs together, so that the roof was green.
>
> (Alison Uttley, *The Country Child*)

Although dried fruits had been exported for centuries (the unseasonable appearance of fresh fruits from other countries is only a recent innovation), the burden of coping with the rich fruit harvests year after year was very much a local affair. No doubt as a result of considerable boredom, a host of imaginative sweetmeats evolved, especially during the nineteenth century. In the cherry-growing areas, fruits were bottled and preserved, candied in sugar or distilled into Kirsch liqueur; some were simply steeped in spirit. Cherries were baked in various pastries or in a type of omelette, layered in open pies or dipped in batters and deep-fried. Each region developed its own specialities. This seasonal and regional glut was no different from that of the oranges and almonds of Portugal and Spain, or of apples from the more northern climes of Normandy and England, the chestnuts of Italy or the plums in Southern Germany, Switzerland and Austria. The problem arose in almost every fruit-growing area in the world.

Fresh fruits are quite the most gratifying of all ingredients in bakery – they are in themselves a recipe for success. The Romans loved them 'covered with a light and perfumed paste'; at a sixteenth-century banquet they might be served for the fourth course of 'Delicacies from the Sideboard' of 'Bean tarts, Quince pastries, one quince per pastry, pear tarts, pears wrapped in marzipan'. However elaborate – in a layered gâteau, or simple in an open-faced tart, fruits have a mouthwatering attraction and lose nothing in their fulfilment.

Of the Baking of Fruit. From Mr. L. M.

It is to be observed, that all Fruits that are ripe require little baking, and those which are of the hardest, or most unripe Sorts, ought to have a long and gentle baking. In Pears, for example, when we have some of those, which ripen in the Autumn, they will bake with a Tart; for as they are ripe of themselves, they require very little baking, for Ripeness is one degree tending to Rottenness; and as that is done by heat gently, so the Oven brings that to a certain height, suddenly, with its safeguard of Sugar; that the Fruit comes to its full flavour, with the additional beauty from the Sugar. It would have done a great deal by Nature itself, if the Tree had stood in a place agreeable; but much more would it be for those baking Pears, as we call them, if they had the advantage of a good Climate; one may guess then how much difference there is between one and the other. In the tough and hard Pears, one ought to bake them twice, that is, once with a little Water and Sugar, in as hot an Oven as they bake Bread in; and then put them in Pyes, and bake them over again, so will they become tender, well tasted, and of a fine colour. But be it as it will, as soon as either of these come out of the Oven, pour some Cream over them, and mix it with them, if they are to be served hot, mashing the Fruit all the while; but if they are to be served cold, then only pour some Cream over them, when they just come from the Oven, and let it remain till you serve it cold.

There is one way which is practised by some, and that is, to break the hard Pears, just when they are taken out of the Oven, in the Pye; for else the outsides, though the Rind is off, will be hard, and tough: then pour on the Cream. It is to be noted, that all ripe Apples require less baking, and less Sugar, than the hard Apples, which do not become ripe till some Months afterwards. When an Apple, or Pear, for example, is as ripe as it can be in our Climate, it will have some softness, and some sweetness in it, and therefore will require less baking, as baking is only a sort of ripening; and so on the other hand: but we are providentially provided with both Apples and Pears, which are, some ripe sooner, and some ripe later; even that by the end of *July*, we have some ripe, and some remain hard and sour till *June*. We ought be apprised of the Sorts, to take them in their several Seasons, and not to take the Winter Fruits, for baking, when we have ripe Fruits by us. Many thousand Bushels of Fruit are lost for want of this Caution.

So at any time, when you use Apples, or Pears, for Tarts, Puddings, or Sauces, let them be all of one Sort, and ripe; for, if they are ripe, or towards it, they will soon soften; and if you put two Sorts together, one will be in Pulp very soon, and the other will be hard for an Hour or two, and at length will not be soft. *Memorandum*, This is not to be disregarded.

(Richard Bradley, *The Country Housewife and Lady's Director*, 1736)

Some Hints on Choosing Fruits for Baking

Apples. It is essential to use apples which do not lose their moisture, which still hold their shape and puff up. Some apples collapse dramatically and become wet and mushy, which will spoil any bakery. I like Bramley cooking apples – their slight tartness blends well with pastry and their characteristics are ideal. Of the dessert apples, Cox's Orange Pippins, Russet and Golden Delicious are the most suitable.

Apples should always be sliced quite thickly, otherwise they become hard and chewy when cooked.

Cherries. Although Kent, the 'orchard of England', used to have many cherry trees, they are now being replaced by more economical stock and the choice of cherry has become very limited. Unfortunately we can usually only choose between black, red or yellow, or best sour or morello. Luckily we are importing some very fine large varieties from the United States which also have a longer season. Cherries are seen mostly in June and July. If you can get them, 'Flemish' and 'Kentish Red' are earlies – while the black sweet dessert 'Early Rivers', 'Bigarreau Napoleon' and 'Bradbourne Black' are also suitable for baking. The paler yellow-red varieties, such as 'White Heart', the barrow boy's delight, are less attractive and the stones more difficult to remove. And if you are able to get hold of the marvellously bitter and acidy Morello you are in for a great treat – though make sure that they are sugared well enough. In America the large black 'Bing' and 'Queen Anne' fruits excel.

Cherries can be left whole for baking but I prefer to remove the stones, although they stain your fingers. I find that a mouthful of stones detracts from the flavour of the cake. (Do suck the stones before discarding them, that is the baker's bonus! They have a lovely taste.)

Tinned and bottled cherries: Morello or black pitted are definitely the best. Avoid the huge black ones, which are tasteless and leave you with a mouthful of stones, and the bright pinky-red ones which are very bland and best eaten with other fruits in a salad.

Plums. Autumn plums are best for baking when they have a slightly sharp flavour, which contrasts so well with sweet pastry. Zwetschken – the Austrian Carlsbad plum – appears around late September, usually imported from Europe for a very short season. It is especially suitable for baking because very little juice is drawn from it. The English yellow-green greengage and the French Reine Claude, which is almost orange, speckled with white, have very different flavours but are excellent tart and pie candidates. If you can find the bright yellow gold Mirabelle, round and small, it tastes wonderfully sweet.

Tinned and bottled plums are not really suitable other than for deep-dish pies.

There are numerous fruit recipes elsewhere in the book: see particularly the selection of pies and tarts (page 220), and also the yeast cakes section (page 119). Soft fruits are especially good with flaky pastries as well as sponges and meringues. Some more uncommon recipes follow.

Sponge Cakes Baked with Fresh Fruit Inside

In England, fresh fruit baked in a pie or a tart is very familiar, but inside a sponge mixture it is quite unusual. In Europe, however, it has been common for decades.

CAKES

The first time I made the plum sponge which follows, I served it at tea to a friend and her eleven-month baby, Sam, who had been off-colour and very miserable all day. Within minutes, the sad expression was transformed as, beaming widely and gurgling with delight, he stuffed pieces of cake into his mouth as fast as he knew how.

It definitely classes as a 'cut and come again' cake; neither too sweet nor too dry, it needs no dressing up and is not too difficult to prepare. The fresh unsweetened fruits give a moist texture and slightly tart richness to the paste, which in its turn adds just sufficient sweetness to the fruits. In fact almost any fruit can be used, although citrus should be avoided as too much moisture and acidity affects the paste.

Apples and *pears* are simple enough – select ripe fruits, peel, core and slice not too thin. *Rhubarb* and *gooseberries* have a marvellous sharp acidity – choose thin sticks of rhubarb which will cook easily, trim and chop into short pieces or cut thick ones finely, and top and tail small gooseberries. Leave *strawberries, bilberries* and *blackcurrants* whole. Naturally the pits should be removed from stone fruits – *plums, greengages, peaches* and *apricots*. Leave *damson* stones intact, they are almost impossible to remove – but *cherries* are better without (cut larger ones in half). Leave small seedless *grapes* whole, but de-pip and halve bigger ones – they taste better that way. You can even use *pineapple* and *banana* slices, but they have little appeal for me.

The fruit must be dried very carefully before it is used.

Here is a basic recipe which you can adapt to the fruit of your choice.

Plum Sponge for Sam

Prepare a rich Genoese sponge (or the ordinary Genoese which uses less butter). Use the method with separately beaten egg whites (see pages 90–1). Use about 750 g (1½ lbs) fruit.

150 g caster sugar	5 oz caster sugar
150 g plain flour	5 oz plain flour
150 g butter, melted and cooled	5 oz butter, melted and cooled
6 egg whites	6 egg whites
6 egg yolks	6 egg yolks
zest 1 lemon	zest 1 lemon

gas 4, 180°C, 350°F/1 hour

FRESH FRUIT CAKES

Prepare the sponge mixture (page 91). Peel, core and slice the fruit — the quantity can vary, depending on the depth of your cake tin. Grease, and dust with flour and sugar a 26 cm (10½ inch) spring-form tin or savarin mould. Pour in just less than half the cake mixture, and put in the preheated oven for about 10 minutes to set the mixture (it will have risen); this stops the fruit from falling to the bottom. (Make sure that the centre is also set or the fruit will stick.)

Take the cake tin out of the oven and gently lay on the prepared fruits; there is no need to sugar them. Pour over the rest of the Genoese mixture and return to the oven. Bake for a further 45 minutes, or until it has browned nicely and shrinks from the sides of the tin.

As an alternative to par-baking a bottom layer, all the cake mixture can be poured into the tin and the fruit gently laid on the surface. It will sink as it bakes. The more fruit you use, the longer it will take to cook; but cover the top with foil if it starts to brown too much.

You may like to enrich the flavour with cinnamon or nutmeg; with a handful of slivered almonds or pistachios or coarsely ground hazelnuts; with chopped candied peel, sprinkled over the fruit layer and even on top. The fresh fruits also taste delicious if they have been previously macerated in Kirsch, rum or Maraschino. Dry the fruits off carefully after about 10 minutes and use.

To serve, scatter some fine slivered zest of orange over the surface and dust with a thick coating of icing sugar.

CAKES

Bilberry Cake

Bilberry tart is very familiar, but this is quite unusual. If you like, soak the fruit in Grand Marnier or Cointreau beforehand — surprisingly good and delightfully restoring — but drain it well. It should be eaten fresh, even while still warm, and whipped cream is a good accompaniment. Don't be alarmed by the amount of cinnamon. The mixture is prepared in two parts which are amalgamated at the end.

140 g butter	5 oz butter
150 g caster sugar	5 oz caster sugar
1 heaped teaspoon cinnamon	1 heaped teaspoon cinnamon
5 egg yolks	5 egg yolks
125 g flaked or nibbed almonds	4½ oz flaked or nibbed almonds
100 g white breadcrumbs, moistened with milk or single cream	3½ oz white breadcrumbs, moistened with milk or single cream
6 egg whites	6 egg whites
50 g plain flour	2 oz plain flour
500 g bilberries, fresh or frozen	generous 1 lb bilberries, fresh or frozen

gas 4, 180°C, 350°F/50 minutes

Mixture (1): Beat the butter and half the sugar until pale and creamy, then mix in the cinnamon. Add the egg yolks one at a time, beating well between each addition, and then add the almonds. If milk has been used to moisten the breadcrumbs, drain any excess; with cream the mass is usually thicker. Beat the breadcrumbs into the mixture thoroughly until all the lumps have dissipated.

Mixture (2): In another bowl beat the egg whites to form stiff snowy peaks, whip in 2 spoonfuls of the remaining sugar, then fold in the rest. Add a couple of spoonfuls of this meringue to the first mixture to lighten it a little before folding into it alternate spoonfuls of sifted flour and prepared fruits.

Combine the second mixture with the first, using a large metal spoon and retaining as much air as possible. Grease and line with siliconed paper a 28 cm (11 inch) spring-form tin; grease again. Pour in the mixture and bake in the preheated oven. Leave to cool in the tin, then dredge with icing sugar and serve.

Raspberries and blackcurrants are also suitable for this recipe.

FRESH FRUIT CAKES

My Mother's German Apple Cake

This unusual pastry is a pleasant alternative to the more familiar crisp crusts of pies and tarts. The soft and crumbly texture is a cross between a cake and a pie paste; self-raising flour helps it rise up, around and between the fruits and the slight sweetness complements fresh fruits particularly well. At the same time any vagrant juices are absorbed into the pastry, which gives it a delicate and fruity flavour. You may make a double quantity of pastry; the rest will keep very well for a week wrapped in foil in the refrigerator.

150 g self-raising flour	5 oz self-raising flour
150 g butter	5 oz butter
75 g sugar	2½ oz sugar
1 small egg	1 small egg
4 cooking apples (750 g)	4 cooking apples (about 1¾ lb)
sugar and cinnamon or nutmeg	sugar and cinnamon or nutmeg

gas 5, 190°C, 375°F/50 minutes

See page 48 for the detailed method of pastry preparation.

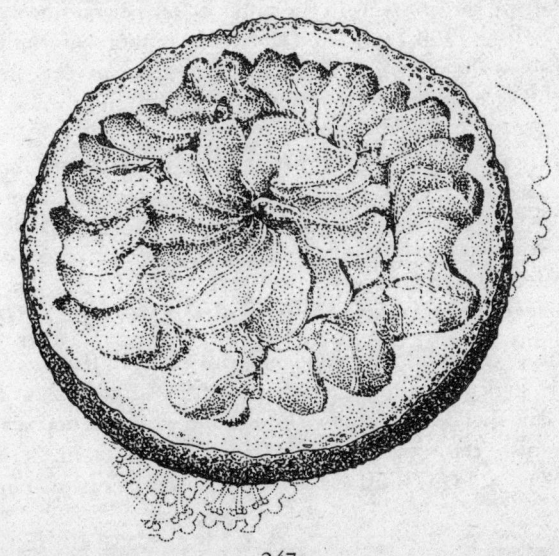

Make the pastry and chill for a short while in the refrigerator. Grease a baking tin 34 × 24 × 1 cm (13½ × 9½ × ½ inch) or a 24 cm (9½ inch) round tin with a loose base. Press the pastry lightly into it with the fingertips, covering the base and sides evenly. Peel and core the apples, slice them not too finely, and lay them on to the pastry base in a regular pattern. Sprinkle with caster sugar and cinnamon or nutmeg between the layers as you progress. Dredge the surface also. Always be generous with the fruit, as it reduces during baking. Bake in the preheated oven until the cake starts to shrink away from the sides of the tin and the fruit is slightly brown at the edges. Leave to cool in the tin, and serve with freshly whipped cream.

Zwetschken or Switzen Plum Cake

Let the plum hang unmolested upon her boughs, till she fatten her delicious flesh, and cloud her polished skin with blue.

(James Hervey, 1746)

A Polish friend tells of her childhood memory when her father used to cut a branch from the Zwetschken tree, laden with ripe fruits still firm on the bough. He would plunge the whole branch into the well at the bottom of the garden, and at Christmas time would lift it out intact. They had fresh plums for the festive season.

Zwetschkenkuchen is considered to be *the* German fruit tart, traditionally baked in large square or rectangular trays and usually on a yeast pastry base. But German pastry is also a perfect base for these lovely plums. Prepare the pastry as in the previous recipe and line a tin. You will need between 750 g and 1 kg (1¾ to 2 lb or more) of fruit (apricots and peaches are also suitable). Wash, dry, halve and stone the fruits, and pack very close together on their sides, and in straight rows, into the pastry base.

The fruit must not be sugared before being baked, as too much juice will be drawn out; it loses its taste and the cake becomes soggy. Bake. Leave to cool in the tin and dredge with icing sugar to serve.

Austrian Sour Cream Pastry with Fruit

Sour cream pastry is another delicious base for fresh fruits. The baked texture has some of the characteristics of puff pastry. In this recipe the fruits are sandwiched between two layers, and while the bottom remains slightly moist, the top rises, flakes a little and becomes crisp. In a similar recipe, Carême finishes the cake with a top crusting of nuts (see

FRESH FRUIT CAKES

below); the combination of this with the crisp pastry and soft tart fruits is extremely good.

This quantity make two 31 × 21 × 2.5 cm (12 × 8½ × 1 inch) baking trays, giving 24 slices. You can halve the amount if you wish.

250 g butter	9 oz butter
250 g plain flour	9 oz plain flour
50 g caster sugar	2 oz caster sugar
1 egg yolk	1 egg yolk
4 tablespoons sour cream	4 tablespoons sour cream
beaten egg white	beaten egg white
750 g plums, cooking or eating apples, pears, etc.	1¾ lb plums, cooking or eating apples, pears, etc.
100 g granulated sugar	3½ oz granulated sugar
40 g raisins (optional)	2 oz raisins (optional)
1 teaspoon cinnamon	1 teaspoon cinnamon

gas 4, 180°C, 350°F/approx 1 hour

Cut the butter into small pieces and rub into the sifted flour to make fine crumbs. Mix in the sugar. Blend in the egg yolk and the sour cream to make a firm paste. Roll into a ball, wrap, and chill for an hour or leave in the freezer for about 15 minutes. Cut into two pieces. Roll out one half 3 mm (⅛ inch) thick, and cut in two. Lay one of the sheets into the greased baking tray and brush lightly with beaten egg white. Slice the fruit quite thickly if using apples, less thickly for other fruit. Pack them close in the base and sprinkle with sugar, raisins and cinnamon; cover with another layer of fruit and sprinkle as before. Lay the second pastry sheet on top, brush with egg white, and sprinkle with granulated sugar or spread with Carême's crusting.

Repeat the process with the second piece of pastry. Bake in the preheated oven. Leave to cool in the tray, and cut into slices to serve.

Carême's Nut Crusting

Chop 100 g (4 oz) of hazelnuts and almonds coarsely; mix with 25 g (1 oz) of granulated sugar and bind into a spreading paste with 2 lightly beaten egg whites. Brush the pastry with egg white and spread the nut mixture over. Sprinkle with a little more granulated sugar before baking.

CAKES
THE CHERRY ORCHARD

'Women and children – those two fragile roots of society were always fond of sweet and delicate cakes', said Alexis Soyer. Queen Elizabeth I was certainly renowned for indulging her sweet tooth, though she was not fragile. Cherry pie was listed among her favourites, and she even commanded that cherry orchards be planted to provide amply for her demands. Cherry 'pyes' and tarts were frequently mentioned during past centuries, with little hint of any other fresh cherry cake apart from the occasional cherry batter. The crystallized cherry on the other hand does feature very often with other dried fruits.

> . . . There being no importation of foreign fruit, the cherries were of prime quality, May dukes, White heart, Black heart, and the Kentish cherry succeeded each other – and, when sold by weight, and not tied on sticks, fetched sixpence, fourpence or threepence per lb., which was at least twopence or threepence less than charged at the shops . . .
>
> (Andrew W. Tuer, *Old London Street Cries*, 1830)

Probably the best known cherry dessert is the popular *clafouti aux cerises*: a traditional dish of the Limousin region in France. Charmingly named, it is not a cake, but simply a glorified pancake. A flour, milk or cream batter is poured over fresh cherries (or any fresh fruit) and baked like a tart. The peasants serve it at harvest meal-times, and although it is quite pleasant eaten warm it tastes rather stodgy once cold – at best a satisfying filler for hungry appetites.

Similar to the fresh fruit sponge (page 258) is the following recipe; an unusual alternative to the ubiquitous 'pyes' and clafouti, it tastes as good cold as hot and is a better 'keeper'.

Fresh Cherry Almond Cake

This contains neither fat nor flour.

7 egg yolks	7 egg yolks
120 g caster sugar	4 oz caster sugar
2 teaspoons lemon zest	2 teaspoons lemon zest
140 g fine chopped almonds	5 oz fine chopped almonds
6 egg whites	6 egg whites

FRESH FRUIT CAKES

a sheet of rice paper
500 g fresh cherries

a sheet of rice paper
generous 1 lb fresh cherries

gas 4, 180°C, 350°F/1 hour

Beat together the egg yolks and the sugar until pale and creamy; add the lemon zest, and mix in the nuts. Beat up the egg whites to form peaks, and fold them into the mixture gently losing as little air as possible. Lay half the mixture into a ready greased, sugared and floured 24 cm (9½ inch) spring-form tin, and cover with the rice paper to prevent the fruits from sinking. Cover with the cherries and pour over the rest of the cake mixture. Bake in the preheated oven. Cool in the tin on a wire rack, then sprinkle generously with sugar before serving.

* *For a chocolate alternative:* Prepare the above mixture. Finish off by folding in at the end 35 g (1½ oz) of grated chocolate, 35 g (1½ oz) of candied lemon peel, chopped small, and 20 g (²/₃ oz) of white breadcrumbs moistened with a little orange juice. Proceed as above, but bake in a slightly cooler oven – gas 3, 170°C, 325°F – for an hour.

QUINCE

There are two distinct varieties of Quince – *Cydonia oblonga* and *Chaenomeles japonica*. Japonica or Japanese quince is the familiar ornamental garden shrub which flowers flamboyantly in English gardens in the spring, bright scarlet, pink or orange, and whose autumn fruits are small, hard, bullet-like and fairly inedible. Cydonia, on the other hand, bears similar beautiful blossoms, but the fruit and the foliage are very different. The fruit has a strong, sweet fragrance and is large and golden, shaped rather like a pear, with a greyish bloom. The yellow flesh turns pink when cooked. Cooking is essential, as the quince is still as bitter today as it was 3,000 years ago, and the raw taste is unforgettable, an 'exquisite torture of the mouth appearing to desiccate and wrinkle under the stringent action of its acid juice'. The quince flourishes in hot climates, although it also grows in cooler, more sheltered, regions. The lower temperatures produce a hard outer flesh which has to be peeled away before being used, but in the Middle East the whole fruit is edible.

In early times the Persians made quinces into a savoury dish, stuffing them with meat in much the same way as they did courgettes and peppers, and, like the Moroccans, also used them chopped in meat stews. For a sweet dish the Europeans added honey, a small amount of rose-water, almonds, spices such as cinnamon and ginger, cream and eggs. But in the eighteenth and nineteenth centuries, the favourites undoubtably were quince cheeses and marmalades, and the hardened pastille made by boiling a quince purée with sugar and lemon juice. The paste was used in pies, or the fruits were left whole, peeled and cooked in honey syrup to soften them, and then baked in pastry. Slices of the dried quince cheese were poached in wine to make a tasty compôte, or mixed with Malaga wine and lemon juice and frozen to make a fine sorbet. Shapes were cut out of the hardened paste for Christmas tree decorations; a mousse was made with sugar, or they were boiled in sugared water with orange zest and rind and made into a clear jelly or a wine. Slices of fruit preserved in vinegar were served as accompaniments to meat dishes. Quince marmalade, also popular for many centuries, is now practically the only use made of the fruit.

Dedicated to Venus, the quince was considered to be a symbol of love and happiness, and it became the custom to send quinces as love tokens and to offer them to a bridal couple at a wedding feast – 'as the eating of a Quince Peare to be a preparative of sweet and delightful dayes between the married persons'.

Quince Mousse for Fillings

Quince mousse is the basis for two of the three recipes which follow. The simplest way is to boil the peeled and cored fruits in lemon-flavoured water; but I prefer the following method, which takes longer but brings out the full flavour and also the pectin which helps it set well.

Peel and core 1 kg (a generous 2 lb) of quinces. Reserve the peels and cores. Cut the fruit into thick slices, and leave in a bowl covered with a little water and a teaspoonful of lemon juice to stop the fruits discolouring.

Boil the peels and cores with 400 ml ($^3/_4$ pint) of water, the juice of half a lemon, and 250 g (9 oz) of granulated sugar for about 30 minutes. The syrup will have thickened to a jelly-like consistency. Strain and return it to the pan, then cook the quince slices in it until they have softened. Pour away the liquid and either push the fruit through a fine sieve or liquidize in a blender or processor. Sweeten and flavour as necessary for each recipe.

FRESH FRUIT CAKES

Quince mousse can be frozen very successfully. Pack it in small freezer bags and seal tightly. It will keep for at least a year.

500 g (1 lb) whole fruit will make 300 g (11 oz) fruit mousse.

Quince Slices

Make a *sweet shortcrust pastry* (page 45) for a 20–22 cm (8–8½ inch) tin with:

130 g plain flour	4½ oz plain flour
90 g butter	3 oz butter
45 g caster sugar	2 oz caster sugar
1 egg yolk	1 egg yolk
pinch salt	pinch salt
½ teaspoon lemon zest	½ teaspoon lemon zest

Filling

50 g almonds, flaked and toasted	2 oz almonds, flaked and toasted
100 g candied lemon peel, chopped fine	3½ oz candied lemon peel, chopped fine
juice ½ lemon	juice ½ lemon
1 teaspoon cinnamon	1 teaspoon cinnamon
30 g caster sugar	1 oz caster sugar
300 g quince mousse	11 oz quince mousse
1 teaspoon orange-flower water	1 teaspoon orange-flower water

Line the base and sides of a 34 × 24 cm (13½ × 9½ inch) shallow Swiss roll tin with two-thirds of the pastry. Bake blind (page 208) in the preheated oven set at gas 6, 200°C, 400°F for 10 minutes, then reduce the temperature to gas 4, 180°C, 350°F for a further 20 minutes until it is a very pale biscuit colour. Allow to cool.

Mix together all the ingredients for the filling and smooth over the pastry base. Roll out the remainder of the pastry 2 mm (under ¹⁄₁₀ inch) thick, and cut into long narrow bands approximately 1.5 cm (½ inch) wide. Make a trellis by laying 4 bands across the length at regular intervals and 6 across the width; press gently into the quince paste. Brush with lightly beaten egg, and bake for 35 minutes longer until the trellis has browned a little. Cut into fingers while still hot, but leave in the tin on a wire rack to cool.

CAKES

A Nineteenth-century Quince Torte

Prepare a sweet shortcrust pastry for a 20–22 cm (8–8½ inch) tin as in the previous recipe.

Line the base only of a spring-form tin with half the pastry, bake blind (brushing with egg white to insulate) and allow to cool. Roll out the rest of the pastry, cut it into a strip the depth of the tin and press it into place (page 209).

Filling

240 g quince paste	8 oz quince paste
40 g caster sugar	2 oz caster sugar
2 teaspoons lemon zest	2 teaspoons lemon zest
1 teaspoon orange-flower water	1 teaspoon orange-flower water

Covering

65 g caster sugar	2½ oz caster sugar
4 egg yolks	4 egg yolks
65 g ground almonds	2½ oz ground almonds
4 egg whites	4 egg whites
20 g plain flour	1 oz plain flour

To make the filling, mix the quince mousse with the sugar, lemon zest and orange-flower water and spread evenly over the pastry base. For the covering, beat the caster sugar and egg yolks together until they are pale and creamy, then mix in the almonds. Whip the egg whites in another bowl to make firm, snowy peaks, and fold them into the mixture. Lightly sift part of the flour over the surface in two stages, and fold in very carefully. Pour over the quince filling, rap the tin sharply on the work-top to disperse any pockets of air, and bake in the preheated oven for 50 minutes at gas 4, 180°C, 350°F. Leave to cool in the tin for about 10 minutes before releasing the spring and removing the base. Cool on a wire rack. Serve with sweetened whipped cream.

Strawberries

> The native strawberry red-ripening grows.
> By nettles guarded, as by thorns the rose
>
> (Richard Savage, *The Wanderer* 1729)

FRESH FRUIT CAKES

> The fruit of any species of the genus Fragaria: a soft bag-shaped receptacle, scarlet to yellowish in colour, full of juicy pulp, and dotted over with small yellow seed-like achenes.
>
> (Oxford English Dictionary)

What a mundane description of a fruit as delectable as this. More appropriate, surely, is the suggestion that, 'Doubtless God could have made a better berry, but doubtless God never did.'

The earliest mention of strawberries in English writings is in a tenth-century Saxon plant list. Where the name originates is not known, although of the two most common suggestions, the straying (stráe) habit of the layering shoots, which root themselves, is more likely. (Protecting plants with straw was common much later when the hybrid fruits were developed.) In 1265 a household scroll belonging to the Countess of Leicester listed the 'straberie', and a century later the London street crier peddled, 'strabery rype, and cherryes in the ryse'.

The first settlers in America learned from the native Indians how to eat the lovely fruits which grew there in abundance. They ate them at breakfast, in soup sprinkled with milkweed dew, and even as seasoning for meat dishes. Medicinally their virtues were also found useful.

It was in America that two strains of strawberry grew which were later crossed by the French to create the larger modern variety. The North American Virginian strawberry had already travelled to Europe in 1629, and almost a hundred years later five plants of the Chilean beach variety were introduced into France. These bore fruit of exceptional size, 'as large as a walnut', were pale red with firm, almost white flesh and had a delicate aroma.

Strawberries always lend a festive air to an occasion – with cream in layers of shortcake, or piled in meringue shells; served at Wimbledon in the traditional way with sugar and cream, or from crystal bowls at Glyndebourne picnics; or simply presented in leaf cones, with their stalks and a dipping of sugar.

They are mentioned frequently in literature. Ben Jonson speaks of 'A pot of Strawberries gathered in the wood to mingle with your cream'; after dinner Parson Woodforde ate 'Almonds and Raisins, Oranges and Strawberries . . . the first gathered this year by me', and the strawberry-picking party in Jane Austen's *Emma* is very familiar.

The nineteenth-century pastrycooks enjoyed using strawberries. Fruits were mostly crushed for cream, bavarois, frozen desserts, fondants and sauces, while whole ones were preferred for cakes such as vacherin, or between layers of Genoese sponge and puff pastries or open flans. As with much of their cuisine, perfumes and liqueurs played a strong part, and strawberries were particularly suitable.

Flavouring Strawberries

We are fortunate to have strawberries for most of the year: the main season is in May, June and July. They vary in shape, size, and flavour, some small and round and very sweet, others enormous and oval, long and pointed, and sometimes with not much flavour.

Freshly picked strawberries have the finest taste and generally need very little or no enhancement – at most a sprinkling of caster sugar – but when they have lost that first fragrance, for instance if bought in a shop or picked slightly unripe and travelled from afar, they improve greatly with a little encouragement. Vanilla sugar is the obvious flavour, while the zests and juices of both sweet orange and lemon work a special magic. But have you thought of pepper? – Kirsch, Cointreau, Curaçao and cognac enhance, and some people like claret or ports.

> to add a redder tincture to their own
>
> (William King, *Mully of Mountown* (1702))

– but I prefer champagne.

Cream, double, single, whipped, flavoured or plain, is the other popular accompaniment, while in France the slightly sour crème fraîche, crème pâtissière and crème frangipane are favourites.

Preparation

Strawberries should be rinsed in very little water before the stems are removed, so that the juices do not wash away.

SOME SIMPLE STRAWBERRY CAKES

A blind baked flan (page 208) filled with strawberries is simple and appealing, but James Beard's peppery 'Strawberries Carcassone' with cream and meringue is more unusual. Toss the fruits in sugar with a little lemon juice. Sprinkle with coarse black pepper and a dash of Armagnac. Macerate for a short time, then drain and mix the excess juices into the sweetened stiffly beaten whipped cream, spread the meringue over, and cover with the saturated fruits.

Hazelnut tart shells (page 322) can be filled with strawberries, or the fruits can be cut and layered with crème pâtissière in slices of puff pastry (page 52).

The Reverend Sydney Smith said, 'What is real piety? What is true attachment to the Church? How are these fine feelings best evinced? The answer is plain; by sending strawberries to a clergyman.'

Strawberry Sponge Cake

Here is a light sponge cake split in layers and filled with strawberries and cream.

Prepare a fatless sponge (page 90) with 6 eggs; 150 g caster sugar; 150 g plain flour; 1 teaspoon lemon zest
(6 eggs; 5 oz caster sugar; 5 oz plain flour; 1 teaspoon lemon zest)

Turn into a lined, greased, sugared and floured 26 cm (10½ inch) spring-form tin, and bake for 40 minutes at gas 4, 180°C, 350°F. Stand on a wire rack to cool for 10 minutes before removing the tin; then leave to cool completely. Split the cake into three layers.

Wash briefly, dry and hull 500 g (1 lb) strawberries. Keep 4 or 5 for decoration and slice the rest. Cover the bottom layer of cake with half the fruits and sprinkle with a tablespoon of Kirsch or Cointreau; cover with a second sheet of sponge and the rest of the fruits, spooning over more spirit. Place the remaining sponge on top and spread 275 ml (½ pint) whipped crème chantilly all over. Scatter a few toasted almond flakes as decoration and finish with the whole strawberries.

Strawberry Fruit Cake with Almonds

Strawberries baked inside a cake mixture are a colourful surprise. Ground almonds replace flour in this recipe; the nuttiness of the pastry enhances strawberries particularly well, also cherries, plums, peaches and apricots. Double cream and eau de vie make it richer and more luxurious.

CAKES

100 g butter	3½ oz butter
100 g caster sugar	3½ oz caster sugar
6 egg yolks	6 egg yolks
zest 1 lemon	zest 1 lemon
100 g coarse ground almonds	3½ oz coarse ground almonds
2 tablespoons double cream	2 tablespoons double cream
3 egg whites	3 egg whites
2 tablespoons toasted white breadcrumbs	2 tablespoons toasted white breadcrumbs
2 tablespoons double cream or Kirsch	2 tablespoons double cream or Kirsch
250 g fresh fruits of choice	9 oz fresh fruits of choice

gas 4, 180°C, 350°F/1 hour

Beat the butter and the sugar together until pale and creamy. Beat in the egg yolks one at a time. Add the grated lemon zest, mix in the ground almonds and 2 tablespoons of double cream, and combine well. Whip up the egg whites in a separate bowl until they stand in peaks, and fold them carefully into the mixture, using a metal spoon, retaining as much air as possible. Finally fold in the breadcrumbs and the rest of the cream or Kirsch. Grease and dust with flour and sugar a 24 cm (9½ inch) spring-form tin and pour in a quarter of the mixture. Par-bake in the preheated oven for 10 minutes to set, then cover with the fruits and the remaining cake mixture. Bake and set on a wire rack to cool. Dredge with icing sugar to serve. The fruits may also be laid in the bottom of the tin and there is then no need to par-bake the cake mixture. In this case cover the upturned fruits with sweetened whipped cream before serving.

Strawberry Shortcake

The Americans have a penchant for strawberry shortcake. Evan Jones in *American Food: The Gastronomic Story* explains:

> Nothing is more American than strawberries freshly picked and drenched in thick cream skimmed from the morning's milk, unless it is strawberry shortcake. There are variations — sometimes this earthy Americanism has been gussied up by the employment of layers of airy white cake, or a bread dough enriched with sugar and eggs, as in old Nantucket kitchens — but an unimpeachable

strawberry shortcake needs a baking powder biscuit-dough lavishly mixed with butter and cream. Baked to flaky perfection, this is carefully split into two layers, the lower of which is usually slathered with butter before accepting its burden of berries with sugar to make a filling that drips in rivulets down the sides. The top half is buttered, still hot, and covers the crushed berries and in its turn is capped with more berries. Some cooks put their strawberry shortcakes back in the oven to ripen for a minute or two and then served the dessert with a pitcher of cream.

Here is a delectable recipe for American Strawberry Shortcake from Anita Borghese's *Just Desserts*. The pastry is rather like an English scone.

Pastry

220 g plain flour
1 tablespoon caster sugar
3 teaspoons baking powder
1/2 teaspoon salt
pinch nutmeg
110 g unsalted butter
1 egg
150 ml double cream or milk
140 g softened butter for spreading on cooked layers

7 1/2 oz plain flour
1 tablespoon caster sugar
3 teaspoons baking powder
1/2 teaspoon salt
pinch nutmeg
4 oz unsalted butter
1 egg
5 fl oz double cream or milk
5 oz softened butter for spreading on cooked layers

Filling

200 g strawberries, crushed
2 tablespoons sugar
1 tablespoon Cointreau or Kirsch
50 g strawberries, sliced

7 oz strawberries, crushed
2 tablespoons sugar
1 tablespoon Cointreau or Kirsch
2 oz strawberries, sliced

Top

250 ml double cream
1 tablespoon caster sugar
whole strawberries for decoration

9 fl oz double cream
1 tablespoon caster sugar
whole strawberries for decoration

gas 8, 230°C, 450°F/20 minutes

Carefully sift all the dry pastry ingredients into a bowl. Coarsely cut the butter, and rub in to form dry crumbs. Lightly beat the egg with the cream and stir into the mixture. Combine well without overmixing. Press the dough into a greased and floured 20–22 cm (8–8 1/2 inch) spring-form tin and pat even. Bake, and cool for a short while on a wire rack. Split the layer in half. Spread the bottom layer with butter and cover with the filling mixture of sliced and macerated crushed fruits. Cover with the other cooked layer which has also been buttered underneath. Cover with the cream, stiffly whipped and with the sugar added, and decorate with the remaining strawberries.

Oranges and Lemons

> Fine Sevil oranges, fine lemmans, fine;
> Round, sound, and tender, inside and rine,
> One pin's prick their virtue shew:
> They've liquor by their weight, you may know.
>
> (Seventeenth-century street cry)

Oranges and lemons are now so familiar that we are inclined to take them for granted, but of all the fruits they are perhaps the most attractive in their natural state. The dark, glossy green leaves contrast dramatically with the shiny, almost fluorescent, coloured fruits, whose tidy symmetry lends an air of unreality.

As to their origin, history is a little uncertain, though the bitter orange is reputed to have come from China and India, and the lemon from further west, maybe from Persia. The Persians loved the fresh tang of the fruit, and flavoured many sweet and sour dishes with citrus as well as with other fruits such as pomegranate and apricot. It was due to the Arabs, who planted trees on their conquering expeditions to the eastern Mediterranean, and to the Crusaders returning from Palestine to Italy and south eastern France, that Europe became familiar with the orange. But it was the bitter orange which they knew, the sweet China fruit being introduced at a much later time, possibly by the Portuguese explorer Vasco da Gama or the fifteenth-century merchants from Genoa. Sweet oranges were first seen in some London markets during the 1660s and known as *portyngales* – having been brought from Portugal.

Citrus fruits were enormously valued in Europe – over a hundred varieties came to be cultivated — and this interest stimulated the development of plant houses in areas where the colder climates proved too severe for the half-hardy trees. The orange, with its attractive close head of deep green foliage on top of a slender trunk, was particularly coveted; pot-grown oranges featured in the gardens of many grand houses and in the winter they were wheeled into orangeries.

In 1736 Richard Bradley had these words to say concerning oranges in his *Country Housewife and Lady's Director*:

> In this Month [February] it may not be unnecessary to observe that Oranges are declining, and waste apace; but they are commonly very cheap, and therefore such as have a great Call for Orange-peel, as Confectioners, etc. now buy them in quantities; but a little Carriage by Land will contribute to their quicker decay. The Orange, tho' it is not found in every Garden, yet I esteem it as a necessary Fruit in many Cakes, and what a Family can hardly be without; and truly considering how good Oranges we might have in our Gardens, and how easily they may be cultivated against Garden-walls, I much wonder that they are not more generally planted with us. There is a very good Instance of their prospering well against a Wall, and thriving in the natural Ground, at Mr *Heather's*, a curious Gentleman at *Twittenham*, which Trees bear very well, and bring very large Fruit.
>
> But as I have observ'd above, that this is the Season when foreign Oranges are generally in the greatest plenty about *London*, it is a good time to preserve their Juice . . .

Zests, Peels and Juices

Zest — the grated rind of citrus fruits — gives an acid tang and a piquant taste. In baking it enriches and enhances other flavours. It also looks attractive — brightly speckled with a clear oily sheen. Zests must be used with a light touch, for they can overpower other flavours and spoil the texture of a cake.

The zest is the coloured part of the skin — the white pithy layer underneath is bitter and unpleasant, so take care to leave it behind. You can grate zest, or better still, use a zester, a handy little nineteenth-century tool which once again is becoming popular, and which cuts and curls fine long slivers of peel.

Rinds can also be grated coarsely and wrung through a cheese-cloth into sugar — but leave to absorb the oils for at least 15 minutes.

Oranges and Lemons in Baking

The role of oranges and lemons in baking is principally to flavour and to perfume. Too much acid moisture will cause a cake to sink and become soggy. Zests and juices flavour creams and icings well; the fruits can be sliced and candied in sugar where the volatile oils are trapped; a sugar and citrus syrup can be poured over a hot freshly baked sponge; lemons, combined with eggs and butter, make a delicious cheese or curd which layers well in a tart or flan. Orange zest enhances the flavour of strawberries and bilberries and blends well with chocolate and with almonds. Choose fruits which have a good, clean strong colour and are free from blemishes. Thin skinned varieties are preferable, for they are generally sweeter and more juicy. Roll the fruit between your hands to soften the skins and make the juices flow more readily. Avoid citrus essences of any sort.

Orange Honey Sponge

A moist and aromatic cake.

50 g butter	2 oz butter
1 tablespoon honey	1 tablespoon honey
80 g caster sugar	3 oz caster sugar
4 egg yolks	4 egg yolks
zest 1 orange	zest 1 orange
50 g potato flour	2 oz potato flour
50 g plain flour	2 oz plain flour
4 egg whites	4 egg whites

gas 3, 170°C, 325°F/40 minutes

Gently melt the butter and honey together and leave to cool. Work the sugar and egg yolks to a pale frothy mixture, and beat in the orange zest. Beat in the butter and honey mixture. Sift the flours well to aerate. Beat up the egg whites to stiff snowy peaks, and fold alternate spoonfuls of egg snow and flour into the mixture, being careful not to lose any air. Pour into a greased and flour-dusted 22 cm (8½ inch) spring-form tin. Bake in the preheated oven. Leave in the tin for 5 minutes before turning out on to a wire rack to cool. Fill with orange-flavoured butter cream (page 64), and dredge with icing sugar to serve, or coat with orange glacé icing.

FRESH FRUIT CAKES
FRESH MINCED ORANGE CAKES

The following two recipes are quite unlike other citrus cakes, as they use fresh whole oranges. In the first recipe they are minced raw, and in the second they are boiled in water for 2 or 3 hours until tender. The texture and flavour of both cakes is completely different. Apart from the varying ingredients, the boiled fruits have a much stronger and slightly bitter taste, which infuses with the ground almonds, rum, sugar and eggs after a couple of days, leaving a very moist cake with a clean, dominating fragrance. The minced raw fruits, prepared in a more conventional type of Genoese sponge, give a much milder flavoured, less moist cake. In both instances it is vital to keep the maximum amount of air in the mixture to counter the effect of the wet, rather heavy, fresh fruits; this means that attention must be paid to careful beating of the egg whites and even more careful folding in.

Because the cakes are made with fresh fruits they will keep for only 4 or 5 days in a cold place.

Minced Orange Sponge Cake

220 g minced oranges	8 oz minced oranges
200 g butter	7 oz butter
4 egg yolks	4 egg yolks
200 g caster sugar	7 oz caster sugar
100 g plain flour	3½ oz plain flour
½ vanilla pod	½ vanilla pod
4 egg whites	4 egg whites
50 g corn or potato flour	2 oz corn or potato flour

gas 5, 190°C, 375°F/50 minutes

Wash and dry the oranges and mince them coarsely. Leave in a colander to drain. Melt the butter on a low heat and set aside to cool. Beat the egg yolks and 100 g (3½ oz) sugar until pale and creamy. Beat in the well sifted plain flour and then the cool butter. Next add the vanilla pod scrapings and the minced oranges, and blend well together. Whip up the egg whites in a separate bowl to form stiff peaks, and beat in the remainder of the sugar, then fold the egg whites and the sifted potato flour in alternating spoonfuls into the main mixture. Pour into a greased and floured 24 cm (9½ inch) spring-form tin. The mixture will be quite soft and runny. Bake in the preheated oven.

Orange and Almond Cake

I am not sure where this type of orange and almond cake originates — possibly the Middle East (Claudia Roden has a similar recipe), or maybe Spain or Portugal, where both fruits and nuts grow in such profusion. My own early twentieth-century recipe comes from Frau Kroschel. She was one of those itinerant cooks who only appeared for special occasions in my grandparents' home. Her cooking was divine and her bakery a constant source of pleasure.

2 large oranges	2 large oranges
150 ml water	5½ fl oz water
110 g slightly coarse ground almonds	4 oz slightly coarse ground almonds
75 g caster sugar	2½ oz caster sugar
1 tablespoon potato flour	1 tablespoon potato flour
2 tablespoons rum	2 tablespoons rum
5 egg yolks	5 egg yolks
5 egg whites	5 egg whites

gas 5, 190°C, 375°F / 45 minutes

Wash the unpeeled oranges and set to boil in a covered pan with the water. Change the water 3 or 4 times to remove any bitterness, and cook for about 2 hours until the fruit is soft and spongy. Leave to cool. Mash, mince or process the cold fruit to a slight coarseness so that it has a pleasant texture. Beat the orange mousse together with the almonds and half the quantity of sugar. Next add the sifted flour and the rum. Beat in the egg yolks one at a time. Whip up the egg whites into peaks, and lightly beat in the rest of the sugar. Fold this into the orange mixture. It will have a surprisingly firm consistency.

Pour into a greased and floured 22 cm (8½ inch) spring-form tin, it will fill it almost to the top, but hardly rises in baking. Bake in the preheated oven. Leave in the tin for a few minutes before turning on to a cake rack to cool. Cover with whipped, sweetened double cream, and decorate with slivers of fresh orange rind.

The cake becomes dark golden brown and shrinks away from the edges of the tin when ready, but test with a skewer carefully before taking it out of the oven as the centre may be slow to cook. Leave in the tin for a few minutes before turning it out to cool. Dredge with icing sugar before serving.

FRESH FRUIT CAKES

Lemon Cake

This is a very popular and simple tea-time treat.

100 g butter	3½ oz butter
100 g caster sugar	3½ oz caster sugar
2 large eggs	2 large eggs
100 g plain flour	3½ oz plain flour
½ teaspoon baking powder	½ teaspoon baking powder
zest and juice of 1 lemon	zest and juice of 1 lemon
2 tablespoons warm water	2 tablespoons warm water
50 g granulated sugar	2 oz granulated sugar

gas 4, 180°C, 350°F/1 hour

Beat the butter and caster sugar until pale and creamy. Mix in the eggs one at a time. Sift the baking powder and the flour together, and combine with the mixture taking care not to overbeat. Add the lemon zest and stir in the water. Turn into a greased 1 kg (2 lb) loaf tin, and bake in the preheated oven. Meanwhile melt the granulated sugar in the lemon juice over a gentle heat to form a syrup.

When the cake starts to shrink away from the sides of the tin and has browned nicely, take it out of the oven and turn out on to a wire rack. While it is still hot, prick it all over with a knitting needle or a skewer, and spoon the lemon syrup over the surface, taking care to catch any escaping juices on a plate set underneath. Pour these over as well until all has been absorbed. Dredge the top with icing sugar to serve.

This cake keeps very well in the freezer for 2–3 months, wrapped well in aluminium foil. Once defrosted it will stay fresh for at least a week.

Orange Mousseline with Farci Curaçao

This light sponge cake of Urbain Dubois, layered with orange flavoured marzipan, is quite unusual.

Cake mixture

70 g potato flour	3 oz potato flour
70 g plain flour	3 oz plain flour
6 egg yolks	6 egg yolks
125 g caster sugar	4½ oz caster sugar
zest 1 orange	zest 1 orange
6 egg whites	6 egg whites
75 g butter, melted and cooled	3 oz butter, melted and cooled
strained apricot jam and orange icing for topping	strained apricot jam and orange icing for topping

Filling

150 g ground almonds	5 oz ground almonds
75 g icing sugar	3 oz icing sugar
egg white	egg white
35 g strained apricot jam	1½ oz strained apricot jam
zest 1 orange	zest 1 orange
2 tablespoons Curaçao or Grand Marnier	2 tablespoons Curaçao or Grand Marnier

gas 3, 170°C, 325°F/50 minutes

First prepare the marzipan filling and chill in the refrigerator while you bake the cake. Mix the ground almonds and the icing sugar together, and bind them with a little egg white, the strained apricot jam, the orange zest and the liqueur. Roll into a ball, wrap tightly and refrigerate.

Sift the flours together to aerate well. Beat the egg yolks and caster sugar until pale and creamy and the ribbon stage is reached. Mix in the orange zest. Whip up the egg whites in another bowl until they hold firm peaks. Use a large metal spoon to fold alternate spoonfuls of sifted flour and egg white into the mixture. Finally fold in the melted butter. Pour into a greased and flour-dusted 24 cm (9½ inch) spring-form tin, and bake. When the cake shrinks away from the sides of the tin and feels springy to the touch, it is ready. Leave on a wire rack for a few minutes in the tin before removing it to allow the cake to cool completely.

FRESH FRUIT CAKES

To finish the cake: Divide the marzipan filling into two, and roll each piece into a circle to fit the cake. Split the cake into two; cover the bottom layer with a circle of marzipan, cover with the other cake and press the second marzipan layer onto this. Brush the whole cake with strained apricot jam and cover with orange glacé icing (page 73). Decorate with fresh orange slices or candied orange pieces.

* For a decorative alternative, brush apricot jam on the sides only of the cake and press in toasted chopped almonds. Lay a circle of orange slices round the perimeter surface only, fixed in place with a dab of jam.

Dried Fruit Cakes

While he, from forth the closet, brought a heap
Of candied apple, quince, and plum, and gourd;
With jellies smoother than the creamy curd,
And incent syrups tinct with cinnamon;
Manna and dates, in argosy transferr'd
From Fez; and spicèd dainties, every one,
From silken Samarcand to cedar'd Lebanon.

(John Keats, *The Eve of Saint Agnes*)

Dried fruits were a vital staple food of most communities from very early times. With origins mainly in the Near East, the fruits (which were buried in the hot desert sand to dry them) were very popular in early Arab cuisine; the sweet and sour element was to have far-reaching influence as the fruits became popular throughout the world. Nutritionally they were of especial importance during the winter months in the colder climes, often forming the main part of a meal, and figs and dates particularly became the chief staple of the poorer peoples. Pastries were stuffed with dried fruit fillings, like the 'Ma'amoul' of Bedouin origin later glamorized by the Abbassid courts; these little tartlets, made of flour, butter and milk and perfumed with orange-flower water, had dates or nuts inside.

Later European fruit cakes consisted of simple bread-like doughs enriched with spices, fruits and butter, which in England were usually known as 'plumb' cakes. The term 'plumb' was a curious one, for hardly a plum or a prune appeared in a cake (usually they were preserved in sugar or dried and offered as sweet-meats). Plumb cakes were invariably made with a selection of dried fruits and lemon and orange peels; Hannah Glasse mentioned in 1760 an ordinary plumb cake made with bread dough to which '. . . You put in the plumbs, and work in as many as you please.' She also gives one recipe for an unyeasted plumb cake, which our rich fruit cake more closely resembles.

DRIED FRUIT CAKES

To make a very fine rich plumb cake.

Take four pounds of the finest flour well dried and sifted, six pounds of the best fresh butter, seven pounds of currants well washed, picked, and rubbed very clean and dry; two pounds of Jordan almonds, blanched and beat in a marble mortar, with sack and orange-flour water, till they are very fine; take four pounds of eggs, leave out half the whites, and add three pounds of double-refined sugar, beat and sifted through a lawn sieve, with mace, cloves, and cinnamon, of each a quarter of an ounce; three large nutmegs beat fine, a little ginger, of sack and French brandy half a pint each, sweetmeats to your liking, lemon and citron; take a large broad pan, beat your butter to a cream before any of your ingredients go in, minding to beat it all one way, or it will turn to oil; put in your sugar, beat it well, and work in your almonds; let your eggs be well beat, put in, and beat all together till it looks white and thick; put in your brandy, sack, and spices, and shake your flour in by degrees; when your oven is ready, put in your currants and sweetmeats, and put it into your hoop; it will take four baking hours in a quick oven.

> *Note:* As you mix it for the oven, you must be mindful to keep beating it all the time with your hand; and your currants, as soon as cleaned, must be put in a dish before the fire, that they may be warm when mixed. The above quantity bakes best in two hoops.

(The Compleat Confectioner, 1760)

Dried Fruits in Baking

Currants, raisins and sultanas are the most common fruits used in baking. Fortunately they are now available ready cleaned and washed. I like to plump raisins and currants a little before baking; as the cut cake looks more attractive and the fruit is less chewy. Steep them in water, to cover, for about 30 minutes, then spread them over a baking sheet, cover closely with foil, and dry out in a moderate oven for 5 minutes. Plump sultanas in a little dark rum or brandy, which gives them more flavour. Glacé cherries should be washed in a little boiling water to dissolve the syrup; dry off very carefully before chopping.

As a change from the conventional fruits you can substitute a similar quantity of any one of the following. The large, stoned, California prunes have a good colour and add moisture – steep them in water for a short time, drain and chop. Dried apricots have an unusual, rather nutty taste – handle in the same way as prunes. Preserved stem ginger with a little of the syrup gives a sharp tang, but be careful, for it can dominate all the other flavours. Dried pears, very common in Switzerland, and dried apples are also unusual; soak pears in cold water for a few hours, but apples only need a short time.

Dried fruits keep well for 2 or 3 months. When they start to deteriorate a whitish bloom appears on the surface, and the fruit dries and hardens. Maggots may also appear.

For specific instructions on nuts see pages 308–41.

To Prevent Fruits from Sinking to the Bottom of the Cake

Dried fruits and nuts are heavy and inclined to drop to the bottom of a fruit cake. Simone Beck and Julia Child, in *Mastering the Art of French Cooking*, Volume II, have found that using strong, plain flour rather than soft flour, and adding a little baking powder, helps to prevent this.

To coat the fruit, mix ½ teaspoon of baking powder with 1 or 2 tablespoons of flour taken from the main quantity. Dry the fruits very carefully, and coat them thoroughly with the mixture.

More Hints

A heavy fruit cake mixture can be left to rest overnight in the refrigerator before being baked.

Lining papers are left in place until a heavy fruited cake has cooled down completely.

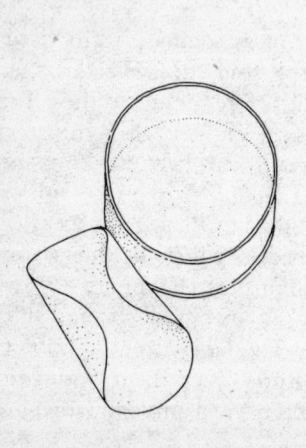

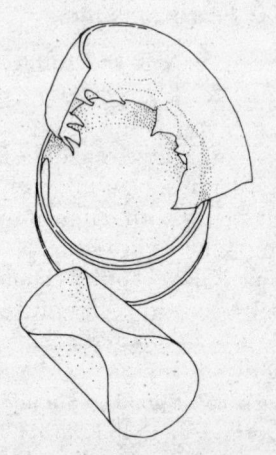

For lighter cake mixtures, the lining paper is peeled off after the cake has cooled for about 10 minutes.

Fruit cakes are great 'keepers', and with time their flavour mellows and improves. The richer the fruit content, and particularly if it is laced with spirit (you can always spoon more over during storage), the longer it will keep.

Lining Tins for Fruit Cakes

Heavy fruit cakes are baked for a long time in a slow to moderate temperature. To prevent the bottom and the sides of the cakes from darkening too much and sticking, the cake tin must be lined with paper. The longer the baking period, the thicker the insulation should be. For a very heavy, rich cake in a deep tin, two layers of brown paper and one of greaseproof are necessary. Where the cooking time is less than 1½ hours, a single layer of greaseproof paper on the sides is enough.

For a round or square tin – how to cut the paper and line the tin. The base and the sides are cut separately. Use the tin as a template; stand it on the paper (which has been folded to give two bases) and draw round it with pencil. With scissors, cut a neat circle to fit inside the tin. Cut two strips of paper a little longer than half the circumference, and 5 cm (2 inches) deeper than the tin. Fold over 2 cm (1 inch) along the length of the paper, and snip diagonally at regular intervals to the crease, to help ease the band around the sides of the tin.

Use a pastry brush to grease the base and sides with melted butter. Press in the first paper circle, then ease the two paper bands into place – they will stand higher than the sides of the tin. Cover the snipped bottom edge of the band with the second paper circle. Brush all the surfaces again with melted butter. (If a double thickness of paper is used to line the walls of the tin, a dab of butter in three or four places will stick them together.)

How to cut the paper and line a rectangular tin. Cut a sheet of paper large enough to cover the base and sides of the tin plus 2 cm (1 inch). Stand the tin in the middle. With scissors, cut in from each corner to the nearest corner of the tin. Grease the base and sides of the tin with butter and press the paper lining into place, letting the corner flaps overlap. Neatly secure them with a dab of butter. Brush all the surfaces with more butter.

Dundee Cake

He had always liked cakes, especially rich Dundees and dark brown home-made fruit cakes tasting elusively of Guinness. He said to the lady at the stall, 'You won't think me greedy if I have another sixpennyworth?'

'No. Please.'

'I should say, then, four pounds eight and a half ounces.'

He was conscious of an odd silence, as if all the afternoon they had been waiting for just this, but hadn't somehow expected it from him. Then a stout woman who hovered on the outskirts gave a warm and hearty laugh. 'Lawks,' she said. 'Anybody can tell you're a bachelor.'

'As a matter of fact,' the lady behind the stall rebuked her sharply, 'this gentleman has won. He is not more than a fraction of an ounce out. That counts,' she said, with nervous whimsicality, 'as direct hit.'

'Four pounds eight ounces,' the stout woman said. 'Well, you be careful, that's all. It'll be as heavy as lead.'

'On the contrary, it's made with real eggs.'

The stout woman went away laughing ironically in the direction of the clothing stall.

(Graham Greene, *The Ministry of Fear*)

The city of Dundee in Scotland became famous for its marmalade well over two centuries ago. Demand was heavy, and the manufacturer urgently needed to use up the left-over peels – what better than a Dundee cake? It is a simple, dark fruit cake made with brown sugar, sultanas and, of course, candied orange peel; but what makes it instantly recognizable is the concentric circles of blanched almonds studded on the surface.

1 teaspoon bicarbonate of soda	1 teaspoon bicarbonate of soda
300 ml water	11 fl oz water
110 g butter	4 oz butter
220 g soft brown or muscovado sugar	8 oz soft brown or muscovado sugar
125 g candied orange peel	4½ oz candied orange peel
375 g sultanas	13 oz sultanas
4 tablespoons brandy or dark rum	4 tablespoons brandy or dark rum
220 g strong, plain flour	8 oz strong, plain flour
2 teaspoons baking powder	2 teaspoons baking powder
2 large eggs	2 large eggs
zest 1 orange and 1 lemon	zest 1 orange and 1 lemon
50 g blanched, split almonds	2 oz blanched, split almonds

gas 4, 180°C, 350°F/1¼–1½ hours

Dissolve the bicarbonate of soda in the water in a pan, then add the butter, sugar, orange peel and sultanas. Set the pan on a low heat and bring to the boil. Stir occasionally and leave to boil gently for 20 minutes. Cool completely, then add the spirit. Sift together the flour and baking powder, and set aside. Whip up the eggs until frothy and mix in the boiled mixture. Add the orange and lemon zests and gradually work in the sifted flour. Butter, line and butter again a deep 20 cm (8 inch) cake tin, and pour in the mixture. Smooth it out carefully, making a slight hollow in the centre – it will flatten out as it bakes. Using the fingertips, lightly smooth a little milk over the surface.

Dip the blanched almonds in milk (this keeps them tender and crisp and prevents them burning during baking), and stud them split side down, in even concentric circles, starting from the middle and working out, into the surface of the cake. Lightly dredge caster sugar over the cake, and set in the preheated oven immediately. The cake will brown evenly and the almonds stay white. When it shrinks away from the sides of the tin, test for readiness; remove from the oven and cool in the tin for 10 minutes before turning out on to a wire rack to cool completely.

CAKES

Dattel Torte

(with fresh dates)

Little dates like pearls, that glisten
On a necklace one by one . . .

(Mahumudibn a-Husain al-Kushajim)

In 1226 the Baghdad Cookery Book contained a method for freshening dates when not in season. 'Take large poor-quality dates with stalks complete. Take a green water-melon, make a hole in the top large enough to admit the hand, then remove the pith, leaving the juice in. Put in the dates as required, replace the top, and leave for a day and a night. Then take out the dates: they will be found to be like fresh-picked dates.'

Obviously fresh dates have a much finer flavour than dried varieties, and are often available during the winter months. Otherwise use dried stoneless dates, but cook them in a little water for a short while to soften them (leave to cool and dry before chopping). Or use the whole fruits that come with their stems — halve them and remove the stones.

This cake makes a rich and luxurious party dessert.

210 g dates, pitted (280 g fresh dates, with stones)	8 oz dates, pitted (10 oz fresh dates, with stones)
8 egg whites	8 egg whites
280 g caster sugar	10 oz caster sugar
30 g candied orange and lemon peel	1 oz candied orange and lemon peel
280 g raw almonds, coarsely chopped	10 oz raw almonds, coarsely chopped

gas 4, 180°C, 350°F/approx. 1 hour

Skin the dates, remove the stones and chop into fine strips — dip the knife frequently into hot water to make it easier. Beat the egg whites to stiff peaks, beat in half the sugar and then fold in the remainder with a large metal spoon as you do with meringue, taking care not to lose any air. Mix the finely chopped candied peels with the dates and fold them into the mixture, then fold in the nuts. Have ready greased and lined with siliconed paper a 28 cm (11 inch) spring-form tin. Pour in the mixture and bake.

The cake will brown well and be quite soft but springy to the touch. Remove it from the oven, place on a wire rack for a few moments, then gently strip away the lining papers taking care not to tear the cake. Invert it on to another rack and remove the bottom paper. Leave to cool.

Split the cake in half; it will be very moist. Fill with stiffly whipped double cream, and spread cream over the top and sides. Decorate with a few chopped nuts and some fresh date slivers.

Carmelite Cake

Almonds replace butter in this very moist cake. Leave it to rest for a few days so that the flavours can mellow, and then cut only thin slices, for it is very rich.

100 g fresh or dried dates	3½ oz fresh or dried dates
100 g dried figs	3½ oz dried figs
100 g strong, plain flour	3½ oz strong, plain flour
50 g raisins	2 oz raisins
9 egg yolks	9 egg yolks
200 g caster sugar	7 oz caster sugar
150 g ground almonds	5 oz ground almonds
60 g plain or bitter chocolate, grated	2 oz plain or bitter chocolate, grated
5 egg whites	5 egg whites
50 g flaked almonds	2 oz flaked almonds

gas 4, 180°C, 350°F/1 hour

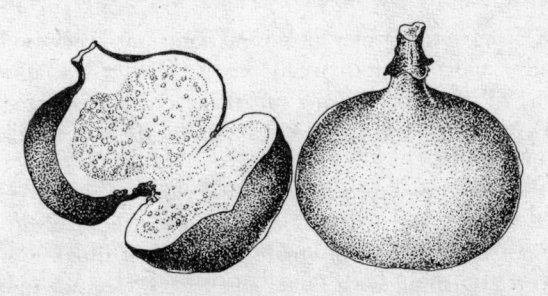

Skin the fresh dates, remove the stones, and chop small (soak dried dates in water for a short time and dry). Chop the figs into small pieces and discard the stalks. Sift 2 tablespoons of the flour into a bowl and drop in the chopped dried fruits and the raisins; dredge with a little more flour and toss all carefully until they are well coated. Set aside. In another bowl beat the egg yolks and sugar until thick, pale and creamy; mix in the ground almonds and grated chocolate. Whip up the egg whites in a separate bowl until they stand in firm peaks. Lighten the first mixture with 2 tablespoons of the beaten whites before folding in the rest using a large metal spoon; finally fold in alternate spoonfuls of the fruits and sifted flour until all is used up. Pour into a square tin 24 cm (9½ inch) buttered, lined and buttered again. Sprinkle the top with the flaked almonds and bake in the warm oven. The almonds will have turned brown. Turn out on to a wire rack after 10 minutes cooling; dredge with icing sugar to serve.

Apricot, Orange and Walnut Loaf

This is a more sophisticated version of the lemon cake on page 265. It also has syrup poured over while it is still warm.

200 g dried apricots	7 oz dried apricots
75 g walnuts, chopped	3 oz walnuts, chopped
250 g strong, plain flour	9 oz strong, plain flour
½ teaspoon salt	½ teaspoon salt
½ teaspoon baking soda	½ teaspoon baking soda
100 ml milk	3½ fl oz milk
100 g butter	3½ oz butter
220 g caster sugar	8 oz caster sugar
2 large eggs	2 large eggs
4 tablespoons orange zest	4 tablespoons orange zest
½ teaspoon orange-flower water	½ teaspoon orange-flower water
320 g granulated sugar	11 oz granulated sugar
125 ml orange juice	4½ fl oz orange juice

gas 3, 170°C, 325°F / 1¼ hours

Soak the apricots in cold water for several hours until they swell; drain, dry carefully, and chop into small pieces. Dredge the apricots and walnuts with a little flour, making sure that each piece is coated. Sift the flour and salt together. Dissolve the baking soda in the milk and set aside.

Cream the butter and caster sugar until pale and fluffy; beat in the eggs one at a time, and stir in 2 tablespoons of orange zest and the orange-flower water. Mix in alternate spoonfuls of sifted flour and the milk mixture, finishing with flour, and taking care not to overbeat.

Fold in the apricot and walnut mixture using a large metal spoon. Pour into a buttered, lined and buttered 1 kg (2 lb) loaf tin and bake in the preheated oven.

While the cake is baking, make the syrup: combine the granulated sugar, orange juice and remaining 2 tablespoons of orange zest in a copper sugar pan and heat on a low flame until all the sugar has dissolved. (Stir very gently, and wash down any sugar crystals off the sides with a wet pastry brush — see page 70.)

Pierce the top of the still warm cake at regular intervals, standing a plate underneath the wire rack to catch any drips, and carefully spoon the syrup all over. Cool. Wrap in plastic film and leave to chill overnight. Next day turn the cake over so that the juices soak well through. Leave for 3 or 4 days before cutting. This cake keeps for at least 3 weeks.

Eccles Cakes

Puff pastry wrapped around a spicy mincemeat filling crops up in various regions of the British Isles and often has a religious origin. The difference is usually in the shape of the pastries. Eccles, Banbury and Coventry God cakes are the most familiar.

The Crusaders are reputed to have brought the recipe from the Holy Land to the thriving market town of Banbury in the thirteenth century. On market days the popular pointed, oval cakes (a classic Eastern shape) were sold to travellers who carried them far and wide — possibly to Coventry. Here in the sixteenth century it became the custom for godparents to send their godchildren the cakes as presents at Eastertide, the size being an indication of their wealth and the triangular shape derived, maybe, from the heraldic three spires of the town.

How they originated in Eccles is not clear either, but apparently this drab outer suburb of Manchester derives its name from 'church' and from the one founded in 1111 A.D. The annual 'Eccles Wakes' celebrated the occasion, of which the flat, round cakes became a feature; but in 1650 the Puritans forbade them both, convinced that the festivities had pagan origins and that the cakes, filled with exotic dried fruits and spices from the East, were too rich. Florence White gives this 'Wakes' song:

> When racing and fighting were all at an end,
> To an ale-house each went with a sweet-heart or friend;

Some went to Shaw's, others Phillips' chose,
But me and my Moll to the Hare and Hounds goes.
Chorus
With music and cakes
For to keep up the wakes
Among wenches and fine country beaux.

Puff pastry trimmings may be used. 500 g (1 lb) puff pastry makes about 16 cakes.

Filling

100 g unsalted butter	3½ oz unsalted butter
100 g molasses or demerara sugar	3½ oz molasses or demerara sugar
1 teaspoon allspice	1 teaspoon allspice
1 teaspoon ground nutmeg	1 teaspoon ground nutmeg
150 g currants	5½ oz currants
100 g candied, chopped peel	3½ oz candied, chopped peel
zest ½ lemon	zest ½ lemon
milk to bind	milk to bind
caster sugar	caster sugar

gas 7, 220°C, 425°F/15 minutes

Cream the butter and sugar with the spices. Add the prepared currants, chopped peel and lemon zest, and bind with a little milk. Roll out the puff pastry to 3 mm (⅛ inch) thickness. Stamp out 10 cm (4 inch) circles with a sharp cutter. Place a teaspoon of the mixture in the centre of each circle, moisten the edges of the paste with water, and draw them up over the filling into the centre, pinching well to seal. Turn the cake over and flatten it slightly with the palm of the hand until the currants start to show through, but keep the shape round. Make three or four slits in the top, for the steam to escape, brush over with milk or egg white and dredge with caster sugar. Allow to stand for 10 minutes. Bake in the preheated oven for about 15 minutes.

Christmas Mincemeat Pies

. . . It was his own room. There was no doubt about that. But it had undergone a surprising transformation. The walls and ceiling were so hung with living green, that it looked a perfect grove; from every part of which, bright gleaming berries glistened. The crisp

> leaves of holly, mistletoe, and ivy reflected back the light, as if so many little mirrors had been scattered there; and such a mighty blaze went roaring up the chimney, as that dull petrifaction of a hearth had never known in Scrooge's time, or Marley's, or for many and many a winter season gone. Heaped up on the floor, to form a kind of throne, were turkeys, geese, game, poultry, brawn, great joints of meat, sucking-pigs, long wreaths of sausages, mince-pies, plum-puddings, barrels of oysters, red-hot chestnuts, cherry-cheeked apples, juicy oranges, luscious pears, immense twelfth-cakes, and seething bowls of punch, that made the chamber dim with their delicious steam. In easy state upon this couch, there sat a jolly giant, glorious to see . . .
>
> (Charles Dickens, *A Christmas Carol*)

Christmas was banned by the Puritans in the seventeenth century; so were mince pies, for these, they claimed, amounted to idolatry. Baked in a cradle-shape (rather like Christstollen) and filled with dried fruits, nuts and spices, an incision was made in the top to make room for a modelled figure of the Infant Jesus. This gave rise to the suggestion that mince pies might have been offered as gifts to the Christ child by the Three Kings, along with the traditional gold, frankincense and myrrh. During the Restoration the pies were brought into official favour once again, though the shape had changed to a circle. Since then, an English Christmas without mince pies has been inconceivable.

The pastries were usually known as minced meat pies, for they contained meat. Ox-heart, ox tongues, sirloin of beef, beef marrow or suet were the most common. The meat was boiled and cut up into small pieces similar in size to the fruits and nuts; apples were usually included, and most important was brandy. Dorothy Hartley mentions one recipe, dating, she suggests, from the mid-seventeenth century, which is made with the piths of oranges and lemons, rather like the marmalades of the time, and unusually, contains no spices. More recently, beef suet has usually remained as the only meat ingredient, and even that is replaced by grapes in one instance, with the recommendation that they make the mincemeat more luscious and more digestible. James Beard has an excellent version which uses both boiled beef and tongue, figs and dates as well as the usual dried fruits. My version is simpler.

CAKES

Mincemeat

This makes about 1.75 kg (4 lb).

250 g beef suet
250 g crisp, tart apples (Bramley or Granny Smith)
250 g seedless raisins
200 g sultanas
200 g currants
120 g candied orange peel
120 g candied lemon peel
100 g blanched almonds, chopped
zest 3 lemons
juice 4 lemons
1/2 teaspoon ginger
1 teaspoon cinnamon
pinch cloves
1/2 teaspoon nutmeg
300–400 ml brandy
100 ml rum or sherry
300 g dark muscovado sugar

9 oz beef suet
9 oz crisp, tart apples (Bramley or Granny Smith)
9 oz seedless raisins
7 oz sultanas
7 oz currants
4 oz candied orange peel
4 oz candied lemon peel
3 1/2 oz blanched almonds, chopped
zest 3 lemons
juice 4 lemons
1/2 teaspoon ginger
1 teaspoon cinnamon
pinch cloves
1/2 teaspoon nutmeg
10 1/2–14 fl oz brandy
3 1/2 fl oz rum or sherry
10 1/2 oz dark muscovado sugar

Carefully wash and dry the suet, shred it and chop small. Peel and core the apples and cut them to about the same size. Assemble all the dried fruits and peel with the suet and apples in a large bowl. Add the nuts, lemon zest and juice. Stir the spices into the spirits, pour them into the bowl, and finally add the sugar. Combine all together very thoroughly — the mixture should be rather loose. Spoon the mincemeat into a large stone crock or mixing bowl and cover tightly. Stand in a cool place for a week, and give the mixture a stir each day, adding more spirit if it has all been absorbed. Turn into sterilized preserving jars and seal as for jam. Store in a dark, cool place. Mincemeat will keep for several months; and if you feed it with brandy now and then, to stay moist, will keep for years.

Leave mincemeat for at least a month before using it.

DRIED FRUIT CAKES
Mincemeat Tarts and Pies for Christmas

For 10 shortcrust pastry tartlets use pastry quantity (2) on page 44. For 12 puff pastry tartlets use pastry quantity (2) on page 51.

Bake at gas 7, 220°C, 425°F/15 minutes

Roll the pastry to 3 mm (^{1}/8 inch) thick, and with a fluted pastry cutter cut 10 to 12 circles one size larger than your patty tins. To make the lids, cut a similar number of circles the same size as the tins from the rest of the pastry, using up the scraps as necessary. Line the tins with the larger circles and spoon in the mincemeat generously, pressing it down gently. Damp the edges of the pastry lids with water and press them on, making sure that the sides have sealed. Cut two small incisions in the middle and brush with lightly beaten egg yolk; dredge with caster sugar and leave to rest for 30 minutes. Bake in the preheated oven.

A Mincemeat and Apple Pie

A layer of apples cooked underneath the mincemeat gives added interest to a large pie. And for a spirited luxury, why not pour a little brandy through the top incisions and bring the pie to the table hot? For an enclosed pie use shortcrust pastry quantity (2) on page 44 and for an open tart quantity (1). Use two-thirds of the first to make a 22 cm (8^1/2 inch) blind shortcrust pastry shell (page 208). Roll out the rest as a lid. Peel and core 6 large, crisp eating apples, and cut them into thick slices. Stew very gently until transparent with 50 g (2 oz) butter, turning occasionally so that they are evenly cooked. Lift out of the pan with a slotted spoon and leave to drain and cool. Brush the pastry shell with a little strained apricot jam, then pack in the apple slices neatly. Cover with a thick layer of mincemeat, about 500 g (1 lb), and press down gently. Dot with a few knobs of butter, and cover with a lid of pastry. Make several incisions for the steam to escape. Brush the surface with beaten egg and dredge with caster sugar. Bake in the oven preheated to gas 5, 190°C, 375°F for about 30 minutes. It should be quite lightly browned. Serve hot with a warm custard or cold with whipped cream. The pastry lid can be left off; in which case brush the baked tart with strained apricot jam when cold and scatter toasted almond flakes over.

Richard Bradley writes in his *Country Housewife and Lady's Director* of an interesting eighteenth-century Christmas custom. The recipe for 'Hackin', containing all the usual mincemeat ingredients, sounds remarkably like a boiled Christmas pudding.

To make a Hackin. From a Gentleman in Cumberland.

SIR,
There are some Counties in *England*, whose Customs are never to be set aside; and our Friends in *Cumberland*, as well as some of our Neighbours in *Lancashire*, and else-where, keep them up. It is a Custom with us every *Christmas*-Day in the Morning, to have, what we call an Hackin, for the Breakfast of the young Men who work about our House; and if this Dish is not dressed by that time it is Day-light, the Maid is led through the Town, between two Men, as fast as they can run with her, up Hill and down Hill, which she accounts a great shame. But as for the Receipt to make this Hackin, which is admired so much by us, it is as follows.

Take the Bag or Paunch of a Calf, and wash it, and clean it well with Water and Salt; then take some Beef-Suet, and shred it small, and shred some Apples, after they are pared and cored, very small. Then put in some Sugar, and some Spice beaten small, a little Lemon-Peel cut very fine, and a little Salt, and a good quantity of Grots, or whole Oat-meal, steep'd a Night in Milk; then mix these all together, and add as many Currans pick'd clean from the Stalks, and rubb'd in a coarse Cloth; but let them not be wash'd. And when you have all ready, mix them together, and put them into the Calf's-Bag, and tye them up, and boil them till they are enough. You may, if you will, mix up with the whole, some Eggs beaten, which will help to bind it. This is our Custom to have ready, at the opening of the Doors, on *Christmas*-Day in the Morning. It is esteem'd here; but all that I can say to you of it, is, that it eats somewhat like a *Christmas*-Pye, or is somewhat like that boil'd. I had forgot to say, that with the rest of the Ingredients, there should be some Lean of tender Beef minced small.

Two Unusual Christmas Cakes

. . . For the people who were shovelling away on the house-tops were jovial and full of glee; calling out to one another from the parapets, and now and then exchanging a facetious snowball – better-natured missile far than many a wordy jest – laughing heartily if it went right, and not less heartily if it went wrong. The poulterers' shops were still half open, and the fruiterers' were radiant in their glory. There were great, round, pot-bellied baskets of chestnuts, shaped like the waistcoats of jolly old gentlemen,

DRIED FRUIT CAKES

lolling at the doors, and tumbling out into the street in their apoplectic opulence. There were ruddy, brown-faced, broad-girthed Spanish onions, shining in the fatness of their growth like Spanish friars, and winking from their shelves in wanton slyness at the girls as they went by, and glanced demurely at the hung-up mistletoe. There were pears and apples, clustered high in blooming pyramids; there were bunches of grapes, made, in the shopkeepers' benevolence, to dangle from conspicuous hooks, that people's mouths might water gratis as they passed; there were piles of filberts, mossy and brown, recalling in their fragrance, ancient walks among the woods and pleasant shufflings ankle-deep through withered leaves; there were Norfolk biffins, squat and swarthy, setting off the yellow of the oranges and lemons, and, in the great compactness of their juicy persons, urgently entreating and beseeching to be carried home in paper-bags and eaten after dinner. The very gold and silver fish, set forth among these choice fruits in a bowl, though members of a dull and stagnant-blooded race, appeared to know that there was something going on; and, to a fish, went gasping round and round their little world in slow and passionless excitement.

The grocers'! oh, the grocers'! nearly closed, with perhaps two shutters down, or one; but through those gaps such glimpses! It was not alone that the scales descending on the counter made a merry sound, or that the twine and roller parted company so briskly, or that the canisters were rattled up and down like juggling tricks, or even that the blended scents of tea and coffee were so grateful to the nose, or even that the raisins were so plentiful and rare, the almonds so extremely white, the sticks of cinnamon so long and straight, the other spices so delicious, the candied fruits so caked and spotted with molten sugar as to make the coldest lookers-on feel faint and subsequently bilious. Nor was it that the figs were moist and pulpy, or that the French plums blushed in modest tartness from their highly decorated boxes, or that everything was good to eat and in its Christmas dress. But the customers were all so hurried and so eager in the hopeful promise of the day, that they tumbled up against each other at the door, crashing their wickerbaskets wildly, and left their purchases upon the counter, and came running back to fetch them, and committed hundreds of the like mistakes, in the best humour possible; while the grocer and his people were so frank and fresh that the polished hearts with which they fastened their aprons behind might have been their own, worn outside for general inspection, and for Christmas daws to peck at if they chose.

CAKES

But soon the steeples called good people all to church and chapel, and away they came, flocking through the streets in their best clothes, and with their gayest faces. And at the same time there emerged from scores of by-streets, lanes, and nameless turnings, innumerable people, carrying their dinners to the bakers' shops . . .

(Charles Dickens, *A Christmas Carol*)

Certosino

This Italian Christmas cake is quite unlike the traditional heavy fruited English version (page 290). Originating with the Carthusian Monks of Bologna, the eggless dough sweetened with honey and flavoured with chocolate and spice is more like Lebkuchen; it mellows and enriches with keeping. Use strained apple or pear mousse or quince fruit for a more distinctive taste.

The recipe comes from Ada Boni's *Italian Regional Cooking*.

70 g white seedless raisins	2½ oz white seedless raisins
1½ tablespoons rum	1½ tablespoons rum
340 g honey	12 oz honey
40 g butter	1½ oz butter
1 teaspoon cinnamon	1 teaspoon cinnamon
1 tablespoon aniseed	1 tablespoon aniseed
370 g plain flour	13 oz plain flour
170 g cooked and sieved apples, pears or quince	6 oz cooked and sieved apples, pears or quince
170 g blanched almonds, coarsely chopped or flaked	6 oz blanched almonds, coarsely chopped or flaked
70 g bitter chocolate, coarsely chopped	2½ oz bitter chocolate, coarsely chopped
170 g candied orange and lemon peel	6 oz candied orange and lemon peel
40 g pine nuts	1½ oz pine nuts
1½ teaspoons bicarbonate of soda	1½ teaspoons bicarbonate of soda
candied fruits and peels, walnuts or pecan halves for decoration	candied fruits and peels, walnuts or pecan halves for decoration

gas 3, 170°C, 325°F/1¼–1½ hours

Steep the raisins in the rum for 30 minutes. Spoon the honey into a heavy pan, add the butter and 3 tablespoons of water, heat gently and stir until liquid. Do not let it boil. Stir in the cinnamon and aniseed. Sift the flour into a mixing bowl, then slowly pour in the honey liquid and stir vigorously until it is well blended. Mix in the fruit mousse and the almonds, chocolate, peels, raisins and rum. Add the pine nuts, but avoid stirring too much so that they do not get damaged. Finally add the bicarbonate of soda dissolved in a little water.

Turn into a generously buttered 24 cm ($9^{1}/_{2}$ inch) loose-based tin or a savarin mould. Bake in the preheated oven, then turn out on to a wire rack to cool. Stud the top with glacé fruits or the nut halves for decoration as you wish using apricot jam to set them in place. Brush apricot jam all over the fruits and the cake to finish. Dry. Store wrapped in foil.

Jane Grigson's Fruit Cake with Brazil Nuts

Jane Grigson calls this a last-minute Christmas cake. It tastes good without requiring lengthy storage.

350 g fresh dates (giving 250 g stoned and skinned)	12 oz fresh dates (giving 9 oz stoned and skinned)
125 g glacé cherries	$4^{1}/_{2}$ oz glacé cherries
250 g Brazil nuts, coarsely chopped	9 oz Brazil nuts, coarsely chopped
125 g self-raising flour	$4^{1}/_{2}$ oz self-raising flour
125 g caster sugar	$4^{1}/_{2}$ oz caster sugar
$1/2$ teaspoon salt	$1/2$ teaspoon salt
1 large egg	1 large egg
2 tablespoons rum, brandy or sherry	2 tablespoons rum, brandy or sherry

gas 2, 150°C, 300°F/$1^{1}/_{4}$ hours

Strip the skins from the dates, cut them in half, and remove the stones. Rinse the excess sugar from the cherries and cut them in half. Mingle the nuts and dried fruits. Sift the flour, sugar and salt together, then sift carefully over the fruits, making sure that they are all well coated, before beating in the egg and the spirit. Turn into a 1 kg (2 lb) loaf tin lined with greaseproof paper (page 271) and bake in the preheated oven.

Wedding Cakes

The wedding cake of today is a grand crusted affair of many heavily fruited layers, decorated with royal icing and columns, bells, horseshoes, doves and flowers – a far cry from the 'mustaceum' familiar to the Romans. Although the symbolic meaning still remains, our cake is at least a little more palatable. The Roman 'bride cake' was made of salt, flour and water or wine, and it was intended merely to represent sharing by the bride and groom with their guests, whilst three wheat ears carried by the bride were the symbol of plenty.

In later times the wheat was baked with the other ingredients into thin, hard biscuits which were broken over the bride's head; and by the time Queen Elizabeth I came to the throne, eggs, milk, sugar, currants and spices, together with flour, were added and formed into small rectangular cakes for throwing at the bride.

It has been suggested that the two-tiered wedding cake – one rich and heavy groom's cake, the other lighter bride's cake, gay with spun-sugar ornaments – spread from France during the seventeenth century. Two centuries later, however, Urbain Dubois, when discussing fruited cakes at some length, maintained that they were little known or used in France and were most popular in England and America. The only cake for weddings and family celebrations in France was the biscuit de Savoie; and a little later the gâteau de Breton also earned Dubois' scorn. Berating his Parisian colleagues (France's cuisine was particularly regional at the time), he suggested that they should create something quite different.

The tradition of the two cakes remained popular in the United States – Fannie Farmer, in her *Boston Cooking School Cookbook* from the late nineteenth century, gives several long and complicated recipes for both cakes. More recently, though, the lighter bride's cake is usurping the fruit cake. In England only the fruited layer remains; but there are several of these, and each is usually covered with marzipan, icing, and decorations all symbolizing the white bride's portion. Mrs Raffald's recipe for 'Bride Cake' in 1769, however, which includes nuts along with the dried fruits and other ingredients, has no decorations other than a plain white icing.

Superstitions

There are several superstitions surrounding the wedding feast and the cake itself. Sampling and sharing the cake with relations and friends spreads good fortune and fertility; the bride who bakes her own wedding cake stalks bad luck; a crumb sampled before the ceremony forfeits the husband's love; a fragment preserved afterwards ensures his life-long fidelity; and as long as the happy couple cut the first slice together and every guest samples a small piece they are ensured of producing a family.

Decoration of Wedding Cakes

Although Mrs Raffald's bride cake had no decoration, only eleven years later in 1780, Hagger, chef to the Prince of Salzburg, was creating raised impressions and decorating pastries in a style reminiscent of what is now considered to be a 'classic' English wedding cake. Queen Victoria's, a century later, was a typical example.

A new era in the history of haute cuisine and grand pâtisserie in France began with Antonin Carême. He trained with the great chef pâtissier Bailly, and pâtisserie remained his first love. His life centred around his profession as he toiled ceaselessly to perfect; he innovated and inspired while feeding the important personages of the time – the Prince of Talleyrand, King George IV, the Russian Prince Alexander. His early labours involved detailed studies and drawings of architecture and sculpture, as he strongly believed these to be the basis of all decoration. Almost a hundred years later Gouffé, greatly influenced by Carême, gave aspiring young pâtissiers the following advice:

> . . . The pâtissier should know the elements of design, of sculpture and architecture. Once these are known he should study good models, both to imitate and to be inspired by their perfections. If he should see in a museum, or a public garden, or a shop display a cup, a vase, or a trophy, he must not neglect to make a sketch and prepare a model. He should examine with care houses, farms, public fountains, bell-towers and rose windows of ogival architecture and engrave the details in his memory or set them on paper, until the occasion arises to reproduce them as an ornament for great tables or family celebration . . .
>
> (*Le Livre de Pâtisserie*, 1873)

These words reflect completely Carême's beliefs, as his highly elaborate 'pièces montées' – table centres – so clearly showed. His 'constructions' were generally made with sugar and pastry, and his cake designs were equally elaborate. Carême's influence and fame spread rapidly, and his work was probably the inspiration for the cake served at the wedding feast in *Madame Bovary*.

> . . . For the tarts and confectioneries they had hired a pastry-cook from Yvetot. He was new to the district, and so had taken great pains with his work. At dessert he brought in with his own hands a tiered cake that made them all cry out. It started off at the base with a square of blue cardboard representing a temple with porticoes and colonnades, with stucco statuettes all round it in recesses studded with gilt-paper stars; on the second layer was a castle-keep in Savoy cake, surrounded by tiny fortifications in angelica, almonds, raisins and quarters of orange, and finally, on the uppermost platform, which was a green meadow with rocks, pools of jam and boats of nutshell, stood a little Cupid, poised on a chocolate swing whose uprights had two real rose-buds for knobs at the top . . .
>
> (Gustave Flaubert, *Madame Bovary*)

Within fifty years France produced several famous chefs and chefs pâtissiers, such as the Gouffé brothers, Urbain Dubois and Pierre Lacam, all of whom felt the urge to record their professional experiences. Of these Dubois was the most prolific on the subject of pâtisserie. He illustrated several 'grands gâteaux de mariage' which followed grandiose lines similar to those of Carême.

Although sugar-craft and decoration are still practised today, those nineteenth-century splendours have virtually disappeared. Modern decoration on wedding cakes often strays from the traditional symbols, and has given way to depiction of the couple's interests, whether tennis or car-racing, football or music – even Queen Victoria had an image of Britannia on her wedding cake.

Marzipan

Marzipan in the Middle Ages belonged to the apothecary's cupboard, and was considered to have exceptional health restorative as well as magical powers. One seventeenth-century tale tells of a young lady overcome with a great passion for a certain learned gentleman, to whom she presented a costly gift of a heart made of marzipan as a token of her affection. Valuing it not at all, he threw it to his pig, who smitten with a sudden overwhelming desire, attempted to storm her house.

WEDDING CAKES

Early mention of the nourishing combination of almonds and sugar was made in a book on foodstuffs by the Persian doctor Rhazes (850–923 A.D.). Arabic poets of the time also wrote of the spoils of the table:

> The perfumed rains of Dschuddhaba subside
> Almond cream follows, sprinkled with sugar.
> Thanks to the heavens for such rain,
> Blessed is the earth, which it pleases.

About the same time, too, a secret society in Basra on the Euphrates recorded the delicious sweetmeat made from raw honey, sugar, almonds and oil; a similar recipe appeared in the thirteenth-century *Baghdad Cookery Book*. By the Middle Ages, softly-textured almond mousses, milks and cheeses were very popular in cookery manuscripts. Possibly the first mention of a moulded marzipan, by the poet al-Matanabbi around 900 A.D., was of an almond fish, but the Baghdad book includes several set in carved wooden moulds in the shapes of cocks, lambs, loaves and fishes. Two hundred years later these moulded versions were very popular in medieval Europe.

Marzipan was the most coveted gift amongst the nobility, and even considered worthy of a gold-leaf covering. On a visit to Cambridge Queen Elizabeth I was presented with two pairs of perfumed gloves, two sugar cones and a piece of marzipan. Another royal offering came from Henry IV of France to Maria de Medici on her journey through Avignon: he gave her 300 small baskets filled with dainty fruit shapes of marzipan and sugar. No Renaissance tables of King or Count went without marzipan, no wedding, funeral, crowning or christening. At the wedding banquet of the Count of Mantua in 1581, three foot-high marzipan sculptures appeared – Hercules wrestling with the Lions, the Steeds of Dioscurus on the Capitol, and a group of dragons and unicorns. A Papal banquet in 1604 included sugar and marzipan pieces which alone cost 4,000 silver pieces.

Today marzipan confectionery is still popular in Germany; there are the small rectangular Brenten printed with a bird or a flower, and the almond spiked pyramid Beethmänchen of Frankfurt, while the Königsberger Tee-Konfekt is heart-shaped. But probably the best known is the traditional scenic embossed and decorated circle or rectangle of Lübeck. Lübeck's connection with marzipan stems as far back as 1407, and from early in the 1800s it was of major economic importance to the town, much as Lebkuchen had become in Nürnberg, with exports throughout the world.

CAKES

In England marzipan now remains only as a topping for a festive cake, or moulded as a simple figure or flower, but in the seventeenth century marchepane was very popular and offered as the most coveted morsel at the end of a banquet. Sir Hugh Plat in *Delightes for Ladies* (1608) gives a recipe for making it.

The origin of the name marzipan has raised much speculation. At first it was thought to have come from the Italian *marzapana* — or *marci-panis* or *pana* meaning bread; but where does *marza* come from? From March — St Marcus? — it was made for Easter; or, as C. Anne Wilson suggests, from a magical, alchemical bread named by the Franks on encountering Saracen cuisine and alchemy. Another suggestion is that the name derives from a Byzantine coin of the first century A.D., *mauthabau*, bearing an engraving of the enthroned Christ. Boxes filled with almond sweetmeats and candied fruits, which arrived in Venice from the Orient, were used as a form of currency, and named *mataban* by the Italians. The boxes as well as their contents are still called *mazapane*, and *mataban* is still the Arabic name for a jar or box.

A Fruited Festive Cake

(for Christmas or a wedding)

125 g glacé cherries	4½ oz glacé cherries
250 g sultanas	9 oz sultanas
250 g raisins	9 oz raisins
250 g currants	9 oz currants
(*or* 750 g mixed dried fruit)	(*or* 1 lb 11 oz mixed dried fruit)
125 g candied chopped peel	4½ oz candied chopped peel
200 ml brandy or dark rum	7 fl oz brandy or dark rum
300 g plain flour	10½ oz plain flour
1 teaspoon cinnamon	1 teaspoon cinnamon
1 teaspoon nutmeg	1 teaspoon nutmeg
125 g blanched, slivered or ground almonds	4½ oz blanched, slivered or ground almonds
250 g lightly salted butter	9 oz lightly salted butter
250 g soft, brown sugar (light or dark)	9 oz soft, brown sugar (light or dark)
1 tablespoon vanilla sugar	1 tablespoon vanilla sugar
4 large eggs	4 large eggs
1 tablespoon golden syrup	1 tablespoon golden syrup

WEDDING CAKES

zest 1 lemon
1/2 teaspoon bicarbonate of soda
1 tablespoon milk

zest 1 lemon
1/2 teaspoon bicarbonate of soda
1 tablespoon milk

gas 2, 150°C, 300°F for 1 1/2 hours – then lower the temperature to gas 1, 140°C, 275°F for a further 3–3 1/2 hours. (If you prefer a smaller cake using the same size tin (20 cm, 8 inches), use half the ingredients but bake for a shorter period. The second period is reduced to 2 1/2 hours cooking time.)

Wash and dry the glacé cherries, then chop them into quarters. Mix them with the dried fruits and peel, and soak them all in the brandy or rum for about an hour before using them; the fruits will swell and the cloying sweetness will be removed.

Sift the flour and spices together two or three times, then dust a small amount over the soaked fruits to absorb a little of the moisture; add the ground almonds.

Beat the butter, sugar and vanilla sugar until light and fluffy. In a separate bowl mix together the eggs, syrup and lemon zest, then add this to the butter and sugar mixture.

Beat spoonfuls of the flour and spices into the egg mixture, alternating with spoonfuls of the fruit and nut mixture. Finally dissolve the bicarbonate of soda in the milk, and beat into the mixture.

Line the base and sides of a 20–22 cm (8–8 1/2 inch) loose-bottomed, high-sided tin with two layers of brown or silicone paper, and finally with one of silicone paper, taking the paper up over the edge as instructed (page 270); make sure it is all well greased. Pour the cake mixture into the tin, smooth it over and slightly hollow out the centre so that it will bake flat.

Remember the unbaked cake will keep overnight in the refrigerator without coming to any harm.

Stand the tin on a flat baking sheet in the oven to give additional protection, and bake as directed at the start of this recipe. Test the cake for readiness with a larding needle, skewer or toothpick – it should come out dry. If the cake seems to be browning too much and is not quite ready, cover it with a layer of brown paper.

Remove from the oven when done. Leave in the tin on a rack to cool down completely. Next day peel off the papers and wrap the cake in fresh paper before storing it in an airtight tin. Although it can be eaten after a week or so, it improves with keeping. Should you wish to enhance the brandy flavour, unwrap it each week and feed the underside with a little more brandy. This type of fruit cake keeps for several months.

CAKES

The cake should be covered with marzipan and iced at least 10 days before it is needed.

The Almond Paste – Marzipan Layer

Flavour the paste carefully, either with a sharp tang of lemon juice or a sweeter oriental perfume, according to taste.

To fit a 20–24 cm (8–9½ inch) cake.

250 g icing sugar	9 oz icing sugar
500 g ground, blanched almonds	1 lb ground, blanched almonds
1 large egg (size 1)	1 large egg (size 1)
3–4 teaspoons lemon juice, rose-water or orange-flower water	3–4 teaspoons lemon juice, rose-water or orange-flower water

Sift the icing sugar into a bowl and mix in the prepared almonds. In a separate bowl beat the egg very thoroughly, then add it to the dry ingredients along with the lemon juice or perfume. Beat together, using a wooden spoon, and when it is all combined, turn out on to a board sprinkled with icing sugar.

Knead the paste until it becomes very smooth. Chill in the refrigerator for a short time, wrapped in foil or plastic film. Leave aside one third of the paste, and roll out the remainder on a sheet of greaseproof paper dusted with icing sugar. Roll it just a little larger than the cake, and cut it to size with a sharp knife, using the cake tin as a guide.

Measure the depth and the circumference of the cake; then roll out the remaining paste to fit, also on a sheet of greaseproof paper dusted with icing sugar.

How to Cover a Cake with Marzipan

The cake must first be coated with an apricot glaze (page 71). Make sure that the cake surface is level and slice a thin layer away if necessary, then brush with heated apricot jam. Pick up the whole cake, invert it on to the prepared circle of marzipan, and press it gently but firmly so that it sticks well all over. Turn the cake back again on to the right side and peel away the paper from the marzipan. Using a rolling pin, lightly roll across the surface to smooth any irregularities, and smooth any excess paste over the top edge on to the side if necessary.

Brush the sides of the cake with the remaining warm jam; trim the sides of the ready-rolled paste to fit. Pick up the cake gently and roll it carefully over the paste making sure that the ends join up. Flatten the paste where necessary with the rolling-pin. Leave to dry out for some days; if it is used too soon, the oil from the almonds will spoil the taste and colour of the icing.

Marzipan makes an excellent finishing layer on its own, simply decorated with an appropriate subject and a ribbon or frill; but the classic finish is of course with royal icing.

Royal Icing with Egg White

This icing should be spread over a marzipan base. It is used for rich wedding and festive cakes and for piped decoration. It sets hard and will keep for a long time.

Before use, the icing can be kept for up to a week in the refrigerator; to prevent it from hardening, close cover with one layer of plastic film on the icing surface and another over the top of the bowl.

For a very special finish, two thinner coats of icing are desirable. Make double the basic quantity, and dry out the first coat thoroughly before applying the second.

Ingredients for a 20–22 cm (8–8 1/2 inch) cake

500 g icing sugar	1 lb icing sugar
2 1/2 egg whites	2 1/2 egg whites
juice 1/2 lemon	juice 1/2 lemon

Ingredients for a 24–26 cm (9–9 1/2 inch) cake

650 g icing sugar	1 lb 7 oz icing sugar
3 1/2 egg whites	3 1/2 egg whites
juice 3/4 lemon	juice 3/4 lemon

How to Cover a Cake with Royal Icing

A palette knife, a long kitchen knife or a ruler can be used; and a turntable makes the work much simpler.

Make sure the icing is well mixed, drop a large spoonful into the centre of the cake, then, holding a large metal palette knife steadily and slightly angled to the top of the cake, rotate the turntable slowly and the icing will spread out. Spread and smooth more icing over the sides of the cake – this is possible with firm icing as it takes much longer to set. If two layers are being applied, the first coat need not be perfect. The finish must be quite level and perfectly smooth. Leave to dry completely before finishing with a second coat or starting decoration.

CAKES

As Francatelli said in 1846, 'When the icing has become perfectly hard, decorate the top and sides of the cake with raised ornaments of gum paste, (stamped out from boards cut for the purpose) and arranged with taste, either in the form of garlands, wreaths, scrolls, etc; or else, the cake may be decorated with piping, using for that purpose some of the icing work somewhat thicker, by adding to it more sugar and a little prepared gum-dragon. The ornaments must be all white, and some blossoms and sprigs – or, even wreaths of orange-flowers should also be introduced' . . .

This type of traditional icing is an art in itself – I suggest that you consult one of the many specialist books devoted to the technique. For a simpler finish, glacé fruits such as orange and lemon pieces, cherries and angelica are attractive, or candied violets, roses, mimosa and silver balls. Coloured imitation fruits and leaves fashioned in marzipan are also interesting. On pages 71–81 there are a few suggestions for some simpler iced ideas.

Baumkuchen – My Family Wedding Cake

Spit cooking was one of the earliest methods of cooking foods; and a wine and flour batter flavoured with spices made a tolerable type of cake. In *Food in England* Dorothy Hartley gives a fifteenth-century recipe which threads dried fruit and nuts on to strings – these were wrapped around a spit, and then had batter ladled over them.

The more northerly countries, and especially the Germans, were particularly fond of this sort of cookery. Originating in the fifteenth-century monastery kitchens, spit-turned tree cakes – Baumkuchen – soon found their way into the kitchens of the nobility as well as middle-class homes. (They earned the name from the shape brought about by the constant rotation as the dripping batters set.) Recipes proliferated, and as the centuries passed both ingredients and methods changed. Apart from strung fruits, as in England, bread dough was rolled out and wrapped over the spit to be basted with egg yolk or with melted fats.

Marx Rumpolt wrote in 1581:

> Take warm milk and beat egg into it; make a dough with good white flour. Take a little beer yeast put butter with it; let it stand for a while at the back of the oven, so that it rises. Knead it down again and salt a little, and roll it out clean, throw over it black

WEDDING CAKES

raisins. Take a roll (wooden) which is nice and warm, and has been brushed with butter and lay it on the dough; wrap the dough around it and tie it up with twine so that it cannot fall off. Set by the fire and turn it round slowly, so will it roast clean. And when it is brown, take a brush and dip it in hot butter and brush the cake with it so it will be nice and brown. And when it is roasted, put it from the spit roll and close both ends with clean cloths so that the heat stays in. Leave it so until it has cooled. Bring it thus cold to the table and it will be crisp and good. And one calls this a spitcake.

But it was not until 1692 that the Brunswick Cookery Book published the first recipe for a batter where the egg whites were whipped up separately from the yolks, and the mixture was ladled over the spit in single layers while it cooked. Indentations were formed in the cakes during baking by studding with almonds and dried fruit slivers.

Since then Baumkuchen has become part of the repertoire of professional confectioners, and a traditional speciality for festive occasions.

The German writer Theodor Fontane, in his childhood reminiscences during the early 1880s, regarded Baumkuchen and its preparation as a major event in his young life. A festive wedding-like atmosphere pervaded his home whenever important visitors were expected; the days of preparation tingled with an anticipation that intensified with the appearance of the itinerant cook. Frau Gaster had a splendid reputation, particularly for desserts. On her arrival he would station himself at a suitable vantage point where all the activities could be observed. The Baumkuchen was always first on her list. 'It is true,' Fontane goes on to say, 'that Baumkuchen still exist today; but they have degenerated into feeble, liquidy, pale imitations, whereas those then had a happy firmness which in the most successful examples was almost crispy, and its colour ranged from the darkest ochre to the palest yellow of the spectrum.'

He continues with the description of a typical spit – of the narrow coke fire just over a metre long in front of which rested a tapered hollow spit on iron supports. A wooden sheath pushed over it was wrapped around with greaseproof paper held in place by egg white. Then, using a long-handled tin spoon, ladling would commence. The batter at first had a thin liquid dripping consistency, and as it thickened and the drips slowed, so 'the hopes were aroused again, and after a couple of hours, it was possible to lift down the magnificent browned and spiky Baumkuchen. Everything about it had a symbolical meaning. On its completion, this splendid show-piece ensured a confidence in the entire success of the celebration. The Baumkuchen was considered to be the Horoscope.'

Frau Gaster's efforts were noble; she was honoured by the local housewives with a special celebration on completion of her thousandth Baumkuchen.

It was also customary to coat Baumkuchen with a lemon- or liqueur-flavoured icing. This was poured on to the hot cake while it was still on the spit, away from the fire, and rotated until the icing had set and the cake cooled down, or it would collapse.

Urbain Dubois must take the prize for the largest Gâteau de Broche – prepared for a 'Buffet de Bal', it used between 260 and 280 eggs and measured over a metre in height. Dubois declared himself as much in favour of the Baumkuchen as English fruit cake, suggesting that both are quite suitable for cutting into small portions and serving on festive occasions.

Baumkuchen became my parents' 'Family classic'. After the war, our home welcomed a constant stream of visitors who enjoyed my mother's cooking. Several couples then engaged to be married persuaded my mother to prepare their various wedding feasts. Unfamiliar with the traditional English wedding cake, she naturally opted for the most important festive cake that she knew, the Baumkuchen.

I remember well the hours she toiled in the kitchen; perched on a stool and crouched low to reach under the grill (a good modern alternative since the open fire spit no longer existed), she spooned and smoothed over the layers of batter patiently, toasting them each in turn. The kitchen grew hotter and hotter. But the efforts were always well rewarded with appreciative exclamations as the first slices were cut and sampled, and the fine layers counted – that became our ritual! (Apparently this method is not as new as we thought: in 1796 a Baumtorte was baked in just the same way.)

The Baumkuchen batter, apart from being rather more extravagant with eggs, is similar to a Sandtorte (page 181); its unusual taste comes from the many fine toasted layers. Although it does not look quite as attractive when baked in a cake tin under the grill, the taste is every bit as good as the spit version. (I suppose you could even try to adapt a barbecue spit for the purpose – but remember to use a drip tray, and beware of flying dust!) I use a 28 cm (10 inch) spring-form tin; the shallow sides make it more accessible.

WEDDING CAKES

Baumkuchen

½ fresh vanilla pod	½ fresh vanilla pod
zest 1 lemon	zest 1 lemon
500 g caster sugar	1 lb caster sugar
500 g butter	1 lb butter
14 egg yolks	14 egg yolks
250 g plain flour	9 oz plain flour
250 g cornflour or potato flour	9 oz cornflour or potato flour
14 egg whites	14 egg whites

Mix the scraped vanilla pod with the lemon zest and sugar. Beat the butter until creamy, add the sugar, then the egg yolks one at a time. Beat thoroughly. Sift the flours together two or three times and beat single spoonfuls into the mixture. Whip the egg whites to form stiff creamy peaks, and lightly fold into the mixture.

Grease a 28 cm (10 inch) spring-form tin, spread 2 tablespoons of the mixture over and push under the grill, preheated to gas 6, 200°C, 400°F (if possible). When golden brown, spoon over more of the mixture and repeat until it is all used up.

Glaze with lemon- or liqueur-flavoured icing when cool.

A nineteenth century Baumkuchen

Cheese Cakes

To make Orange or Lemon Cheesecakes, another way. From the same.

Take the Rind of a large Lemon or Orange, and boil it in four or five Waters till it is quite tender, and free from its Bitterness; then either shred it or beat it very fine in a Marble Mortar with the Yolks of eight hard Eggs, six Ounces of Loaf-Sugar finely powder'd, and a spoonfull of Orange-Flower-Water: mix this then with as much Cream, and two Eggs beat, as will render it of the Consistence of Cheesecake-meat before it is baked; then put it into your Coffins, and bake them in a gentle Oven. You may put in Currans if you please, but they are generally omitted: however, if you like to have them, let them be first plump'd a little over the Fire in Sugar and Water.

The best way for these Cheesecakes is to make the Coffins in Patty-Pans, and fill them with the Meat near an Inch thick. The Proportions mention'd above will serve to direct for a large quantity.

(Richard Bradley, *The Country Housewife and Lady's Director*, 1581)

Traditionally, cheese cakes are baked from fresh soft cheeses, cream, eggs, butter, sugar and spices on a shortcrust pastry base – not made of crushed biscuit crumbs with a gelatined, plastic, uncooked, cream cheese topping as is the current fashion. Some may find the latter aesthetically more attractive, but for me the promise of home-made goodness, of which no other cake smacks quite so obviously, has a far greater appeal. Inevitably, due to the high proportion of fat and despite the absorbing qualities of the dry goods, cheese cakes have a tendency to collapse after baking, while cooling. This, together with the cracked golden surface (possibly enhanced by a thin extra layer of cream before baking) is characteristic of a real cheese cake.

Made with cream, cottage or curd cheese; Quark, Topfen or Schotten; ricotta, mascapone, pot, myzithra, fromage blanc or Eishta; from cow's, sheep's, or goat's milk, or sometimes as in the Middle East with buffalo's milk, the cakes are essentially regional and, despite the large variety, basically the same. It is the nuances of flavour, their combinations and presentation which characterize the different origins.

Cheese for Baking

Three cheeses – cottage, curd and cream – are most commonly available.

The commercial *cottage cheese* has large firm curds and contains only 4 per cent butter fat. Be sure to drain cottage cheese very thoroughly and sieve it before using it for baking. Too much moisture will spoil the cake.

Curd cheese contains about 12 per cent butterfat. I find it the most practical for baking. Both the flavour and the texture are good, and not too rich to interfere with other ingredients. Curd cheese need not be drained, nor is it essential to sieve it.

Cream cheese is a soft cheese made of renneted double or single cream; the butterfat can vary – 25–55 per cent. It has to be very well drained, and can be tricky to handle in baking because of the high fat content. I prefer not to use it.

Cheeses must be absolutely fresh when used, for a hint of sourness will taint and spoil a cake completely. Baked cheese cakes are best eaten fairly quickly – they keep fresh for at the most 2 or 3 days in a cool place.

Freezing Cheese Cakes

All these cakes freeze very successfully. They should be frozen without wrappers, then wrapped in suitable freezer containers. They may be kept for up to 3 months. Unwrap before thawing so that the cheese surface is not damaged when the papers are removed. Thaw at room temperature for 3–4 hours, or overnight in the refrigerator.

Cheese cakes are frequently associated with Jewish cuisine. Pentecost or Shavuoth, the early harvest festival which usually falls in June, fifty days after passover (Succot celebrates the late harvest) has the strongest link with dairy foods – cheese cakes and blintzes (thin egg pancakes filled with cheese, and fresh or dried fruits) in particular are baked then.

Pentecost brings to a close the successful gathering of the ripened barley and wheat (in the Middle East the grains planted in the previous autumn ripen at this time). The other 'early fruits' of the Middle East – grapes, figs, pomegranates, olive oil and honey – are also celebrated.

Shavuoth in biblical times was purely an agricultural festival, but from the second century B.C. it principally commemorated the giving of the Ten Commandments and the Torah to Moses on Mount Sinai. During the Seleucid era, 312 B.C. – 65 B.C., and the collapse of the second Temple in 70 A.D., near Asia was heavily peopled by immigrant Macedonians and Greeks. Their cosmopolitan cities, strongly characteristic of the Hellenistic age, admitted Jews and Syrians to citizenship.

Pentecost was an extremely popular Jewish festival and people would flock to offer their first fruits:

> Ye shall bring out of your habitations two wave loaves of two tenth deals; they shall be of fine flour; they shall be baken with leaven; they are the first fruits unto the Lord.
>
> (Leviticus 23:v.17)

Although the agricultural nature of the festival then diminished, the Middle Ages again saw young trees and plants being arranged around the synagogues in some communities, while others offered flowers to the worshippers, and some sprinkled perfumed water on scattered fresh herbs. Today, and despite the religious significance, the echo of nature still lingers.

When the custom of eating dairy foods for the feast began is unclear, although folk tales abound. Perhaps it was as a personal penance that the Jews abstained from eating meat on the day before the Torah was given; or perhaps the study of the holy scriptures was as sweet and nourishing as milk and honey and so served as an effective substitute. Or is it possible that the Jews owed their love of cheese, with honey and nuts, to Greek civilization, and simply adapted it for their religious observance?

Already before the destruction of Jerusalem in 70 A.D. the Diaspora of the Jewish peoples from the East had begun. Their religions and no doubt their culinary traditions accompanied them through Western Europe.

CHEESE CAKES

Simple Cheese Cake

pâte sucrée or shortcrust pastry for 22 cm base (page 45)
500 g cottage or curd cheese
150 ml sour cream
3 egg yolks
175 g caster sugar
zest 1 lemon
3 egg whites

pâte sucrée or shortcrust pastry for 8½ inch base (page 45)
1 lb cottage or curd cheese
5 fl oz sour cream
3 egg yolks
6 oz caster sugar
zest 1 lemon
3 egg whites

gas 4, 180°C, 350°F/1 hour

Bake blind a pastry shell (page 208), and allow to cool. Carefully sieve the cheese into a mixing bowl, then beat in the sour cream, egg yolks and sugar until thick and creamy. Mix in the lemon zest. In another bowl whip the egg whites to stiff snowy peaks, then fold them into the cheese mixture using a large metal spoon. Pour into the flan case, and bake in the preheated oven for 40–45 minutes. It should have a rich golden appearance and start to shrink away from the sides. Do not be tempted to overcook it or it will be tough when cold. Turn the oven off, and leave the cake inside to cool down for about 20 minutes with the door ajar. This will not prevent the cake collapsing but may stop it from splitting.

Dust with icing sugar before serving. As an added touch flaked almonds may be sprinkled over the cheese filling before it is baked. Sour cream may be spread on the surface to serve.

* For a spectacular after-dinner dessert heap soft fruits on to the top of the cake. Try cranberries or blackcurrants for a change, and cover with softly whipped double cream.

Cheese Cake with Almonds

This recipe dates from 1794; and differs from other cheese cakes since it is made without a pastry base. The large quantity of nuts, which give it body and enhance the fine taste of the cheese, help prevent the cake from sinking as it cools down.

I have also tried a French whipped cream cheese – fromage blanc – (40 per cent butterfat content), which has an unusually distinctive taste and a fine creamy texture which lightens the cake very successfully.

350 g curd or cottage cheese
50 g caster sugar
2 egg yolks
2 teaspoons lemon zest
1 tablespoon plain flour
1 tablespoon cornflour
50 g raisins
80 g almond flakes or nibs
1 tablespoon chopped candied lemon peel
4 egg whites

12 oz curd or cottage cheese
2 oz caster sugar
2 egg yolks
2 teaspoons lemon zest
1 tablespoon plain flour
1 tablespoon cornflour
2 oz raisins
3 oz almond flakes or nibs
1 tablespoon chopped candied lemon peel
4 egg whites

gas 8, 250°C, 450°F for initial heating then gas 3, 160°C, 325°F for 40–45 minutes

Beat the cheese well with the sugar. Add the egg yolks one at a time, then the lemon zest. Sift in the flours. Add the raisins, the almonds and the candied peel. Beat the egg whites in a separate bowl, until they stand in stiff snowy peaks. Fold them into the main mixture, using a large metal spoon. Pour into a well-greased 24 cm (9½ inch) springform tin, and set in the preheated oven immediately. Turn the temperature down and bake. Do not open the oven door during the cooking time.

Talmouses and Maids of Honour

Fifteenth-century France saw little choice of pâtisserie, and talmouses de St Denis were much coveted by Louis XI. These cheese savouries, now hors d'oeuvre, were then considered to be cakes — a song was even composed extolling their virtues. The filling for the puff pastry base was generally made of a choux paste flavoured with Brie or Parmesan, sometimes Gruyère, cream and icing sugar.

In England people had been buying sweetened cheese cakes from stalls set in front of the medieval houses since the fourteenth century, but it was probably Henry VIII's reputed involvement two centuries later which started a long and popular fashion. Maybe the King's French connections introduced them to him, but legend tells of a Richmond festivity which he attended with members of his entourage, among whom was Anne Boleyn, maid of honour to his sister. Apparently overwhelmed by her charms, and pleased with the unfamiliar cakes, the King gallantly dedicated them in her favour.

CHEESE CAKES

Various curd cakes featured subsequently at the great country fairs. Yorkshire tarts in particular were well known:

> Nice Yorkshire Cakes!
> Nice Yorkshire cakes, come buy of me,
> I have them crisp and brown;
> They are very good to eat with tea,
> And fit for Lord or clown.
>
> (London cry)

A certain confectioner in Richmond had the exclusive right of the recipe for 'Maids of Honour'. It was suggested that he bought the secret for £1,000, and he might even have baked them for the famous banquet; his fortune was made whatever the case, and his cakes were sent far and wide for many centuries. It was customary to use puff pastry as the basis for curd cakes, but I prefer shortcrust pastry. Here is a fifteenth-century recipe. Brandy improves the flavour.

shortcrust pastry to make 10 tartlet cases (page 44)	shortcrust pastry to make 10 tartlet cases (page 44)
120 g curd cheese	4 oz curd cheese
90 g butter	3 oz butter
2 egg yolks	2 egg yolks
2 tablespoons brandy	2 tablespoons brandy
90 g caster sugar	3 oz caster sugar
60 g ground almonds	2 oz ground almonds
pinch nutmeg	pinch nutmeg
juice ½ lemon	juice ½ lemon
zest 1 lemon	zest 1 lemon

gas 6, 200°C, 400°F/approx. 25 minutes

Make the pastry and line the tartlet moulds. Prick the bases with a fork. Sieve the cheese if necessary; beat the butter until it is smooth then mix in the cheese. Beat in the egg yolks and the brandy, then the sugar and the almonds. Mix in the nutmeg and lemon juice and zest. Fill each tartlet case just a little more than half full, otherwise they will brim over as they bake, then set in the preheated oven and bake. They will rise and puff. When they have browned lightly and the pastry has also coloured, take them out of the oven taking care not to jerk or handle them roughly; in any case they will collapse a bit as they cool.

CAKES

Pear and Cheese Sponge

4–5 dessert pears	4–5 dessert pears
juice ½ lemon	juice ½ lemon
1 tablespoon sugar	1 tablespoon sugar
400 g curd cheese	14 oz curd cheese
100 g caster sugar	4 oz caster sugar
3 egg yolks	3 egg yolks
zest 1 lemon	zest 1 lemon
4 tablespoons cornflour	4 tablespoons cornflour
1 teaspoon baking powder	1 teaspoon baking powder
3 egg whites	3 egg whites
shortcrust pastry for 24 cm spring-form tin	shortcrust pastry for 9½ inch spring-form tin

gas 4, 180°C, 350°F / 45 minutes

Peel, quarter and finely slice the pears, and mix with the lemon juice and 1 tablespoon of sugar to prevent discoloration. Beat the sieved cheese with the sugar, egg yolks and lemon zest until creamy. Sift in the cornflour and baking powder. Beat the egg whites to form stiff peaks. Drain the excess liquid from the pears and fold into the egg mixture together with the egg whites. Turn into the prepared tin which has been lined with the shortcrust pastry. Bake until the cheese has slightly coloured. Leave to cool in the tin; it will collapse but has a very creamy texture.

Rose Cheese Cake from Poland

Honey and spices are typical of cream cheese pastries in the Old World. *Borekias* from Turkey parcel the mixture in their traditional filo pastry, and *Queijadas de Évora* from central Portugal, influenced by the Arab invaders, are small puff pastry shells filled with the same. Elizabeth David's cinnamon-spiced *Siphniac honey pie*, made with myzithra sheep's cheese and eggs, is also sweetened with honey, as was the less tasty Savillum pie of the early Romans. *Knafe* (page 340), a local Jerusalem delicacy with halumi cheese filling (from goat's and sheep's milk), has a perfumed syrup poured over. The difference between the sweet tooth of the east and the more savoury of the West is well bridged in this unusual old recipe which comes from Poland. Despite the history of hostilities with Turkey, Turkish cooks were often to be found in the kitchens of their adversaries.

CHEESE CAKES

The re-discovery of this recipe revived a host of forgotten memories for my Polish housekeeper. She remembered the cellar in her parents' home, which was always well stocked with garden produce. Sterilized jars were filled with pickled Saffron Milk-cap mushrooms, with sliced green tomatoes, tiny gherkins and onions; sauerkraut and sweet and sour cucumbers were marinaded in barrels, as well as spiced and vinegared sides of wild pig. *Bryndza*, the cheese pressed with caraway seeds and salt and made from sheep's milk curds brought by the mountain shepherds, was packed tightly in a wooden barrel. A huge glass jar was layered alternately with sugar and the passing season's fruits and topped up with rum. Bottling jars brimmed with Morello cherries, with apples and with pears. A selection of jams and the pale pink crystallized candy of roses, which kept for years, completed the picture.

In the spring the family of eight children used to collect the petals of the wild rambling eglantine roses in the garden and hedgerows for the rose conserve, and more were bought from the peasants in the local market. The white points beneath the petals were snipped away, and the remainder was crushed with icing sugar in a huge bowl and stirred and pounded into a thick paste. This was poured into clean glass jars and covered, to be stored for months in the dark cellar.

It was and still is a very popular candy in Poland. The preserve was a classic filling for doughnuts, where the delicate aroma and taste harmonized mouth-wateringly with the warm yeast pastry. Often it sandwiched a cream-covered Bishop's sponge cake but a layered combination of cream cheese, short pastry and rose conserve was more unusual.

Roses are fairly uncommon in old cookery books. They were generally used as cake decoration, when the petals were dipped in or brushed with sugar. Mrs Leyel has a rose jelly recipe, and of course rose-flower water was familiar as a perfume.

I found this one in Otto Bierbaum's *Cake Encyclopedia*. 'Rose conserve in the Turkish manner' uses 625 g (1 lb 6 oz) of icing sugar with 250 g (9 oz) of fresh picked rose petals. The preparation is similar to the Polish one, although the suggestions for drying the paste are less practical. 'Stand the open jars in a place where the sun shines strongly, cover them at sunset and bring them inside each night for four weeks.'

The wild old-fashioned single-petalled eglantine rose which blooms in the spring is the most suitable – the cultivated garden varieties have a chewy texture and almost no flavour.

CAKES
Sernik z Ucierana Róza (Cukrowa)

(Cheese cake with rose preserves)

Pastry

1 egg	1 egg
2–3 tablespoons sour cream	2–3 tablespoons sour cream
1 teaspoon baking powder	1 teaspoon baking powder
200 g plain flour	7 oz plain flour
80 g butter	3 oz butter
80 g icing sugar	3 oz icing sugar
150–200 g rose preserve	5½–7 oz rose preserve

Filling

150 g butter	5 oz butter
750 g curd cheese	1¾ lb curd cheese
300 g caster sugar	11 oz caster sugar
6 egg yolks	6 egg yolks
30 g candied orange peel	1 oz candied orange peel
zest ½ lemon	zest ½ lemon
50 g currants (optional)	2 oz currants (optional)
vanilla	vanilla
6 egg whites	6 egg whites
30 g semolina or ground almonds	1 oz semolina or ground almonds
1 teaspoon rose-water	1 teaspoon rose-water

gas 4, 180°C, 350°F/15 minutes, then 1 hour

Pastry: Mix the egg and the sour cream. Sift the baking powder with the flour. Crumb the flour with the butter and the other ingredients except the rose preserve and blend to a fine paste. Chill. Roll out the pastry, line the bottom and sides of a 26 cm (10½ inch) baking tin, and prick. Weigh down with aluminium foil or greaseproof paper and par-bake until set and a pale biscuit colour. Take out of the oven and spread the rose conserve over. Cover with the prepared cheese filling (see below). Bake for an hour. Switch off the oven and leave the cake in for a further 15 minutes.

Filling: Cream the butter and mix with sieved cheese, sugar and yolks. Add peel, lemon zest, currants and vanilla. Beat egg whites to form stiff peaks and fold into the cheese mixture alternating with spoonfuls of semolina or ground almonds. Fold in the rose-water.

CHEESE CAKES

If rose conserve is not available, a variation of this recipe uses an almond layer. Moisten 150 g (5 oz) of sugar with water and boil to the fine thread stage. Into this mix 150 g (5 oz) of blanched, ground almonds, and allow to cool until thick.

Nuts

In Persia since early times, powdered nuts, almonds, walnuts and pistachios were used extravagantly to thicken sweet and savoury sauces as accompaniments to various meat dishes. This tradition was eagerly adopted by the Romans, and later by the Arabs and the crusaders, who planted nuts as they returned from the East to Europe.

The general enthusiasm for nuts inspired many unusual dishes, and especially an interest in nut cakes and sweets, which reached a crescendo in mid nineteenth-century Europe, when nuts were frequently used in preference to flour. Cookery books of the time were filled with pages of nut recipes, as each culture developed its regional specialities. Interest is still sustained today, though to a lesser degree.

In the Middle East, almonds, walnuts, pine nuts and pistachios are still loved and much used in pastries. Vermicelli-like doughs and fine pastry layers are wrapped or rolled around delicately perfumed and powdered nut pastes. In Italy, 'mandoletti' almond pastries, macaroons and sweet chestnut cakes are especially popular. The French, on the other hand, have a regional, more insular approach and the emphasis in their use of nuts is on appearance rather than on flavour. They are used mainly in fillings and as decoration, and only occasionally in pastes. The Swiss seem to favour closely textured pastry-like cakes which, though delicious, are a little heavy.

In England the approach is also very restrained – a hint of a nut in a basic pastry, a traditional almond pattern on a Dundee cake, a handful of nuts in a mincemeat filling, a marzipan layer on the simnel cake, or combined with other fruits in a plain fruit and nut loaf. But the Austro-Hungarians and the Germans, with their sweet tooth, still have a passion for nuts, and the finest recipes from Europe and the Middle East have been absorbed into their repertoire. The full rich flavours of the nuts are delicately and considerately enhanced with perfumes and liqueurs, vanilla, coffee and chocolate. Coarsely or finely ground, they are blended with eggs and sugar and baked in layers, in light sponges, pastries and biscuits. Filled and covered with equally flavoursome creams and icings, the combinations are endless and imaginative.

A particular characteristic of these nut cakes is that many need no butter – the fats in the nuts replace it; and often only a little flour is necessary, or none at all. Eggs are generally separated, and the stiffly beaten whites, which are usually folded in last of all, give air and lightness to the mixtures. Although the cakes tend to rise only a little, the fatty richness of the nuts imparts a moist texture, and when layered with creams, they make unusual desserts.

Selection and Storage

> . . . It was an amazing sight. One hundred squirrels were seated upon high stools around a large table. On the table were mounds and mounds of walnuts, and the squirrels were all working away like mad, shelling the walnuts at a tremendous speed.
>
> 'These squirrels are specially trained for getting the nuts out of walnuts' Mr Wonka explained.
>
> 'Why use squirrels?' Mike Teavee asked. 'Why not use Oompa-Loompas?'
>
> 'Because,' said Mr Wonka, 'Oompa-Loompas can't get walnuts out of walnut shells in one piece. They always break them in two. Nobody except squirrels can get walnuts whole out of walnut shells every time. It is extremely difficult. But in my factory, I insist upon using only whole walnuts. Therefore I have to have squirrels to do the job. Aren't they wonderful, the way they get those nuts out! And see how they first tap each walnut with their knuckles to be sure its not a bad one! If it's bad, it makes a hollow sound, and they don't bother to open it. They just throw it down the rubbish chute . . .'
>
> (Roald Dahl, *Charlie and the Chocolate Factory*)

When selecting nuts, choose those which are large and unblemished, and free from dust and debris. Bruises and marks (unless they are from the United States, where cracking is done mechanically) may have been caused by vermin and should be discarded. Buy them in shops where the turnover of stock is rapid and you may be sure of fresh produce. Since all nuts are rich in butter, fats and oils they are fresh for only a relatively short time and then have a tendency to turn rancid, which gives a bitter unpleasant taste. Health food stores and supermarkets are particularly reliable. Avoid buying in too great bulk, unless you bake frequently; the initial saving will only be lost in wastage.

Most nuts will keep satisfactorily in a cool, dry place, sealed in an airtight box or jar, for up to 4 or 5 months (almonds up to a year).

Walnuts are particularly susceptible to rancidity and should be kept for no more than 2 months. If your storage area is suspect and inclined to changes in temperature, avoid using metal containers – these tend to cause condensation, which hastens deterioration. Avoid storing nuts in a domestic freezer, as the controlled degree of humidity, which is essential to prevent nuts becoming mouldy, is difficult to maintain in home conditions.

Almonds

Early in the New Year branches of the almond tree are softened by a delicate froth of pink blossom. This premature awakening of spring is honoured in the Greek fable of Demophoon – stricken with remorse on finding his dead love Phyllis turned to an almond tree because of his betrayal, he clasped the barren tree in an embrace, whereupon it burst into full bloom.

In early times, as with anything new, almonds were regarded with suspicion; they were used only for medicinal purposes to cure insomnia and dysentery, and even as an antidote for the influence of witchcraft and the evil eye. Known as 'Greek nuts', they were particularly coveted by the Romans, and used extensively in their general cuisine as well as in cakes and pastries, but Jordan almonds were the most valued as sweet dessert nuts. Coated in sugar and honey, they were offered as tokens of rejoicing to celebrate family births and marriages, a custom which is still common in Europe today. A few raw almonds eaten before drinking alcohol were also considered excellent for preventing drunkenness and hangovers.

The immense popularity of almonds has been sustained throughout the centuries; so much so that in the nineteenth century Otto Bierbaum's cake encyclopedia featured over 250 almond recipes alone.

There are over a hundred varieties of almond, but only four are widely available. These are Jordan, Valencia and California almonds, all sweet varieties, and bitter almonds which are less common.

Jordan Almonds. The name derives from the French jardin, and they are grown in Malaga and Alicante in Spain. Considered to be the best and the sweetest of the dessert varieties, they are sometimes referred to as 'finger' almonds because of their long and slender shape. The larger sized nuts are most common, as the smaller ones are generally used by the trade for producing sugared almonds and other confectionery.

Valencia Almonds. Though less sweet than Jordan almonds, these have a good full flavour. They grow in Spain and Portugal, and are broader, shorter and heart-shaped. Their skins are rougher and tougher, and the nuts are usually imported in their shells. They are mostly used for baking purposes, where the rather indigestible coarse skin is removed by blanching.

Californian Almonds. These do not have as full a flavour as the Spanish almonds, but their appearance is excellent. Quite short and oval in character, they are clean and uniformly attractive. They are often much cheaper than the Mediterranean nuts.

Preparing Almonds

Almonds may be bought in many different forms – in the shell; whole, natural or raw; whole blanched; sliced, flaked or slivered; chopped or nibbed; and ground. .

Be particularly careful when buying ground almonds. Sometimes a proportion of peach kernels is mixed with the almonds, and they do not have as good a flavour. (Consumer protection laws now make this less likely.) Often a lower price will reflect this. I prefer to prepare almonds myself, as I need them, to ensure freshness and the best flavour.

Raw Almonds. A number of recipes use raw almonds – those which have their brown skins left on. Take a damp tea-cloth and rub the dry nuts gently to remove any particles of dust.

Blanched Almonds. Bring a large saucepan of water to the boil, and drop in a few nuts at a time, so as not to slow the boiling. Allow to boil for 2 or 3 minutes longer and drain through a sieve. The brown skins will easily slide off with gentle pressure between the thumb and fingers. Spread the almonds on a large baking sheet, and dry off in a cool (gas 1, 140°, 275°F) oven for about an hour.

Pounded or Ground Almonds. Great care must be taken to avoid releasing the natural oils in the nuts, as they will make the nuts moist and gritty, tasteless and difficult to handle.

Pound the nuts in a mortar, adding a little granulated sugar and water, or a perfumed water, such as orange-flower or rose, to moisten. (A small amount of egg white or cream may be chosen as an alternative.)

A slightly coarser texture will be achieved if you use a hand grinder or mincer; moisten with sugar and water as before.

Almonds may be pulverized in a liquidizer, and once again particular care should be taken. Use only about 100 g (4 oz) at a time, and grind at top speed for about 30 seconds. The food processor is particularly efficient for this operation, as the oils are less easily released in the larger bowl. Drop the nuts through the feeding spout on to the rotating cutting blade, stop very briefly every few seconds so that the larger pieces may fall back into the centre, moisten occasionally, and continue until the desired texture is obtained. The grating blade of a processor will give a coarser texture, which is sometimes more desirable.

Shop-bought ground almonds may be rather dry and bland; this is why egg whites, double cream or a perfumed flower water are often used to moisten them.

Split, Sliced and Slivered Almonds. Prepare while the almonds are still warm and moist after blanching. Use a wooden chopping board and a sharp knife, or the slicing blade of a food processor.

Chopped or Nibbed Almonds. Chop by hand, using a long sharp pointed knife; rest the tip on a wooden board and chop through the nuts, swinging the handle round in a half circle and back again. Alternatively, drop the nuts on to the rotating blades of a processor or liquidizer and chop to the correct texture.

Roast Almonds. These are often used in European recipes. Coarsely chop blanched almonds, then lightly toss and stir in a frying pan over a low heat until the nuts are an even toasted brown. Alternatively, spread the nuts on a baking sheet and set in a gas 4, 180°C, 350°F oven for about 10 minutes. Stir often to avoid burning.

Almond Praline (Caramelized Almonds). This delicious marriage of caramelized sugar and almonds is frequently used as a flavouring for cakes, fillings and ice-creams, as well as for decoration. Although it is quickly prepared, pay particular attention that the sugar does not burn.

Praline may be stored for several weeks in an airtight container.

Almond Praline (1)

Boil 100 g (4 oz) of granulated sugar with 2 tablespoons of water in a copper sugar boiler until caramel forms (page 70). Toss in 100 g (4 oz) of chopped toasted almonds, and stir lightly to coat them with the sugar. As soon as the mixture boils, pour on to an oiled baking tray, spread out, and leave to cool. Break the praline into pieces, and coarsely chop or grind — it may also be pounded or pulverized.

Almond Praline (2)

Stir together 100 g (4 oz) of caster sugar and 100 g (4 oz) of whole raw unblanched almonds in a copper sugar boiler over the heat, until the sugar has melted into a dark brown caramel and has well grilled the almonds. Pour on to an oiled marble slab or baking sheet and leave to cool. Break up and pound or grind as before.

Whipped Almond Cake

This is very simple to prepare. Beat very thoroughly between each addition, and fold the separated, beaten egg white very lightly and carefully, but swiftly, into the mixture so as not to lose any air. Do not open the oven door until 10 or 15 minutes before the end of the cooking time, as this type of cake is especially susceptible to draught, will collapse and become wet and soggy.

You can use blanched or raw ground almonds. Raw almonds give a pleasant chewiness.

6 egg yolks	6 egg yolks
140 g caster sugar	5 oz caster sugar
140 g ground almonds	5 oz ground almonds
4 egg whites	4 egg whites

gas 3, 170°C, 325°F/1 hour

Beat the egg yolks and sugar together until light and creamy. Mix in the ground almonds and beat again thoroughly. In a separate bowl, beat the egg whites until they stand in peaks, then using a large metal spoon fold the white into the basic mixture. Pour into a well greased and floured 24 cm (9½ inch) spring-form tin, and bake in the preheated oven.

* For an orange flavour, add the grated zest of an orange, and mix the juice of the orange with 25 g (1 oz) of white breadcrumbs before combining with the nuts.

CAKES
Gâteau de la Reine

The flavour of this rich, closely textured but moist cake is delicately enhanced by the perfumed water. Serve it cut in thin slices; it will keep for at least 2 weeks.

There is no need to decorate the cake if you sprinkle flaked almonds over the cake base before you pour the mixture into the tin. Turn it over when cold, then dredge with icing sugar to serve.

200 g butter	7 oz butter
200 g caster sugar	7 oz caster sugar
4 egg yolks	4 egg yolks
100 g ground almonds	3½ oz ground almonds
1 teaspoon orange-flower water	1 teaspoon orange-flower water
140 g potato flour	5 oz potato flour
1 teaspoon cinnamon	1 teaspoon cinnamon
zest ½ lemon	zest ½ lemon
3 egg whites	3 egg whites
170 ml double cream, whipped	6 fl oz double cream, whipped
flaked almonds to sprinkle over the base (optional)	flaked almonds to sprinkle over the base (optional

gas 3, 170°C, 325°F / 1 hour

Beat the butter and the sugar until pale and creamy, then mix in the yolks one at a time. Add the nuts and then the orange-flower water. Sift the potato flour and beat it into the mixture with the cinnamon and lemon zest. Whip the egg whites in a separate bowl until they stand in stiff peaks, and fold them gently into the mixture using a metal spoon. Finally fold in the whipped cream. Turn the cake into a greased and sugar-coated gugelhopf mould or a base-lined, 24 cm (9$^1/_2$ inch) tin, and bake in the preheated oven. When cool coat with apricot jam and glaze with glacé icing, or fill and cover with whipped cream, and sprinkle with praline.

Almond Slices

These crunchy almond slices use up the surplus egg yolks which often pose a problem after baking meringue and nut cakes. The slices will keep for at least 2 weeks.

150 g caster sugar	5 oz caster sugar
1 whole egg	1 whole egg
6 egg yolks	6 egg yolks
150 g ground, blanched almonds	5 oz ground, blanched almonds
150 g plain flour	5 oz plain flour
150 g butter, melted and cooled	5 oz butter, melted and cooled
2 egg whites	2 egg whites
100 g icing sugar	3$^1/_2$ oz icing sugar
50 g flaked almonds for decoration	2 oz flaked almonds for decoration

gas 3, 170°C, 325°F for 30 minutes, then gas $^1/_4$, 100°C, 225°F for 2 hours or more

Beat together the sugar and whole egg with the egg yolks until light and fluffy. Add alternate spoonfuls of ground almonds, sifted flour and cooled melted butter, and beat well together. Spread the mixture evenly over two well-greased baking trays 34 × 24 cm (13$^1/_2$ × 10$^1/_2$ inches) and bake in the preheated oven for 30 minutes. When golden coloured, remove from the oven, cut the biscuit into slices about 7 × 3 cm (2$^1/_2$ × 1 inch) and loosen from the tray. Turn down the oven temperature.

Using the egg whites and icing sugar, make the meringue in the usual way (page 108) and spread over the almond biscuit base, making sure that all the corners are covered. Roughen slightly with a fork, and scatter the flaked almonds all over, pressing them down gently where necessary. Run a knife along the lines where the biscuit has been previously cut; this makes it very easy to separate after baking. Put the trays back in the cool oven to dry out slowly. You may even leave them overnight if need be — but turn the oven to its lowest setting and leave the door ajar.

My Mother's Bienenstich (Bee Sting)

A yeast pastry base is traditional for Bienenstich. It tastes delicious while still warm, but unfortunately keeps fresh for only 1 or 2 days: however, it stores well for up to 4 weeks in the freezer.

20 g fresh yeast	$2/3$ oz fresh yeast
1 teaspoon caster sugar	1 teaspoon caster sugar
100 ml warm (blood-heat) milk	$3^{1}/_{2}$ fl oz warm (blood heat) milk
360 g strong, plain flour, slightly warmed	12 oz strong, plain flour, slightly warmed
1 teaspoon salt	1 teaspoon salt
110 g butter	4 oz butter
110 g caster sugar	4 oz caster sugar
2 small eggs (or 1 large egg and 1 yolk)	2 small eggs (or 1 large egg and 1 yolk)
1 teaspoon lemon zest	1 teaspoon lemon zest

Almond layer

100 g butter	$3^{1}/_{2}$ oz butter
200 g granulated sugar	7 oz granulated sugar
250 g flaked almonds	9 oz flaked almonds
4 tablespoons milk	4 tablespoons milk

gas 4, 180°C, 350°F / approx. 30 minutes

Crumble the yeast and the teaspoon of caster sugar into half the warmed milk. Leave to stand for 10 minutes until it starts to foam. Sift the flour and salt into a large bowl and make a well in the centre. Beat the butter and sugar until light and fluffy; lightly whisk the eggs in a cup. Pour the yeast into the flour, draw some of the flour over it, then add the butter and sugar mixture, the egg, lemon zest and the rest of the milk. Gently work all the ingredients together, lightly kneading and drawing the yeast through. Work the mixture until the dough starts to roll off the sides of the bowl and looks very shiny. Cover with a damp cloth, or place in a large lightly-oiled polythene bag and seal. Leave in a warm place to rise and double in bulk for about 20–30 minutes. Knock the dough back down again and roll it out lightly to fit two greased baking trays with 3 cm (1¼ inch) deep sides and 34 × 24 cm (13½ × 9½ inches) wide. Leave to rise again, uncovered, for a further 30 minutes and prepare the almond layer meanwhile.

Almond layer: Gently melt the butter, then mix in the sugar and stir until it has all dissolved. Beat in the flaked almonds, and add enough milk to make the mixture slightly stiff but of a spreading consistency. Allow to cool.

Spread the yeast pastry with the almond mixture and bake for about 30 minutes in the preheated oven until rich and golden in colour. Cut into strips whilst still warm.

A *butter pastry base*

This alternative base is a fine butter pastry which has the advantage of keeping fresh for at least 5 days.

Melt 250 g (9 oz) of butter and set aside to cool. Beat with 250 g (9 oz) of caster sugar until light and fluffy, then beat in 4 eggs one at a time, beating well between each addition (should the mixture start to curdle add a spoonful of flour). Mix in the zest of a lemon. Finally sift 275 g (10 oz) of plain flour and 125 g (a generous 4 oz) of potato or cornflour with a teaspoon of baking powder and blend with the rest. Divide the mixture between the two baking sheets as above, and smooth even. Spread the almond layer over, and bake in the preheated oven set at gas 3, 170°C, 325°F for about 30 minutes until rich and golden coloured. Cut in slices while warm, and leave in the tin to cool.

Almond Strudel or Fila

Traditionally this Austrian filling is for a strudel dough; use a portion of dough (page 55), or substitute shop-bought fila pastry (page 336). You need 8 sheets of fila pastry (remember to re-pack the remainder immediately, so that it does not dry out), and 100 g (3½ oz) of unsalted butter to brush over. This will make two strudels. Lightly brush the first paper-thin fila sheet with melted butter, cover with the second sheet and brush again; repeat with two more. Use the remaining sheets in the same way for a second roll.

Make the Filling: Beat 100 g (4 oz) of butter with 5 egg yolks and 100 g (4 oz) of caster sugar until pale and creamy. Mix in 100 g (4 oz) of ground almonds. Whip up 5 egg whites into stiff, snowy peaks, and fold them into the mixture.

CAKES

Spread the mixture over the prepared dough, fold in the edges, and roll up lightly with the open side underneath. Make sure that the edges are well sealed, or the filling will leak out. Brush the top with melted butter. Bake in the oven preheated to gas 6, 200°C, 400°F for 30 minutes. When cold, dredge with icing sugar to serve.

Hazelnuts and Filberts

> Conspiring with him how to load and bless
> And fill all fruit with ripeness to the core
> To swell the gourd, and plump the hazel shells
> With a sweet kernel.
>
> (John Keats)

Blanching and Roasting Hazelnuts

Most cake recipes use roasted hazelnuts, as this brings out their full flavour. Spread raw hazelnuts over a baking sheet and leave for about ten minutes in a gas 4, 180°C, 350°F oven. Shake gently from time to time. When the brown skins start to split and darken, remove from the oven. Cool slightly, then roll a few nuts at a time between the fingers, or in a coarse towel, to remove the skins. Shake through a coarse sieve to separate. It does not matter if any skins remain. If they need further toasting, return to the oven and roast until golden brown.

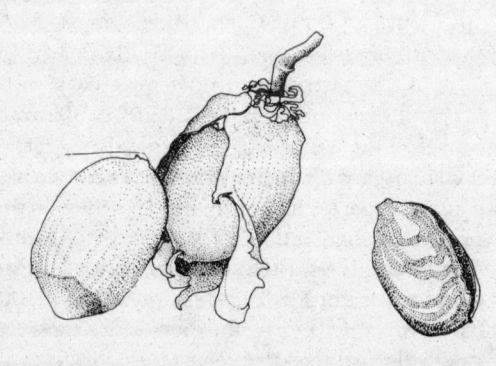

Grinding Hazelnuts

Although hazelnuts are not quite as oily as almonds, care must still be taken not to extract the natural oils. Follow the same method for grinding as for almonds (page 311). Hazelnuts may also be bought ready ground.

Whipped Hazelnut Cake

6 egg yolks	6 egg yolks
180 g caster sugar	6 oz caster sugar
220 g coarsely ground hazelnuts	8 oz coarsely ground hazelnuts
2 teaspoons lemon zest	2 teaspoons lemon zest
6 egg whites	6 egg whites

gas 4, 180°C, 350°F/1 hour

Beat the egg yolks and sugar until light and creamy; beat in the nuts and lemon zest. Whip the egg whites in a separate bowl until they hold firm peaks and fold them lightly, using a metal spoon, into the mixture. Turn into a greased and floured 24 cm (9½ inch) spring-form tin, and bake in the preheated oven. When the cake starts to shrink away from the sides of the tin, take it out of the oven, leave to rest for 5–10 minutes before releasing the clip, and turn the cake out on to a wire rack to cool completely. The cold cake can be glazed with vanilla glacé icing (page 72) and decorated with a few whole caramelized hazelnuts or covered all over with stiffly whipped cream.

For a dinner party dessert the hazelnut cake is good filled with Kirsch-flavoured whipped cream and layers of fresh loganberries and raspberries – the sharpness of the loganberries contrasts very pleasantly with the coarsely chopped nuts. Fresh strawberry or raspberry cream is also good.

Strawberry Cream Filling

You need at least 250 g (9 oz) of fresh or frozen strawberries. Reserve 2 or 3 whole fruits for decoration and chop another 3 or 4 to give texture to the finished cream. Sieve the rest of the strawberries and stir in 2 tablespoons of icing sugar. Mix into 500 ml (1 pint) of stiffly whipped double cream flavoured with 3 tablespoons of Cointreau or Kirsch.

Split the cake in two and spread a third of the cream on the bottom layer; sandwich with the top and spread the rest of the cream lavishly all over. Decorate with the whole fruits, and dredge with icing sugar just before you serve the cake.

Hazelnut Filling

Mix 140 g (5 oz) of caster sugar with the same amount of coarse ground toasted hazelnuts. Fold into 500 ml (1 pint) of whipped double cream and flavour with liqueur as above or with rum. Fill the cake shortly before serving, and decorate with chocolate shavings and toasted caramelized hazelnuts.

Hazelnut and Chocolate Torte

100 g plain flour	3½ oz plain flour
½ teaspoon baking powder	½ teaspoon baking powder
1 teaspoon ground cinnamon	1 teaspoon ground cinnamon
1 teaspoon ground cloves	1 teaspoon ground cloves
180 g unpeeled ground hazelnuts	6 oz unpeeled ground hazelnuts
150 g butter	5 oz butter
180 g caster sugar	6 oz caster sugar
4 egg yolks	4 egg yolks
110 g dark plain chocolate, grated	4 oz dark plain chocolate, grated
4 egg whites	4 egg whites
2 tablespoons rum	2 tablespoons rum

gas 4, 180°C, 350°F/approx. 1 hour 20 minutes

Sift the flour with the baking powder and the spices. Rub the unpeeled nuts in a towel to clean them, and grind coarsely. Beat the butter with 120 g (4 oz) of the sugar until pale and fluffy, then beat in the egg yolks one at a time. Mix in the nuts and the grated chocolate. Whip up the egg whites in a separate bowl until they stand in peaks, sprinkle over the rest of the sugar, and beat for a few seconds until the snow is stiff and shiny. Beat half of the meringue into the main mixture to lighten it, then fold in the rest, alternating with portions of sifted flour. Fold in the rum. Pour the mixture into a prepared greased and base-lined 22 cm (8½ inch) spring-form tin and bake. Leave to cool in the tin for about 10 minutes before turning out on to a wire rack to chill.

Split the cake and soak the bottom layer with 3 tablespoons of rum, then spread with 2 tablespoons of sour jam such as redcurrant or morello cherry jam. Sandwich, brush the top with the same jam, and glaze with rum-flavoured glacé icing (page 73).

NUTS
Hungarian Hazelnut Roulade

I prefer a roulade made with nuts to a plain sponge. The oily nature of the nut gives a much softer texture when baked; but make sure that it is well browned before attempting to peel the foil or paper off the back, for it has a tendency to stick. I usually use greased foil for nut roulades.

4 egg yolks	4 egg yolks
65 g caster sugar	2½ oz caster sugar
4 egg whites	4 egg whites
65 g toasted ground hazelnuts	2½ oz toasted, ground hazelnuts
150 ml whipped double or whipping cream	5 fl oz whipped double or whipping cream
150 g chocolate (plain, dessert)	5½ oz chocolate (plain, dessert)

gas 4, 180°C, 350°F/15–20 minutes

Cut a sheet of foil to line a baking sheet 25 × 36 cm (10 × 14 inches); let the ends overhang, and grease. Beat together the egg yolks and sugar in a bowl over hot water until the ribbon stage is reached; draw away from the heat and carry on beating until the mixture has cooled, thickened and trebled in volume. Whip up the egg whites to form a stiff snow, and gently fold them together with the ground nuts into the egg yolk mixture. Spread the mixture 1.5 cm (⅝ inch) thick on the lined baking sheet, making sure that it goes into all the corners. Bake in the hot oven.

The sponge will feel very soft to the touch even when it has browned. Take out of the oven and turn immediately on to sugar-dredged paper. Peel off the backing, trim the edges, replace a piece of paper and roll it up until it is cold. Cover with a slightly moist cloth. When cold, unroll carefully, remove the paper and spread thickly with the whipped cream. Roll up again. Gently melt the chocolate and pour immediately over the roulade, spreading it with a hot spatula. Leave a slightly rough surface for decoration.

This can also be filled with Kirsch-flavoured whipped cream and chopped strawberries. Dust the top with icing sugar.

Walnut Roulade

Use the same recipe as above, substituting walnuts for the hazelnuts. Enhance the walnut flavour with coffee: grind 8 dark, roast coffee beans to a powder, or use 1 tablespoon coffee syrup (page 85) or 1 heaped teaspoon of instant coffee powder. Beat into the egg and sugar mixture of the above recipe. Flavour the cream filling with 1 teaspoon of coffee syrup, and dredge the surface with icing sugar.

The *roulade au chocolat* on page 150 is a richer version, made with chocolate, butter and raw almonds.

Hazelnut Short Pastry

This pastry is very short and crumbly, as there is no egg or water to bind it; this makes it a little difficult to handle, though it can be patched if need be. It can be moulded into tartlet shells or baked as a flat disc. Bake it for only a very short time — it will still feel rather soft — otherwise it scorches and gets a bitter taste. It will keep fresh for 2–3 weeks stored in an airtight container, but once exposed to air it becomes soggy after a few hours.

140 g plain flour	5 oz plain flour
100 g butter	$3^{1}/_{2}$ oz butter
75 g caster sugar	3 oz caster sugar
75 g ground hazelnuts	3 oz ground hazelnuts

gas 3, 170°C, 325°F/10–15 minutes

Rub the flour and butter to make fine crumbs, blend in the sugar and the nuts. Gently press the mixture together until it stays in a fairly compact ball. There is no need to chill it.

Hazelnut and Chocolate Sandwich

Prepare the pastry as above; roll out to 2 mm (under $^{1}/_{10}$ inch) thickness and stamp out rings of pastry 5 cm (2 inches) in diameter. You should get about 50 circles (25 sandwiches). Lay them on a greased and floured flat baking sheet and bake at gas 4, 180°C, 350°F for 10 minutes. They will colour only very slightly. Remove from the oven and lay on a wire rack to cool.

Make the filling

Boil 50 ml (or 2 fl oz) of water with 120 g (4½ oz) of granulated sugar to the thread stage (page 70), pour it on to a mixture of 200 g (7 oz) of fine ground hazelnuts and 30 g (1 oz) of butter, and beat well.

When the biscuits have cooled, sandwich them in pairs with the filling. Melt 50 g (or 2 oz) of plain dark chocolate gently, drop a dot in the middle of each sandwich top, and sprinkle with a little chopped pistachio while still warm. They will keep for 2–3 weeks in an airtight tin.

Hazelnut Galette

Raspberries blend very well with this pastry, and combined with whipped cream it is a spectacular party confection. You need at least 350 g (¾ lb) of fresh or frozen fruits.

Prepare the basic pastry, and roll out two similar large circles of about 3 mm (⅛ inch) thick and 20 cm (8 inches) diameter. Bake as before. While still hot, cut one circle into 8 equal triangular sections (very carefully, for it is very delicate at this point), and leave to cool.

Whip 250 ml (½ pint) double cream until it holds soft peaks, and whisk in 2 tablespoons of caster sugar; flavour the cream with Kirsch or rum. Smooth the cream all over the plain base, and embed the triangles of pastry on their sides in the cream with the points meeting in the middle. Support each triangle on either side with raspberries, and cover the rest of the cream surface with the remaining fruits. (See Dobos torte, page 169, for method of decoration.)

You can also make tartlet shells with this pastry. Cut the rolled pastry to fit the cases and lay each disc over the back of the tin (page 210). Bake, then cool for a few seconds before turning them over and dropping them into the hollows to chill.

The tartlets taste good filled with fresh soft fruits. Insulate the base of each pastry with a little apricot jam before filling. Pipe whipped cream for decoration, and serve. They start to soften after 4 or 5 hours.

CAKES
Walnuts

> I went down to the nut orchard,
> to look at the blossoms of the valley . . .
>
> (The Song of Solomon, 6:v. 11)

The walnut tree grows to a height approaching 30 m (100 ft), has a span of some 20 m (60 ft) and is known to have survived as long as 300 years. The trunk is thick and massive, and although the timber is very brittle it lends itself admirably to the delicate inlaid and veneered marquetry which is so familiar in European furniture of the late nineteenth century. The honey tones and shaded variations of the fine woods were particularly valued and eagerly sought at great expense by the skilled craftsmen of the time.

The fruit of the walnut tree is particularly oily – it is much valued in cooking, and also by painters for mixing gold sizes and varnishes. The leaves and barks are effective as laxatives and astringents and possibly even against poison. Nicholas Culpeper gives the recipe as follows:

> Take two dry walnuts, and as many good figs, and twenty leaves of rue, bruised and beaten together with two or three corns of salt and twenty juniper berries, which take every morning fasting, preserves from danger of poison, and infection that day it is taken . . .
> – The kernels, when they grow old, are more oily, and therefore not fit to be eaten, but are then used to heal the wounds of the sinews, gangrenes and carbuncles . . . the said kernels being burned, are very astringent . . . being taken in red wine, and stay the falling of the hair, and make it fair, being anointed with oil and wine. The green husks will do the like, being used in the same manner . . . a piece of the green husks put into a hollow tooth, eases the pain.

He also suggests that 'if they [the leaves] be taken with onions, salt, and honey, they help the biting of a mad dog, or the venom or infectious poison of any beast, etc.'.

There are many varieties of walnut. The hickory and black walnut are natives of North America, whereas in England the common walnut is familiar. The tree was probably brought here early in the sixteenth century, but previously the nuts had been carried from the East in English trading ships, and were for a time known erroneously as 'English' walnuts.

There are several grades of nuts from which to choose. Generally the lighter the colour and the larger the size, the better the quality. Walnuts have a particularly distinctive flavour which blends very successfully with orange, chocolate and coffee. Take care when grinding not to extract the oils, which are very bitter and concentrated.

Whipped Dark Walnut Torte

This dark Torte is a speciality of my grandmother's.

1 tablespoon white breadcrumbs	1 tablespoon white breadcrumbs
1 teaspoon cinnamon	1 teaspoon cinnamon
1 tablespoon cocoa powder	1 tablespoon cocoa powder
180 g caster sugar	6 oz caster sugar
5 egg yolks	5 egg yolks
180 g ground walnuts	6 oz ground walnuts
70 g raw ground almonds	2 oz raw ground almonds
5 egg whites	5 egg whites

gas 4, 180°C, 350°F/50 minutes

Mix the breadcrumbs with the cinnamon and cocoa. Beat the sugar with the egg yolks until pale and creamy, then mix in the ground walnuts and almonds and the breadcrumb mixture. Beat well. In a separate bowl whip up the egg whites until they stand in peaks, beat 2 tablespoons into the basic mixture, then gently fold in the rest of the snow using a metal spoon, and taking care not to lose any air. Pour into a greased and floured spring-form tin 24 cm (9½ inches) in diameter, and bake in the preheated oven.

Like all nut cakes, this can be served simply as it is, dredged with icing sugar and offered with whipped sweetened double cream. A more elaborate finish is with a chocolate coating (page 148). The cake can also be split, filled with walnut filling (2) (page 66), and glazed.

> For lo! the board with cups and spoons is crowned,
> The berries crackle and the mill turns round;
> On shining altars of Japan they raise
> The silver lamp; the fiery spirits blaze:
> From silver spouts the grateful liquors glide,
> While China's earth receives the smoking tide:
> At once they gratify their scent and taste,
> And frequent cups prolong the rich repast.
> Straight hover round the fair her airy band;

Some o'er her lap their careful plumes displayed,
Trembling and conscious of the rich brocade.
Coffee (which makes the politicians wise,
And see through all things with his half-shut eyes)
Sent up in vapours to the Baron's brain
New stratagems, the radiant lock to gain.

(Alexander Pope, *The Rape of the Lock*, 1712)

Mrs Wosiek's Walnut Coffee Cake

Walnuts and coffee complement each other very well in this Polish recipe.

4 egg yolks
110 g icing sugar
1 tablespoon fine white breadcrumbs
1 tablespoon cocoa powder
1 tablespoon moka or coffee syrup
175 g coarsely chopped walnuts
4 egg whites

Filling

1 portion of Moka coffee cream (page 66) made with:
2 tablespoons coffee syrup
1 tablespoon powdered medium roast coffee beans
3 egg yolks
75 g caster sugar
2 teaspoons potato flour
100 g unsalted butter

4 egg yolks
4 oz icing sugar
1 tablespoon fine white breadcrumbs
1 tablespoon cocoa powder
1 tablespoon moka or coffee syrup
6 oz coarsely chopped walnuts
4 egg whites

Filling

1 portion of Moka coffee cream (page 66) made with:
2 tablespoons coffee syrup
1 tablespoon powdered medium roast coffee beans
3 egg yolks
3 oz caster sugar
2 teaspoons potato flour
$3^{1}/_{2}$ oz unsalted butter

gas 4, 180°C, 350°F/45 minutes

Cream the egg yolks and the icing sugar until thick and fluffy; beat in the fine breadcrumbs and the cocoa powder together with the coffee flavouring. Add the nuts and mix well together. Whip up the egg whites to snowy peaks and fold them into the mixture. Pour into a greased and floured 26 cm ($10^{1}/_{2}$ inch) spring-form tin, and bake in the preheated oven. When the cake starts to shrink away from the sides of the pan, withdraw from the oven and leave to cool.

Meanwhile prepare the filling. Split the cool cake and spread inside and on top with a layer of butter cream. Decorate with walnut halves and coffee beans.

Engadiner Nusstorte

The sugar bakers of the Engadin in Switzerland are world-famous. In earlier times many of them were obliged to seek employment elsewhere, due to a shortage of work locally, and only the rich and successful were able to return to the homeland to live out their final days. In a well-known Konditorei in Pontresina a small sign hangs which says 'Früher gingen unsere Vorfahren ins Ausland . . . Heute schicken wir unsere Engadiner Nusstorte in die Welt!' [In earlier times our forefathers went to foreign lands . . . today we send our Engadiner Nusstorte into the world.]

It is ideal, too, as a take-home present, a gastronomic memory of the country; the casing of short pastry filled with walnuts, enriched with honey and cream, travels well and keeps well.

The variations are numerous. Sometimes the base may be firm, sometimes short; sometimes the base will be brushed with jam, the walnuts may have pine nuts mixed in, and particularly refined recipes add candied orange and lemon peel. The following is a classic recipe; firm and compact, this cake will keep for up to a month, and the flavour improves with age.

Short pastry

300 g plain flour	10^1/$_2$ oz plain flour
210 g butter	7 oz butter
pinch salt	pinch salt
110 g granulated sugar	4 oz granulated sugar
1 teaspoon lemon zest	1 teaspoon lemon zest
2 small eggs	2 small eggs

Filling

250 g granulated sugar	9 oz granulated sugar
240 g walnuts, coarsely chopped	8 oz walnuts, coarsely chopped
300 ml double cream	^{1}/$_2$ pint double cream
1 tablespoon honey	1 tablespoon honey

gas 4, 180°C, 350°F/1 hour

Make the short pastry (page 44), and chill for at least 20 minutes wrapped in foil or plastic film.

Meanwhile prepare the filling. Drop the sugar into a heavy-based frying pan and heat gently, while stirring, until a pale brown caramel forms. Toss in the coarsely chopped nuts and roast together for 2–3 minutes. Next pour in the cream; as soon as the caramel has blended with the cream, mix in the honey. Set aside to cool.

Divide the pastry into a third and two-thirds, and roll out the greater to 3 mm ($^1/_8$ inch) thickness. Press into a greased 24 cm ($9^1/_2$ inch) loose-based cake tin, and gently ease the paste up the sides to about 5 cm (2 inches). Brush the base with lightly beaten egg white and spread the nut mixture evenly over the bottom. Roll a lid from the remaining paste the same size as the tin; gently fold the pastry edge over the nut filling and brush with water. Lay the lid in place, taking care to stick down the sides well, and prick all over with a fork – this is the traditional pattern. Bake in the preheated oven. The cake should hardly colour; if necessary, cover with foil towards the end of the cooking time. Cut after 3 or 4 days.

Chestnuts

The sweet chestnut is the least oily, the most floury and the easiest to digest of all nuts. The Swiss and Italians are particularly fond of them, and use them lavishly. In England, however, apart from the occasional luxury of an expensive French *marron glacé*, chestnuts have been rather sadly neglected.

Known in earlier times as 'Acorns of Sardis', the sweet chestnut is said to originate in Sardis Asia Minor, and the town of Castanis in Thesaly, where it grew in great numbers, gives the name Castanea.

The horse-chestnut is no relation, although the tree is of like stature; its similar fruits are rather inedible and foliage quite different.

Fresh chestnuts have the finest flavour, particularly those from Spain. They should be stored in a cool, airy, frost-free spot, and will keep fresh for up to 3 months. They contain very little oil and are not prone to rancidity, but will shrivel and dry, or go mouldy and start to decay. Chestnuts should not be eaten raw as they contain an unpleasant amount of tannic acid. Discard any buggy or holed nuts, as they will spoil the flavour of the rest.

Peeling chestnuts for baking — the conventional way.

500 g (1 lb) chestnuts will yield about 375 g (12 oz) peeled nuts. Drop the nuts, without incisions, into a pan of lightly salted boiling water and cover. Boil for 15–25 minutes, by which time the outer casing and inner skin should peel away quite easily. Test with gentle pressure between the fingers. Peel the nuts while still warm, and drop any stubborn ones back into the water for a little longer. Never leave the inner skin, as it has a bitter unpleasant taste.

For sieved chestnuts, boil peeled nuts in fresh water until they collapse. Drain and mash.

Peeling chestnuts — the Chef's Quick Method

The traditional method is rather laborious and very time-consuming. This is the professional way — with a hint of caution! *Take care not to overheat the oil and not to drop in too many nuts at once.*

Rub the chestnut skins clean with a slightly damp cloth, and dry well. Make an incision with a sharp knife, all the way round the fat part of the raw chestnut. Heat up a deep pan of fat or oil to 175°C, 350°F (any oil will do, and it can be used again, but filter it well). Plunge in a few chestnuts at a time — they will crackle and sputter, but after 2 or 3 minutes the shells will split wide open. Lift them out of the oil with a slotted spoon and lay them on absorbent kitchen paper to dry off. Peel away the outer and inner skins quickly; they just pop off, leaving a whole raw nut. Neither the appearance nor the taste are affected by the hot fat. Dry off any excess oil and leave to cool. Boil the nuts in water or milk as instructed, to soften.

Chestnuts Boiled in Milk

Some recipes for cakes and purées suggest chestnuts be boiled in milk. In this case, boil the nuts in water to start, until the peels can be removed (or use the quick method), then boil in milk, enough to cover fruits, until they collapse. Drain excess milk and sieve as before.

Dehydrated chestnuts have some advantages over fresh chestnuts, although their flavour is not as good. Apart from finer quality control, and not having to peel them, they will keep for up to 18 months and have been kept for up to 4 years (although I would not recommend it).

To reconstitute: soak overnight in warm water until they may easily be cut with a knife, or bitten. Boil up in a pan of cold water and simmer until they crumble – about 30 minutes. Strain and mash.

Tinned chestnut purée from France has an excellent flavour and is available sweetened or un-sweetened. The texture is rather soft, and not suitable for cakes or pastries, although it is quite successful in fillings.

CHESTNUT CAKES

Use only freshly sieved chestnut, which is very floury, in a cake batter.

The simplest chestnut torte of all is made in exactly the same way as the whipped almond cake on page 313. Flavour it with 1 teaspoon of instant coffee powder. Here is a more unusual recipe.

Chestnut Torte with Almonds and Quince Slices

500 g fresh quinces or Cox's apples	
140 g chestnuts, sieved (200 g raw)	1 lb fresh quinces or Cox's apples
	5 oz chestnuts, sieved (7 oz raw)
100 g butter	3½ oz butter
5 egg yolks	5 egg yolks
70 g caster sugar	2½ oz caster sugar
½ teaspoon cinnamon	½ teaspoon cinnamon
70 g ground almonds	2½ oz ground almonds
zest ½ lemon	zest ½ lemon
3 egg whites	3 egg whites

gas 4, 180°C, 350°F / 1 hour

Prepare the quince slices using the method on page 252, but leave the fruits sliced. Set aside to cool. (If using apples – peel, core, slice not too thin, sprinkle with lemon juice and dredge with caster sugar. Leave in a bowl to draw, then drain before using.)

Sieve the chestnuts, which should first have been cooked in milk (see page 330). Beat the butter with the egg yolks and sugar, until pale and creamy. Mix in the chestnuts. Sift the cinnamon with the almonds and beat into the mixture with the lemon zest. Whip up the egg whites in a separate bowl until they stand in peaks, and gently fold them into the chestnut mixture. Grease a 22 cm (8½ inch) spring-form tin, carefully lay the prepared cold fruits in an even pattern across the bottom, and pour over the cake batter. Brush lightly with beaten egg yolk and dredge with caster sugar. Bake.

When the cake has browned a little and starts to shrink away from the sides of the tin, lift out of the oven and set on a wire rack for a few minutes before turning out to cool. You can have either the fruited surface on top or the chestnut one. Serve with whipped cream. The cake keeps fresh for 4–5 days in a cool place.

Radetsky Torte

Named after Josef Graf von Radetsky (1766–1858), the famous Austrian Commander in Chief, this is a spectacular party cake. The chestnuts for the filling should be boiled in milk (page 330) for a better flavour.

120 g butter	4 oz butter
160 g caster sugar	6 oz caster sugar
8 egg yolks	8 egg yolks
sparing 1 teaspoon fine ground high roast coffee *or* 1 teaspoon instant coffee powder	sparing 1 teaspoon fine ground high roast coffee *or* 1 teaspoon instant coffee powder
160 g chestnuts, sieved (280 g raw)	6 oz chestnuts, sieved (8 oz raw)
8 egg whites	8 egg whites
20 g potato flour	1 oz potato flour
1 tablespoon rum	1 tablespoon rum

Filling

100 g sieved chestnuts (130 g raw)	4 oz sieved chestnuts (5 oz raw)
80 g caster sugar	3 oz caster sugar
1 tablespoon rum	1 tablespoon rum
2 egg whites	2 egg whites
chocolate glacé icing (page 73)	chocolate glacé icing (page 73)

gas 4, 180°C, 350°F/45 minutes

Beat the butter and sugar until light and fluffy; whip in the egg yolks one at a time, then add the coffee and chestnut. Whip the egg whites in a separate bowl until they hold firm peaks, and gently fold them into the mixture. Finally dredge the potato flour across the surface and fold it in with the rum. Pour into a greased and floured baking tin 26 cm (10½ inches) in diameter, and bake in the preheated oven. Invert on to a wire rack to cool.

Make the filling by beating the sieved chestnuts with the sugar and rum. Whip up the egg whites until stiff and fold them into the mixture.

Split the cooled cake carefully into 3 layers; spread the filling over two and lay the unfilled one on top. Brush the top lightly with apricot jam and coat with the chocolate glacé icing.

* For a particularly luscious dessert you can inset an extra layer of crisp meringue; fill this with sweetened whipped cream, and coat the top of the cake and the sides also, rather than glaze it. This will keep for only 1 day.

Chestnut Creams and Vermicelles in Pastries

Chestnut creams and purées are delicious and versatile as fillings, in a whole range of pastries. Layered or sandwiched, combined with puff or short pastries or with sponges, the scope is endless. This chestnut cream has a thick texture and is very suitable for piping, or to be pressed through a large-holed sieve or a mincing machine to form vermicelli-like strands. It keeps well in the refrigerator for 3–4 days.

200 ml milk	7 fl oz milk
½ vanilla pod	½ vanilla pod
300 g sieved chestnuts, boiled in milk (approx. 500 g raw)	11 oz sieved chestnuts, boiled in milk (1 lb raw)
50 g caster sugar	2 oz caster sugar

NUTS

50 ml double cream
1 tablespoon Kirsch or brandy

2 fl oz double cream
1 tablespoon Kirsch or brandy

Scald the milk with the vanilla pod; add the sieved chestnut and boil very gently for about 15 minutes, stirring all the time so that it does not burn, until a thick mousse forms. Add the sugar and cream and cook a few moments longer. Set aside to cool. Remove the vanilla pod and mix in the liqueur. Use as directed.

Suggestions for use

* Cut a sheet of sponge (page 90) into two equal strips, brush one with sieved apricot jam, cover the other with icing and sandwich both layers together with the chestnut cream.
* A Genoese sponge (page 91), filled and covered with chestnut cream, sprinkled with praline (page 312) and pistachios, was dedicated to La Carmago, a famous and successful eighteenth-century Belgian dancer, who even inspired Voltaire to compose a verse in her honour.
* Choux pastries filled with chestnut cream taste good. Ice them with plain melted chocolate.
* The most successful combination is layers of meringue, filled with both chestnut vermicelles and chocolate butter cream, and topped with crème chantilly. It is an irresistible party dessert.

Meringue Pavlova with chestnut vermicelles

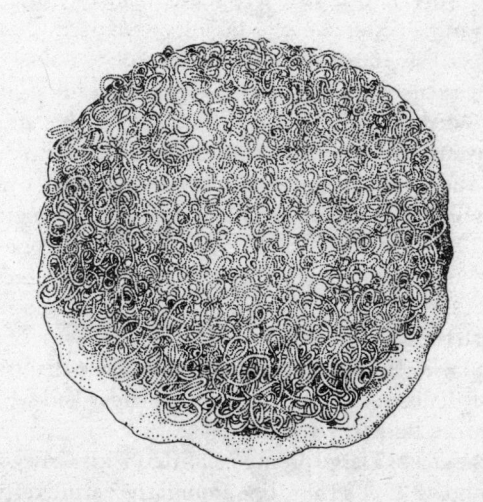

Tea at Fortnum's, enviously watching a mannequin weaving her way between the tables with a quick step that seemed to cover no distance, 'A mink stole is slimming', Isabella would think, breaking open a chestnut meringue with her fork and wishing that she was not about to eat it and hoping that she would not have another when it was gone . . .

(Elizabeth Taylor, *The Sleeping Beauty*)

Meringue with Chestnut, Chocolate and Whipped Cream

Bake four 26 cm (10½ inch) pavlovas a little thinner than usual, using 8 egg whites and 400 g (16 oz) of caster sugar (see page 110). Leave to cool.

Prepare a portion of Chestnut Cream Vermicelles (see page 332) with: 400 g (14 oz) boiled and sieved chestnuts (500 g (1 lb) raw); 150 ml (¼ pint) milk; ½ vanilla pod; 65 g (2½ oz) caster sugar; 65 ml (2½ fl oz) double cream; 1½ tablespoons Kirsch, brandy or rum.

Make Chocolate mousseline butter cream (1) (egg yolks: page 63) with: 50 g (2 oz) granulated sugar; 40 ml (1½ fl oz) water; vanilla pod; 2 egg yolks; 110 g (4 oz) unsalted butter; 50 g (2 oz) plain dark, chocolate; 1 tablespoon water.

Crème Chantilly: 250 ml (9 fl oz) double cream or whipping cream; 2 tablespoons vanilla caster sugar; 1 tablespoon Kirsch, brandy or rum.

20 g (1 oz) coarse grated chocolate or chocolate flakes.

Assemble the cake, apart from the whipped cream topping, the day before it is needed, and leave to chill overnight in the refrigerator: this allows the flavours and fillings to 'ripen' and mellow with the meringue. It also takes the meringue past the stage of stickiness which develops after a few hours as the moisture from the fillings penetrates.

Reserve 3 or 4 tablespoons of chestnut cream for decoration. Smooth half the chestnut cream over a meringue base and gently press the second sheet in place; spread all of the chocolate mousseline filling over this and sandwich with the third meringue. Spread over the rest of the chestnut cream and top with the last meringue. To make the chantilly, whip the cream until it holds soft peaks, beat in the sugar and whip until it is stiff. Fold in the liqueur.

Fill with the cream a large piping bag fitted with a rose-shaped nozzle and pipe as follows: Pipe a thick line around the perimeter, then a trellis pattern across the meringue centre. Pipe with a plain nozzle 5 mounds of vermicelles evenly apart. Finish by scattering chocolate flakes over all.

Brazil Nuts

Brazil nuts, enjoyed both as dessert nuts at Christmas time and as candy-covered sweets, seem to have been almost totally neglected in most European cake recipes. They are, however, greatly enjoyed in South America where the tree grows wild in the swampy Amazonian forests; and cakes which are especially loved there follow the Moorish tradition of using eggs, and particularly egg yolks, very lavishly. Many recipes were developed in the kitchens of the great houses of the sugar plantations of Bahia in Brazil.

Brazil nuts may be bought ready shelled in health food stores; otherwise a little time and patience will be needed to crack them out of their rather unyielding shells. Grind or grate as usual (page 311).

My friend Elisabeth Lambert Ortiz, who has enriched our cookery repertoires with books on Caribbean and South American foods, has given me this recipe from *A Book of Latin American Cooking*. The cake has a very rich, sweet and juicy flavour, and the combination of Brazil nuts with the egg-yolk filling and chocolate frosting makes an unusually moist and luscious after-dinner dessert.

Torta de Castanhas-do-pará
Brazil Nut Cake

12 egg whites	12 egg whites
225 g caster sugar	8 oz caster sugar
225 g Brazil nuts, finely ground	8 oz Brazil nuts, finely ground

Filling

225 g caster sugar	8 oz caster sugar
100 ml water	3½ fl oz water
6 egg yolks	6 egg yolks

gas 4, 180°C, 350°F/40 minutes

Beat the egg whites until they form stiff and creamy peaks. Beat in half the sugar and fold in the rest together with the nuts, working lightly and swiftly. Turn into two greased and floured 26 cm (10½ inch) spring-form tins and bake. The cakes will puff up, and fall as they cool. Spread the bottom layer generously with the filling, sandwich the cakes together and glaze with a chocolate icing.

Filling: Combine the sugar and water in a copper sugar pan and cook to the soft ball stage (115°C, 240°F on a sugar thermometer). Whip the egg yolks until thick and lemon-coloured, and beat into the cooled syrup. Cook the mixture in a double boiler over the heat, stirring constantly until the mixture thickens. Cool before using.

Three Middle Eastern Nut Pastries

It was only when we moved house and found ourselves neighbours of Claudia Roden that I began to appreciate the true pleasure of these delectable little pastries. Watching Claudia pound and mix the fine nut pastes, and expertly roll and fold the fila doughs, I realized how easy it is to make them, and most important, that the finest home-made pastries are not so sticky, nor quite so sweet as the commercial ones.

Nuts are greatly coveted in the Middle East, and this particularly influences the attitude to baking, with the emphasis on filling rather than on the doughs wrapped around them. This basic approach makes the pastries quite distinctive. The nuts are lightly flavoured with perfumed flower-waters and with spices, or sprinkled with sweet syrups. Made with almonds or pistachios, walnuts or pine nuts, the fillings are characteristically wrapped or rolled, folded and layered in a variety of plain doughs. Acting as an inexpensive and generally unsweetened frame-work, these may be made only of flour and water, and at most include a little butter or oil.

Fila Dough

Fila is certainly the best known of the doughs: fine and paper-thin, it is extremely popular throughout the Middle East and used most notably in baklava as well as in an infinite number of savouries. Nowadays in England, it is even being used as a substitute for strudel dough, since it is essentially the same.

Although the dough itself is quite easy to make (a mixture of flour and water kneaded to a fine, firm, elastic mass), pulling the wafer-thin sheets is a highly skilled operation, and even in the Middle East this rare and disappearing family art is being left to the pastry experts. In fact the tradition now is to buy it ready-made. The dough is usually cut into standard-sized sheets, 30 × 40 cm (12 × 20 inches), and comes wrapped and sealed in polythene in weights of 250 g (9 oz) and 500 g (1 lb). (The larger size gives about 24 large sheets of pastry.) It can be bought in many Greek stores and pastry shops. Sheets of fila pastry can be stored in a freezer for 2 or 3 months. After this time, although they cannot spoil, they are inclined to become damp and stick together, and are then only suitable for use in large pies and tarts which need little handling.

Allow the fila to defrost slowly in the wrapping and refrain from using while still hard, as the fine pastry will break. Once fila sheets are exposed to the air they tend to dry out very quickly and crumble when folded. Assemble and prepare all ingredients and grease the baking tray. Only then remove the fila from the polythene wrapping, a few sheets at a time; cut and use as quickly as possible. Once prepared, and despite their fragile nature, fila and konafa pastries may be stored unbaked in a refrigerator for 2 or 3 days, or in a freezer for up to 4 months, which is especially useful for party occasions. They will keep for several days after baking too.

BAKLAVA AND KONAFA (KADAIFI)

These are probably the best known and most elaborate of Middle Eastern pastries and they

> are present at every party and served at every occasion. No bakery or café could be without them. They even go in donkey carts on those national day-long picnics to the cemeteries, filling the huge baskets alongside the pickles, bread, lettuce and falafel. They are part of the celebrations, the rejoicing with the dead, tokens of love for the departed, who are believed to come out from the tombs to play on see-saws and swings, and to enjoy the merry dancers, musicians, jugglers and gala-gala men with their relatives. Baklava and Konafa are always brought to be shared in these happy reunions.
>
> (Claudia Roden, *A Book of Middle Eastern Food*)

CAKES

Baklava

It is important to use unsalted butter in this recipe, otherwise a salty taste will taint the delicate flavour of the pastry.

I also like to make up a larger quantity of syrup to store in my refrigerator. It keeps indefinitely, and is always at hand well chilled.

500 g fila pastry	1 lb fila pastry
225 g unsalted butter, melted	8 oz unsalted butter, melted

Filling

225 g pistachios, walnuts or almonds, coarsely chopped	8 oz pistachios, walnuts or almonds, coarsely chopped
2 tablespoons granulated sugar	2 tablespoons granulate sugar

Syrup

225 g granulated sugar	8 oz granulated sugar
150 ml water	1/4 pint water
1 tablespoon lemon juice	1 tablespoon lemon juice
1 tablespoon orange-flower water	1 tablespoon orange-flower water

gas 3, 170°C, 325°F/1/2 hour
gas 8, 230°C, 450°F/1/4 hour

Syrup: Dissolve the sugar in the water and lemon juice and simmer until it thickens to coat the back of a spoon. Stir in the orange-flower water, and simmer for 2 minutes longer. Cool and chill. This syrup gives sweetness to the finished pastry.

Filling: Lightly mix the nuts with the sugar.

Carefully brush the sides and base of a deep, square or round baking tin with melted butter. Halve the quantity of fila baking sheets and lay one half in single layers into the tin, brushing melted butter all over each, folding in and overlapping the sides as necessary. Spread the nut filling evenly across, and cover with the remaining sheets, brushing butter over and folding each layer as before. Finally brush melted butter on the surface. With a sharp knife cut squares, rectangles or lozenge shapes. Place into the preheated oven and bake for 30 minutes, then raise the heat for 15 minutes longer.

The baklava should be puffed up and a light golden colour. Remove from the oven and quickly pour the chilled syrup over the hot pastry. When cold, cut out pieces along the markings.

Konafa

This dough is usually bought ready-made; it looks like soft white strands of uncooked vermicelli. The shops that sell fila usually make konafa too.

500 g konafa pastry	1 lb konafa pastry
225 g unsalted butter, melted	8 oz unsalted butter, melted

Filling

225 g walnuts, pine nuts or pistachios, coarsely chopped	8 oz walnuts, pine nuts or pistachios, coarsely chopped
2 tablespoons granulated sugar	2 tablespoons granulated sugar

Syrup

225 g granulated sugar	8 oz granulated sugar
150 ml water	¼ pint water
1 tablespoon lemon juice	1 tablespoon lemon juice
1 tablespoon orange-flower water	1 tablespoon orange-flower water

gas 4, 180°C, 350°F for 45 minutes
gas 8, 230°C, 450°F for 10–15 minutes

Prepare syrup as for baklava. Leave to chill. Mix the nuts and sugar for the filling.

Grease a deep square or round baking tin. Turn the konafa pastry into a bowl and separate the strands as much as possible, by gently teasing them apart with the fingers. Pour over the cooled melted butter and lightly turn the pastry strands over and around, to coat them entirely with the butter.

Lay half the pastry in the prepared baking tin and spread the nut filling over the surface. Cover with the remainder of the pastry in an even layer and gently press down with the heel of the hand or a large fork. Place in the preheated oven, and after 45 minutes turn the heat up for another 10 or 15 minutes until the pastry is light and golden in colour. Remove from the oven and immediately pour the chilled syrup over the hot konafa. Cool, cut into slices and serve.

As an alternative, konafa may be filled with a cream mixture:

Cream filling

3 tablespoons ground rice	3 tablespoons ground rice
2 tablespoons sugar	2 tablespoons sugar
500 ml milk	18 fl oz milk
150 ml double cream	¼ pint double cream

Mix the ground rice and sugar with half the milk, to a smooth paste. Boil the rest of the milk and mix in the rice paste, beating continuously. Continue stirring, and allow to simmer until the paste becomes very thick. Set aside to cool, then mix in the double cream.

In Jerusalem the local version, called Knafe, is filled with slices of Halumi cheese, which when melted has a rather elastic stringy texture. The combination of this and the sweet syrup is quite unusual.

Assabih bi Loz (Almond Fingers)

These almond fingers rank very high on my list of favourites. The light, crisp sugar-dusted fila combined with the fragrance of the almond filling is delicious. The fingers may also be filled with walnuts, pine nuts or pistachios (I find the delicate perfume of rose-water better suited to the subtle flavour of the pistachio). Known as *Lauzinaj* in medieval times, the fingers were also fried and sprinkled with syrup, rose-water and chopped pistachios.

225 g fila pastry	8 oz fila pastry
110 g unsalted butter, melted	4 oz unsalted butter, melted

Filling

225 g ground almonds, chopped pine nuts, pistachios or walnuts	8 oz ground almonds, chopped pine nuts, pistachios or walnuts
110 g sugar, granulated	4 oz sugar, granulated
1 tablespoon orange-flower water	1 tablespoon orange-flower water
ground cinnamon, *or* rose-water	ground cinnamon, *or* rose-water

gas 3–4, 170–180°C, 325–350°F/20 minutes

Filling: Mix the ground almonds or pine nuts with orange-flower water and sugar, or walnuts with cinnamon and sugar, or pistachios with rose-water and sugar.

Cut sheets of fila into 4 rectangles and brush the centre of each with melted butter. Heap a teaspoon of the nut filling at one end of each rectangle, fold the longer sides in, slightly over the filling, and roll up into a cigar shape. Lay on a greased baking sheet and bake for about 20 minutes until very lightly coloured. Take particular care not to overcook, as they spoil very easily. Serve cold, sprinkled with icing sugar.

The pastries may also be deep-fried. Drop into moderately hot oil for a very short time, until lightly coloured. Drain on absorbent kitchen paper and dust with icing sugar. Serve hot or cold.

The Spice Box

Ah, que j'aime t'ouvrir cher tiroir aux épices,
Souffle d'Orient gratis, voyage inespéré,
Colombo et Ceylan aux magiques caprices,
A défaut de vous voir, je puis vous respirer.

(Roger Lecuyer, in Savarin, *La Vraie Cuisine*)

The herbs were springing in the vale;
Green ginger plants and liquorice pale
  And cloves their sweetness offer,
With nutmegs too, to put in ale
No matter whether fresh or stale,
Or else to keep in coffer . . .

(Geoffrey Chaucer, *The Tale of Sir Topaz*)

Did you know that cinnamon grows in dark and silent valleys guarded by fearful serpents? Or that the phoenix builds his nest of cinnamon twigs high up in the remote reaches of the mountains, where man can only clamber at great risk? And that natives also try to lure the monstrous birds with chunks of their favourite donkey meat, which cause the nests to collapse under the weight? Of course we know now that the stories of their mystical origins and of all the other spices were spread from very early times by the Arabs, who, acting as middlemen, completely monopolized a very lucrative expanding trade.

The spices actually originated in India and China, and by the first millennium A.D. ginger, pepper, cinnamon, cardamom — grains of delight, as they were known — nutmeg, cumin, mace and cloves were being imported from the Indonesian archipelago, and coriander and cumin from the eastern Mediterranean.

Spices in Foods

While the early civilizations of India and China also valued the medicinal virtues of spices, they quickly appreciated the culinary pleasures.

Savoury relishes for meat, fish, fruit and vegetables were mixed with crushed spices which added a zest to the tedious staples of wheat, barley and rice. Later the Romans also discovered that strong spices, and particularly pepper, gave a good flavour to many foods and cakes, but meats especially, even disguising the foul tastes of rancidity and contamination – which in later times was to prove very important.

An Arab Spiced Bread

In the thirteenth century the Arabs showed a passionate interest in all the foreign foods which passed their way. The handwritten manuscript (1261) of *Kitab al wusla ila l-habib fi wasfi t-tayyibati wat-tib* (Book of the bond with the friend, or description of good dishes and perfumes) is an astonishing revelation of their contemporary customs and manners, as well as of culinary dishes on which their Eastern neighbours had a strong influence; it also highlights the willing assimilation of the new commodities into their own cuisine.

Apart from the spices of Asia, there were raisins from Jerusalem, chestnuts and saffron from Southern France, Syrian apples and Persian pistachios; sesame from India, and poppy seed, which grew locally. The beloved rose-water came from their own rose gardens, and cheese came from Crete and Sicily. There is a wide choice of spice recipes, and this one is typical; a basic bread dough is filled as follows:

> Take one third of flour, and knead it with *samn* (clarified butter) in the same way as one does for *ka'k* (small breads). Leave to rise. Make a round loaf raised at the edges. Next take an egg, break it into a bowl and throw in a little salt, ground pepper, ginger, grains of sesame seed, hempseed, anis, caraway grilled with some cumin, equal to all that in whole grains, poppy seed. Mix all with the egg. The pepper must be abundant so that one can smell the 'heat'. Add some fresh leaves of rue and some grated cheese. Add to this saffron, poppy, pistachios and spread over the top of the bread. The whole should be of a fine thickness. Bake. This recipe is excellent . . .

Spices in Europe

By the fifteenth century pepper and ginger had become most popular in Europe, and spiced breads and cakes were the traditional much loved fare for all religious and secular occasions. More important, though, spices could mask the unpleasant flavours of putrid food and also add taste to the dried and salted ones. This had become a serious problem, since the towns and cities were now expanding so fast that fresh foods had become impossible to find during the winter months. While the poor folk could afford only tiny amounts, if any, of spices (which cost them several weeks' wages) to enhance their tasteless fare, the wealthy people, who brought their meats from the country for the season, relied heavily on generous quantities to disguise their rotting produce. Spices became so important that in the households of the royalty and noblemen a clerk of spicery was kept, and under him a yeoman powderbeater, who no doubt ground the spices for daily use. Pepper, ultimately, was depended on to such an extent that it became a currency as negotiable and common as silver. The 'peppercorn rent' which today implies an insignificant sum, then accounted for a considerable amount. No wonder spices were kept under lock and key.

Subtle Spicery

In the seventeenth century during the reign of Louis XIV a new style of cooking evolved when François Pierre de la Varenne published his three cookery books. Their most striking feature was the lack of spices, and an appreciation of ingredients such as vegetables for their own sake rather than as adjuncts to meats and soups. Europe was also getting tired of spices in savoury dishes – the spices were becoming cheaper anyway and more easily available, but their popularity in sweet baked goods remained strong.

Today the role of spices in the kitchen is a subtler affair. Apart from some ethnic foods which depend heavily on and owe their tradition to spices, their use is no longer to serve as a disguise for contaminated foods, but to enhance in a positive manner and bring out special flavours to the best advantage.

Special Points about Spices for Baking

Whole spices ground freshly in a mortar or mill have a much stronger flavour and fragrance than ready-ground ones, which tend to lose their aroma very quickly once they are exposed to the air.

For cinnamon, allspice, cardamom, clove, black pepper, cumin: grind whole spices with a pestle in a mortar or in an electric mill, together with a small amount of sugar taken from the recipe. This makes the task easier and prevents any oils from being left behind.

Nutmeg: grate on a very fine grater.

Fresh ginger root is only suitable for moist, sponge-type cakes. It can be stored in a freezer and grated finely when needed without de-frosting.

Powdered ginger must be used in hard biscuits and gingerbreads. Make sure that the container is tightly stoppered.

Saffron: Dry out the filaments on a small plate in a warm oven, until they crumble between the fingers. Infuse in a little warm milk or water until the liquid is a rich, strong yellow colour. Strain if you wish.

Special Spiced Cakes

GINGERBREAD

> They fetched him first the sweetest wine,
> Then mead in mazers they combine
> With lots of royal spice,
> And gingerbread, exceeding fine,
> And liquorice and eglantyne
> And sugar, very nice . . .
>
> (Geoffrey Chaucer, *The Tale of Sir Topaz*)

Gingerbread is reputed to have been invented by a Greek baker from Rhodes, and it is said to be the oldest cake-bread in the world. In Europe spiced honey cakes originated in the monasteries and convents, where the honey was also produced. Gingerbread, the spiced bread of England, was popular very early on; a recipe is included in the *Forme of Cury* written around 1390 by the master cooks of King Richard II. Sugar, and later treacle, was preferred as sweetener, but since punitive taxes were levied on sugar only the nobility and wealthy people were able to enjoy it.

Some of the early recipes used grated stale bread as the basic ingredient; sugar gave sweetness, pepper gave spice to it and saffron gave colour. In 1609 Sir Hugh Plat offered this recipe in *Delightes for Ladies* – the inclusion of liquorice seems to have disappeared in later times. Manchets were bread rolls made with white wheat flour.

> *To make Ginger bread.* Take 3 stale Manchets, and grate them: drie them, and sift them thorow a fine sieve: then adde unto them one ounce of Ginger, beeing beaten, and as much Cinamon, one ounce of Liquorice and Anniseedes being beaten together, and searced, halfe a pound of sugar, then boile all these together in a posnet, with a quart of claret wine, till they come to a stiffe paste with

often stirring of it; and when it is stiffe, mold it on a table, and so drive it thin, and print it in your moldes: dust your moldes with Cinamon, Ginger, and Liquorice, beeing mixed together in fine powder. This is your Gingerbread used at the Court, and in all Gentlemens houses at festival times. It is otherwise called drie Leach.

Fairings. During the fourteenth century gingerbread began to appear on pedlar's trays in the street, at markets and fairs. At Bartholomew Fair they were sold at 20 a penny and called *fairings* (a gift from the fair). For centuries they remained popular among street traders. In 1614 a gingerbread woman in Ben Jonson's play *Bartholomew Fair* sold 'gingerbread, very good bread, comfortable bread . . .'; other street criers offered, 'hot spiced gingerbread, smoking hot! . . .' Hot and smoking in this context must have referred to the sharpness of the spices which warm the blood. A most colourful itinerant gingerbread tradesman also appeared in the seventeenth century. Andrew W. Tuer writes of Tiddy Diddy Doll in *Old London Street Cries*:

> 'Tiddy Diddy Doll, lol, lol, lol' was a celebrated vendor of gingerbread and, according to Hone, was always hailed as the king of itinerant tradesmen. It must be more than a century since this dandified character ceased to amuse the populace. He dressed as a person of rank – ruffled shirt, white silk stockings, and fashionable laced suit of clothes surmounted by a wig and cocked hat decorated with a feather. He was sure to be found plying his trade on Lord Mayor's day, at open-air shows, and on all public occasions. He amused the crowd to his own profit; and some of his humorous nonsense has been preserved.
>
> 'Mary, Mary, where are you now, Mary?'
>
> 'I live two steps underground, with a wiscom riscom, and why not. Walk in, ladies and gentlemen. My shop is on the second floor backwards, with a brass knocker at the door. Here's your nice gingerbread, your spiced gingerbread, which will melt in your mouth like a red-hot brickbat, and rumble in your inside like Punch in his wheelbarrow!' He always finished up by singing the fag end of a song – 'Tiddy Diddy Doll, lol, lol, lol;' hence his nickname. . . .
>
> (Andrew W. Tuer, *Old London Street Cries*, 1978)

Tiddy Diddy doll

Diane's Ginger Biscuits for the Fair

350 g self-raising flour	12 oz self-raising flour
2 teaspoons ginger powder	2 teaspoons ginger powder
1 teaspoon mixed spice	1 teaspoon mixed spice
1 teaspoon bicarbonate of soda	1 teaspoon bicarbonate of soda
175 g butter	6 oz butter
175 g caster sugar	6 oz caster sugar
175 g golden syrup	6 oz golden syrup
1 egg	1 egg

gas 4, 180°C, 350°F/20 minutes

Sift the flour with the spices; dissolve the bicarbonate of soda in a spoonful of water. Rub the butter with the flour to crumbs, and blend in the sugar. Combine all the ingredients with the syrup and the egg and finally add the bicarbonate. Roll into small olive-sized balls and place them on a greased baking sheet – space them well apart, for they spread out flat as they bake. Makes 60 biscuits.

Moulded and Gilded Gingerbreads. While the gingerbread of the street folk was baked in simple moulded shapes, flat and oblong or square, the more affluent preferred decorated versions. From the middle of the fifteenth century onwards, wooden rolling pins heavily engraved with patterns were used, later to be replaced by wooden moulds from Europe which were suitably carved to represent the occasion. While still

CAKES

hot the cakes were gilded with Dutch leaf, hence the expression 'the gilt on the gingerbread'. Gilding of gingerbread figures was of religious significance and was already to be found as early as 1123; the offerings for the Lord had to be as glowing and bright as possible, hence the ginger and gilt.

The decoration on the moulds in Georgian times was more elaborate still, but of a secular nature, depicting the status or interest of the giver. They were works of art carved in different shapes out of various hard woods. Today the heart-shaped gingerbread is still popular. Here is what Alison Uttley had to say about the moulds:

> Gingerbread men were made and sold in country places at Easter Fairs and Autumn Wakes week, and they are still fashioned in old moulds . . . I have one of the prints for making these little figures, but mine dates back to the time of the Napoleonic Wars. It is a solid block of beech wood, close-grained and hard, with seven designs cut and carved with intricate and delicate accuracy, four on one side and three on the other.
>
> There is a farmer with his sheaf of corn and a sickle, an admiral with a shock of hair and a tricorne hat, a marine with a sword, a little church with three windows and a tower, a bird on a tree, a basket of fruit and sportsman . . .
>
> In my childhood we had small moulds of heavy blocked tin, with designs of a horse, a tree, a leaf, and a man . . .
>
> The gingerbread men at the fairs were not gilded as in Elizabethan days, but they had coloured hats and scarlet buttons on their coats or white buttons of sugar.
>
> (Alison Uttley, *Recipes from an Old Farmhouse*, 1968)

Gingerbread Man

This is not a moulded figure, but one that is stamped out with a shaped cutter.

150 g honey	5½ oz honey
100 g sugar	3½ oz sugar
25 g butter	sparing 1 oz butter
pinch cinnamon	pinch cinnamon
½ teaspoon cardamom	½ teaspoon cardamom
pinch ground cloves	pinch ground cloves
pinch ground black pepper	pinch ground black pepper

375 g plain flour	13 oz plain flour
70 g blanched, chopped almonds	3 oz blanched, chopped almonds
40 g candied lemon peel	2 oz candied lemon peel
1 egg yolk	1 egg yolk
1 teaspoon bicarbonate of soda	1 teaspoon bicarbonate of soda
50 g icing sugar	2 oz icing sugar
½ teaspoon lemon juice	½ teaspoon lemon juice
6 whole blanched almonds	6 whole blanched almonds

gas 3, 170°C, 325°F/15 minutes

Stir the honey, sugar and butter together gently over heat until the mixture is smooth and the sugar has dissolved; add the spices and allow to cool. Sift two-thirds of the flour into a bowl, stir in the chopped almonds, the candied peel and the egg yolk, and mix well. Pour in the cooled honey mixture and thoroughly combine before adding the bicarbonate of soda which has been dissolved in a tablespoon of warm water. Finally knead in enough of the remaining flour for the paste to roll off the sides of the bowl. Roll out the pastry on a floured surface approximately 2 cm (¾ inch) thick, and cut out the gingerbread men. Lay on a greased and floured tray and bake in the preheated oven.

Meanwhile mix the icing sugar with the lemon juice and a teaspoon of hot water until it is smooth; spread over the warm men and decorate with the halved almonds.

Sponge Ginger Cakes. In the seventeenth century treacle was introduced to England, and shortly thereafter Hannah Glasse incorporated it in her gingerbread recipes. For centuries the basic ingredients and methods of preparing the cakes had remained the same, but in 1789 Elizabeth Moxon gave a recipe for gingerbread cake and gingerbread in small pans which differed from those baked in moulds. This was one of the earliest mentions of the soft, sponge-type cakes.

In early times ginger, ground from the dried roots or rhizome of the perennial ginger reed plant, had made its journey across the continents on camel back; it arrived dry and dusty in Europe and was sometimes adulterated still further by the greedy wholesale merchants before it reached the kitchen. Apart from the lavish quantities that added piquancy to savoury dishes, its fiery tang gave a sharp richness to gingerbreads, spiced pastries, preserves and sweetmeats. Later, during the eighteenth century, when the East India Company started trading profitably, they were able to carry large stone jars in their ships' holds, filled with succulent lumps of ginger steeped in dripping syrup. What a difference their pungent moisture made to the fruited and spiced sponge-type gingerbreads which were being introduced.

Today the ginger cakes seem to be more typically English than the earlier moulded ones. The cake mixture has quite a different texture, like a thick batter before cooking, and is very moist and spongy when baked.

Here are two sponge-type recipes.

NOTE: Because of the quantity of sugary ingredients they are liable to burn, and the oven heat must be quite low. Care must be taken not to open the oven door too early, as the mixture does not set quickly and may sink.

June's Ginger Cake

This is an inexpensive cake, enough for two 500 g (1 lb) loaf tins.

225 g granulated sugar	8 oz granulated sugar
2 large eggs	2 large eggs
250 ml corn or sunflower oil	9 fl oz corn or sunflower oil
250 ml golden syrup	9 fl oz golden syrup
350 g plain flour	12 oz plain flour
1 teaspoon bicarbonate of soda	1 teaspoon bicarbonate of soda
250 ml hot water	9 fl oz hot water
2 teaspoons ground or fresh grated ginger	2 teaspoons ground or fresh grated ginger
pinch mixed spice	pinch mixed spice
75 g finely chopped preserved ginger (optional)	3 oz finely chopped preserved ginger (optional)

gas 2–3, 150–170°C, 300–325°F/45 minutes

Cream the sugar and the eggs until light and fluffy: beat in the oil, the syrup and the flour a spoon at a time. Dissolve the bicarbonate of soda in the hot water and mix into the rest of the ingredients along with the remaining spices. Add preserved ginger if used. Turn into greased baking tins and bake in the preheated oven. Cool on a wire rack, and ice with a plain white icing (page 72) when cold.

An Excellent Gingerbread

Heat 350 g (12 oz) of treacle with 100 g (3½ oz) of demerara sugar until the sugar has dissolved. Melt 110 g (4 oz) of butter in another pan and leave to cool down slightly. Beat well together the yolks and whites of 3 eggs, and then gradually add the treacle and sugar mixture. Next beat in the melted butter. Sift 20 g (1 oz) of ginger and 270 g (10 oz) of plain flour into a bowl, gradually beat in the other ingredients and blend well together. Finally add the thinly grated rind of 1 lemon and 20 g (1 oz) fine chopped candied ginger. Grease a 30 × 21 × 2 cm (12 × 8 × ¾ inch) baking tin and pour in the mixture. Bake in the oven, preheated to gas 2, 150°C, 300°F, for about an hour. When cold, brush with apricot jam and ice with a thick white icing. Cut into squares before storing in an airtight tin.

CINNAMON

> . . . While cinnamon, of condiments the king,
> Unblemished hue, unrivalled seasoning,
> Like musk in subtle odour rises there,
> Tempting the palate, sweetening the air . . .
>
> (Ibn al-Mutazz)

I remember the jar of cinnamon sugar that stood in the condiment cupboard in my mother's kitchen when I was a child. I would lift the stopper and sniff the lovely scent, and when her back was turned, dip in a moist finger to taste it.

Cinnamon is the bark of a tree indigenous to Ceylon and Malabar and for centuries played almost as important a role as pepper and ginger. Medicinally its exttacted essential oil – oil of cinnamon – was considered to be of great value as a tonic for the human system — heart, liver, kidneys, stomach, gall and even nerves. It sedated mothers during childbirth, and alleviated heartburn and nausea. Culinarily the spice featured in sauces, both sweet and sour; as seasoning for vegetables, and

Cinnamon scrolls

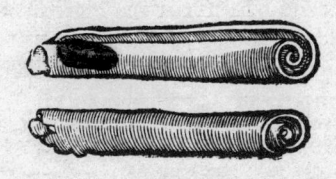

to flavour meat dishes. Mixed with other spices it perfumed much sweet bakery; during the eighteenth, nineteenth and early twentieth centuries cinnamon was the dominant flavour in several cakes, biscuits and tarts. Why these recipes should have been cast aside I fail to understand. Let me re-introduce them for your pleasure; they have certainly been greeted with unanimous approval by my friends.

Cinnamon Chocolate Cake

The Swiss and Germans frequently use grated black bread in cake recipes. If your local baker does not sell dark, rye bread, you can usually buy imported packets at delicatessen shops.

80 g plain chocolate, melted	3 oz plain chocolate, melted
225 g caster sugar	8 oz caster sugar
2 teaspoons ground cinnamon	2 teaspoons ground cinnamon
1/2 teaspoon ground cloves	1/2 teaspoon ground cloves
6 egg yolks	6 egg yolks
6 egg whites	6 egg whites
80 g grated black bread	3 oz grated black bread

gas 2, 150°C, 300°F/1 hour

Gently melt the chocolate in a bowl over warm water. Cool, and while still soft mix in the sugar and the freshly ground spices. Beat in the egg yolks one at a time, until the mixture is very thick and forms a ribbon. Whip the egg whites to make moist, firm, snowy peaks and lightly fold them, along with the grated black bread, into the spiced chocolate combination. Turn into a greased (use unsalted butter) 22 cm (8 1/2 inch) spring-form tin, and bake in the preheated oven. Cool in the tin on a wire rack before turning it out.

Cinnamon Torte

A seventeenth-century recipe.

pâte sucrée (page 45, for 23 cm tin)	pâte sucrée (page 45, for 9 inch tin)
140 g caster sugar	5 oz caster sugar
4 egg yolks	4 egg yolks
140 g blanched, coarsely chopped almonds	5 oz blanched, coarsely chopped almonds
zest 1/2 lemon	zest 1/2 lemon

30 g raisins (soaked in 1 tablespoon rum)	1 oz raisins (soaked in 1 tablespoon rum)
1½ teaspoon ground cinnamon	1½ teaspoon ground cinnamon
4 egg whites	4 egg whites

gas 4, 180°C, 350°F/1 hour

Line the base and sides of a shallow baking tin with the pastry, prick the bottom and weigh down with pebbles. Par-bake (page 209) in the preheated oven (gas 5, 190°C, 375°F) until set; cool slightly. Lower the oven temperature. Meanwhile beat together the sugar and egg yolks until pale and creamy, then mix in the almonds. Add the lemon zest, the drained, plumped raisins and the spice. Beat up the egg whites until they are slightly firm but peaked, then gently mix 2 tablespoons into the almond mixture to soften it, and fold in the rest taking care not to lose the air. Pour into the slightly cooled flan case and return to the oven to bake. When cold, cover with whipped cream just before serving. It makes a particularly good after-dinner dessert.

Zimmt Kuchen

An eighteenth-century recipe from Germany. This moist sour cream pastry rises little while baking, but has an exotic flavour with a classic blend of oriental perfumes. Serve it with coffee.

140 g blanched, ground almonds	5 oz blanched, ground almonds
2 tablespoons rose-water	2 tablespoons rose-water
140 g caster sugar	5 oz caster sugar
1 egg	1 egg
75 ml sour cream	2¾ fl oz sour cream
1½ teaspoons cinnamon	1½ teaspoons cinnamon
zest ½ lemon	zest ½ lemon
20 g candied lemon peel, finely chopped	⅔ oz candied lemon peel, finely chopped

gas 4, 180°C, 350°F/1 hour

Line only the base of a shallow baking tin with 3 mm (⅛ inch) of shortcrust pastry (page 44), then par-bake (page 209) until pale. Cool. Moisten the almonds with the rose-water, then mix together with the sugar. Add the remaining ingredients and combine well. Pour into the

CAKES

prepared cake base and bake. Serve cut in squares and dusted with icing sugar.

Honey and Spice

Mel (Honey)
Storie for Table-Talke

'All honny is made of Dewe. For out of flowers the Bees gather that which they make their Combes: of the gum which droppeth from trees, they make waxe: of Dewe they make Honny. So that Dewe is congealed together and crassified either by liuing creatures, and is made Honny: or of it owne accord, which also is Honny, usually tearmed Dry Manna: or is not thickened at all, which they call liquid Manna. Whereof there is great store about Hormus, a Cittie in Arabia Feliz.'

(Mrs Groundes-Peace's *Old Cookery Notebook*)

Honey is the oldest natural sweetener – cave paintings of Neolithic man show that already he searched out the honey from the bees' nests, and the sophisticated civilization of the Ancient Egyptians held honey in such esteem as to give the title of 'bee-man' – Byati – to their king. They even placed sealed jars of it in their burial chambers. (Thousands of years later when these were discovered, the honey had hardly deteriorated.) Paintings also show how honey was collected by smoking the bees from their nests; its use in cooking for honey breads and pastries made with honey, flour and oil; for sacrificial offerings, and as medicine.

In 171 B.C. many of the cake shops newly established in Rome were baking recipes, translated from earlier Greek writings, or cakes made with flour, eggs, and wine or oil, sometimes currants, and almonds, poppy seed or sesame seed, various herbs and, of course, honey. The Oriental influence was strong. They were expensive sweetmeats, cut in a variety of fanciful shapes, and made for sacrificial offerings, feasts and celebrations. Sometime later the surfaces of the cakes were decorated with imprints appropriate to the occasion, and later still, special clay moulds were used. For the Roman New Year fair, the Saturnalia and the Sigillaria, figures were made of honey cake and flavoured with aniseed.

In Ancient Britain, or the 'Isle of Honey' as it was once known, the sweetener was appreciated just as much. At first it was most loved in 'mead', a fermented mixture of water, honey and ginger – one of the oldest alcoholic beverages in the world. Everyone from the King to the poorest peasant imbibed, and only when the Normans conquered Britain was it ousted from popularity by wine and later by beer.

It is difficult to believe that honey, which was used over much of Europe, India and China, South and Central America very early on, was unknown in North America. The North American Indians used an excellent syrup made from the boiled-down sap of the bird's eye or sugar maple, a tree indigenous to the temperate zones of the north. Perhaps the bees were there, but no one felt the need for their nectar. It is said that European settlers introduced bees in the sixteenth century, and as late as 1853 to California. Today the state has the largest honey output in the whole of the United States.

> My son, eat thou honey, because it is good; and the honeycomb, which is sweet to thy taste . . .
>
> (Proverbs: 24, 13)

Honey is a very rich and concentrated food, full of sugars, floral essences, minerals and other substances. It is the sweet liquid manufactured in the sac of the worker bee from the pollen and nectar of open flowers which he transfers to the cells of the hive. The number of flowers from which the nectar is gathered is impossible to count, and even then the same flowers are affected by different soil conditions, so that no two batches of honey are identical. The quality, the aroma and the flavour of each flower species is also different. There are a few which give especially fine honey.

The Best Honeys

No doubt the most renowned honey is that from Mount Hymettus in Greece, made from the nectar of wild thyme; it has a distinctive and fine flavour and dark, brown, rich tones. The French Narbonne golden-yellow honey is made with rosemary; the clear, pale lemon acacia honey has a bitter sweet perfumed taste. The monks of Buckfast Abbey collect the nectar from the heathered moorlands of Exmoor for their granular, half-bitter variety, and this, together with white-clover honey which has a delicate flavour, is probably the most popular in England. Orange-blossom creamy-white honey from California is most loved in the United States, with alfalfa and buckwheat close runners-up.

Eucalyptus and pine honeys are strong and dominating – the pine almost unpleasant, with its resinous aroma and flavour. Honeycomb is of course the purest honey, untampered with and unadulterated. These last three are best appreciated on their own for their particular taste, and are least suitable for baking purposes.

Honey is difficult to describe, since everyone has his own preference. I like the bitter-sweet, slightly perfumed sort which has a definite flavour, such as orange-blossom. I dislike the innocuous blandness of the cheap honeys, which are blended from several perfumes and are sometimes so sweet that your tongue curls in distaste. Avoid using them for baking, as honey should enhance and improve the taste of a cake, not dominate or act only as undefined sweetener.

Buy local produce from small apiaries, if possible, for they pride themselves on the 'organic' purity of their goods, and each jar will vary slightly from the next. Larger producers sacrifice some of the floral essences and individual flavours by heating and liquefying the honeys, to achieve uniformity of colour and texture.

Storing Honey

Honey will keep more or less indefinitely. Store in a dry place with an even temperature, such as a kitchen cupboard. Keep in an airtight container otherwise the aroma will be lost and moisture be absorbed. Sometimes as honey ages it crystallizes or granulates, and this can also happen if it is kept in too cold a place. This has no adverse effect – put the jar in a pan of warm water until the crystals disappear.

Honey in Baking

Honey improves both the taste and the keeping qualities of cakes. It imparts a slight chewiness to the texture, and its brown, mellow colour is especially attractive. Baked goods made with rye flours, if stored in airtight containers for some months or even a year, will develop an incomparable bouquet of spices and fruits. Made with white flour they keep less well, and are inclined to dry out after about 5 weeks.

Some points to watch

* Always bake spiced honey cakes at least 2–4 weeks before you need them, so that they can mature and the flavour may develop.
* Honey must be liquid – reliquify by warming, if necessary.
* Spices are usually added to the warmed honey – but remember to cool it before adding to the other ingredients.
* Honey doughs should be rolled no thinner than 0.5 cm (¼ inch), otherwise the cut shapes will be dry, brittle and short. Prick the pastry

with a fork to prevent air bubbles forming during baking, which spoils the appearance of the finished goods.

* Due to the high sugar content honey cakes tend to burn easily during baking. Be careful with heat below – bake in the centre of the oven and place another tray underneath if necessary.

* Sliced honey cake dries out very easily when exposed to air – wrap carefully in an airtight container.

Recipes for honey cakes vary from region to region. In the countries of the Middle East they sprinkle pastries with honey; the Italians and the Spanish like a nougat-type texture; the Swiss and the Germans developed a spiced flour-based dough, enriched with nuts and candied fruits, and left it to mature overnight before baking it in fanciful wooden moulds, carved in intricate detail. These were an important aspect of their trade. The French 'pain d'épices' is a simple affair much akin to bread, usually served sliced and spread with butter; made with warm honey and flour, the pliable dough was emptied into a wooden box and set in a cellar to rest for a month before it was used. In some regions this is still done. Potash was used for leavening, and carbonate of ammonia for a lighter texture. In England ginger biscuits and gingerbread cake, made with eggs, honey and later treacle or syrup and butter, spiced with a large amount of ginger became favourites.

> On her way home she usually bought a slice of honey-cake at the baker's. It was her Sunday treat. Sometimes there was an almond in her slice, sometimes not. It made a great difference. If there was an almond it was like carrying home a tiny present – a surprise – something that might very well not have been there. She hurried on the almond Sundays and struck the match for the kettle in quite a dashing way.
>
> (Katherine Mansfield, *Miss Brill*)

CAKES
Walnut Honey Cake

After 2 or 3 weeks maturing, this cake has a very pleasant sweet honey taste which is complemented by the crunchy walnuts. It is good spread with butter.

120 g caster sugar	4 oz caster sugar
250 g honey	9 oz honey
pinch cloves	pinch cloves
1 teaspoon cinnamon	1 teaspoon cinnamon
3 eggs	3 eggs
150 g plain flour	5 oz plain flour
250 g walnut quarters	9 oz walnut quarters

gas 4, 180°C, 350°F/50–60 minutes

Dissolve the sugar in the honey over a gentle heat, then blend in the spices and transfer to a mixing bowl to cool. Add the eggs one at a time, then the sifted flour and finally the broken walnuts. Beat very thoroughly to give air (the old cookery books say for an hour, but when using a machine about 10 minutes will do). Pour into a greased and floured square or guttered cake tin, and bake in the preheated oven until golden brown.

Honey cakes and pastries are traditionally served on Rosh Hashanah, the Jewish New Year festival which falls some time during September. The celebrations call for soul searching and mutual forgiveness, and carry the hope of goodness in the New Year. This yearning for a new sweet life is symbolized by serving foods made with honey, a custom apparently introduced by the prophet Nehemiah. In Persia is was the tradition to sprinkle a slice of raw apple with fresh honey – a custom which is still practised today by the Jews of the East.

Jewish Honey Cake – Honiglekach

80 g sultanas	3 oz sultanas
125 g chopped walnuts	4½ oz chopped walnuts
65 g each chopped candied orange and lemon peels	2½ oz each chopped candied orange and lemon peels
4 tablespoons rum	4 tablespoons rum
2 tablespoons liqueur or cognac	2 tablespoons liqueur or cognac
4 whole eggs	4 whole eggs
pinch salt	pinch salt
400 g dark honey	14 oz dark honey
175 g butter or flavourless oil	6 oz butter or flavourless oil
200 g caster sugar	7 oz caster sugar
500 g (approx.) plain flour	generous 1 lb (approx.) plain flour
1 teaspoon baking powder	1 teaspoon baking powder
1 teaspoon cinnamon	1 teaspoon cinnamon
½ teaspoon powdered cloves	½ teaspoon powdered cloves
½ teaspoon ginger	½ teaspoon ginger
80 g cocoa	3 oz cocoa

gas 4, 180°C, 350°F/50–60 minutes

Prepare the dried fruit and nuts the night before, and soak them in the spirit of your choice.

Warm the honey with the melted butter or the oil and the sugar, cool, then beat the eggs into the mixture one at a time. Sift part of the flour with the baking powder, the spices, and the cocoa. Sift gradually into the honey mass and beat until the consistency of a thick honey is achieved. It is difficult to be exact about the flour quantity. The texture should not be like that of a dough – you should still be able to stir it even if with difficulty. You may also like to add the spirit in which the fruits have been soaked. The fruits should be drained and then dusted with flour before being added to the mixture; mix them into the dough at the end.

Have ready two 24 cm (9½ inch) spring-form cake tins, lined with paper that has been brushed with oil and dusted with flour. Fill them only two-thirds full, as they rise well. Smooth over the surface with the wet hand and bake for about an hour. Take care not to over-bake and they will keep fresh for some weeks. Cut after 2 or 3 days.

CAKES

Polish Honey Cake

450 g honey	1 lb honey
250 g granulated sugar	9 oz granulated sugar
100 g melted butter	3½ oz melted butter
½ teaspoon cinnamon	½ teaspoon cinnamon
½ teaspoon powdered cloves	½ teaspoon powdered cloves
½ teaspoon ground allspice	½ teaspoon ground allspice
4 whole eggs	4 whole eggs
50 g each chopped hazelnuts and walnuts	2 oz each chopped hazelnuts and walnuts
70 g raisins	3 oz raisins
50 g chopped angelica	2 oz chopped angelica
450 g plain flour	1 lb plain flour
1½ teaspoons baking powder	1½ teaspoons baking powder
1 teaspoon instant coffee powder	1 teaspoon instant coffee powder
1 teaspoon bicarbonate of soda	1 teaspoon bicarbonate of soda
1 tablespoon milk	1 tablespoon milk
2 tablespoons brandy	2 tablespoons brandy

gas 3, 170°C, 325°F/10 minutes
gas 5, 190°C, 375°F/50 minutes

Boil the honey and dissolve the sugar in it, then add the melted butter. Blend in the spices and allow to cool a little. Beat in the eggs one at a time. Dredge the nuts and dried fruits with a little flour, then sift the remainder with the baking powder. Pour the honey mixture over the flour, and mix well. Blend in the coffee, the fruit and nuts, and the bicarbonate of soda which has been dissolved in the milk. Finally mix in the brandy. Grease and line a 24 cm (9½ inch) baking tin, and bake in the oven as indicated above. Turn on to a wire rack and cool with the tin still in place. Serve in slices, or spread with butter.

Nürnberger Lebkuchen
(spiced honey biscuits)

Lebkuchen made with honey originated as peppercakes – Pfefferkuchen – in the monasteries of Germany and Austria around the eleventh century. In time the honey cakes became very popular, and by the fourteenth century the town of Nürnberg had already gained a reputation for the best Lebkuchen in the land – due, it was suggested, to the 'water and the air', but more likely because of the fine honey gathered from the long-flowering vegetation which grew in the huge Reichswald forest surrounding the town. Nürnberg earned the title of 'bee-garden of the Kaiser and the State'.

Situated both at the heart of the Holy Roman Empire of German nations and geographically central in Europe, the town was the principal trading point between North, South, East and West. Among the numerous commodities exchanged were spices, nuts and dried fruits; and the gingerbread bakers – Lebzelter as they were known – were quick to capitalize on these unique advantages. They baked quite exceptional spiced cakes, which they exported everywhere and which were eagerly snapped up by the trading visitors.

The popularity of the spiced honey pastries grew dramatically in 1486 when Kaiser Frederick III visited the town; he gave to 4,000 children gifts of Lebkuchen moulded with a portrait of himself sitting on a throne. In 1587 an order was placed for supplying a wedding feast – '82 Nürnbergische Pfefferküchlin, 12 Tutzent [dozen] Zünglin und 63 grosse [large] Pfefferkuchen für Suppen und Saucen [soups and sauces]' – Pfefferkuchen were grated and mixed with *Most* (unfermented grape juice), vinegar and herbs to baste dry meats roasting on the spit.

The Nürnberg Union of Lebzelter (Gingerbread Bakers)

Until the seventeenth century there had been no particular division of labour between the Lebzelter and the bakers, with the Zelter happily using the baker's facilities as they needed them. But in 1629 the Zelter saw distinct advantages in forming their own guild. It proved to be extremely powerful. The first rule insisted that every Lebküchner must have his own oven. Those 'imposters' who had previously used the ovens of their nearest baker were no longer allowed to sell their goods at any fair or market, and could only trade from their own homes. There were controls on sales venues and conditions, times of sale, types of produce and prices; later they in turn were forced to pay levies of Lebkuchen for their market stalls. A code of practice was established which controlled ingredients and even appearance – with fines imposed if these were not fulfilled. Eventually the guild tightened its grip so firmly that in 1677 one of their members was not even allowed to emigrate.

By 1643 there were fourteen masters in the Nürnberg union, and no more houses were allowed to be established; the control on apprentices was strict. No one was allowed to be replaced until the last had been

CAKES

gone for three years. The apprentices had to pay substantial fees for their tuition, but those who had married into, or were offspring of, the masters were considered more favourably. The training was extensive — four years initially, followed by another four acting as partner with different masters, and another two years of travel. The qualifying examination then took a minimum of eight days, during which time they had to prepare entirely without supervision:

> 6 dozen spiced cakes;
> 6 dozen almond cakes;
> 6 dozen double thickness spiced cakes;
> 6 dozen double thickness almond cakes;
> a further 2 curved cakes; and 12 pieces of long cake.
>
> His time must be well planned, nothing must be wasted or spoiled neither must anything be forgotten.

Many other towns throughout Europe also produced spiced cakes, and each bore its local name. Basel had *Leckerli*, Thorn had *Katharinchen*; from Aachen came *Printen*; Breslau and Liegnitz produced high, round *Bomben*; Cologne *Pfefferbrot* and Nürnberg the *Lebkuchen*. Strife also existed concerning their wares, which culminated eventually in a 200-year so-called 'Lebkuchen war', finally resolved in 1927 in the Berlin County Court, which ruled that 'Nürnberger Lebkuchen' might only be so called if they were made in the town itself. This of course also applied to the specialities of the other towns. It was their copyright, just as Champagne in France established its own, in more recent times.

Nürnberger Lebkuchen

From the sixteenth century until the end of the thirty-year war in 1648, raw sugar was also imported from the Indies and refined in Nürnberg. Maybe the use of sugar and syrup in German baking originated then; for by the seventeenth century sugar, rather than honey as in English gingerbreads, appeared in many Lebkuchen recipes.

It is now customary to spread the Lebkuchen mixture over or sandwich it between 'Oblaten' — round thin wafers. I use rice paper.

300 g raw almonds	11 oz raw almonds
3 eggs	3 eggs
200 g caster sugar	7 oz caster sugar
100 g plain white flour	3½ oz plain white flour
1 teaspoon cinnamon	1 teaspoon cinnamon
pinch cloves	pinch cloves

pinch mace
zest ½ lemon
50 g candied orange peel (or lemon, or half and half)
2 drops pure bitter almond essence
Oblaten wafers or rice paper
rose-water

Icing

125 g icing sugar
1 egg white
1 tablespoon water
30 g coloured sugar crystals
pistachios (optional)

pinch mace
zest ½ lemon
2 oz candied orange peel (or lemon, or half and half)
2 drops pure bitter almond essence
Oblaten wafers or rice paper
rose-water

4½ oz icing sugar
1 egg white
1 tablespoon water
1 oz coloured sugar crystals
pistachios (optional)

gas 3, 170°C, 325°F/25–30 minutes

Grind the almonds coarsely with their skins on. Beat the eggs and the sugar for 20 minutes until pale, frothy and very thick. Add the flour, spices, the lemon zest and the candied peels, together with the almonds and essence. The mixture should be quite firm. Spread it onto rice paper about 1 cm (⅜ inch) thick, and leave to dry out for an hour in a warm place. Brush with rose-water, and bake until light brown. While still hot cover with the icing.

Mix the icing sugar, sieved with egg white and water, until thick. Spread over the baked mixture, sprinkle with sugar crystals and pistachios, and dry out near the warm oven.

* For a brown version of this Lebkuchen mix 40 g (1½ oz) of finely grated dark chocolate with the other ingredients, and cover with a chocolate glaze.

Simple Lebkuchen

Though the Lebzelter's art has virtually perished, spiced cakes and pastries are still very much a European Christmas speciality. As the saying goes, 'Without peppercakes no Christmas feast; indeed where would the world be, without peppercakes?'

> Baking week belonged beneath a lucky star, which began with *pepper* and *sugar nuts* and ended with *Brezeln, Ring* and *Flat* cakes. We were not allowed in the baking kitchen, which smelled so temptingly of bitter almonds and grated lemons; but we children received spe-

cially prepared for us as a Christmas pre-taste, generous amounts of small cakes. 'I know,' said my mother, 'that these will ruin your appetite, but that is better than depriving you. Everyone should have at this time pleasurable anticipation of the feast, and a feast cake gives this best.'

(Theodor Fontane, *Meine Kinderjahre*)

Lebkuchen are often used for Christmas tree decorations, cut into stars, diamonds, hearts, etc. They can be iced or dipped in chocolate and sprinkled with edible decorations. The dough can be kept for several weeks in a cool place before it is used, and indeed improves in the keeping. When baked, they should be wrapped and stored in an airtight tin. After 2 or 3 weeks they soften, and the flavour improves and mellows. This simple recipe uses rye flour.

140 g rye flour	5 oz rye flour
90 g caster sugar	3 oz caster sugar
$1/2$ teaspoon cinnamon	$1/2$ teaspoon cinnamon
pinch cloves	pinch cloves
pinch ginger	pinch ginger
40 g dark honey	2 oz dark honey
1 egg	1 egg
$1/2$ teaspoon bicarbonate of soda	$1/2$ teaspoon bicarbonate of soda

gas 6, 200°C, 400°F/10 minutes

Line the ungreased baking sheet with 2 or 3 sheets of brown paper as additional protection.

Sift the flour and sugar together. Mix the spices with the honey and add to the flour mixture, then knead in the egg and the bicarbonate of soda which has been dissolved in a tablespoon of water. Knead very thoroughly until the dough is firm and hard. Divide into two and cover each portion well. Set aside in a cool place to rest overnight, or longer if wished. Roll out to 3 mm ($1/8$ inch) and cut into shapes, brush with egg and lay on a greased and floured cake tray. Pierce with a hole if to be used for tree decoration, then bake in the preheated oven. While still hot, brush with a light lemon- or vanilla-flavoured glacé icing (pages 72–3), and decorate with hundreds and thousands, silver balls, coloured sugars or crystallized flowers. Makes about 40 pieces.

Spiced Honey Biscuits with Hazelnuts

The filling of hazelnuts with candied orange and lemon adds a special flavour to the heavily spiced dough.

125 g dark honey	4½ oz dark honey
40 g butter	1½ oz butter
60 g caster sugar	3 oz caster sugar
3 ground cloves	3 ground cloves
1½ tablespoons cinnamon	1½ tablespoons cinnamon
pinch allspice	pinch allspice
250 g whole wheat flour	9 oz whole wheat flour
1 egg	1 egg
½ teaspoon bicarbonate of soda	½ teaspoon bicarbonate of soda
1 tablespoon rum	1 tablespoon rum
zest ½ lemon	zest ½ lemon
split, blanched almonds for decoration	split, blanched almonds for decoration

Filling

100 g raisins	3½ oz raisins
1 tablespoon rum	1 tablespoon rum
50 g honey	2 oz honey
125 g hazelnuts	4½ oz hazelnuts
50 g grated chocolate	2 oz grated chocolate

gas 4, 180°C, 350°F/30 minutes

Gently heat the honey and butter until dissolved; stir in the sugar and spices then leave to cool. Sift the flour, then pour in the honey, the egg, the bicarbonate of soda which has been dissolved in a tablespoon of water, the rum and the lemon zest. Mix well. Set aside to rest in a cool place overnight. Roll out to 3 mm (⅛ inch) thickness, and stamp shapes.

Spread the filling over half the shapes and sandwich with the other half. Brush with lightly beaten egg and decorate with half a blanched almond. Bake in the preheated oven.

Filling: Soak the raisins in the rum for an hour. Mix together the warmed honey with the grated nuts, chocolate and drained raisins.

Makes about 30 4 cm (1½ inch) pieces.

CAKES

Liegnitzer Bombe (Spiced Honey Cake)

A rival to the Nürnberger Lebkuchen.

250 g golden syrup	9 oz golden syrup
1½ tablespoons honey	1½ tablespoons honey
190 g granulated sugar	7 oz granulated sugar
55 g butter	2 oz butter
½ teaspoon cardamom	½ teaspoon cardamom
pinch cloves	pinch cloves
440 g wholemeal flour	1 lb wholemeal flour
pinch salt	pinch salt
2 teaspoons baking powder	2 teaspoons baking powder
½ teaspoon lemon zest	½ teaspoon lemon zest
½ teaspoon orange zest	½ teaspoon orange zest
1 egg	1 egg
55 g candied lemon peel	2 oz candied lemon peel
55 g candied orange peel	2 oz candied orange peel
55 g currants	2 oz currants
55 g nibbed or chopped almonds	2 oz nibbed or chopped almonds
1 tablespoon dark rum	1 tablespoon dark rum
250 g apricot jam	9 oz apricot jam
marzipan (optional, page 292)	marzipan (optional, page 292)

gas 4, 180°C, 350°F/35–40 minutes

Heat gently the syrup, honey, sugar and butter until the sugar has dissolved and the butter melted. Take off the heat and stir in the spices. Set aside to cool. Sift the flour with the salt and baking powder twice, then into a bowl. Stir in the melted ingredients, and add the lemon and orange zest and the egg. Combine well. Next add the candied peels, fruits, and nuts, and finally the rum. Pour the mixture into 2 greased and floured deep rectangular trays (31 × 21 × 2 cm, 12 × 8 × ¾ inch); they should only be about half full, as the mixture rises well in baking.

Bake in the preheated oven, then set on a wire rack to cool for 10 minutes in the tin before turning out. Split each cake in half when cool. Spread a quarter of the apricot jam over the bottom layer and cover with a layer of cake. Roll the marzipan on a sheet of greaseproof paper dredged with icing sugar, to fit the cake. Brush the cake first with more apricot jam, then sandwich the marzipan with it. Cover with another layer of cake which has first been coated with apricot jam, brush jam on the top of this too, and cover with the last piece of cake.

Ice the whole of the cake with chocolate glacé icing (page 73), and decorate with a few split almonds. The cake will keep for at least 2 months if well wrapped in aluminium foil. Keep for 2 weeks before cutting.

Haselnussleckerli (Hazelnut Biscuits)

120 g ground hazelnuts
120 g ground raw almonds
240 g sugar
1 teaspoon cinnamon
pinch star aniseed
20 g flour
2 tablespoons finely chopped candied lemon peel
2 tablespoons finely chopped candied orange peel
1½ teaspoons lemon juice
1 tablespoon honey
2 egg whites
30 g caster sugar
65 g icing sugar
2 tablespoons plum spirit (Zwetschkenwasser), if possible, or Kirsch

4 oz ground hazelnuts
4 oz ground raw almonds
8 oz sugar
1 teaspoon cinnamon
pinch star aniseed
1½ oz flour
2 tablespoons finely chopped candied lemon peel
2 tablespoons finely chopped candied orange peel
1½ teaspoons lemon juice
1 tablespoon honey
2 egg whites
1 oz caster sugar
2½ oz icing sugar
2 tablespoons plum spirit (Zwetschkenwasser), if possible, or Kirsch

gas 6, 200°C, 400°F/5–7 minutes

Dry roast the hazelnuts in a frying pan until light brown, and allow to cool. Grind them, and mix with the almonds, sugars, spices, flour, lemon juice, candied fruits and honey. Beat the egg whites to stiff foamy peaks, and fold in the nut mixture. Work to an even dough by hand, then leave to rest for an hour. Sprinkle the caster sugar on the work surface, and roll out the paste to 6 mm (¼ inch) thickness. (Dust the pin with sugar to prevent it sticking.) Cut out small square shapes and lay them on a buttered tray. Dry out for 3–4 hours, then place in the preheated oven on the highest rack and let them dry out for 5–7 minutes; larger ones may need 2 or 3 minutes more. Brush the still hot pastries with a glaze made by stirring the icing sugar with the spirit. Makes 35 pieces.

Hänsel and Gretel

In 1893 Engelbert Humperdinck wrote a new opera, based on the fairy tale written by the Brothers Grimm. All the childish dreams of a 'land of milk and honey' were re-awakened by the magic of the spiced peppercake house. The Lebzelter were quick to seize the new opportunity. Hänsel and Gretel houses appeared everywhere. The walls and roofs were made of Pfefferkuchen dough – even the oven was there; the house was decorated outside with white sugar icing, and long icicles hung from the eaves; thin waffle cakes were used for shutters, and bonbons and slivers of chocolate were stuck all over. Neither were the figures of the wicked witch and the two children forgotten – they were made of tragant and elaborately painted. Today we can still buy spiced houses around Christmas time – they come in cardboard cut-out form. With Pfefferkuchen and Lebkuchen some are even moulded (though these are miserable imitations of their past splendours); they are stuck on the house and even icing sugar is provided.

> . . . as they came nearer, they saw that the house was built of bread, and covered with cakes; but the windows were of light-coloured sugar. 'We must have some of that,' said Hänsel, 'and enjoy a tasty meal. I will eat some of the roof, Gretel, you can have part of the window as it tastes sweet.' Hänsel reached up high and broke off a piece of the roof to see how it tasted, and Gretel stood next to the window and nibbled off a piece. Then, from inside the room, a high voice called,
>   'Crack, crack, crunch,
>   who is nibbling at my house?'
> The children answered,
>   'The wind, the wind,
>   the heavenly wind'
> and carried on eating, without concern. Hänsel, who found the roof especially good, tore down a large piece for himself, and Gretel pushed out a complete round window pane, and sat down again to enjoy it . . .
>
> ('Hänsel and Gretel', *Grimm's Fairy Tales*)

Hänsel and Gretel's Gingerbread House

This is a lovely centrepiece for a Christmas table, but of course you can make it for a child's birthday cake as well, when the decorations should be varied with favourite sweets.

Dough for the House

500 g honey	1 lb honey
250 g sugar	9 oz sugar
250 g butter	9 oz butter
50 g cocoa powder	1½ oz cocoa powder
3 teaspoons ground cinnamon	3 teaspoons ground cinnamon
3 teaspoons ground cardamom	3 teaspoons ground cardamom
1½ teaspoons ground cloves	1½ teaspoons ground cloves
1 kg plain flour	generous 2 lbs plain flour
2 eggs	2 eggs
2 teaspoons bicarbonate of soda	2 teaspoons bicarbonate of soda
2 tablespoons rose-water (optional) or water	2 tablespoons rose-water (optional) or water

CAKES

Icing sugar to stick the house together

3 egg whites
approx. 750 g icing sugar

3 egg whites
approx. 1 lb 10 oz icing sugar

Decorations for the house

14 × 4 cm red leaf gelatine or red tissue paper (for the windows)
100 g split almonds
100 g chocolate drops or dragees
100 g candied cherries, orange and lemon peel
candied mimosa for the bells
silver confectionery balls

5½ × 1½ inches red leaf gelatine or red tissue paper (for the windows)
4 oz split almonds
4 oz chocolate drops or dragees
4 oz candied cherries, orange and lemon peel
candied mimosa for the bells
silver confectionery balls

One portion shortbread biscuits (see page 382), cut into hearts, iced or dipped in chocolate.

gas 6, 200°C, 400°F/10 minutes for thinner slices
15 minutes for thicker slices

The dough: Gently heat the honey with the sugar and butter until they have melted and dissolved. Stir in the cocoa powder and the ground spices, then leave to cool. Sift the flour into a bowl, and pour in the cooled honey mixture. Add the eggs, and the bicarbonate of soda dissolved in the rose-water. Mix well together and knead to a firm, smooth dough. Wrap in aluminium foil or cling film and store in the refrigerator for 2 or 3 days to mature. Knead the dough lightly again and divide into 3 pieces; then roll each out to 3 mm (⅛ inch) in thickness.

Cut a large 22 × 30 cm (8½ × 12 inch) rectangle for the house to stand on.

Cut the side walls, the two roof surfaces and the chimney from the rest of the dough as in the diagram.

Roll the left-over pastry pieces to 2 mm (1/12 inch) thickness, and cut out the witch and her cat, stars, bells and diamonds for the decorations.

Lay out all the cut shapes on greased baking sheets and bake in the preheated oven. The thinner pieces will take less time. Transfer on to wire racks to cool.

Prepare the icing: Whip up the egg whites to stiff snowy peaks, then beat in the sifted icing sugar a little at a time. It should be quite stiff but

THE SPICE BOX

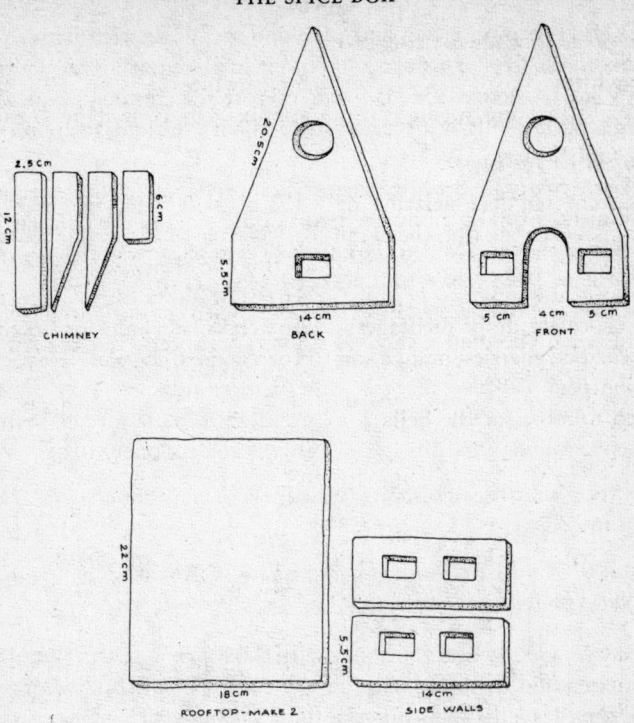

still malleable. Put the icing into an airtight plastic box – it hardens very quickly once it is exposed to the air. Fill the icing into a large piping bag fitted with a medium sized round or rosette type nozzle (page 383) and follow the instructions for assembling the house.

Building Instructions

(1) Stick the windows of red gelatine or paper inside. Pipe one edge of the front wall with icing and fix the side wall to it.

(2) Pipe icing along the edge of the opposite side and stick the second side wall to it. Pipe the last two edges and stick in the back wall. Leave to dry well. Pipe a thick line on to the base and firmly embed the house in it. Leave to harden overnight.

CAKES

(3) Refill the piping bag and pipe one roof edge with icing.

(4) Set in the first roof slope and hold it in place until it has set firm.

(5) When the second side is fixed, prepare the chimney. Pipe along two edges of the straight piece and stick on both the long straight edges of the angled pieces.

(6) Leave to dry for a while, then stick on the remaining short piece.

(7) Finish by piping along the two sloping sides of the chimney and stick it on to the roof. When the chimney is in place, seal the gap tidily between it and the roof with another line of icing.

(8) Cover the roof and walls of the house with the various honey and short biscuits, chocolates, candied cherries and peels. Use the icing to fix and pipe icicles.

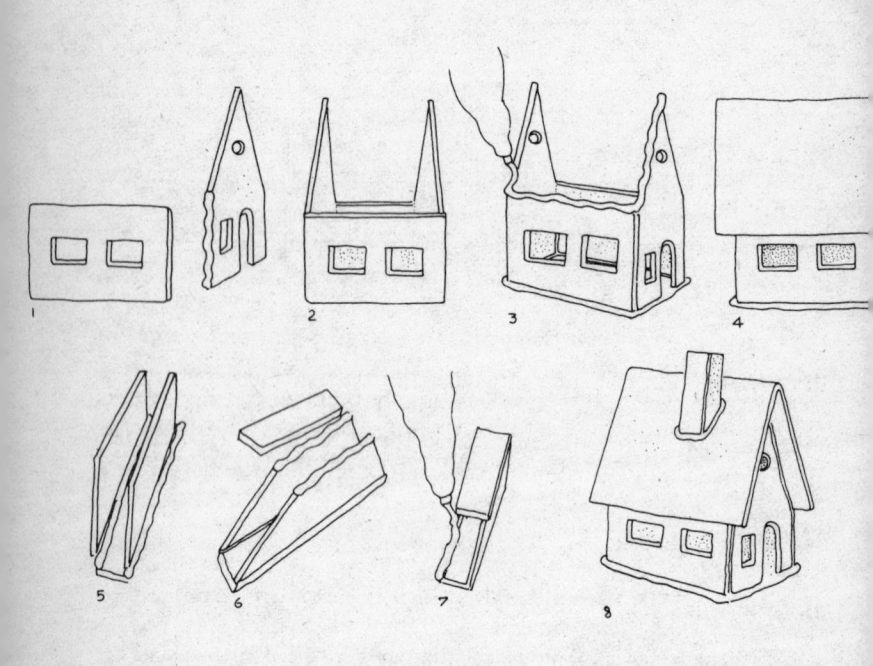

Friandises and Biscuits

'Les hommes se passionnent pour les femmes qui
savent leur cuisiner de bonnes friandises.'

(Honoré de Balzac)

Macaroons

The familiar small, round and flat almond macaroons are now a well loved classic. Made of sugar, egg white and sweet or bitter almonds, they may be flavoured with spices and perfumes. There are numerous variations from many cultures; made with hazelnuts or walnuts or coconut; flavoured with chocolate or coffee, with orange or lemon. The quantities vary from recipe to recipe, and from one country to the next. The basic mixture is also used in layers between other pastries for Torten as well as for large individual macaroon cakes.

There are two schools of thought concerning the preparation of macaroons – the first cooks the nuts with sugar and egg whites in a double boiler over heat; the second simply beats all the ingredients together. As both methods produce equally good results, I have used the quicker one. It is essential that the mixture be very thoroughly beaten.

Macaroons

These can be made with almonds, which is customary, hazelnuts or walnuts. A food processor makes very light work of macaroons, but be careful not to overgrind walnuts for they are very oily. If you haven't a processor, use a pestle and mortar. The almond paste needs a lot of pounding to be very smooth, so add the egg white as you work or the oils will be drawn out of the nuts. Macaroons should be crisp on the outside and slightly soft in the centre. The quantity makes 25 pieces.

150 g ground blanched almonds	5 oz ground blanched almonds
150 g caster sugar	5 oz caster sugar
1 drop pure vanilla essence, or ½ vanilla pod	1 drop pure vanilla essence, or ½ vanilla pod
1 tablespoon orange-flower water	1 tablespoon orange-flower water
2 egg whites (approx.)	2 egg whites (approx.)

gas 7, 220°C, 425°F/approx. 7–10 minutes

If using a processor, grind the almonds and sugar with the flavourings until fine. Add a little egg white while the blades are rotating, and continue until the paste is slightly soft but not runny; you might need a little more egg white, especially if you are using shop-bought ready-ground almonds.

If using a mortar, pound the almonds with a little egg white until the paste is smooth; work in half the sugar, then add the rest together with the egg white and blend the mixture well.

Either spoon the paste into a piping bag fitted with a large plain nozzle and pipe, or pinch off olive-sized pieces and roll into smooth balls. Place about 4 cm (1½ inches) apart on greaseproof, silicone-coated or edible rice paper on a flat baking sheet. Slightly flatten each macaroon, brush with cold water and sprinkle a little caster sugar over. Bake immediately in the preheated oven. Transfer to a wire rack to cool.

Leave the macaroons to cool completely on the paper turn the greaseproof sheet with the biscuits over, and moisten the underside with a damp cloth. After a few minutes the paper will peel off easily. Those on silicone paper should simply slide off. Tear edible rice paper away from the edges of each macaroon.

The basic mixture can be flavoured in the following ways:

* Stir 50 g (2 oz) of finely chopped *candied orange and lemon peel* into the finished mixture.
* Use *raw ground almonds*, and add 1 flat tablespoon of ground cinnamon to the sugar in the basic paste.
* *Apricot macaroons* are more decorative. Add 1 teaspoon of lemon zest to the basic paste and bake as usual. While still warm, gently press the centres and fill with a teaspoonful of strained apricot jam. Cool. Lay a silver confectionery ball in the centre and sprinkle chopped pistachios around the outside.
* *Chocolate macaroons* are also made with raw ground almonds. Use 130 g (4½ oz) raw ground almonds; 3 egg whites; 50 g (2 oz) slightly

softened and finely grated dark plain chocolate; 180g (6oz) caster sugar. Decorate with a split almond. Beat the chocolate into the finished mixture and bake as usual. Makes 30 pieces.

Swedish Macaroons

These include whole eggs and potato flour, and the chopped nuts give a slightly courser texture. This quantity makes 30 pieces.

170g finely chopped blanched almonds	6oz finely chopped blanched almonds
50g ground blanched almonds	1¾oz ground blanched almonds
50g potato flour	1¾oz potato flour
220g caster sugar	7¾oz caster sugar
1 egg	1 egg
zest 1 orange	zest 1 orange
split blanched almonds for decoration	split blanched almonds for decoration

Gas 7, 220°C, 425°F/approx 7–10 minutes

Sift the potato flour. Prepare the macaroon mixture in the usual way (page 374); the paste will not be as smooth as before. Roll walnut-sized balls, press lightly and moisten; then press half a blanched almond in the top of each, brush with water, sprinkle with icing sugar and bake.

Bitter Almonds. In a *Treatise of Foods* in 1705, Louis Lémery, docteur régent in the faculty of the Royal Academy of Sciences in Paris, wrote:

> Bitter Almonds (AMYGDALŒ AMARGŒ) are irritants, detersives, aperients, and diuretics. They prevent the formation of gravel. They cause the death of storks, pigeons, cats and dogs and parrots. The oil is not as bitter as the fruit. They are never used as food, but to lift the taste of gentle sweetmeats.

Bitter almonds are certainly bitter to the taste, and poisonous (owing to the content of prussic acid) if eaten in any quantity. Although used extensively in old cookery books, they are no longer generally available. The oils and essences, however, are valuable, and are used in minute amounts (a few drops) for confectionery, to enhance the flavour of sweet almonds. These are quite distinct from the ordinary almond essences. Use only 'pure' bitter almond essence.

CAKES

Amaretti

These bitter macaroons are made with bitter almond essence and are often served with ice-cream desserts. The shop-bought variety lack the rustic charm of these home-made ones. Make smaller biscuits than for macaroons.

150 g blanched ground almonds	5 oz blanched ground almonds
2–3 drops pure bitter almond essence	2–3 drops pure bitter almond essence
150 g caster sugar	5 oz caster sugar
1–2 egg whites	1–2 egg whites

gas 4, 180°C, 350°F/15–20 minutes

Make the basic recipe and flavour with the essence. Set coffee spoonfuls or roll olive-sized balls on the lined baking sheet, press, brush with water, dust with icing sugar and bake.

Biscuits

Shenkele

(A speciality of Alsace)

They stopped at a corrugated iron hut and sure enough the man who presumably lived there made us an omelette with fried potatoes and a cup of real coffee, so rare in those days that at once I realized that the officers must have brought their own provisions with them and that we were sharing them. And then I remembered the two boxes of cakes the *abbé's* mother had sent to us the day before. So we got them out of Auntie. The little Alsatian cakes were of her own baking and delicious. We took a few of each kind and gave them to the officers whose unwitting guests we had been.

(*The Alice B. Toklas Cook Book*)

Almond Shenkeles and Laekerlis made with honey are the 'little Alsatian cakes' – though the Swiss actually lay claim to the latter. Shenkele keep very well, packed in an airtight container. This quantity makes 30 pieces.

FRIANDISES AND BISCUITS

50 g butter
120 g icing sugar
2 teaspoons lemon zest
3 eggs
70 g ground blanched almonds
1 tablespoon Kirsch
250 g plain flour
1/2 teaspoon cinnamon

2 oz butter
4 1/2 oz icing sugar
2 teaspoons lemon zest
3 eggs
3 oz ground blanched almonds
1 tablespoon Kirsch
9 oz plain flour
1/2 teaspoon cinnamon

Beat the butter and sugar until pale and fluffy, then add the lemon zest, and the eggs one at a time. Beat very well. (A food processor is ideal for preparing this recipe.) Mix in the ground almonds and the Kirsch, then the sifted flour and cinnamon. The dough should be firm but still moist. Cover closely and leave in the refrigerator overnight. Roll long sausages of dough about 1 cm (3/8 inch) in diameter, and cut into cigar shapes about 8 cm (3 inches) long. The dough will seem very sticky, but if you are very light-handed and dust it well with flour it will handle with surprising ease. Deep fry (page 136) slowly at first until they start to swell, then quicker until they are coloured golden. Drain on absorbent kitchen paper, and dredge with icing sugar to serve when cold.

Simple Sugar Biscuits

250 g plain flour
250 g butter
125 g caster sugar
1 teaspoon lemon zest
1 egg
1 egg for brushing on top

9 oz plain flour
9 oz butter
4 1/2 oz caster sugar
1 teaspoon lemon zest
1 egg
1 egg for brushing on top

gas 5, 190°C, 375°F/20 minutes

Rub the sifted flour with the butter to fine crumbs. Fork in the sugar and lemon zest, then combine into a pastry with the egg. Wrap and chill in the refrigerator for 30 minutes. Dust the pastry board with flour and roll the pastry out 3 mm (1/8 inch) thick. Using various pastry cutters — hearts, crescents, diamonds and circles — cut out and lay biscuits on a greased and floured baking sheet. Roll up the scraps of pastry and use in the same way. Brush the top of each biscuit with lightly beaten egg, and scatter a little granulated sugar over.

Bake in the preheated oven until golden; cool on wire racks. These biscuits will keep in an airtight tin for 2–3 weeks. Makes about 50 pieces.

Hazelnut Slices

100 g butter	3½ oz butter
150 g flour	5 oz flour
50 g icing sugar	2 oz icing sugar
½ teaspoon ground ginger	½ teaspoon ground ginger
1 egg white	1 egg white
50 g whole hazelnuts	2 oz whole hazelnuts

gas 6, 200°C, 400°F/10 minutes

Rub the butter and flour to form fine crumbs, then work in the sugar, ginger and egg white to form a paste. Knead in the whole shelled hazelnuts. Form into a roll, wrap in foil, and refrigerate for 1½ hours. Cut into thin slices and lay them on a greased baking tray. Bake. Makes 40 pieces.

Feuilles de Palmiers

These have a lovely crunchy texture with a sugar caramel flavour. This is because of the granulated sugar used during the latter stages of rolling and folding. Remember to space the pastries well apart on the baking sheet, as they will grow to more than twice their original size. Left-over paste may be used. In this case omit the first 3 folds, and only make the ones using sugar. (See page 51f for quantities and technique.)

gas 7, 220°C, 425°F/15–20 minutes

Prepare the puff pastry and make the first three folds as usual. Brush away all the surplus flour, and sprinkle granulated sugar generously on the work surface. Dust the pastry with sugar, roll, fold and turn. Repeat once. Chill if necessary. Finally roll the pastry out into a rectangle, dust with sugar and lightly press it in with the rolling pin. Give the paste a 'double fold' – into four. Fold both narrow ends in half to meet in the middle, dust and press in more sugar, and then fold them on each other. Press with a rolling pin to hold the layers closer together. It should measure about 7–8 cm (roughly 3 inches) in width. Trim and discard

FRIANDISES AND BISCUITS

each end, then cut slices 6–7 mm (a good ¼ inch) in width. Arrange them on a dry baking sheet. Lightly spread each out in a fan shape, or turn the ends in. Dust with granulated sugar; cover and chill for 30 minutes.

Set in the preheated oven. After 6–7 minutes remove from the oven and turn each palmier over, otherwise the additional sugar will brown too much, caramelize and burn. Dust again with sugar, and finish baking. They should be lightly coloured. 325 g (11½ oz) dough will give about 12 pieces.

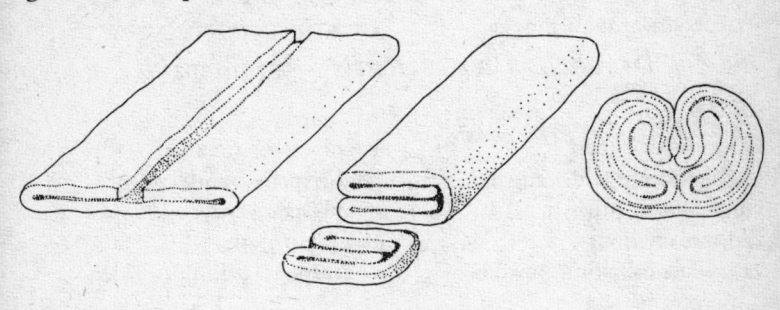

Remove from the oven, and transfer from the hot surface immediately to a cold rack to prevent the sugar from sticking. They will crisp as they cool. Stored in an airtight tin they will keep crisp for several days.

Friandises

Marion's Shortbread

These are good served with fresh soft fruits after dinner.

110 g butter	4 oz butter
35 g caster sugar	1¼ oz caster sugar
1 tablespoon vanilla sugar	1 tablespoon vanilla sugar
1 teaspoon hot water	1 teaspoon hot water
110 g plain flour	4 oz plain flour
25 g chopped walnuts	1 oz chopped walnuts

gas 3, 170°C, 325°F/25 minutes

Cream the butter and sugars until pale and fluffy; mix in the hot water and stir in the well sifted flour with a wooden spoon. Add the walnuts. Roll into a long sausage shape about 2 cm (³/₄ inch) in diameter and 15 cm (6 inches) long, wrap in foil, and chill in the refrigerator for an hour. Cut slices 0.5 cm (¹/₄ inch) thick with a sharp knife, or break off pieces of the dough and shape small crescents. Space at 2 cm (³/₄ inch) intervals on a greased and floured baking sheet, and bake until slightly coloured. Transfer to a rack to cool. Dredge with icing sugar, and store in an airtight tin between layers of greaseproof paper. Makes 30 pieces.

Brown Butter Biscuits – Heidesand

140 g butter	5 oz butter
125 g caster sugar	4¹/₂ oz caster sugar
1 tablespoon vanilla sugar	1 tablespoon vanilla sugar
1 tablespoon milk	1 tablespoon milk
190 g plain flour	7 oz plain flour
¹/₂ teaspoon baking powder	¹/₂ teaspoon baking powder

Melt the butter in a large flat pan, and let it brown without burning; leave to cool and solidify. Beat the butter with the sugars until foamy, then beat in the milk, and continue to beat until the mass is white and fluffy. Sift the flour with the baking powder, and beat about two-thirds of it into the mixture. Knead in the rest. Roll the pastry into a 3 cm (1¹/₄ inch) diameter sausage, wrap tightly, and set in a cool place to chill. After 2 hours cut into thin slices and bake in the preheated oven set at gas 3, 170°C, 325°F for 15 minutes. Makes 50 pieces.

Tuiles

A 'tuile' is a thin wafer wrapped over a rolling pin or a bottle to give it the classic curved shape of a French roof tile. It can be plain, but an almond or a walnut flavour is more interesting and Carême scattered pistachio on his. Once it has baked you have to work very quickly, as the soft pastry crisps up within a few seconds of leaving the oven. Rest the pin on a damp cloth to stop it rolling, and make small batches 5 or 6 at a time.

130 g flaked almonds	5 oz flaked almonds
110 g ground walnuts	4 oz ground walnuts

120 g caster sugar	4½ oz caster sugar
30 g plain flour	1 oz plain flour
2 egg whites	2 egg whites
50 g melted and cooled butter	2 oz melted and cooled butter
1 tablespoon Kirsch or rum	1 tablespoon Kirsch or rum
20 g chopped walnuts	1 oz chopped walnuts

gas 3, 170°C, 325°F/6–8 minutes

Assemble the almonds, and ground walnuts, sugar and sifted flour in a bowl. Lightly fork the egg whites separately before stirring them and the melted butter gently into the nut and flour mixture. Add the spirit. Leave to rest for a few hours in the refrigerator. Grease a baking sheet, then drop heaped teaspoonfuls of the mixture at 12 cm (5 inch) intervals. Flatten evenly to about 2 mm (less than 1/10 inch) in depth with a fork dipped in cold water. Scatter a few chopped walnuts over the top, and bake for a few minutes until golden.

Lift the tray out of the oven, scoop up each wafer with a spatula and lightly press over the curved surface (see above) for 2 or 3 minutes before cooling on a wire rack. You can of course leave them flat. Make sure that the baking sheet is cold when you use it again, and that the oven has returned to the correct temperature. Store in an airtight tin.

Suvretta Friandises

The Suvretta House, in St Moritz, Switzerland, has gained a world-wide reputation for its cakes and pastries in recent years, and particularly due to the painstaking efforts of Hans van den Klinkenberg. Each year the demand for the delicious array increases both at lunch and après-ski, as well as at dinner, when the dessert is always accompanied by a tray of 'friandises'. Hundreds of these delectable mouthfuls are produced each morning in the pâtisserie, by the apprentices who pipe, and knead, chop and roll the many different shapes. When they have been baked the little cakes are locked in a tall cupboard lined with ten or twelve drawers – they have to be kept under lock and key, for apart from the staff themselves, any visitor to the kitchen will surreptitiously try to sneak a mouthful when the chef's back is turned. All friandises will keep for several weeks if stored in airtight containers.

Here is a small selection.

CAKES

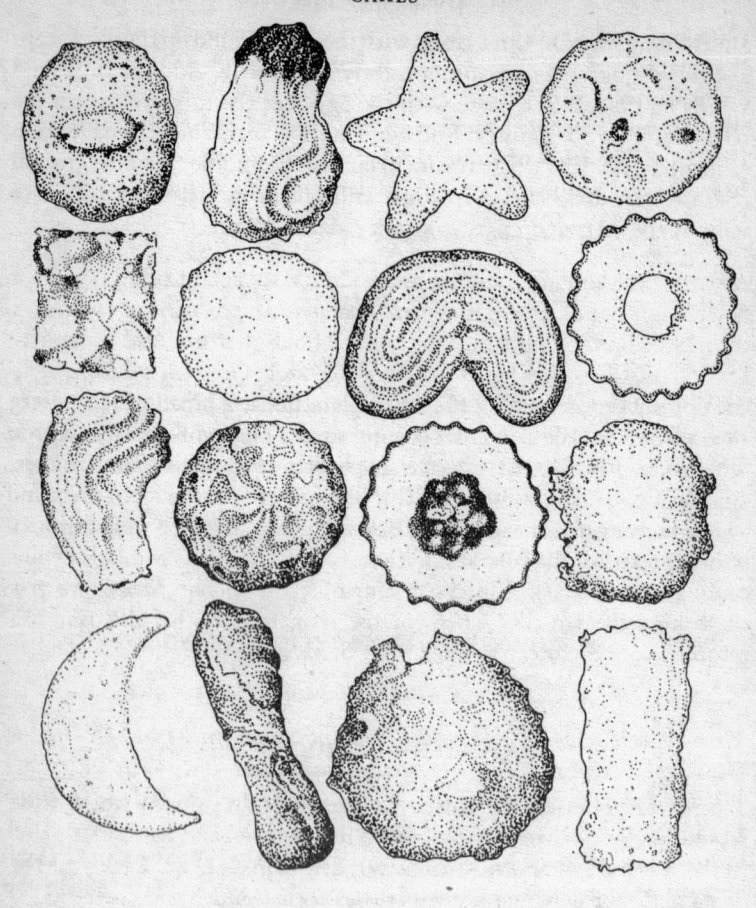

Iced Biscuits – Owis Molis

125 g plain flour
pinch salt
100 g butter
40 g icing sugar
vanilla pod
1 egg yolk

4½ oz plain flour
pinch salt
3½ oz butter
1½ oz icing sugar
vanilla pod
1 egg yolk

gas 6, 200°C, 400°F/10–12 minutes

Sift the flour twice or three times with the salt. Mound on the work-top, and rub the butter pieces into it lightly and swiftly. Add the sugar and vanilla and blend to a paste with the egg. Let the mixture rest in the refrigerator for 30 minutes. Roll out 3 mm ($^1/_8$ inch) thick, and cut 5 cm (2 inch) circles. Cut a 1 cm ($^3/_8$ inch) hole in the middle. Lay on a greased baking sheet and bake. Dip while still hot in vanilla-flavoured glacé icing (page 72), and cool on a rack. Makes 40 pieces.

Sablé

(Sand biscuits)

Make a pastry with 340 g (12 oz) of plain flour, a pinch of salt, 230 g (8 oz) of butter, 100 g (3$^1/_2$ oz) of icing sugar, 1 egg yolk and 1 teaspoon lemon juice. Roll into a sausage shape 4 cm (1$^1/_2$ inches) in diameter, dust with caster sugar and chill. Cut into pieces 1 cm ($^3/_8$ inch) thick and lay on a greased baking sheet. Bake at gas 6, 200°C, 400°F for 10 minutes. Makes 40 pieces.

Florentiner Mandel Plätzchen

(Almond Florentines)

First make the filling. Heat 50 g (2 oz) of honey with 100 g (3$^1/_2$ oz) of butter and 100 g (3$^1/_2$ oz) of granulated sugar until the sugar has dissolved and the butter melted. Remove from the heat and stir in 100 g (3$^1/_2$ oz) of nibbed almonds. Allow to cool.

Make pâte sucrée (2) (page 45) with 30 g (1 oz) sugar; 65 g (2$^1/_2$ oz) butter; 100 g plain flour (3$^1/_2$ oz); 1 egg yolk; a pinch of salt; 1 teaspoon lemon zest.

Roll out 2 mm (less than $^1/_{10}$ inch) thick and line a 31 × 21 × 2 cm (12 × 8$^1/_2$ × $^5/_8$ inch) baking sheet. Par-bake for 10 minutes at gas 6, 200°C, 400°F, brush with strained apricot jam and cover with the cooled filling, spreading the mixture evenly over the apricot surface. Bake for a further 10 minutes, and leave in the tin to cool. Cut into 3 cm (1$^1/_4$ inch) squares while still hot. Makes 60 pieces.

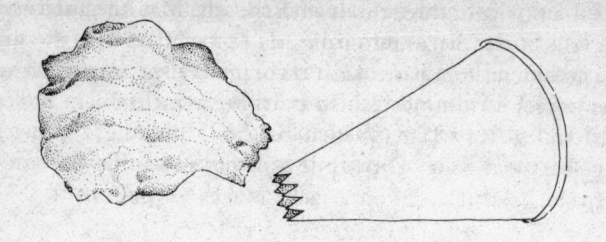

Hazelnut Biscuits — *Hoefeiser*

110 g butter	4 oz butter
75 g caster sugar	3 oz caster sugar
1 egg	1 egg
1 egg white	1 egg white
150 g plain flour	5 oz plain flour
pinch salt	pinch salt
90 g ground hazelnuts	3½ oz ground hazelnuts

gas 6, 200°C, 400°F / 10 minutes

Beat the butter and sugar until light and fluffy, then beat in the egg and the egg white. Next add the sifted flour and salt, but avoid beating too much. Finally mix in the nuts. Fill a piping bag fitted with a star nozzle and pipe 50 curved swags at 2 cm (¾ inch) intervals on to a greased baking sheet. Pipe half facing one way and half the other. Bake for 10 minutes and cool on wire racks. Sandwich in pairs with the chocolate filling (2) (page 65), and dredge with icing sugar. Makes 25 pieces.

Spritsjes

(piped biscuits)

80 g butter	3 oz butter
40 g icing sugar	1½ oz icing sugar
50 ml double cream	3½ oz double cream
130 g plain flour	4¾ oz plain flour
½ teaspoon lemon zest	½ teaspoon lemon zest
pinch salt	pinch salt

gas 6, 200°C, 400°F / 10 minutes

Beat the butter with the icing sugar, then whip in the cream. Sift the flour with the zest and the salt and add them to the mixture. Fill a piping bag fitted with a star nozzle, and pipe 50 straight swags on to a buttered baking sheet at 2 cm (³/₄ inch) intervals. Bake for 10 minutes, cool on racks, then sandwich in pairs with apricot jam and dip the pointed end in melted chocolate. Makes 25 pieces.

This mixture can also be piped in simple star shapes.

Marrons Glacés

It would be foolish to pretend that marrons glacés can be made at home as well as the professional confisiers are able to. Using their specialized equipment they can achieve perfect crystallization by simmering the fruits very slowly in a flavoured sugar syrup for up to 2 days. The syrup thickens as it evaporates. It is a time-consuming and fiddly task; no wonder marrons glacés are so costly.

Nevertheless this homely method also works well and the taste is as good, though the texture may be a little uneven and the finished sweetmeats may not look quite as handsome.

Choose chestnuts of a similar size so that they cook more evenly — if you can find large fat fruits the method is more successful. The traditional method of boiling must be used, for the inner casings are essential to hold the nuts together in the water.

Peel off the hard outer casing of 500 g (1 lb) chestnuts: use a small, pointed kitchen knife and make an incision all around the fat part of the chestnut (if possible try and graze the inner casing as well as this will help it slip off more easily later). Slide the tip of the knife under the cut and ease the outer casing off. It will come away quite easily.

Lay the chestnuts in a deep, heavy-bottomed but narrow pan if you have one, as this reduces the possibility of the chestnuts rolling around and breaking up as the water, and later the syrup, simmers. *Cover the nuts with cold water* and add 2 teaspoons of flour. Bring slowly to the boil, and when it starts to simmer reduce the heat so that there is only the smallest movement. Barely simmer for 8–10 minutes, or a little longer if the chestnuts are very large. Test one by lightly pressing it between finger and thumb — it should give a little and feel slightly soft.

Have ready another large bowl filled with fresh boiling water and carefully transfer the chestnuts, using a slotted spoon, to it. This prevents discoloration. Lift out one nut at a time (for as soon as they start to cool the skins stick), and remove the inner casing with the knife point very carefully, for while still hot the nuts are also very prone to fall apart.

Lay on a wire rack to cool. When they are cold they become much firmer.

Make the syrup: For 500 g (1 lb) chestnuts use 500 g (1 lb) granulated sugar, 250 ml (8 fl oz) water and half a vanilla pod for flavouring. Use the same pan as before. Put the water in the pan first, then add the sugar and vanilla pod and bring to the boil on a gentle heat until all the sugar has dissolved. Raise the heat and boil for 2 or 3 minutes until the syrup coats the back of a spoon (or a drop on a cold plate feels tacky).

Use the slotted spoon to lay the peeled chestnuts in the syrup; bring slowly back to a bare simmer and cook for 10 minutes. Lift off the heat, take out the vanilla pod, and transfer the chestnuts very carefully, to a cold pan if possible, or a heat-proof bowl. Pour the hot syrup over them, and leave to stand for 24 hours.

Next day, carefully transfer the chestnuts and syrup back to the pan (if they have been in a bowl, otherwise leave them in the pan). Bring slowly to the boil, simmer for 1 minute, remove from the heat, and transfer the chestnuts and syrup back to a clean pan or bowl again. Leave to cool overnight. Repeat this three more times, by which time much of the syrup will have been absorbed and what remains will have a thin crust on the top. Transfer the marrons glacés to a wire rack to dry off. Wrap each crystallized fruit in aluminium foil, and store in an airtight container.

Bibliography

Foreign Books:

Bierbaum, Otto, *Conditorei-Lexikon* 1898, Strassburger Druckerei und Verlagsanstalt, Strasbourg

Dubois, Urbain, *La Pâtisserie d'aujourd'hui*, 1894

Dubois, Urbain, *Le grand Livre des pâtissiers confiseurs*, 1883, Éditions Joinville, Paris

Gouffé, Jules, *Le Livre des conserves*, 1869, Hachette, Paris

Hausen, Hans Jürgen, *Die Kunstgeschichte des Backwerks*, 1968, Gerhard Stalling Verlag-Oldenburg, Hamburg

Hess, Olga und Adolf, *Wiener Küche*, 1926, Franz Denticke, Leipzig und Wien

Hoffmann, Maria und Lydtin, Helmut, *Bayerisches Kochbuch*, 1974, Birken-Verlag, Munich

Kaltenbach, Marianna, *Ächti Schwizer Chuchi*, 1977, Hallwag Verlag, Bern und Stuttgart

Kochbuch der Deutschen Kochschule in Prag, 1914, 10th edition, Gustav Neugebauer, Prague

Lacam, Pierre, *Le Mémorial des glaces*, 1902, 2nd edition, Paris

Le Mémorial historique de la pâtisserie, 1888, Paris

Leitich, Ann Tizia, *Das Süsse Wien*, 1964, E. Hunna Verlag, Vienna

Pratto, Katharina, *Die Süddeutsche Küche*, 1929, Verlagsbuchhandlung Styria, Graz and Vienna

Rokitansky, Marie von, *Die Österreichische Küche*, 1899, Vienna; 14th edition 1923, Leykam Verlag, Graz

Rumpolt, Marx, *Ein New Kochbuch*, 1581, facsimile edition 1980, Olms Presse Hildesheim, New York

English and American Books:

Beard, James, *Beard on Food*, 1974, Alfred Knopf, New York

Delights and Prejudices, 1971, Simon and Schuster, New York

CAKES

Bradley, Richard, *The Country Housewife and Lady's Director*, 1736, facsimile edition, 1980, Prospect Books, London

Fance, Wilfred J. (Editor) *The New International Confectioner*, 1976, Virtue and Co Ltd. London

Glasse, Hannah, *The Compleat Confectioner*, 1760, London

Grigson, Jane, *Food with the Famous*, 1979, Michael Joseph, London

Harris, H.G. and Borella, S.P., *All about Gâteaux, and Dessert Cakes*, Maclaren and Sons Ltd, London (undated, early 20th century)

Hartley, Dorothy, *Food in England*, 1954, Macdonald, London

Jones, Evan, *American Food: The Gastronomic Story*, 1981, Random House and Vintage, New York

Soyer, Alexis, *The Pantrophean or History of Food and its preparation from the Earliest ages of the World*, 1853, London

Tannahill, Reay, *Food in History*, 1973, Eyre Methuen Ltd, London

Roden, Claudia, *A Book of Middle Eastern Food*, 1970, Penguin Books, London

White, Florence, *Good Things in England*, 1932, Jonathan Cape, London

Index

Acton, Eliza *Modern Cookery for Private Families* 32, 108
Almonds, 308-318
    varieties and preparation, 310-121
    apricot: nut bread, 190; yeast cake, 126
    amaretti – bitter macaroons, 376 yeast cake, 126
    Austrian carrot cake, 200
    Berliner Crème Torte, 112
    Bienenstich: butter base, 317; yeast base, 316
    bilberry cake, 246
    biscuit – sponge, 94
    Butterbrot mit Schokolade, 190
    carmelite cake (dates, figs), 275
    cheese cake, 301; tartlets, 302
    chestnut Torte with quince slices, 330
    chocolate caracas, 155
    cinnamon Torte, 352
    Dattel Torte (fresh dates), 274
    fillings 67-8; orange and, 68; baklava, for, 338; fila fingers, 340; marzipan, 288-90, 292; potize, for, 131; pralinée, crème, 68
    fingers – assabih bi loz, 340
    florentines – Mandel Plätzchen, 383
    fresh cherry sponge: chocolate, 250-1
    gâteau de la reine, 314
    gooseberry and, flan, 222
    grapes and, in meringue, 239
    Haselnussleckerli, 367
    hazelnut gâteau praline, 174
    Kirschtorte, 166
    Linzertorte, 216
    Lacam, Le, 179
    macaroons, 373-5
    maids of honour (cheese), 302
    malakoff, 172
    meringues à la reine, 111
    mincemeat, 280
    Nürnberger Lebkuchen, 360-3
    orange cake, with, 264; mousseline with farci curaçao, 266
    paste with apple flan, 233
    praline 1 and 2, 312; see also *praline*
    shenkele (biscuits), 376
    slices, 315; with chocolate, 153
    strawberry fruit cake, 257
    Streussel (crumb covering), 123
    Strudel or fila, 317
    Sydney Smith's tart, 214
    tuiles (curved nut wafers), 380
    tartlettes amandines, 213
    wedding cake, 290
    whipped cake, 313
    Zampa Kipfel, 111
    Zimmt Kuchen, 353
Allspice: preparation for baking, 344
Aluminium ware and *P.T.F.E.*, 19-20
Amaretti (bitter almond macaroons), 376
Angelica, candied, 86; in honey cake, 360
Aniseed: in certosina, 284
Antoinette, Marie, 111
Apples: 241-2; see also *fruits, fresh*
    choice and preparation of, 241-2
    certosina, mousse in, 284
    flan with, 227; with almond paste, 233
    layered on yeast dough, 123
    mincemeat, in, 280; apple pie, 281
    mother's German cake, 247
    pound cake, 184
    tart from Basel, 232; tarte tatin, 224
Apricots, dried:
    jam glaze, 71
    in macaroons, 344
    nut bread, 190
    orange and walnut loaf, 276
Apricots, fresh: see also *fruits, fresh*
    flan, 227
    pound cake, 184
    sponge, upside-down, 93
    Streussel flan, 227
    yeast cake with almonds, 126
Arab spiced bread, 343
Aromatics, see *Perfumes*
Assabih bi loz, 340
Austrian sour cream pastry with fruit, 248

Baba au rhum, see *yeast dough*
Baking
    area and planning, 13–22
    blind, 208
    failure in, 39
    par-baking, 208–9
Baklava: 55; recipe, 338
Baltimore, Lady, cake, 175

CAKES

Barquettes (meringue boats), 111
Bartholomew Fair, 346
Basel; apple and almond tart, 232
Baumkuchen, see *Wedding Cake*
Beard, James: *Beard on Food*, 181, 227, 256, 279
Bee sting, 316
Beigli, Hungarian yeast roll, 140; filling for, 141
Berliner Crème Torte, 112
Bernois, le (pistachio, almonds), 167
Bienenstich (yeast, almonds) 316; butter base, 317
Bilberry cake, 246
'Biscuit', 94-7 see also *sponge cakes; roulades*
    almond or hazelnut, 94; with chocolate, 96; with gooseberries, 96; de Savoie, 95; plain, 94; fillings for, 95
Biscuits, 373-86
    amaretti, 376
    brown butter, 380
    feuilles de palmiers, 378
    florentines, 383
    ginger, Diane's. 347
    hazelnut, 384; slices, 378
    Lebkuchen, 363
    macaroons and variations, 373-4
    marrons glacés, 385
    owis molis, 382
    sablé – sand, 383
    Shenkele, 376
    shortbread, Marion's, 379
    spiced honey, 360; with hazelnuts, 364
    Spritsjes – piped, 384
    sugar biscuits, 377
    tuiles, 380
Blackberries:
    flan and apples, 227; Seamus Heaney, 228
Black Forest Kirschtorte, 164
Blanching: almonds, 311; hazelnuts, 318
Boni, Ada, *Italian Regional Cooking*, 284
Borghese, Anita, *Just Desserts*, 258
Bowls, mixing, 17; for whisking egg-white, 35
Bradley, Richard, *The Country Housewife and Lady's Director*, 181, 193, 241, 261, 282, 298
Brazil nut: 335; bread, 191; cake, 335; fruit cake, 285
Breads see *tea*
Brillat-Savarin, Jean Anthelme, 132, 144
Bûche de noël (Christmas log), 176
Butter: 31-2; brown biscuits, 380; for puff pastry, 50
Butterbrot mit Schokolade (tea bread), 190
Buttercream see *creams*

Candied and crystallized fruits see *fruits; perfumes*
Caracas, chocolate almond cake, 155
Caramel, 70; glaze for Dobostorte, 170
Caracassone, 256
Carême, Antonin, *Le Pâtissier Royal (1815)*, 49; 105; 287; recipes of, 59, 82, 108, 194, 206, 229, 249
Carey, John, *Thackeray — Prodigal Genius*, 214
Carmago, la (chestnut cream and sponge), 332
Carmelite cake (figs, dates, almonds), 275
Carrot cakes: 193-5, 200-2
    history 193-5;
    American loaf (walnuts), 202
    Austrian cake (almonds), 200
    Portuguese roll, 201
Certosina (Italian Christmas fruit cake), 284
Chantilly, crème, see *creams, fresh*
Chaucer, Geoffrey, *The Tale of Sir Topaz*, 342, 345
Cheese: history; selection for baking, 298-300
Cheese cakes: 298-307
    almonds (fromage blanc), with, 171
    freezing, 299
    pear sponges and, 304
    Pentecost, for, 301
    Polish rose cake, rose conserve, 304-7
    simple, 301
    talmouses and maids of honour, 302
    yeast curd cake, 125
Cherries, candied: preparation of, 269
    in brazil nut cake, 335
    fruited festive cake, 290
Cherries, fresh: choice for baking, 242-3; 250; preparation, 244
    in almond sponge, 250; with chocolate, 251
    black forest Kirschtorte, 164
    Kuchen with Streussel, 124
    pavlova, 110
    pound cake, 184
    yeast cake, 127
Chestnuts: 328-35
    boiled in milk, 330
    candied-matrons glacés, 385
    creams and vermicelles, 332; butter cream, 64; choux pastry, in, 333; la carmago, 333; malakoff, in, 172; meringue and chocolate, 333; on pavlova, 110; in sponge, 333
    dehydrated, tinned, 330
    peeling, 329
Chestnut cakes:
    Torte with quince slices and almonds, 330
    Radetsky Torte, and filling, 331
Children's favourites:
    apple cake, German, 247
    apricot nut bread, 190
    carrot loaf, 202
    doughnuts, 137
    ginger, biscuits, 347; -bread man, 348; -house, 369
    lemon cake, 265
    meringues, 108
    Potize, 130
    pound cake, 181

INDEX

raisin bread, 187
shortbread, 379
sponges: buns, 93; chocolate, 92; jam roll, 97;
  plum, for Sam, 244
sugar: biscuits, 377; cake, 185
Yorkshire treacle tart, 212
Chocolate: 143-157 see also *cocoa*
  almond slices, 153
  American devil's food cake, 157
  biscuit de Savoie, 96
  black forest Kirschtorte, 164
  Butterbrot mit Schokolade, 190
  caracas, with almonds, 155
  cherry and almond sponge, 250
  and cinnamon cake, 352
  decorations: cake covering, 148; caraque curls or
    flakes, 148; egg white cake, and, 115;
    grated, 148
  fillings: (2), (3) with cocoa, 65; (1) ganache, 64;
    mousseline butter cream, 63, 156; nut
    and, 67; Potize, in 131
  fudge frosting, 75
  ganache Torte, 154
  hazelnut sandwich, and, 322
  hazelnut Torte, and, 320
  history, 143-6
  icing, soft, 75
  macaroons, 374
  marjolaine, 171
  meringue: 111; pavlova, 110
  mikado Torte, 167
  Mohr im Hemd, 151
  Napoleon Torte with spices, 152
  potato flour sponge, 196; dark sponge, 92
  pound cake, 183
  roulade with nuts, 150
  Sachertorte, 150
  storage, 147-8
  truffles; truffle cake, 156
Choux pastry see *pastry, choux; pastries*
Christmas:
  bûche de noël, 176
  certosina, 284
  Dresdener Christstollen, 138
  fruit cake with brazil nuts, 285
  fruited festive cake, 290
  mincemeat: pies, tarts and, 156-7
  Stephen's Beigli, 140
Cinnamon: 351-4
  for baking, 344
  sugar, 84
  Streussel – crumb covering, 123
  toasted pound cake, 185
Cocoa: in Devil's food cake, 157
  filling, 65
  pound cake, 183
  sponge cake, 93
Coffee; see also *Tea Breads*

Austrian pound cake, 183
meringue, 111
moka crème, 66; butter cream with walnuts, 113
Mrs. Wosiek's walnut cake, 326
sour cream coffee bread with nuts, 192
spiced and pecan cake, 183
syrup, 85
Coolidge, Susan, *What Katy Did*, 206
Cooling cakes, 37-8
Cranberry jam, fresh, 219; in Himmelstorte, 174
Creams, fresh and cooked: see also *fillings*
  butter cream 161-2; chestnut, 64; chocolate
    mousseline, 63; coffee creme, moka, 66;
    crème pralinée, 68; with lemon or
    orange, 64; mousseline, 62-3; piping
    technique, 81; quick, 64
  custard creams, cooked, 59-62; frangipane aux
    amandes, 61-2; pâtissière with vanilla
    and alternative flavours, 59-60; St.
    Honoré, 62
  fresh creams, double, single, whipping, 57-8;
    chocolate ganache, 64-5; creme chan-
    tilly, 59; sahne crème, 163
Cristal-Palace (Dubois), 159
croquembouche, 105
crumb covering, 123
Culpeper, Nicholas, 324
curd, see also *cheese*
  and lemon cheese, 237

Dahl, Roald, *Charlie and the Chocolate Factory*, 143,
  309
Dates:
  brazil nut cake, in, 335
  carmelite cake, 275
  Dattel Torte, 274
  fruit cake with brazil nuts, 285
David, Elizabeth, *English Bread and Yeast Cookery*,
  121, 187
Decorations, see *icings and; chocolate decorations*
Devil's food cake with cocoa, 157
Diaz, Bernal, 143
Dickens, Charles, *A Christmas Carol*, 278, 282
Dobostorte (chocolate filling, caramel), 169
Double-boiler, 18,90
Dough:
  fila: 55, in Middle Eastern pastries, 336-40
  Strudel, 54,55 almond filling for, 317
Doughnuts, 135-8; 121; deep frying, 136
Dresdener Christstollen, 138
Dubois, Urbain, *La Pâtisserie d'Aujourd'hui*, 88,
  103, 159, 162, 171, 231, 236, 266, 286,
  288, 296
Dufour, Philippe Sylvestre, *Traitez nouveaux et
  ancieux du cafe, du thé, du chocolat*, 145
Dull, Mrs S.R., *Southern Cooking*, 103
Dundee cake, 272

CAKES

Eccles cakes, 277
Éclairs, 102
Eggs: 32-6, 90
Egg whites: whisking, folding, methods of, 35-6
Egg white cakes:
   chocolate, 115
   Lady Baltimore cake, 175
   in macaroons, 373
   in meringues, 108,
   Rumpolt's Marx 'Piscoten . . .', 87
   snow cake, 114
egg yolk, glaze, 76
Endter, Wolfgang Moritz, *Vollständiges Nürnbergisches Koch Buch*, 160
Engadiner Nusstorte, 327
equipment, choosing, care of, 13-22
Ertoffeltorte, 197

Failure in baking, reasons, 39
Faschingskrapfen, 137
Feuilles de palmiers, 378
Fila dough see *dough*
Filberts see *hazelnuts*
Fillings: 64-8 see also 57-64
   almond, 67-8; with orange, 68; in malakoff, 68; for almond fingers, 340; crème, pralinée, 68
   chestnut for Radetsky Torte, 332; for vermicelles, 332
   hazelnut, 67; for hazelnut cake, 320; for Lebkuchen, 365; nut and chocolate, 67
   lemon, cooked, 237
   for Potize, 131
   quince mousse, 252
   rice, cream for konafa, 340
   strawberry, for hazelnut cake, 319
   walnut, 66
Fingers, almond, 340
Flans: see also *baking; fruits, fresh* and *tarts and pies*
   apple with almond paste, 233; tart from Basel, 232
   apricot Streussel, 227
   berried fruits, 228; in meringue, 238; grapes in meringue, 239
   glazed orange slices, 235
   gooseberry and almond, 222
   lemon meringue, 236
   peach or greengage, 234
   poires frangipane, 231
   rhubarb and hazelnut meringue, 238
Flaubert, Gustave, *Madame Bovary*, 288
Flockensahnetorte, 163
Florentiner Mandel Plätzchen, 383
Flour: selection, types, storage, 29-31
Flower waters, 82-4
Folding, 36
Fontane, Theodor, *Meine Kinderjahre*, 295, 363
Food processors, 47

Francatelli, Charles Elmé, *The Modern Cook, a practical guide to the culinary art*, 161, 294
Frangipane, crème aux amandes, 61; in flan de poires, 231
Freezing: see also individual recipes
   basic pastries, 42;
   cheese cakes, 299
   Gugelhopf, 129
   puff pastry, 54
   savarin and baba au rhum, 133
   yeast, 118
Friandises and biscuits 373-86; see *biscuits*
Fromage blanc in cheese cake, 301
Frosting, seven-minute, 176; fudge, 75
Fruits: candied and crystallized, 85-6
   certosina, 284
   decorations for glacé icing, 77-9
   Dundee cake, 272
   Eccles cakes, 277
   fruit cake with brazil nuts, 285
   mincemeat, 280
   orange yeast Gugelhopf, 129
   wedding cake, 290
Fruits, dried: 268-86
   general hints, history, 150-1
   preparation for baking, 269
   apricot, orange and walnut loaf, 276
   English fruited: in pound cake, 184
   carmelite cake, 275
   certosina, 284
   Dundee cake, 272
   Eccles cakes, 277
   fruit cake with brazil nuts, 285
   fruited festive cake, 290
   Honiglekach, 358
   mincemeat, 280-1
   pound cake, 184
Fruits, fresh, 203-27 see individual names also; see *Tarts and pies*,
   baked in sponge cakes, 243
   cakes, in, 240-68
   choice and preparation of, 221, 241-3
   double crust pastry, in, 207
   Austrian sour cream pastry, in, 248
   berried in flans, 228; in meringue flan, 238
   flans, in, 227-39
   lemon and orange cakes, 260-7
   millefeuille with crème chantilly, 231
   pound cake, in, 184
   yeast doughs, on, 123
Fudge frosting, chocolate, 75
'Fysshe tarte' medieval, 205

Galette, hazelnut with raspberries, 323
Ganache Torte, 154; filling, 64
Gâteaux and Torten, 158-81
   history, 158-62
   Berliner crème Torte (layered nut meringue), 112

INDEX

Bernois, le (pistachio marzipan, almonds), 167
Black Forest Kirschtorte (chocolate, cherries), 164
bûche de noël (chocolate roll), 176
cinnamon Torte (almonds, sour cream), 352
Dattel Torte (fresh dates, almonds), 274
Dobostorte (chocolate filling, caramel), 169
Engadiner Nusstorte (walnuts), 327
Flockensahnetorte (choux, Streussel, and crème), 163
ganache Torte (chocolate filling), 154
gâteau de la reine (almonds), 214
hazelnut and chocolate Torte, 320
hazelnut gâteau praliné, (see recipe) 174
Himmelstorte (biscuit, jam, cream), 174
Katalani Torte (spiced nut meringue), 114
Kirschtorte (macaroon, Kirsch), 166
Lady Baltimore Cake (potato flour, egg white), 175
le Lacam (nuts, liqueurs), 179
Linzertorte (jam, almond pastry), 216
malakoff (sponge, almond filling), 172
marjolaine (nuts, creams, chocolate), 171
meringue with chestnut and chocolate, 333
mikado Torte (sponge, chocolate cream), 167
Napoleon Torte (chocolate, spices), 152
périgourdine, la (walnut, coffee), 170; with fresh fruit, 171
quince Torte, 254
Radetsky Torte (chestnut), 331
Sachertorte (chocolate), 150
St Honoré parisien (choux pastry, cream), 103
whipped dark walnut Torte, 325
Gelatine, to stiffen cream, 58
Genoese sponge, 91
Gerard, John, *Catalogus*; *The Herball or Historie of Plants*, 193
German pastry see *pastry, German*; *pastries*
Ginger: see also *honey and spice*
  biscuits, 347; cake, 350
Gingerbread, 345–51
  excellent, 351; house, 369; man, 348
Glacé icing see *icings and decorations*
Glasse, Hannah, *Compleat Confectioner*, 88, 221, 268, 349
glaze for fruit flans, 210; see also *egg yolk glaze*
Goethe, Johann Wolfgang von, 155
Gooseberries: see also *fruits, fresh*
  almond flan, 222
  biscuit de Savoie, 96
  prize meetings, 222
  syrup, in, 96
Gouffé, Jules, *Le Livre de Pâtisserie*, 102, 104, 287
Grapes, flan, 227; in meringue, 239; in apple tart, 233
Greene, Graham, *The Ministry of Fear*, 272
Greengages, 243; flan, 227; or peach, 234
Grigson, Jane, *Food with the Famous*, 214, 224, 285

Grimm, the Brothers, *Fairy Tales*, 368
Groundes-Peace, Mrs, *Old Cookery Notebook*, 354
Gugelhopf, 127-9; tins and moulds, 21

'Hackin', 282
Hagger, Conrad, *Neues Saltzburgisches Koch=Buch*, 160, 216, 287
Hannsen, *Allerley kochen von Maister Hannsen des von Würtenberg Koch*, 216
Hänsel and Gretel, gingerbread house, 214-5
Harris, H.G. and Borella S.P. *All about Gâteaux and Dessert Cakes*, 91, 176
Hartley, Dorothy, *Food in England*, 41, 205, 215, 279, 294
Hazelnuts: and filberts: 318-23
  blanching, roasting, grinding, 318-20
  biscuit – sponge, 94
  cake, whipped with strawberry, hazelnut filling, 319-20
  chocolate sandwich, and, 322; Torte, 320
  fillings, 67; for spiced honey biscuits, 365
  galette with raspberries, 323
  gâteau praline, 174
  Haselnussleckerli (almonds, spices, peels), 367
  Hoefeiser, 384
  honey cake, 360
  Hungarian roulade, 321
  japonais, 113
  praline on pavlova, 110
  and rhubarb meringue flan, 238
  short pastry, 322; tartlet shells, 322, 256
  slices, 367
  Vienna pound cake, 185
Heaney, Seamus, *Blackberry Picking*, 228
Heavenly cake, 174
Hefeteig, see *yeast dough*
Heidesand, 380
Hervey, James, 248
Himmelstorte, 174
Hoefeiser, 384
Honey and spice: 354-72 see also *spices*
  general, 355-7
  gingerbread man, 348
  Hänsel and Gretel house, 368
  hazelnut biscuits, and, 364
  Jewish honey cake, 359
  Lebkuchen, simple, 363
  orange sponge, 262
  Polish cake, 360
  walnut honey cake, 358
Honoré St, crème, 62; in gâteau parisien, 103
Hungarian roulade (hazelnuts), 321; yeast roll, 140

Icing and decorations: 71-82
  American, boiled, 76
  chocolate: covering, plain, 148; icing, 74; soft icing, 75; fudge frosting, 75
  egg yolk glaze, 76

393

CAKES

glacé icing: and flavourings, 72-3; how to glacé ice a cake, 73
iced cakes; decorative ideas, 77-81
icing sugar decoration, 71
royal icing, 236, 293

Jam, cranberry, 219
roll – sponge, 97
tarts 214–6
Japonais, 113
Jarrin, G.A. *The Italian Confectioner*, 158
Jewish honey cake, 358
Jones, Evan, *American Food, the Gastronomic Story*, 206, 211, 258
Joris, Mrs, 111, 150
Judhab al-rutab, 203

Katalani Torte, 114
Keats, John, *The Eve of Saint Agnes*, 268
Kipfel, Zampa, 111
Kirsch, eau de vie, in Black Forest Torte, 164; Kirschtorte, 166
Kiwi fruit sponge roulade, 98
Klinkenberg, Hans van den, 163; 381-4
Knafe, 40, 340
Kneading yeast dough, 120
Konafa, 337-40

Lacam, Pierre, *Le Memorial des Glaces*, 71, 82, 134, 167, 179, 229
Lady Baltimore cake, 175
Lear, Edward, *Amblongus Pie*, 203
Lebkuchen, Nürnberger, 360-4; spiced honey biscuits with hazelnuts, 364
Lecuyer, Roger, *La vraie cuisine* (savarin), 342
Lemon: fresh, and oranges, 260-5 see also *fruits, fresh* and *fruits, candied*
general, 261-2
cake, juice poured over, 265
curd or cheese, 237
in macaroons, 374
meringue flan, 236
zests, 261
Liegnitzer Bombe, 366
Lining tins: for fruit cakes, 270–1; for sponge cakes, 89; for Swiss roll and roulades, 97; see also *baking*
Linzertorte, 216
Loaf, prune and walnut, 189
Loudon, John, *Encyclopedia of Gardening*, 222

Macaroons: Swedish, 373-5, bitter, 376; Kirschtorte, 166
Maids of honour, 302
Malakoff (sponge, almond), 172
Mango in meringue flan, 238
Mann, Thomas, *the Magic Mountain*, 178
Mansfield, Katherine, 7,9,99,357
Margarine, 32

Marjolaine, 171
Marperger, Paul Jacob, *Vollständiges Küch=und Keller=Dictionarium*, 161
Marrons glacés, 385
Marshall, Arthur, 102
Marzipan, 288-90, 292
Mousseline with farci curaçao, 266; of pistachios, le Bernois, 167
Measuring and weighing equipment, 15-16
Meringues: 33, 108-116
preparation, 108-10
Berliner Crème Torte, 112
with chestnut, chocolate and cream, 333
grapes in, 239; berries in, 238
japonais, 113
Katalani Torte, 114
lemon flan, 236; rhubarb and hazelnut, 238
small with chocolate, coffee, pistachio, à la reine, Zampa Kipfel, 111
pavlova and variations, 110; strawberries Carcassonne, 256
Middle Eastern nut pastries: 336-9
mikado Torte, 167
millefeuille crème chantilly, 231
mincemeat, 278-81
Mohnkunchen, 124
Mohr im Hemd, 151
Moka coffee crème, 66; syrup, 85
Molasses:
measuring hints, storing, 27
pecan pie, 211
walnut bread, 118
Moor in a nightshirt, 151
Moulds, cake, 21
Mousseline butter creams, see *creams*
Moxon, Elizabeth, 349
Muhammed-al-Baghdadi, *Baghdad Cookery Book*, 203,274,289

Napoleon Torte 152
Nürnberger Lebkuchen see *Lebkuchen*
Nuts: 308-342 see individual names also
general, 308-10
grinding, 311
Carême's nut crusting, 249
layered nut meringues, 112-4
Middle Eastern pastries, 336-9
nut and chocolate filling, 67

Oranges; see *lemons*; *fruits, fresh*; *fruits, candied*
general, 261-2;
in baking, 82
almond and, cake, 264
candied, yeast gugelhopf, 129
glazed slices, flan with, 235
Orange fillings:
almond and, 68
butter cream, 64

394

INDEX

flower water, 84
honey sponge, 262; with minced, fresh, 263
in macaroons, 373
mousseline with farci curaçao, 266
peel sugar, 84
pound cake with juice, 183; toasted, 186
syrup for savarin, 134
Ortiz, Elisabeth Lambert, *A Book of Latin American Cooking*, 191,335
Ovens, 37-40
Owis Molis, 382

Panade in choux pastry, 101
Par-baking, 209
Paris Brest, 99
Pastries: see also baking; *flans*
general hints, master recipes, 41-57
double crust tarts and pies, 207
moist fillings, protection against, 208
storing, freezing, 43-4
Pastry: choux, 99-108
baking times, small and large puffs, 101
croquembouche, pyramid, 105
éclairs, 102; fillings: chestnut cream, 333; cream whipped, 102
Flockensahnetorte, 163
grillés aux amandes pralinées, 102
Paris Brest and rings, 99
profiteroles au chocolat, 103
St. Honoré parisien, 103
Pastry: German, 48; apple cake, my mother's, 247; Zwetscken plum cake, 248
Pastry: hazlenut short, 322; and chocolate sandwich, 322; galette with raspberries, 323; tartlet shells, 256
Pastry: puff, 49-53
blitz puff pastry, 53
trimming, freezing, 54
shop bought, frozen, 50
Eccles cakes, 277
feuilles de palmiers, 378
millefeuilles, 231
vol au vent, 229
Pastry: shortcrust, 44
Pastry: sourcream, 248
Pastry: sweet shortcrust, 45; with almonds, 46
Pâte brisée, see *pastry, shortcrust*
Pâte feuilletée, see *pastry, puff*
Pâte sucrée, see *pastry, sweet shortcrust*
Pâtissière, crème with vanilla, 59
Pavlóva meringue, 110
Peach; upside down sponge, 93; or greengage flan, 234; on pavlova, 110; on yeast dough, 123
Pears: see also *fruits, fresh*
in certosina, 284; and cheese sponge, 304; flan de poires frangipane, 231
Pecan: and coffee cake, spiced, 178; Lady Baltimore cake, 175; pie, 211

Pepper, black, history, 344; strawberries carcassonne, 256
Perfumes, 82-7; see also *aromatics and candied fruits*, 82-87
Périgourdine, la, 170; with fresh fruit, 171
Pies, see also *tarts and pies*; *tarts with fresh fruits*
pecan, 211
pumpkin, 227
mincemeat: and apple, 281
Pineapple: sponge roulade with raspberry and kiwi, 98
Pine nuts: decoration on cake icing, 77; in carrot cake, 200; in certosina, 284; filling in Konafa, 339
Piping: bag, 17; to fill, 77
butter creams: technique, 81
cone, paper to make and use, 76
history, 161-2
nozzles and cornets, 161
Pistachio: chocolate almond slices, 153; filling in baklava, konafa, 338-9; marzipan in le Bernois, 167; meringue, 111
Plat, Sir Hugh, *Delightes for Ladies*, 345
Plums: see also *fruits, fresh*
choice and preparation, 243
cake: on Germany pastry, 248
flan, 227
in pound cake, 184
sponge for Sam, 244
with Streussel, 124
Poaching; pears in wine, 232; gooseberries, 96
Pope, Alexander, *The Rape of the Lock*, 325
Poppyseed:
Beigli, filling for, 141
to grind, 125
Mohnkuchen, yeast cake, 124; on butter pastry, 317
Potize, filling for, 131
Portuguese carrot roll, 201
Potato: general, 30, 193-5
and carrot cakes, 193-5
boiled: in Ertoffeltorte, 197; in Rosa's American cake, 199
Potato flour in:
Baumkuchen, 194
biscuit: almond and hazelnut, 94; de Savoie, 95
carrot cake, 200
chocolate egg white cake, 115
gâteau de la reine, 214
le Lacam, 179
orange honey sponge, 262; mousseline farci curaçao, 266
potato flour sponge: with chocolate, 195-6
pound cake, 182
snow cake, 114
zephyrs, 197
Potize, 130
Pound cakes, 181-7

395

CAKES

basic mixture and variations, 182-3
 Austrian coffee, 183
 chocolate or spices, 183; cinnamon toast, 185
 dried/fresh fruits, 184
 orange, 183; making toast with, 185
 sugar cake, 185
 Vienna nut cake, 185
Praline: almond, 312; on pavlova, 110
 crème pralinée, 68
 hazelnut gâteau, 174
Profiteroles au chocolat, 103
Protecting pastry against moist fillings, 208
Prunes and walnut loaf, 189
Puff pastry, see *pastries*; *pastry*, *puff*
Pumpkins, 226; pie, James Beard's, 227

Quince: 251-4
 in certosina, 284
 chestnut Torte with almonds, 330
 mousse for fillings, 252
 nineteenth century Torte, 254
 slices, 253
Quirl, 16, 146

Radetsky Torte, 331
Raisins, bread, 187
Raspberries: see also *fruits*, *fresh*
 flan case, 228; meringue flan, 238
 hazelnut galette, 323; cake, 319
 millefeuilles, 231
 pavlova, 110
 Périgourdine, la, 171
 sponge layers, 92; roulade with kiwi, pineapple and, 98
Red currants: sponge layers, 92; la Périgourdine, 110; pavlova, 110
Reine, gâteau de la, 214
Rhubarb: see also *fruits*, *fresh*
 gâteau à la, 221; and hazelnut meringue flan, 238; pound cake, 184
Ribbon trail, 90
Roden, Claudia, *A Book of Middle Eastern Food*, 264, 336-9
Rolls, sponge see *roulades*
Rose cheese cake from Poland, rose conserve, 304-5
Rose water, 84
Rostand, Edmund, *Cyrano de Bergerac*, 213
Roulades: how to prepare, 97
 au chocolat with nuts, 150
 Hungarian hazelnut, walnut, 321
 with jam, 97
 Portuguese carrot, 201
 raspberry, kiwi and pineapple, 98
Rum: syrup of for babas, 135; Mansfield, 7
Rumpolt, Marx, *Ein new Köchbuch*, 87, 193, 216, 294

Sablé — sand biscuits, 383

Sachertorte, 150
Sade, Marquis de, 88, 240
Saffron, 345
Sahne crème, 161
Sand biscuits, 382
Sandtorte, see *pound cake*, 181
Savage, Richard, *the Wanderer*, 254
Savarin, 132
Savoie, biscuit de: history, 88; with chocolate, 95-6
Seed cake — brawn brack, 183
Shenkele, 376
Shortbread, Marion's, 379
Shortcake, strawberry, 258
Shortcrust pastry, see *pastries*
Slices:
 almond, 315; with chocolate, 153
 hazelnut, 378
 quince, 253
Smith, Sydney, 214, 257
Snow cake, 114
Sour cream:
 almond tart, 214
 in apricot nut bread, 190
 in cheese cake, 301; rose cheese cake, 304
 coffee bread, 192; coffee and pecan cake, 178
 pastry with fruit, 248
 Zimmt Kuchen, 353
Southey, Robert, 222
Soyer, Alexis, 205, 250
Spices, 342-73 see also individual names
 history, preparation, 342-5
 certosina, 284
 coffee and pecan cake, 178
 fairings, 346
 Haselnussleckerli, 367
Spices and Honey 354-72; see also *honey and spice*
 Katalani Torte, 114
 Liegnitzer Bombe, 366
 Napoleon Torte, 152
 Nürnberger Lebkuchen, 360-2
 pound cake, 183
 special spiced cakes, 345-54
 spiced honey cake, 366
Sponge batter, 119
Sponge cakes, 87-99; see also *biscuit* and *roulades*
 basic recipe, fatless, 90
 buns, 93
 cherry and almond, 250
 with chestnut cream, 333
 with chocolate or cocoa, 92
 dressing up a sponge, 92
 fresh fruit baked inside, 240
 genoese, fine, 91
 minced oranges and, 263; and honey, 262
 peach or apricot upside down, 93
 pear and cheese, 304
 plum sponge, 244
 potato flour: chocolate, 195

INDEX

with strawberries and cream, 257
Spritjes, 384
Spun sugar, 72
Stephen's Beigli, 140-1
Strawberries, 254-6; see also *fruits, fresh*
   flan case, 229
   filling for hazelnut cake, 319
   fresh with almonds, cake, 257
   in hazelnut tartlets, 323
   meringue flan, 238
   millefeuilles, 231
   pavlova, 110
   Périgourdine, la, 171
   shortcake, American, 258
   sponge and cream, 257; in layers, 92
   vol au vent, 229
Streussel: apricot flan, 227; cinnamon, almond, 123; Flockensahnetorte, 163; Kuchen, on yeast dough, 123
Strudel, see *dough*
Sugar 23-8; see also *icings and decoration; syrups*
   boiling, 69-70 general, 23-8
   filling for potize, 131
   perfumed, 82
   spun, 72
Sugar biscuits, 377
Sugar cake, 185
Suvretta friandises, 381-85
Sweet shortcrust pastry see *pastries*
Switzen see *plums*
Syrups; see also *sugar*
   measuring hints for, 27
   for baklava and konafa, 338-9
   coffee powder, instant, 85; moka, 85
   orange for savarin, 134
   for baba au rhum, 135; method of soaking, 133

Talmouses, see *maids of honour*
Tartar, cream of in sugar syrup, 69
Tartlets: see also *baking, pastries*
   hazelnut short crust pastry, 256, 322
   mincemeat, 281
   maids of honour, 302
Tartlettes Amandines, 213
Tarts: and Pies, 203-20; see also *baking, pastries, and pies, tarts with fresh fruits*
   freezing, 44
   history, 203-6
   preparation of double crust tarts and pies, 207
   almond tart, Sydney Smith's, 214
   jam tarts, 215
   Linzertorte, 216
   Yorkshire treacle tart, 212
Tarts with fresh fruits: 221, 241-3
   choosing and preparation of, 118
   apple tart from Basel, 232; tarte tatin, 224
   gâteau à la rhubarbe, 221
   gooseberry and almond flan, 222

grape meringue, 239
James Beard's pumpkin pie, 227
mincemeat, and apple, 281
nineteenth century quince Torte, 254
Tatin, tarte (apples), 224
Taylor, Elizabeth, *The Sleeping Beauty*, 334
Tea breads and coffee cakes, 187-93
   apricot (dried) bread, 190
   brazil nut bread, 191
   Butterbrot mit Schokolade, 190
   prune and walnut, 189
   raisin bread, 187
   sour cream coffee cake, 192
   walnut bread, 188
Temperatures: for baking, 37
   basic pastries, 42
   choux pastries, 101
   flan cases, 209
   meringue, 109
   sugar boiling, 70
Testing cake for readiness, 37
Thackeray, William Makepeace, 214
Thermometers and timers, 18, 37
Thompson, Flora, *Lark Rise to Candleford*, 129, 146
Tiddy Diddy Doll, 346
Tin ware, 19-21; see also *lining; baking*
Toklas, Alice B., 376
Tools for baking, 16; care of, 22; for whisking egg white, 17, 35
Torta de Castanhas-do-pará, 335
Torten: see *gâteau and*
Treacle: measuring hints, 27;
   pecan pie, 211;
   tart, Yorkshire, 212
Troisgros, 98
Truffles: and chocolate cake, 156
Tuer, Andrew W., *Old London Street Cries*, 250, 346
Tuiles, 380

Upside-down sponge, 93
Uttley, Alison, *The Country Child*, 240; *Recipes from an Old Farmhouse*, 348

Vanilla pod: 83-4
Varenne, François Pierre de la, 344
Vermicelles – chestnut cream, 332
Victoria sandwich see *pound cake*, 181
Vienna pound cake, 185
Vol au vent: Carême history, 124; see also *pastry, puff*

Walnuts, 324-8
   apricot and orange, loaf, 276
   bread, with molasses, spices, 118
   and carrot loaf, 202
   coffee and, cake, 326
   dark, whipped Torte, 325
   Engadiner Nusstorte, 327

filling, 66; in baklava, konafa, 338-9; for Beigli, 141; for Potize, 131
general information, 324
honey cake; 357; Jewish, 359; Polish, 360
and prune loaf, 189
roulade, 321
in tuiles, 380
Wedding cake, 286-98; Baumkuchen, 294-7
Weighing and measuring equipment, 15-16
White, Florence, *Good Food in England*, 205, 277
Wine, red: poaching pears in, 231; in prune and walnut loaf, 189
Wine, white: in gâteau à la rhubarbe, 221; in gooseberry and almond flan, 222
Wohlbewerth's mit Fleiss zusammengetragenes Kochbuch aus dem Jahr 1778, 152
Woodforde, Parson James, *The Diary of a Country Parson*, 223, 255

Yeast baking, 117-43
handling, freezing, use of, 117-121

Yeast dough – *Hefeteig*,
basic mixture, with fruits, 122-3
apricot cake, 126
Bienenstich, 316
curd cheese yeast cake, 125
Gugelhopf, 127; with candied orange, 129
Dresdener Christstollen, 138
Mohnkuchen, 124
Potize, and fillings, 130
savarin and baba au rhum, 132-4
Stephen's Beigli, walnut and poppyseed filling for, 140-1
Streusselkuchen, 123

Zwetschken or cherry Kuchen with Streussel, 124
Zampa Kipfel, 111
Zephyrs, 197
Zest, see *lemon, general*
Zester; citrus, tool for, 16
Zimmt Kuchen, 353
Zola, Emile, *Gervaise*, 95
Zwetschken, see *plums*

MORE ABOUT PENGUINS, PELICANS
AND PUFFINS

For further information about books available from Penguins please write to Dept EP, Penguin Books Ltd, Harmondsworth, Middlesex UB7 0DA.

In the U.S.A.: For a complete list of books available from Penguins in the United States write to Dept DG, Penguin Books, 299 Murray Hill Parkway, East Rutherford, New Jersey 07073.

In Canada: For a complete list of books available from Penguins in Canada write to Penguin Books Canada Ltd, 2801 John Street, Markham, Ontario L3R 1B4.

In Australia: For a complete list of books available from Penguins in Australia write to the Marketing Department, Penguin Books Australia Ltd, P.O. Box 257, Ringwood, Victoria 3134.

In New Zealand: For a complete list of books available from Penguins in New Zealand write to the Marketing Department, Penguin Books (N.Z.) Ltd, P.O. Box 4019, Auckland 10.

In India: For a complete list of books available from Penguins in India write to Penguin Overseas Ltd, 706 Eros Apartments, 56 Nehru Place, New Delhi 110019.